SWEAT AND SOAP

VOL. 7

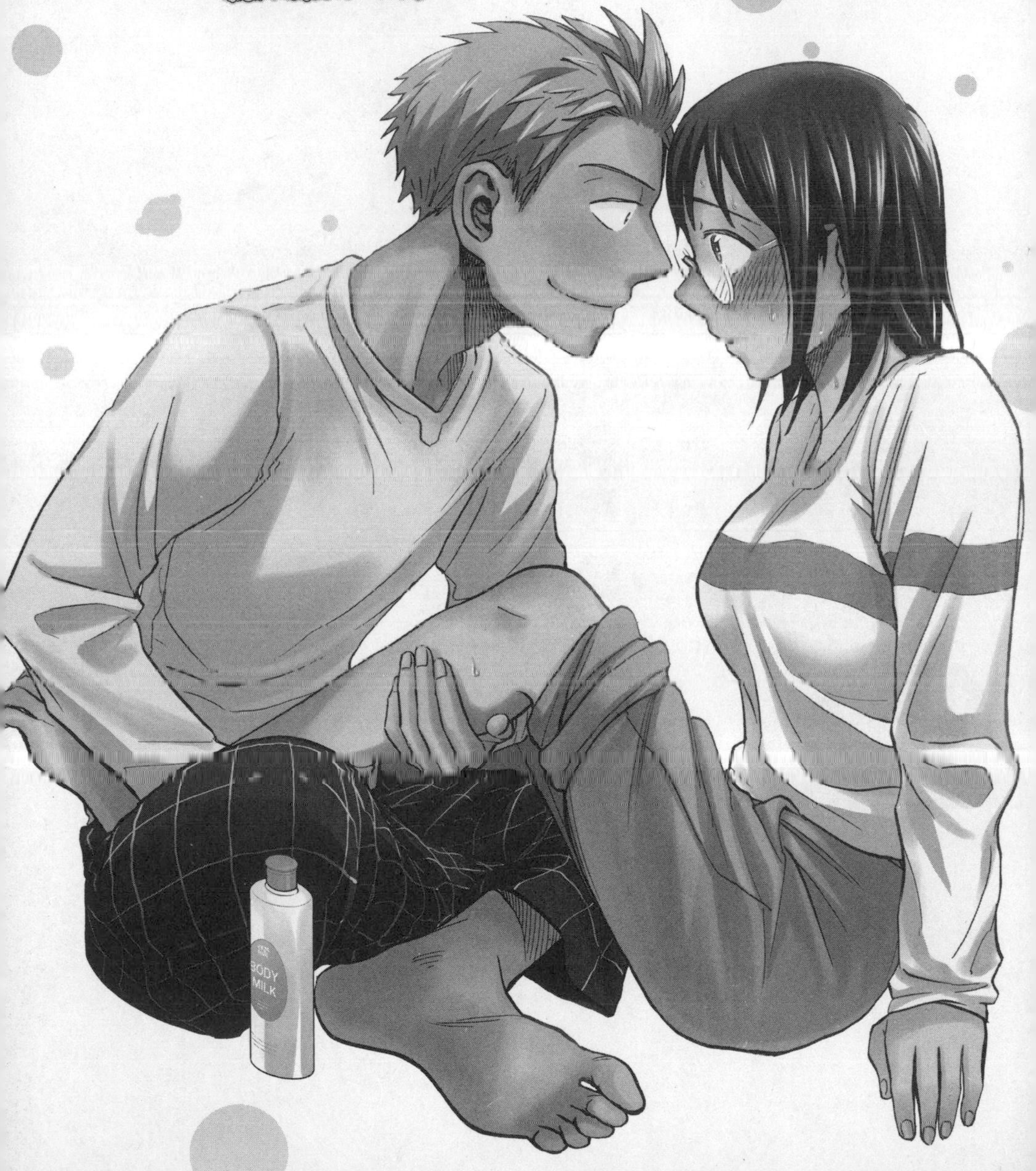
BODY
MILK

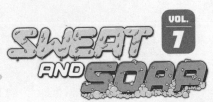

CONTENTS

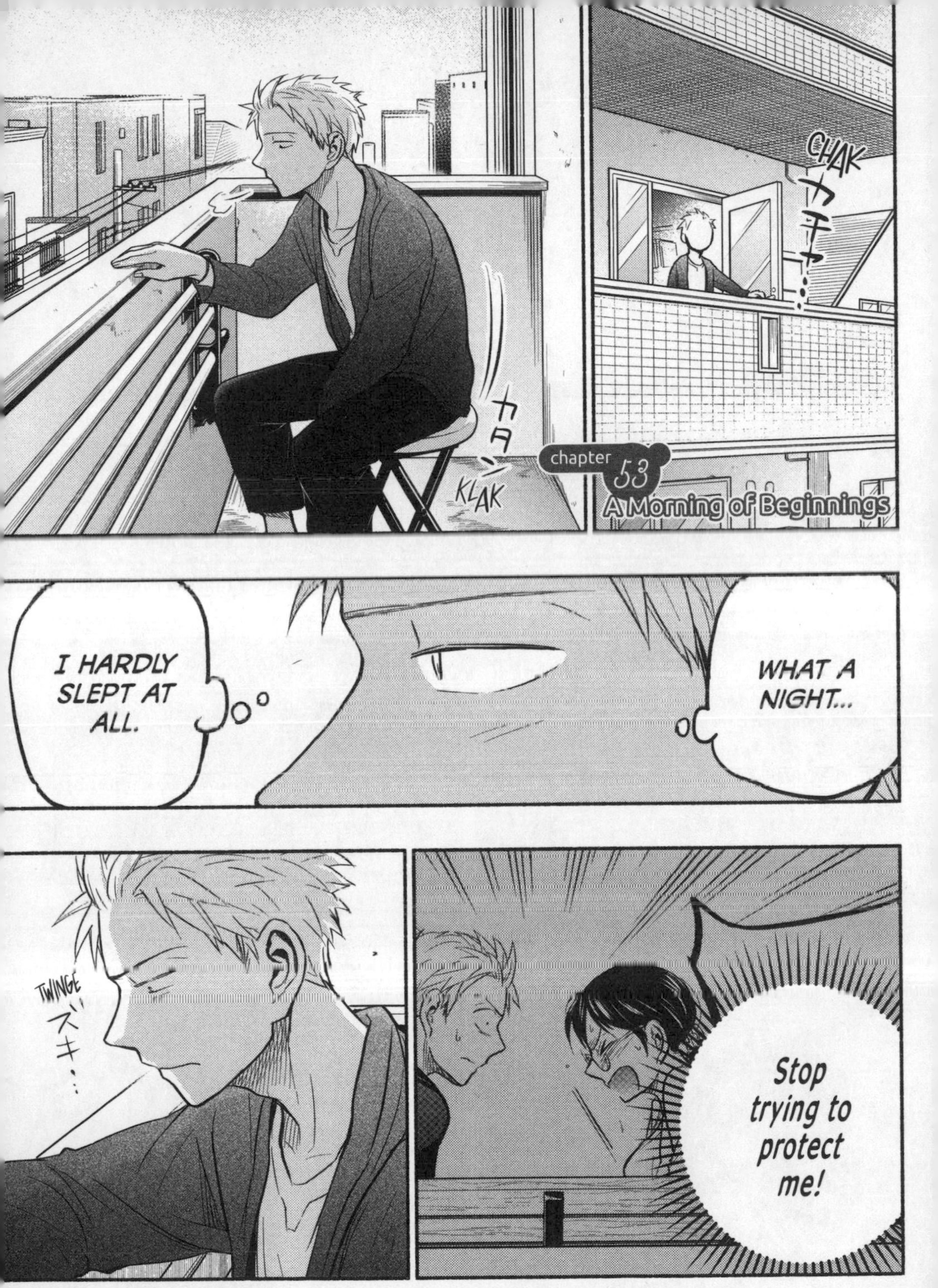
CHAK
カチャ…
chapter 53
A Morning of Beginnings
カタン
KLAK
WHAT A NIGHT...
I HARDLY SLEPT AT ALL.
Stop trying to protect me!
TWINGE
ズキ…

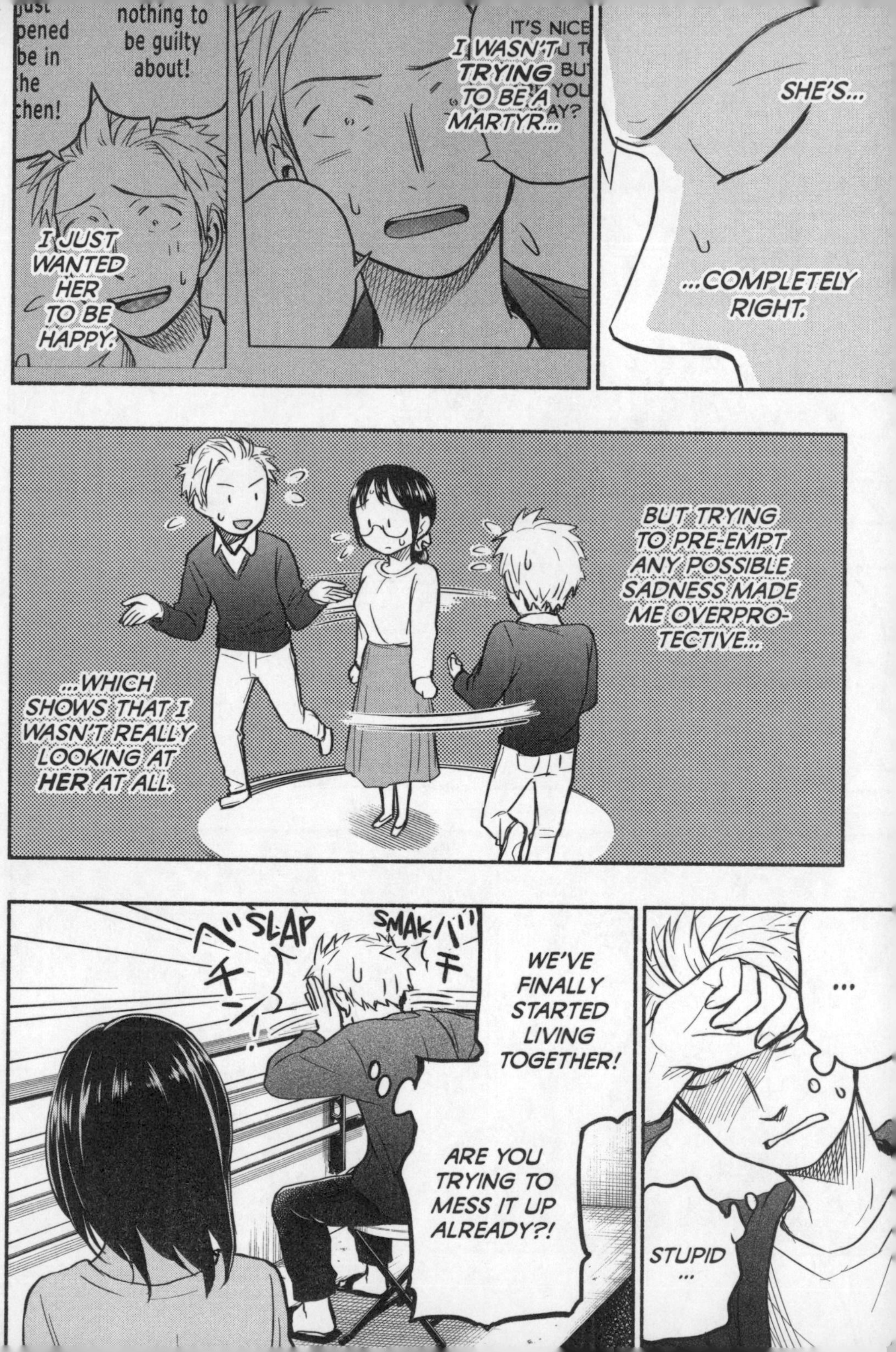
SHE'S...
...COMPLETELY RIGHT.
I WASN'T TRYING TO BE A MARTYR...
nothing to be guilty about!
I JUST WANTED HER TO BE HAPPY.
BUT TRYING TO PRE-EMPT ANY POSSIBLE SADNESS MADE ME OVERPRO-TECTIVE...
...WHICH SHOWS THAT I WASN'T REALLY LOOKING AT HER AT ALL.
...
STUPID ...
SMAK
SLAP
WE'VE FINALLY STARTED LIVING TOGETHER!
ARE YOU TRYING TO MESS IT UP ALREADY?!

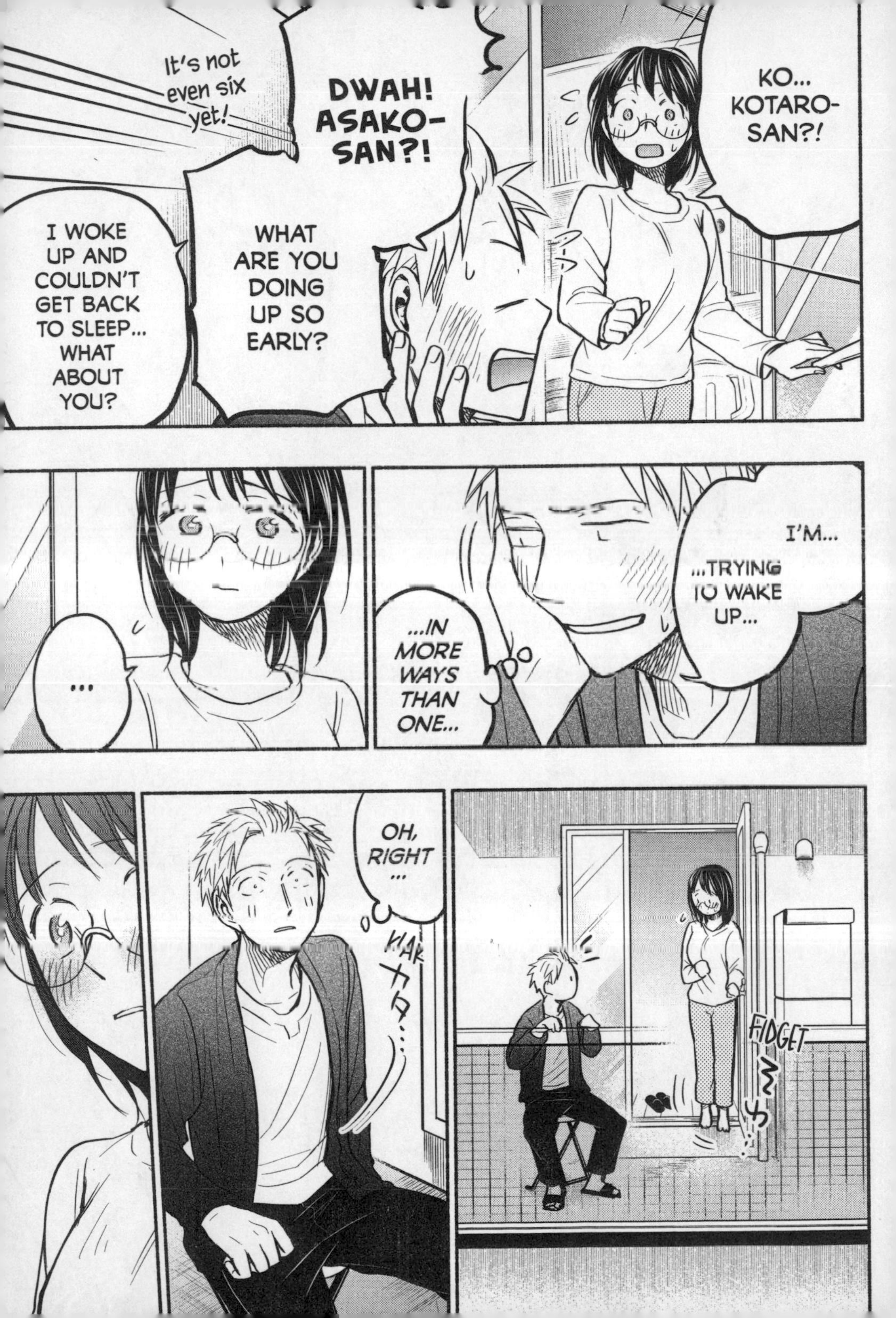
KO... KOTARO-SAN?!
DWAH! ASAKO-SAN?!
It's not even six yet!
WHAT ARE YOU DOING UP SO EARLY?
I WOKE UP AND COULDN'T GET BACK TO SLEEP... WHAT ABOUT YOU?
I'M...
...TRYING TO WAKE UP...
...IN MORE WAYS THAN ONE...
...
FIDGET
OH, RIGHT ...
KLAK
カタ...

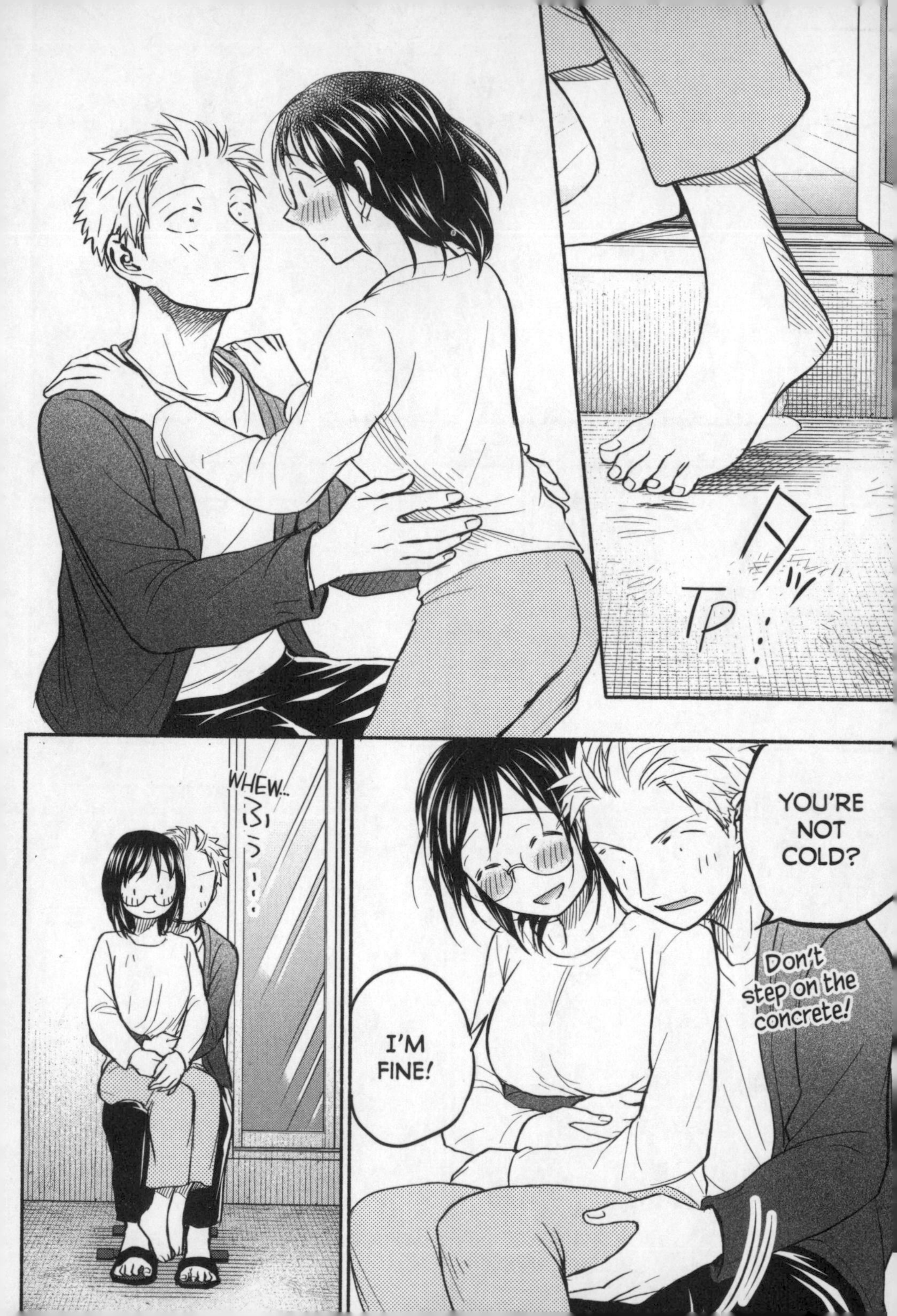
タッ
TP
YOU'RE NOT COLD?
Don't step on the concrete!
I'M FINE!
WHEW...
ふぅ…

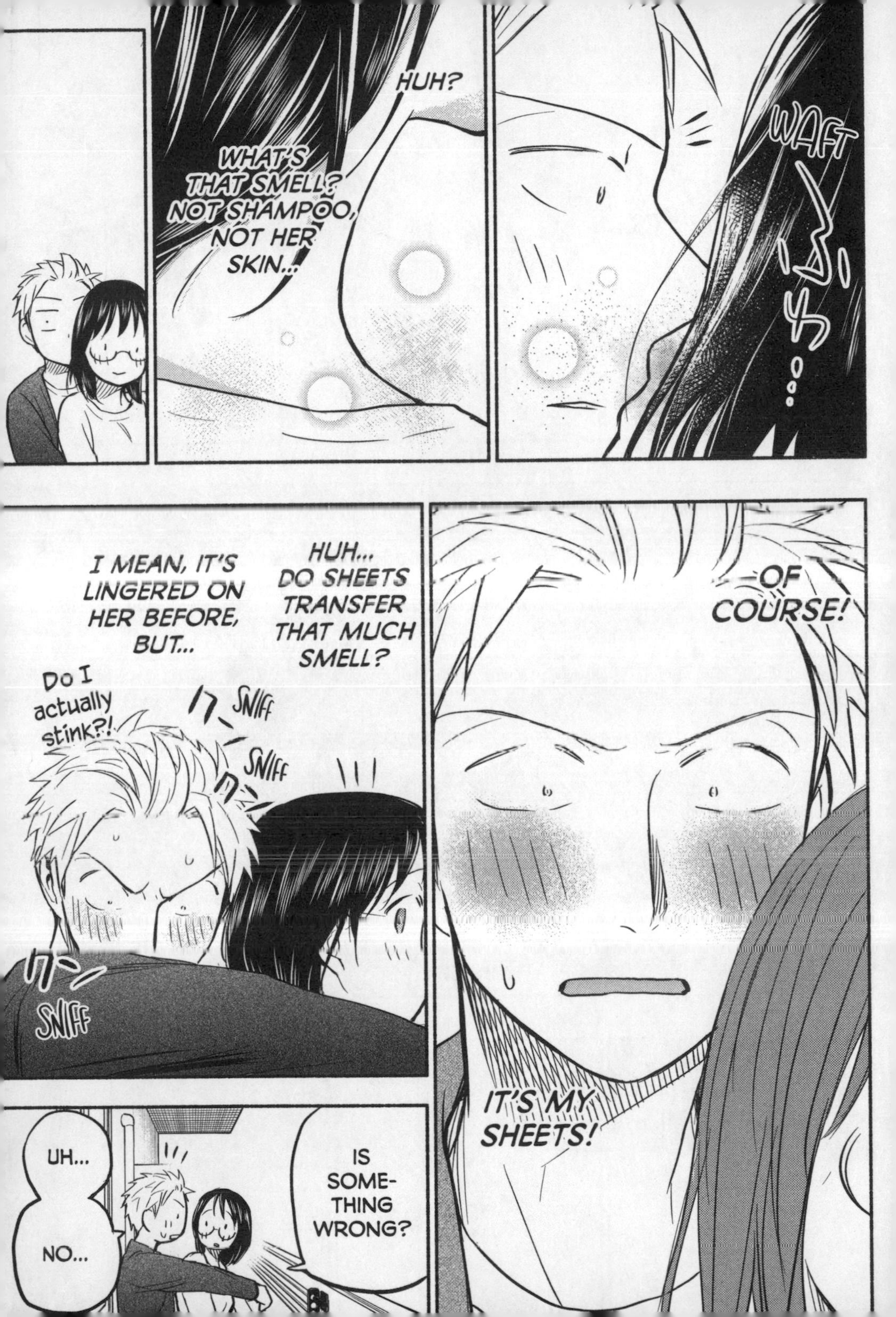
WAFT
HUH?
WHAT'S THAT SMELL? NOT SHAMPOO, NOT HER SKIN...
—OF COURSE!
IT'S MY SHEETS!
HUH... DO SHEETS TRANSFER THAT MUCH SMELL?
I MEAN, IT'S LINGERED ON HER BEFORE, BUT...
Do I actually stink?!
SNIFF
SNIFF
SNIFF
IS SOME-THING WRONG?
UH... NO...

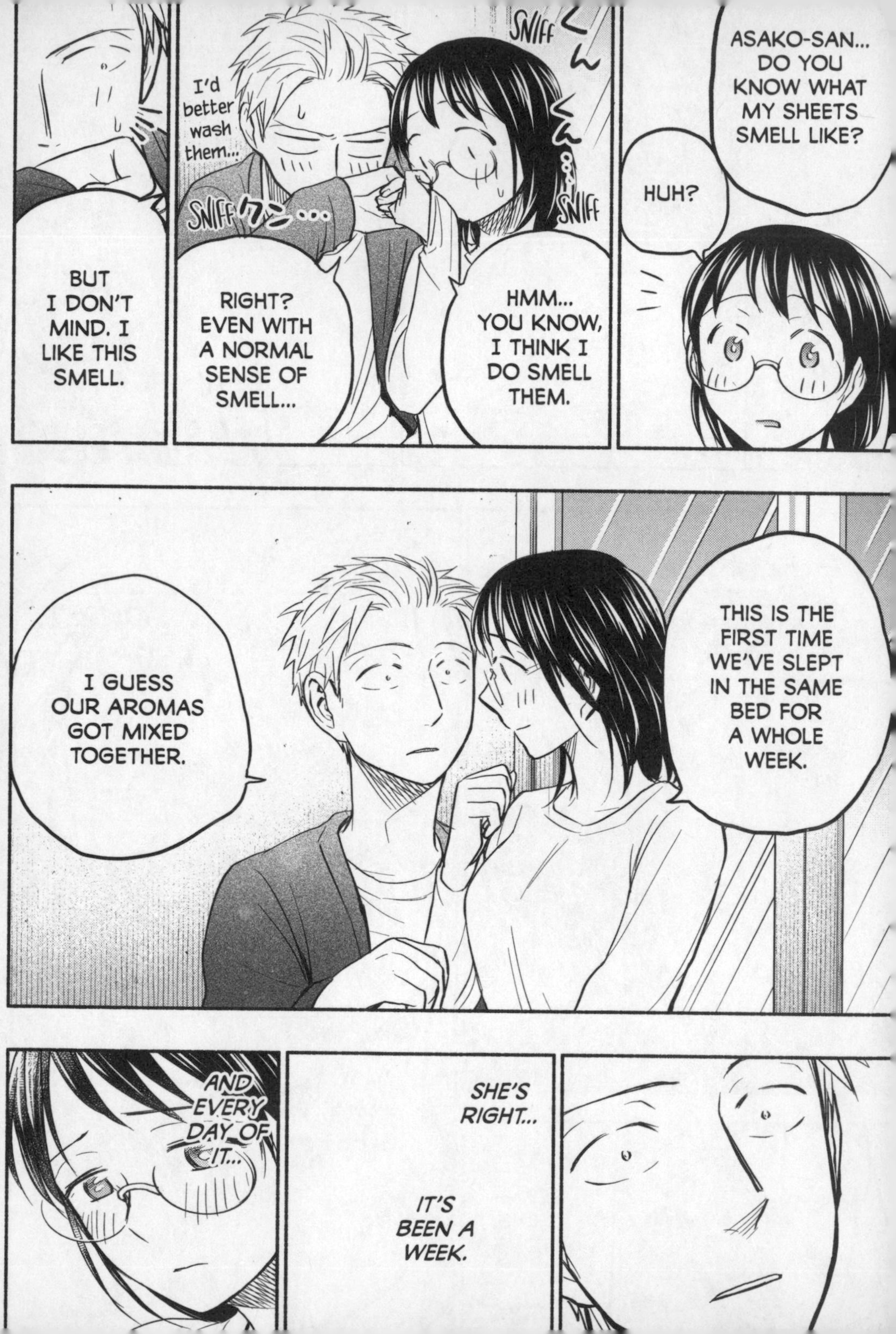
ASAKO-SAN... DO YOU KNOW WHAT MY SHEETS SMELL LIKE?
HUH?
SNIFF くん
くん...SNIFF
HMM... YOU KNOW, I THINK I DO SMELL THEM.
RIGHT? EVEN WITH A NORMAL SENSE OF SMELL...
I'd better wash them...
SNIFF クン...
BUT I DON'T MIND. I LIKE THIS SMELL.
THIS IS THE FIRST TIME WE'VE SLEPT IN THE SAME BED FOR A WHOLE WEEK.
I GUESS OUR AROMAS GOT MIXED TOGETHER.
SHE'S RIGHT...
IT'S BEEN A WEEK.
AND EVERY DAY OF IT...

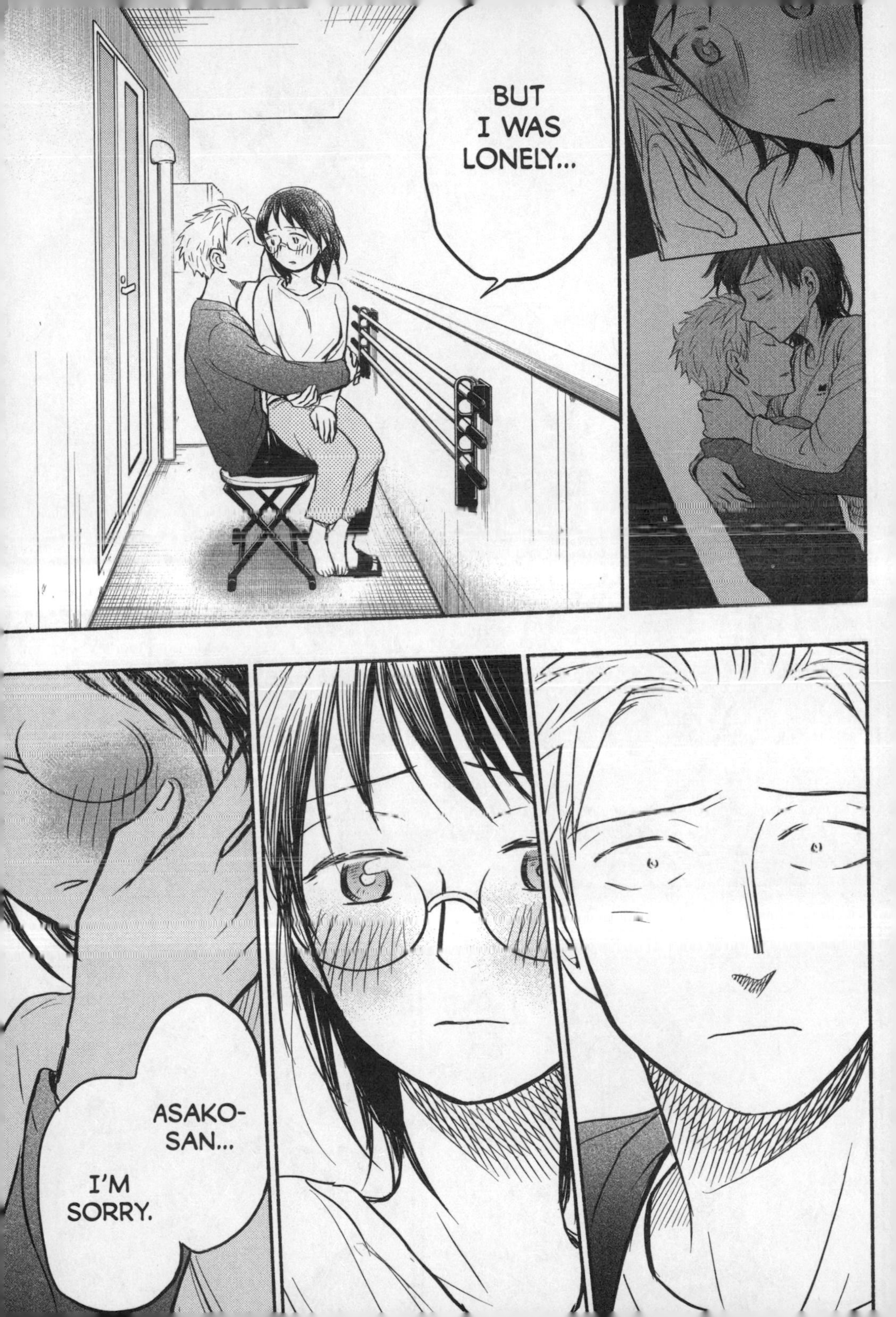
BUT I WAS LONELY...
ASAKO-SAN...
I'M SORRY.

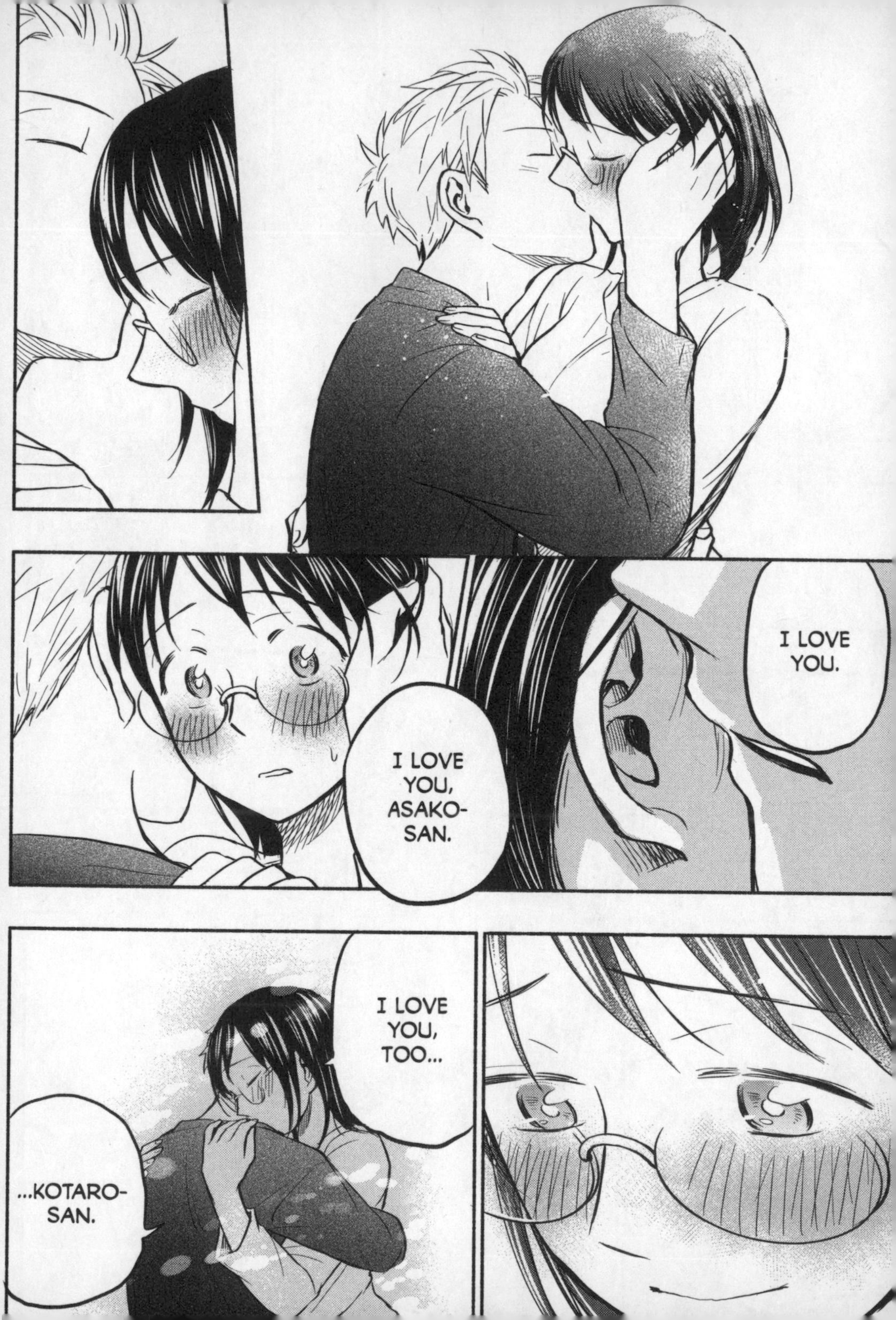
I LOVE YOU.
I LOVE YOU, ASAKO-SAN.
I LOVE YOU, TOO...
...KOTARO-SAN.

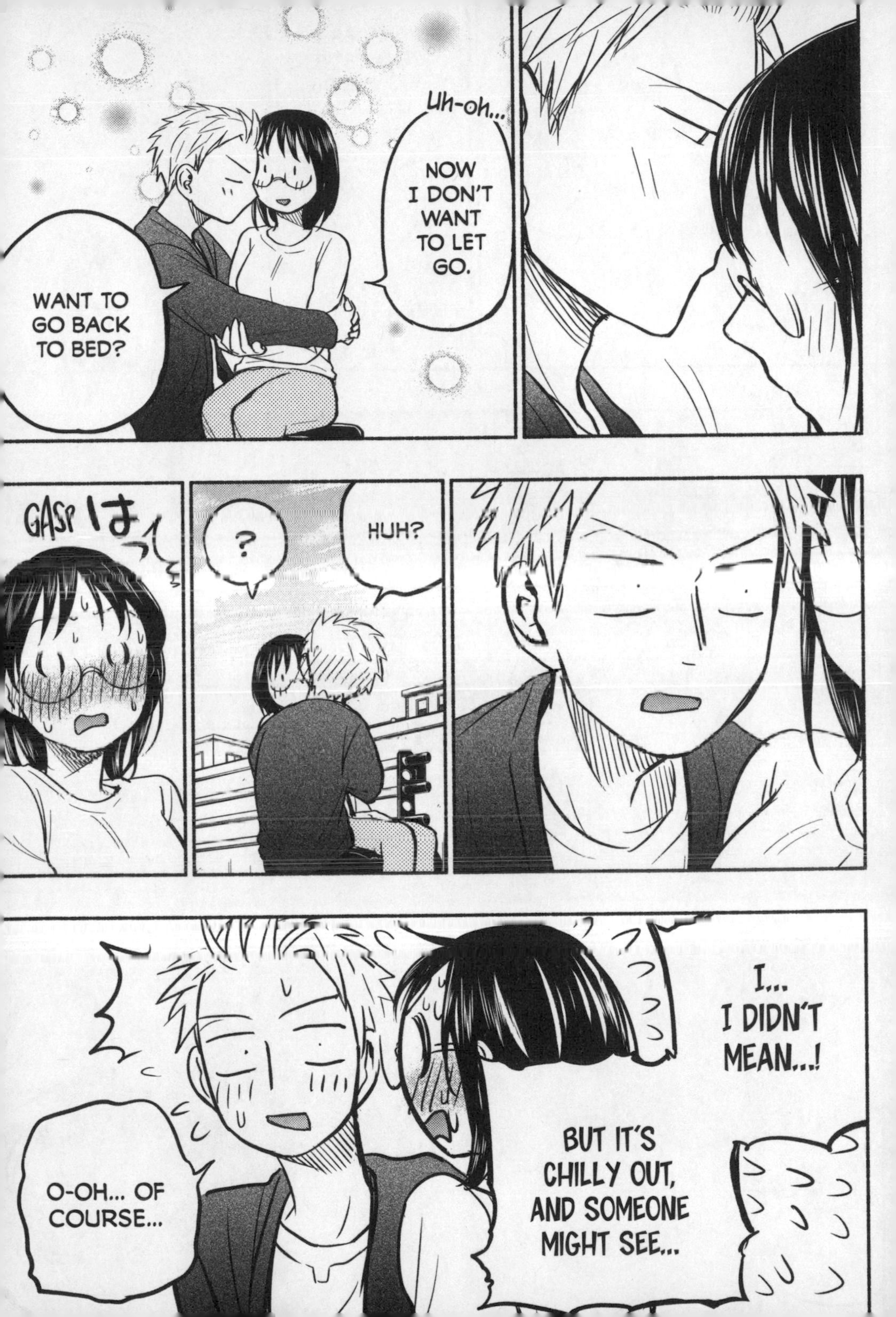
Uh-oh...
NOW I DON'T WANT TO LET GO.
WANT TO GO BACK TO BED?
HUH?
?
GASP
はっ
I... I DIDN'T MEAN...!
BUT IT'S CHILLY OUT, AND SOMEONE MIGHT SEE...
O-OH... OF COURSE...

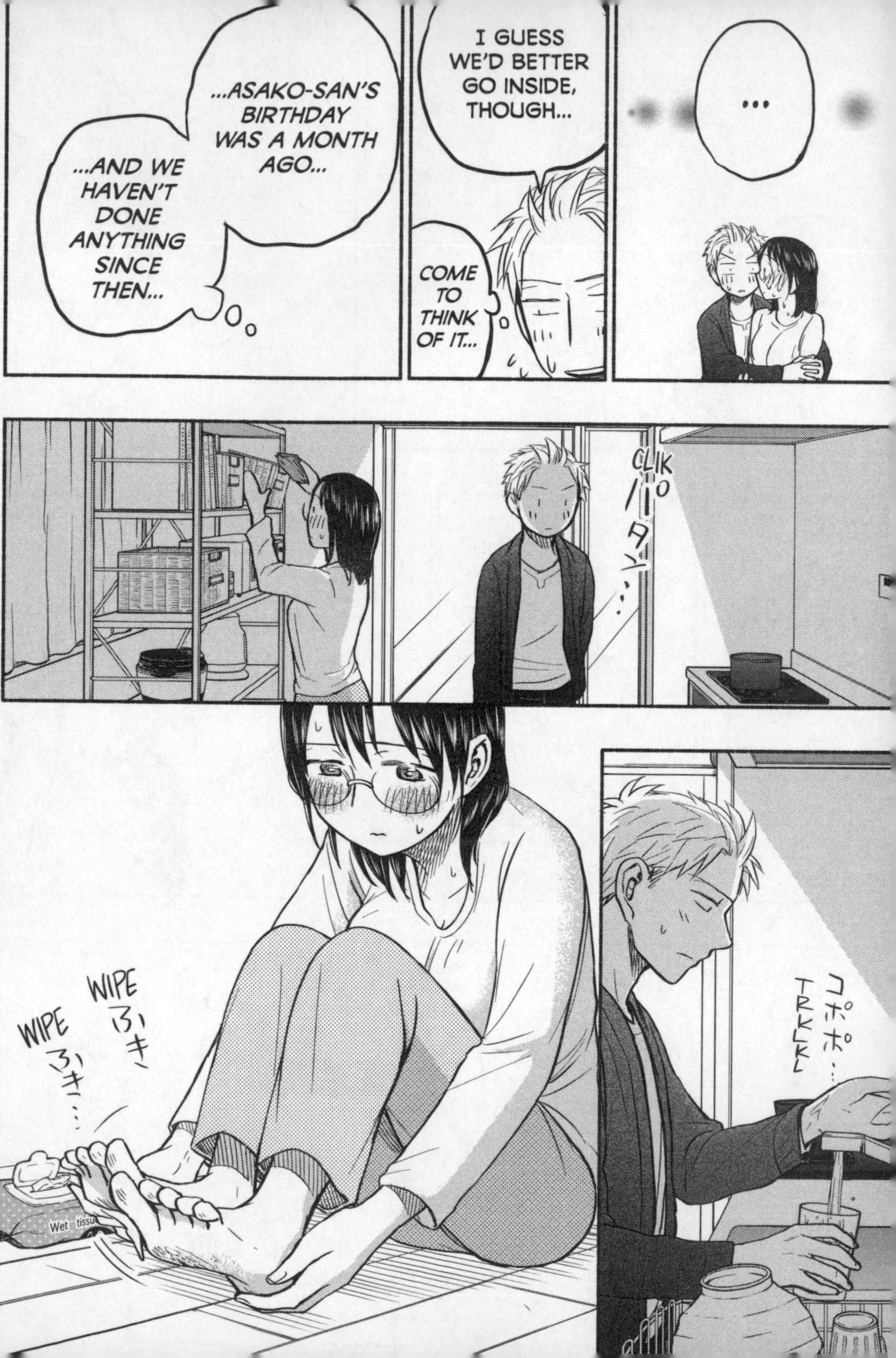
...
I GUESS WE'D BETTER GO INSIDE, THOUGH...
COME TO THINK OF IT...
...ASAKO-SAN'S BIRTHDAY WAS A MONTH AGO...
...AND WE HAVEN'T DONE ANYTHING SINCE THEN...
CLIK
パタン…
TRKLKL
コポポ…
WIPE
ふき
WIPE
ふき…
Wet tissu

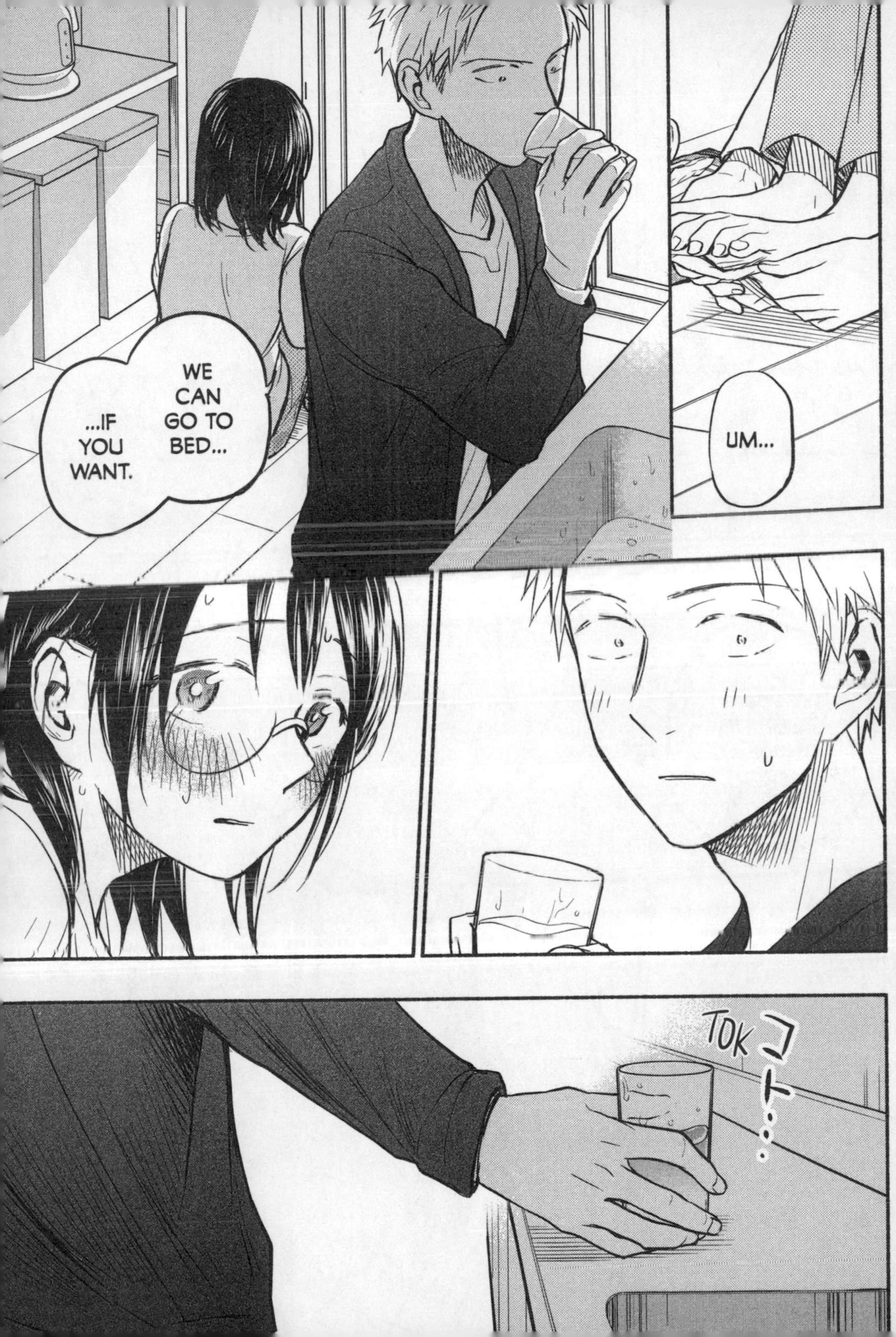
UM...
WE CAN GO TO BED...
...IF YOU WANT.
TOK
コト…

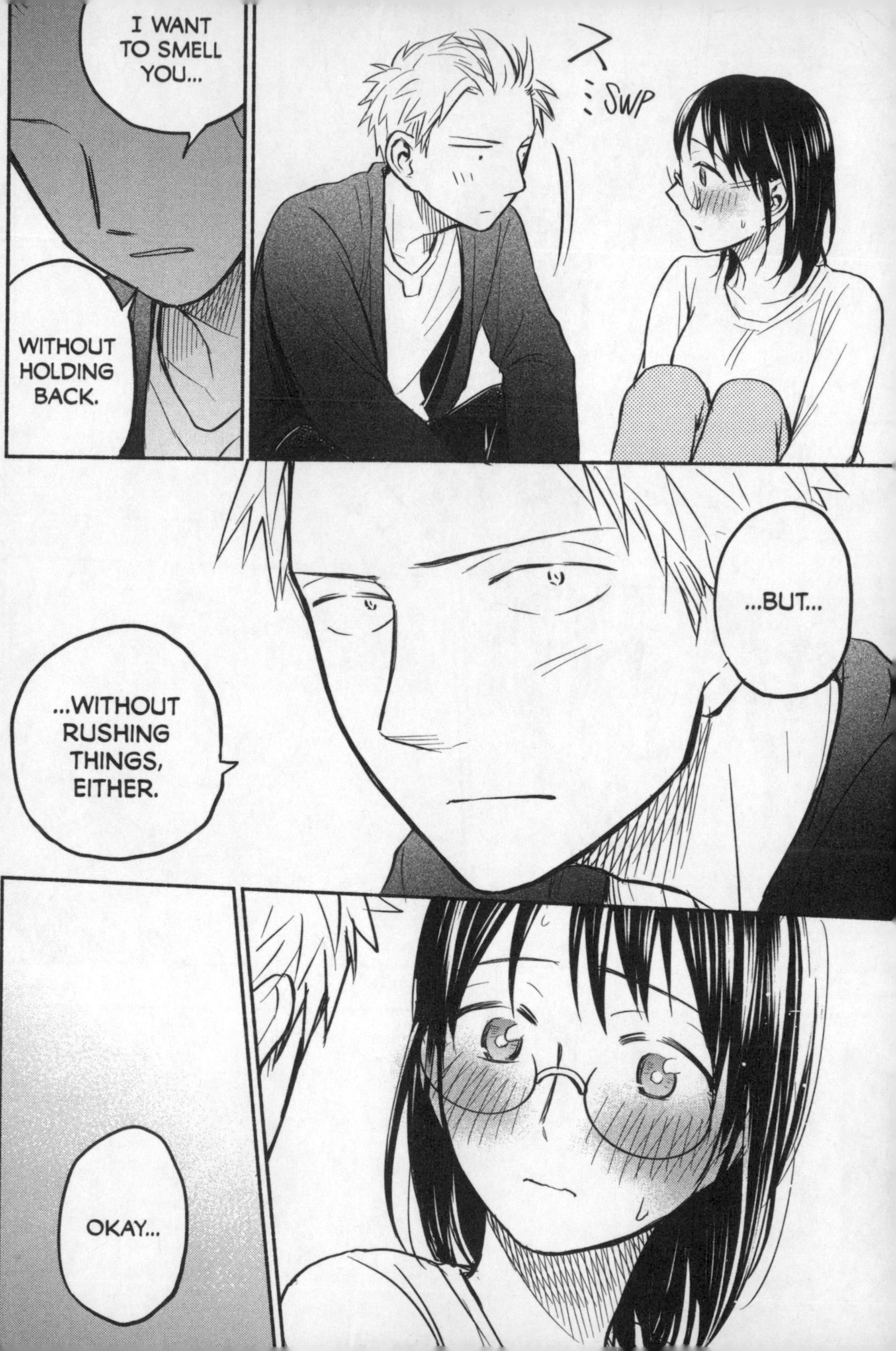
ス
SWP
I WANT TO SMELL YOU...
WITHOUT HOLDING BACK.
...BUT...
...WITHOUT RUSHING THINGS, EITHER.
OKAY...

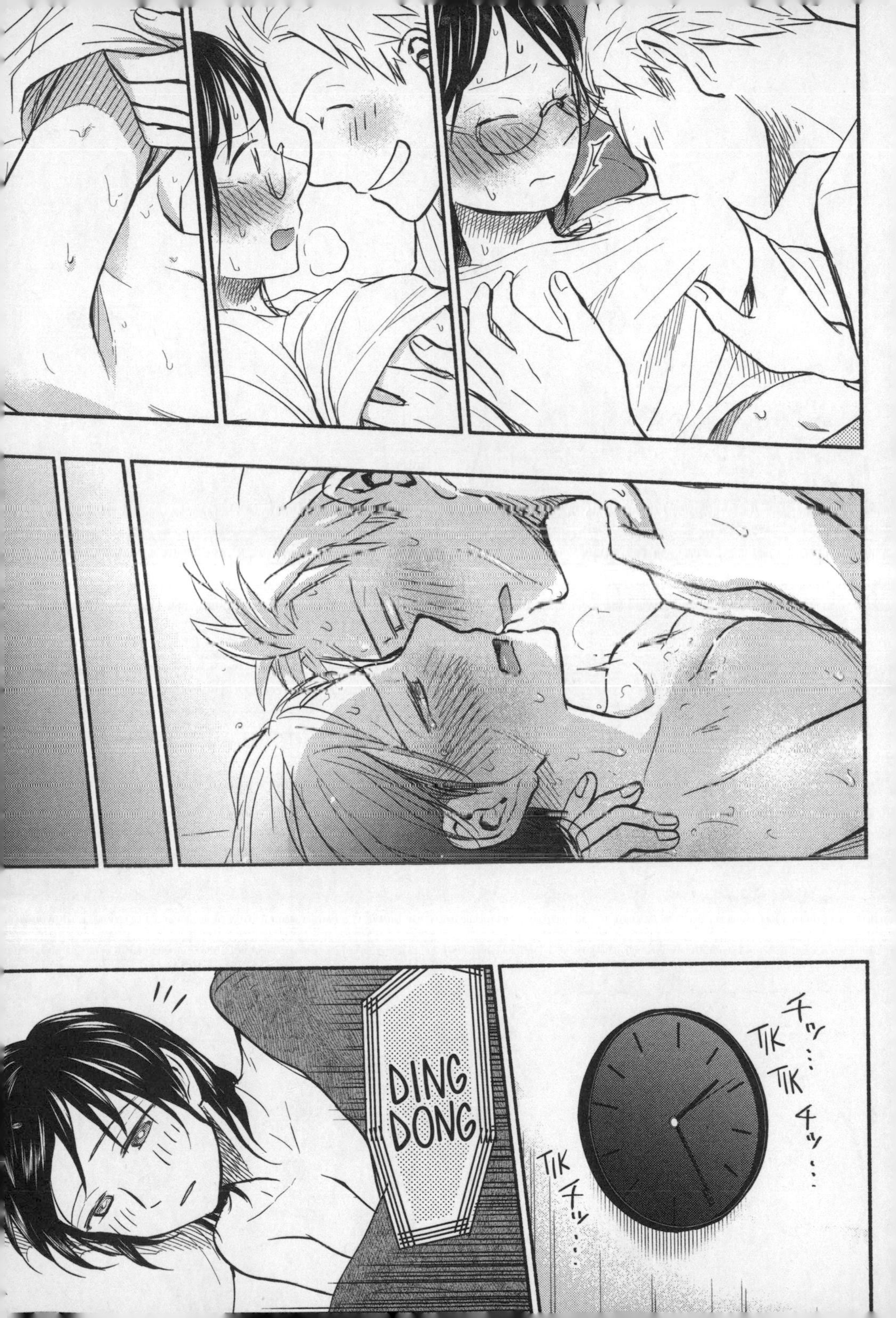
チッ…
TIK
TIK
チッ…
TIK
チッ…
DING
DONG

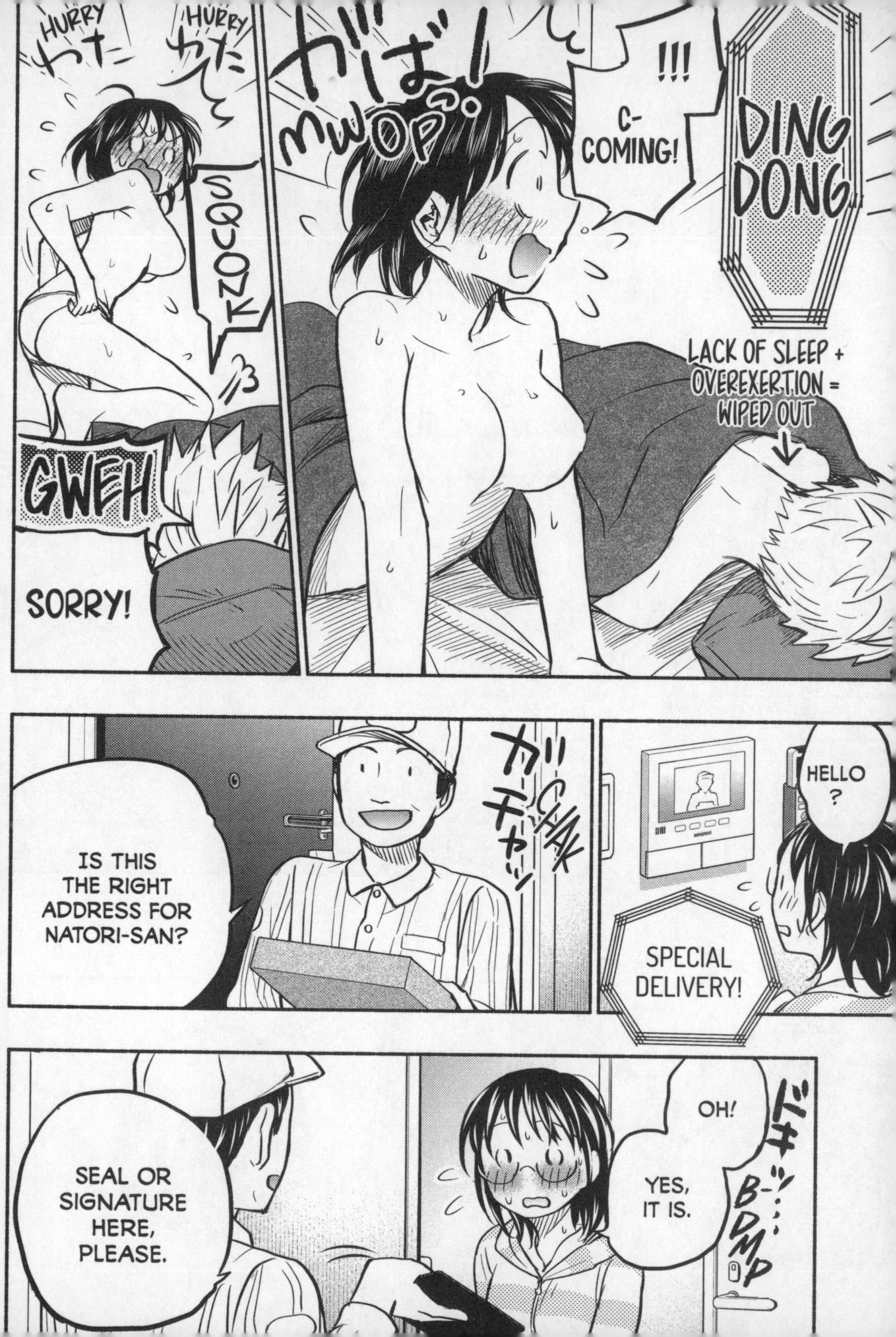
DING DONG
LACK OF SLEEP + OVEREXERTION = WIPED OUT
!!!
C- COMING!
がばっ!
MWOP
HURRY HURRY
わた わた
SQUONK
GWEH
SORRY!
HELLO ?
SPECIAL DELIVERY!
ガチャッ
CHAK
IS THIS THE RIGHT ADDRESS FOR NATORI-SAN?
ドキッ
B-BDMP
OH!
YES, IT IS.
SEAL OR SIGNATURE HERE, PLEASE.

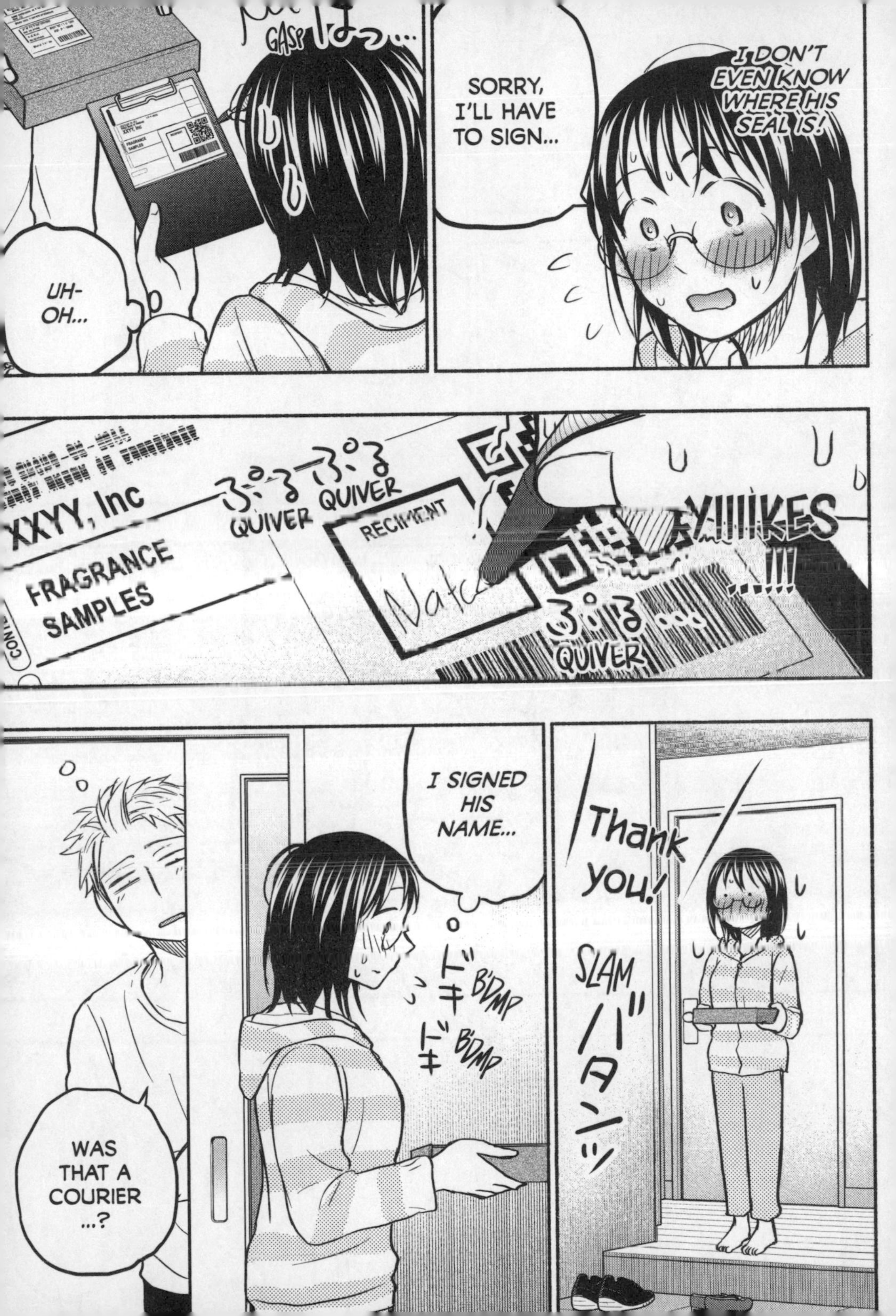
I DON'T EVEN KNOW WHERE HIS SEAL IS!
SORRY, I'LL HAVE TO SIGN...
GASP はっ…
UH-OH...
XXYY, Inc
FRAGRANCE SAMPLES
YIIIKES
ぷるぷる QUIVER
ぷるぷる QUIVER
ぷる QUIVER
Thank you!
SLAM バタンッ
I SIGNED HIS NAME...
ドキ B'DMP
ドキ B'DMP
WAS THAT A COURIER ...?

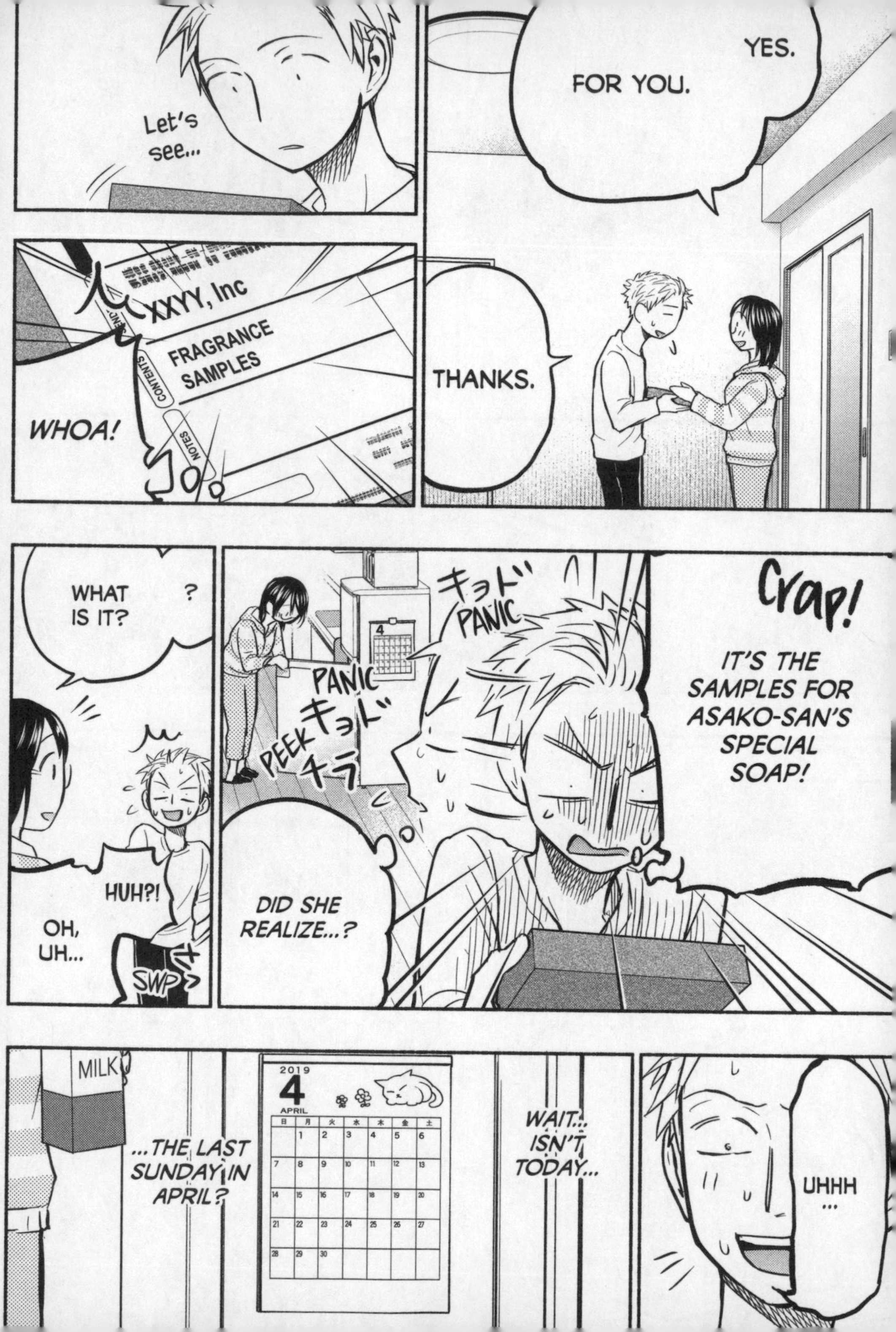
YES.
FOR YOU.
Let's see...
THANKS.
XXYY, Inc
CONTENTS
FRAGRANCE SAMPLES
NOTES
WHOA!
Crap!
IT'S THE SAMPLES FOR ASAKO-SAN'S SPECIAL SOAP!
キョド PANIC
PANIC キョド
PEEK チラ
DID SHE REALIZE...?
WHAT IS IT?
?
HUH?!
OH, UH...
SWP サッ
UHHH...
WAIT... ISN'T TODAY...
2019
4
APRIL
...THE LAST SUNDAY IN APRIL?
MILK

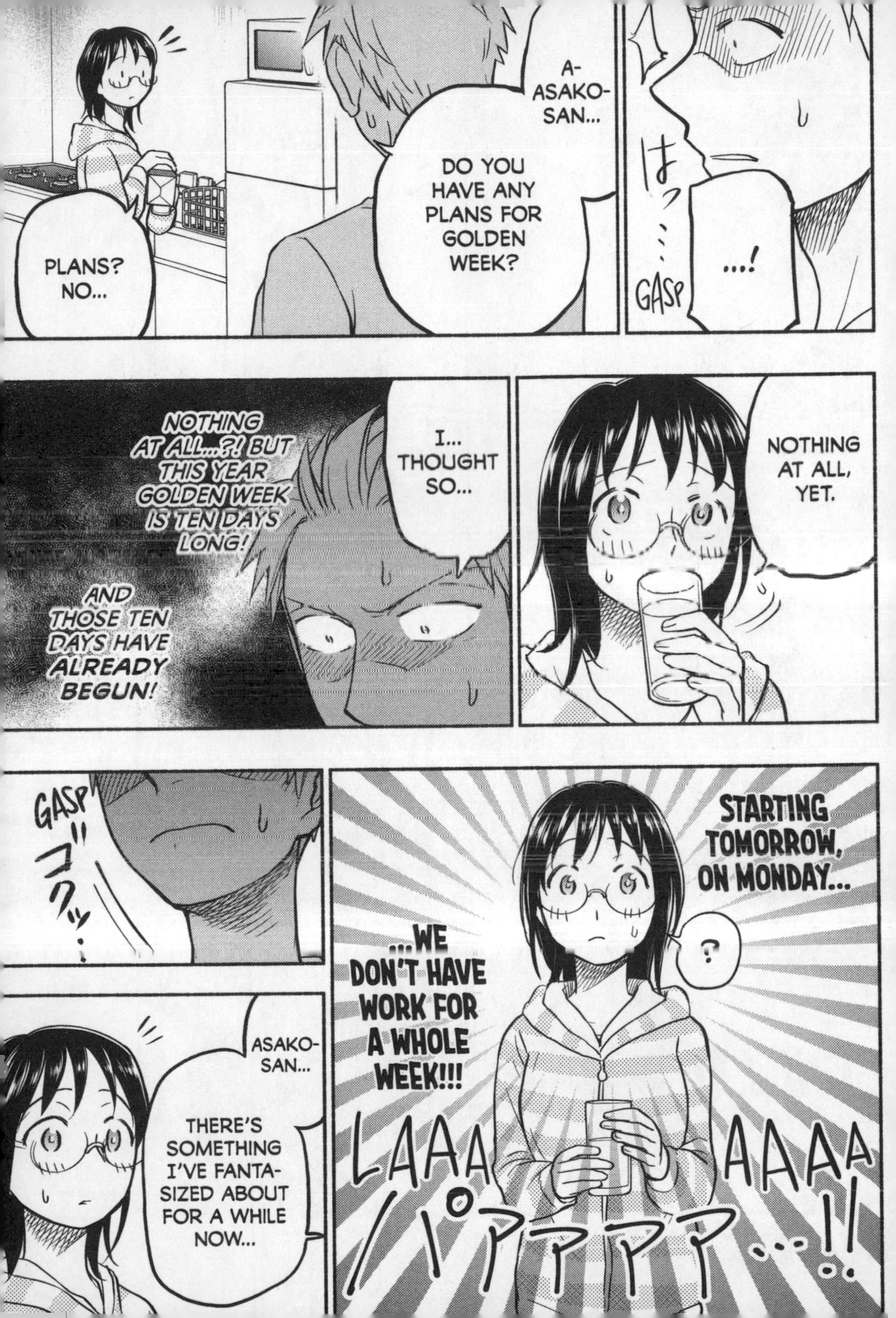
はっ……
GASP
...!
A- ASAKO-SAN...
DO YOU HAVE ANY PLANS FOR GOLDEN WEEK?
PLANS? NO...
NOTHING AT ALL, YET.
I... THOUGHT SO...
NOTHING AT ALL...?! BUT THIS YEAR GOLDEN WEEK IS TEN DAYS LONG!
AND THOSE TEN DAYS HAVE ALREADY BEGUN!
STARTING TOMORROW, ON MONDAY...
?
...WE DON'T HAVE WORK FOR A WHOLE WEEK!!!
LAAA AAAA
パアアアア…!!
GASP
ゴクッ…
ASAKO-SAN...
THERE'S SOMETHING I'VE FANTA-SIZED ABOUT FOR A WHILE NOW...

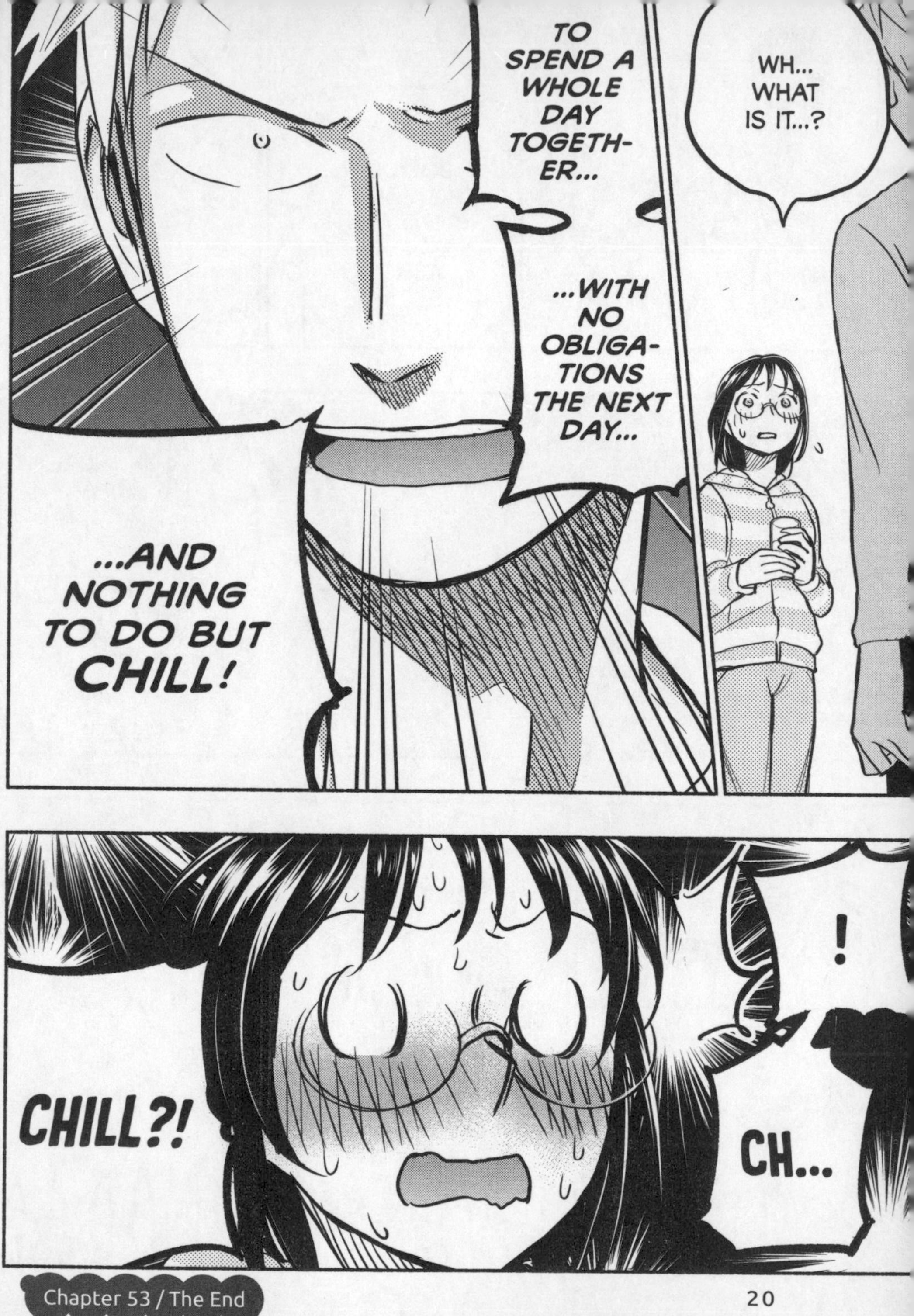
WH... WHAT IS IT...?
TO SPEND A WHOLE DAY TOGETH-ER...
...WITH NO OBLIGA-TIONS THE NEXT DAY...
...AND NOTHING TO DO BUT CHILL!
!
CH...
CHILL?!

Chapter 53 / The End

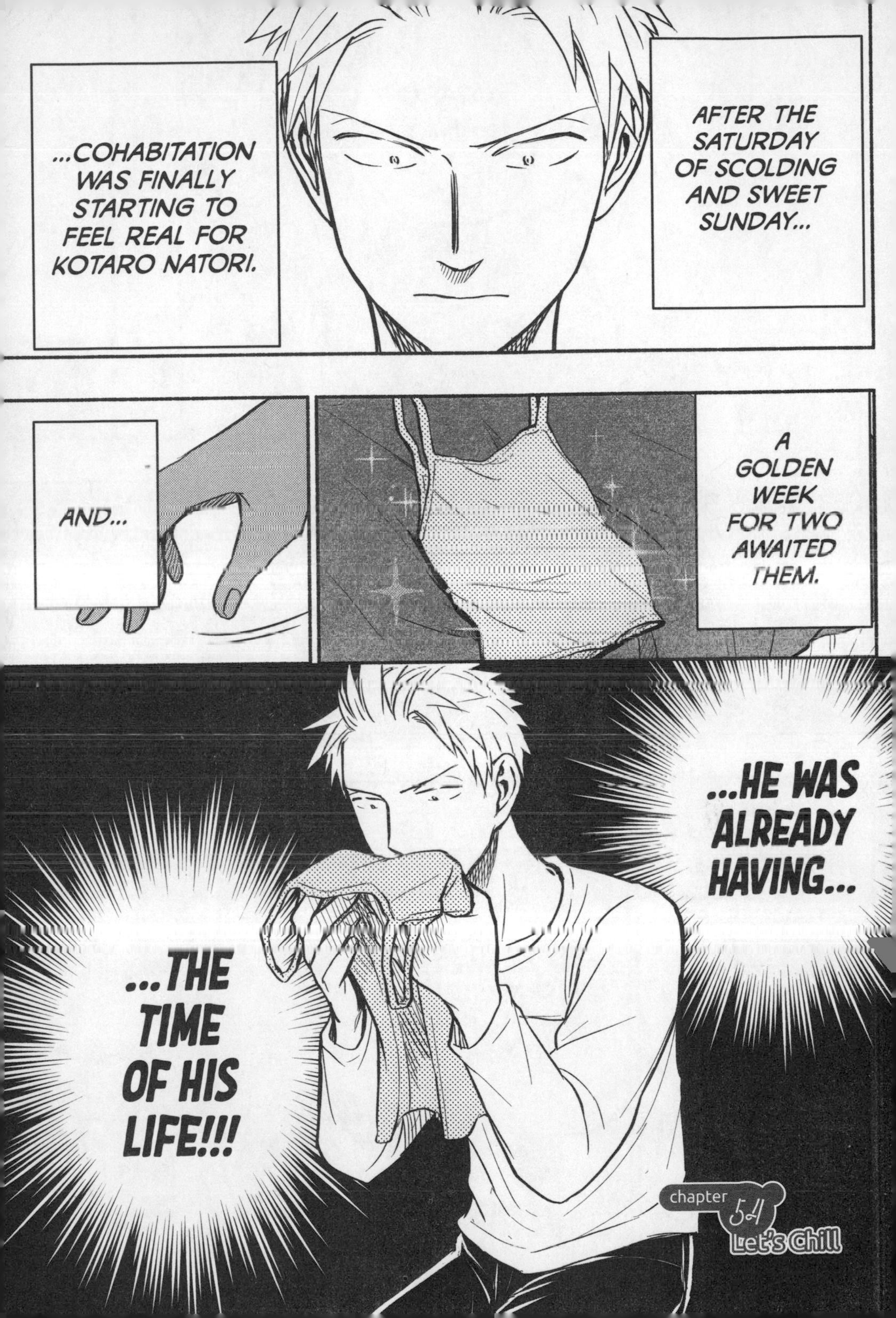
AFTER THE SATURDAY OF SCOLDING AND SWEET SUNDAY...
...COHABITATION WAS FINALLY STARTING TO FEEL REAL FOR KOTARO NATORI.
A GOLDEN WEEK FOR TWO AWAITED THEM.
AND...
...HE WAS ALREADY HAVING...
...THE TIME OF HIS LIFE!!!
chapter 54
Let's Chill

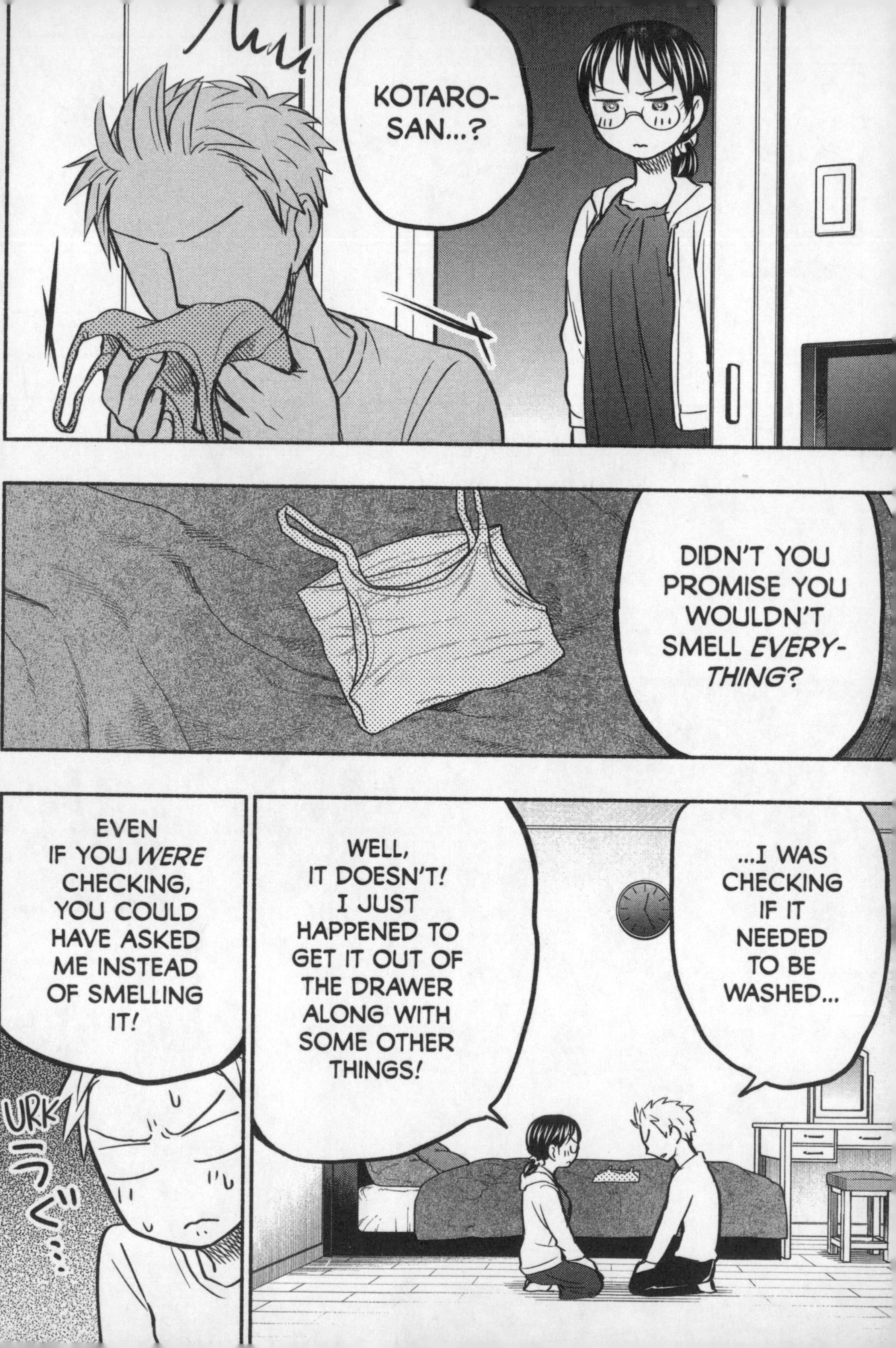
KOTARO-SAN...?
DIDN'T YOU PROMISE YOU WOULDN'T SMELL *EVERYTHING*?
...I WAS CHECKING IF IT NEEDED TO BE WASHED...
WELL, IT DOESN'T! I JUST HAPPENED TO GET IT OUT OF THE DRAWER ALONG WITH SOME OTHER THINGS!
EVEN IF YOU *WERE* CHECKING, YOU COULD HAVE ASKED ME INSTEAD OF SMELLING IT!
URK
うぐ…

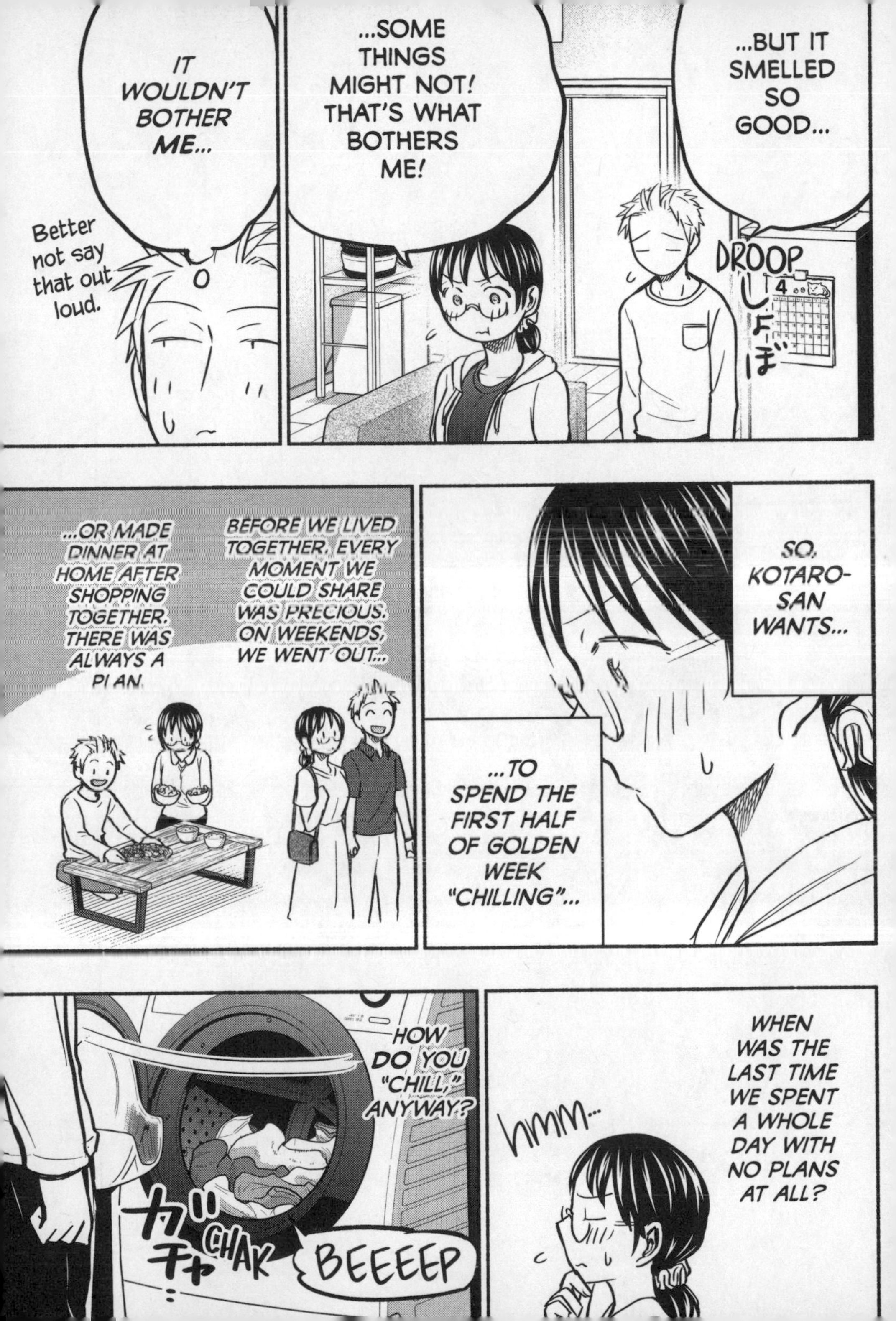
...BUT IT SMELLED SO GOOD...
DROOP
しょぼ
...SOME THINGS MIGHT NOT! THAT'S WHAT BOTHERS ME!
IT WOULDN'T BOTHER ME...
Better not say that out loud.
SO, KOTARO-SAN WANTS...
...TO SPEND THE FIRST HALF OF GOLDEN WEEK "CHILLING"...
BEFORE WE LIVED TOGETHER, EVERY MOMENT WE COULD SHARE WAS PRECIOUS. ON WEEKENDS, WE WENT OUT...
...OR MADE DINNER AT HOME AFTER SHOPPING TOGETHER. THERE WAS ALWAYS A PLAN.
WHEN WAS THE LAST TIME WE SPENT A WHOLE DAY WITH NO PLANS AT ALL?
hmm...
HOW DO YOU "CHILL," ANYWAY?
BEEEEP
カチャ
CHAK

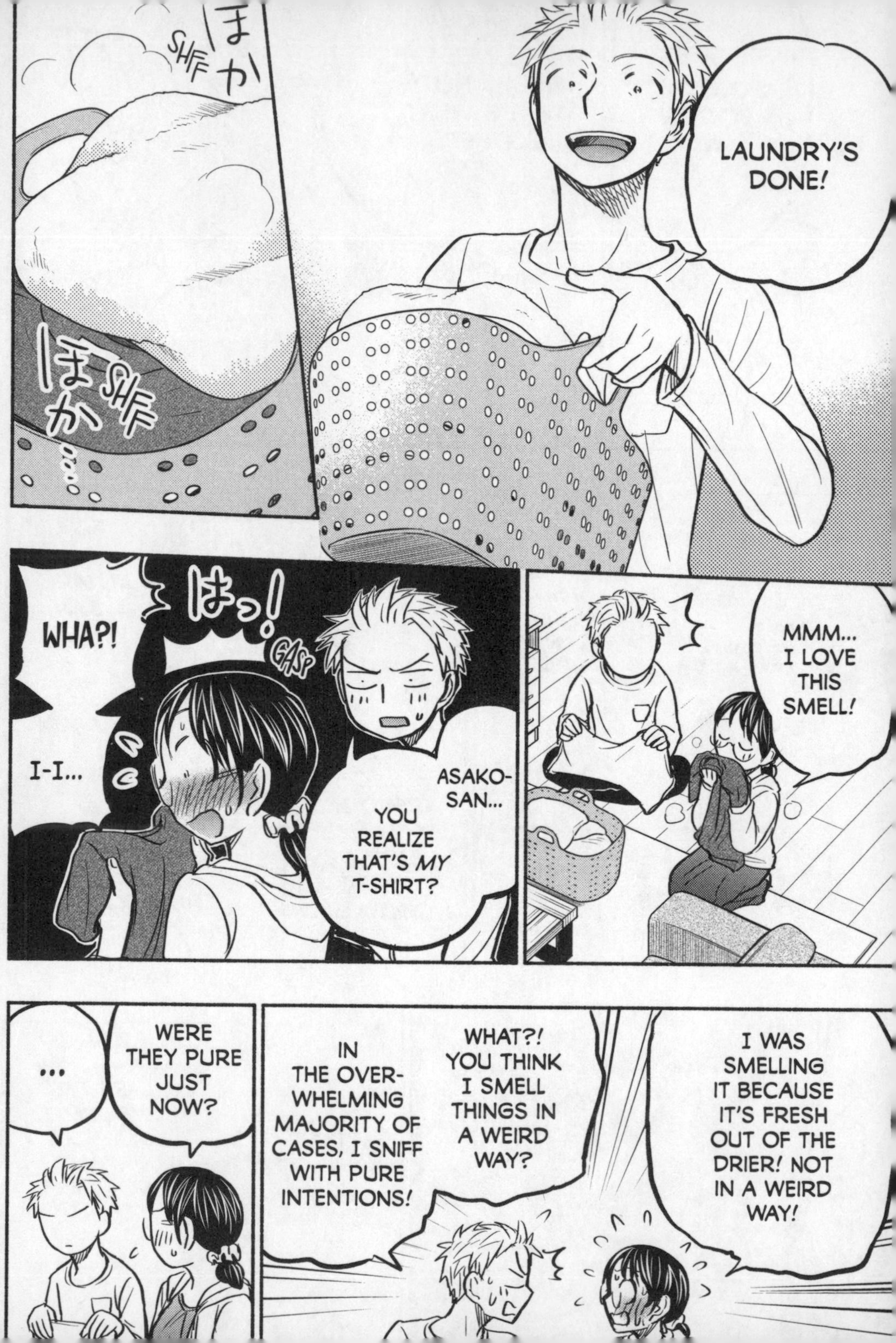
LAUNDRY'S DONE!
ほか
SHFF
ほか
SHFF
MMM... I LOVE THIS SMELL!
ASAKO-SAN...
YOU REALIZE THAT'S *MY* T-SHIRT?
はっ!
GASP
WHA?!
I-I...
I WAS SMELLING IT BECAUSE IT'S FRESH OUT OF THE DRIER! NOT IN A WEIRD WAY!
WHAT?! YOU THINK I SMELL THINGS IN A WEIRD WAY?
IN THE OVER-WHELMING MAJORITY OF CASES, I SNIFF WITH PURE INTENTIONS!
WERE THEY PURE JUST NOW?
...

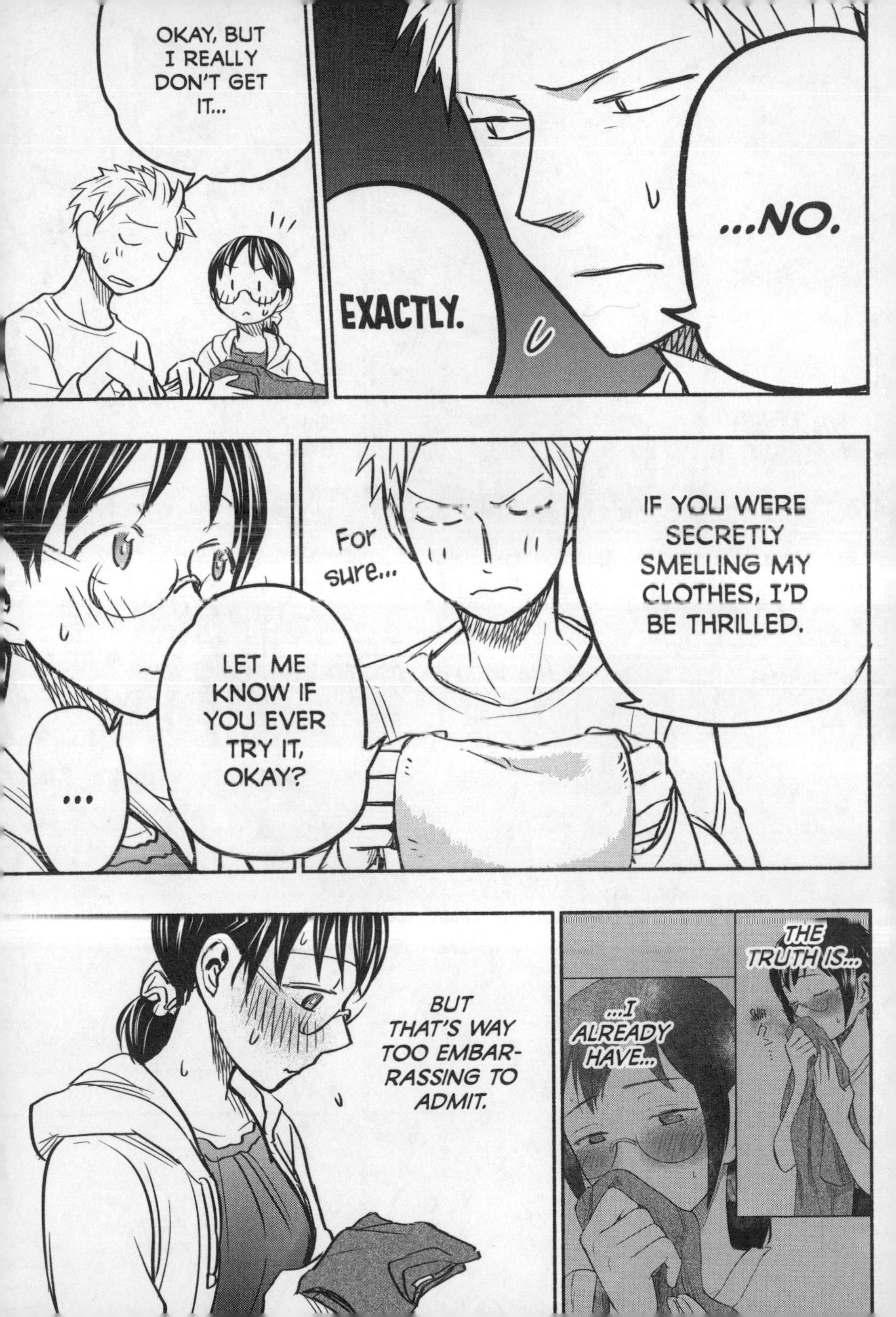
...NO.
EXACTLY.
OKAY, BUT I REALLY DON'T GET IT...
IF YOU WERE SECRETLY SMELLING MY CLOTHES, I'D BE THRILLED.
For sure...
LET ME KNOW IF YOU EVER TRY IT, OKAY?
...
THE TRUTH IS...
...I ALREADY HAVE...
SNIFF
BUT THAT'S WAY TOO EMBARRASSING TO ADMIT.

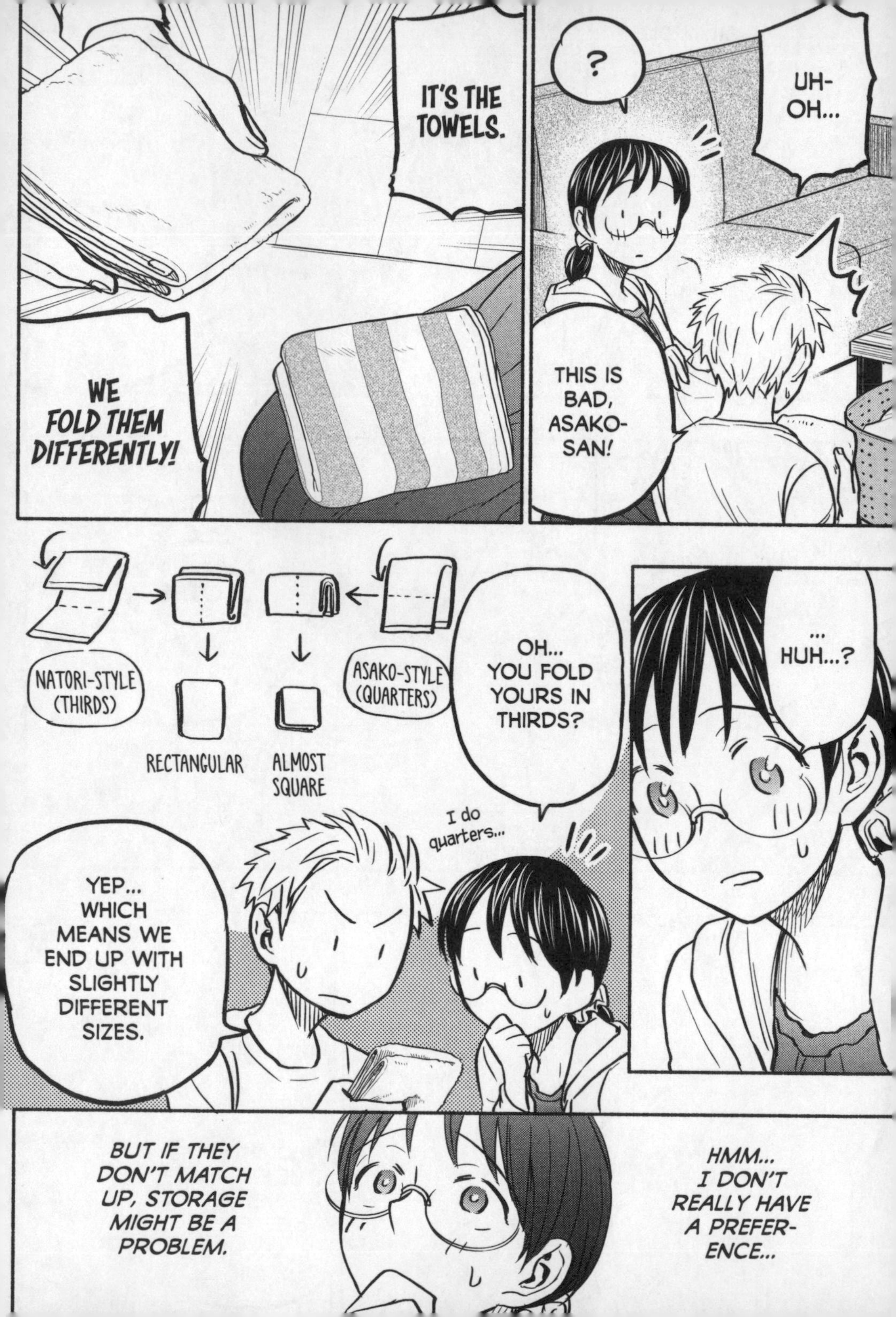
UH-OH...
?
THIS IS BAD, ASAKO-SAN!
IT'S THE TOWELS.
WE FOLD THEM DIFFERENTLY!
... HUH...?
OH... YOU FOLD YOURS IN THIRDS?
ASAKO-STYLE (QUARTERS)
NATORI-STYLE (THIRDS)
ALMOST SQUARE
RECTANGULAR
I do quarters...
YEP... WHICH MEANS WE END UP WITH SLIGHTLY DIFFERENT SIZES.
HMM... I DON'T REALLY HAVE A PREFER-ENCE...
BUT IF THEY DON'T MATCH UP, STORAGE MIGHT BE A PROBLEM.

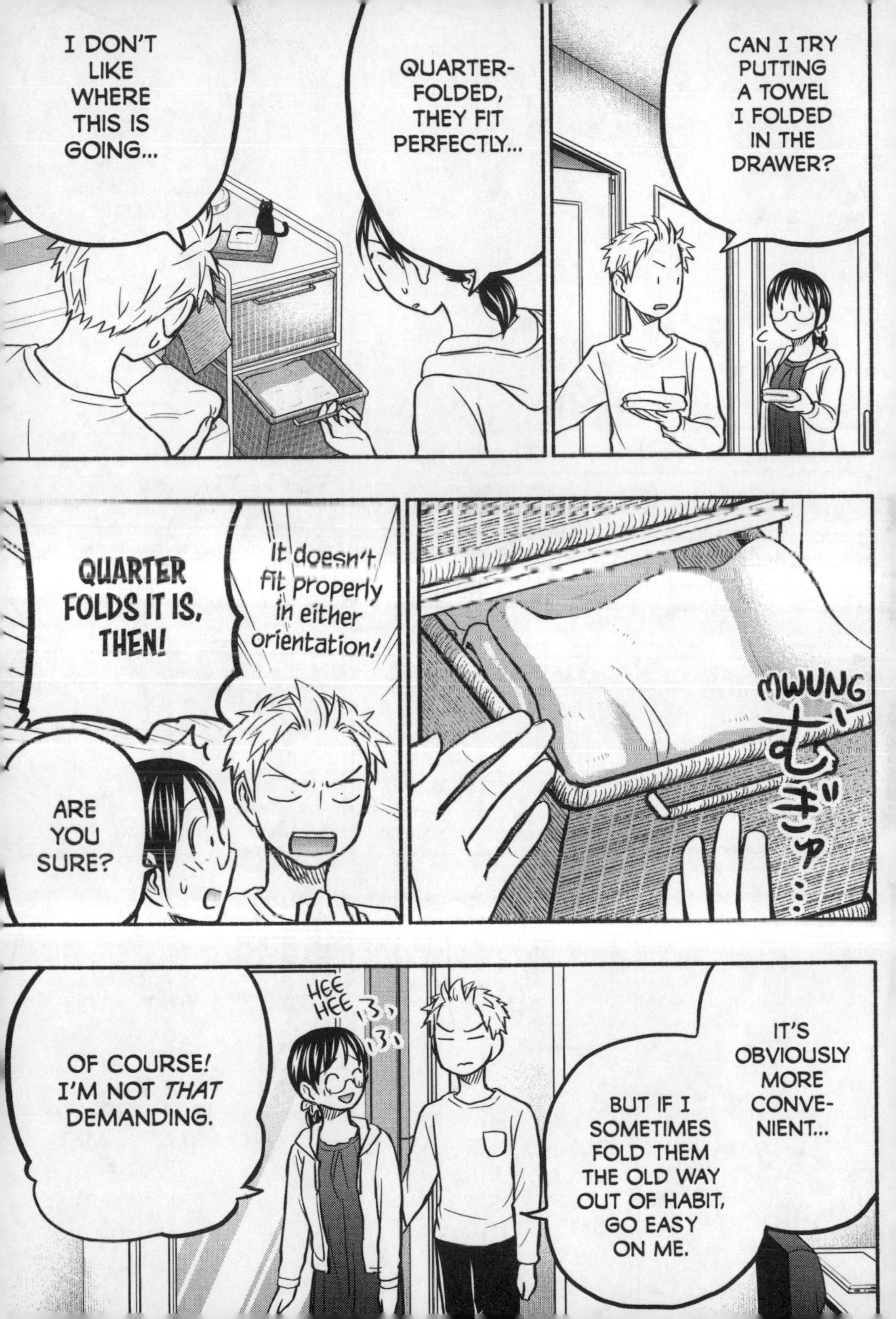
CAN I TRY PUTTING A TOWEL I FOLDED IN THE DRAWER?
QUARTER-FOLDED, THEY FIT PERFECTLY...
I DON'T LIKE WHERE THIS IS GOING...
MWUNG
むぎゅ…
It doesn't fit properly in either orientation!
QUARTER FOLDS IT IS, THEN!
ARE YOU SURE?
IT'S OBVIOUSLY MORE CONVENIENT...
BUT IF I SOMETIMES FOLD THEM THE OLD WAY OUT OF HABIT, GO EASY ON ME.
HEE HEE
ふふ
OF COURSE! I'M NOT *THAT* DEMANDING.

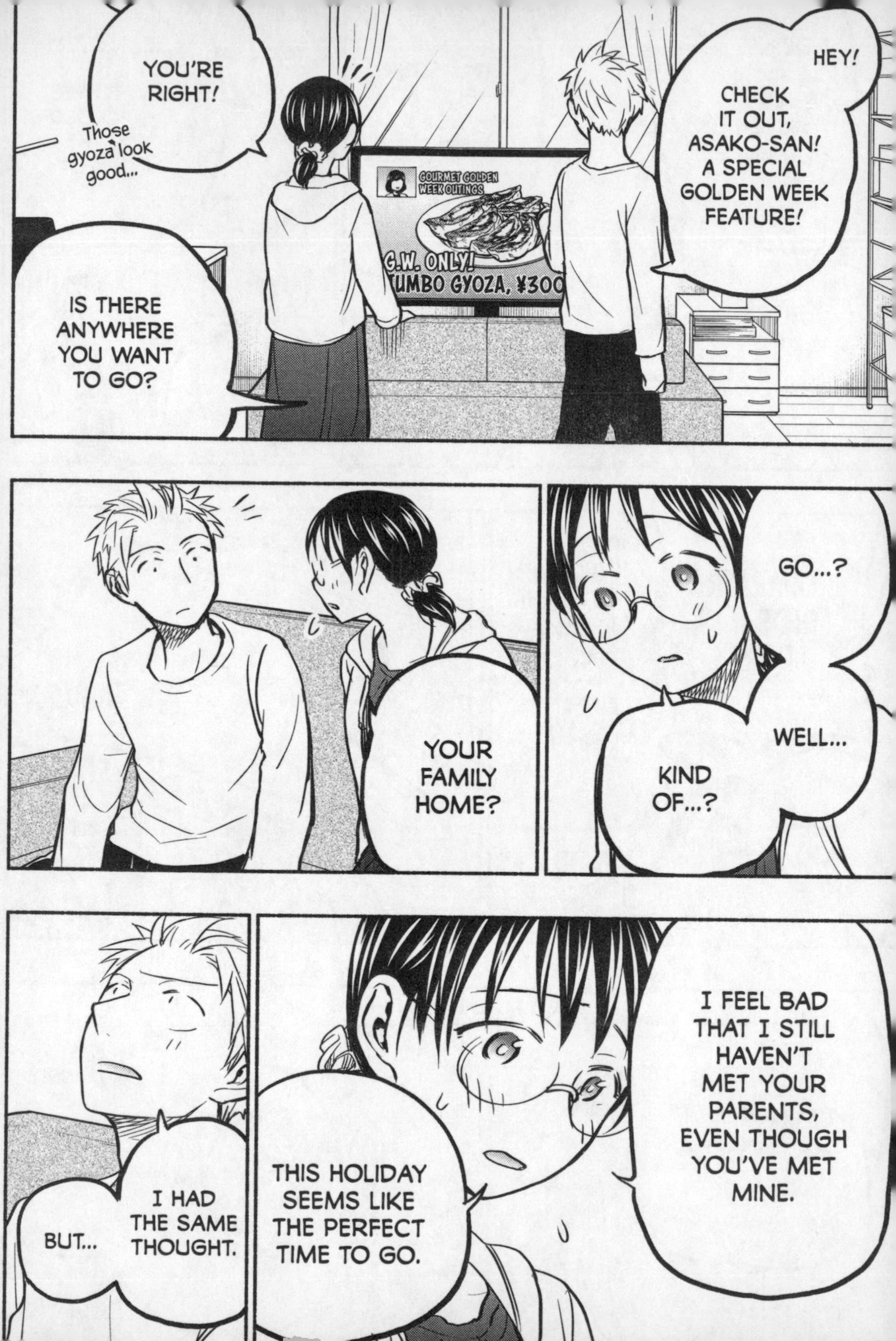
HEY!
CHECK IT OUT, ASAKO-SAN! A SPECIAL GOLDEN WEEK FEATURE!
GOURMET GOLDEN WEEK OUTINGS
G.W. ONLY!
JUMBO GYOZA, ¥300
YOU'RE RIGHT!
Those gyoza look good...
IS THERE ANYWHERE YOU WANT TO GO?
GO...?
WELL...
KIND OF...?
YOUR FAMILY HOME?
I FEEL BAD THAT I STILL HAVEN'T MET YOUR PARENTS, EVEN THOUGH YOU'VE MET MINE.
THIS HOLIDAY SEEMS LIKE THE PERFECT TIME TO GO.
I HAD THE SAME THOUGHT.
BUT...

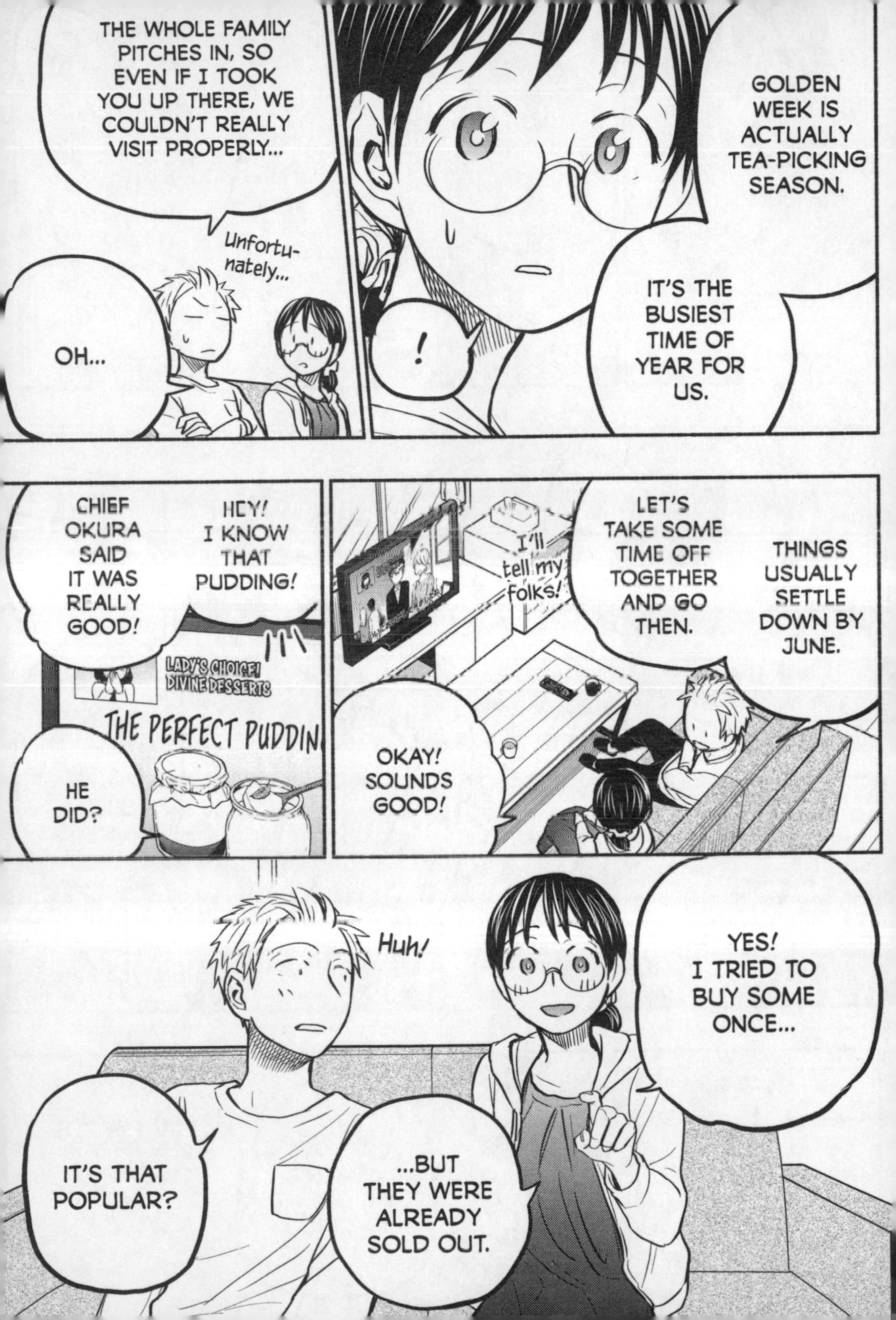
GOLDEN WEEK IS ACTUALLY TEA-PICKING SEASON.
IT'S THE BUSIEST TIME OF YEAR FOR US.
!
THE WHOLE FAMILY PITCHES IN, SO EVEN IF I TOOK YOU UP THERE, WE COULDN'T REALLY VISIT PROPERLY...
Unfortunately...
OH...
THINGS USUALLY SETTLE DOWN BY JUNE.
LET'S TAKE SOME TIME OFF TOGETHER AND GO THEN.
I'll tell my folks!
OKAY! SOUNDS GOOD!
HEY! I KNOW THAT PUDDING!
CHIEF OKURA SAID IT WAS REALLY GOOD!
LADY'S CHOICE! DIVINE DESSERTS
THE PERFECT PUDDIN
HE DID?
YES! I TRIED TO BUY SOME ONCE...
...BUT THEY WERE ALREADY SOLD OUT.
Huh!
IT'S THAT POPULAR?

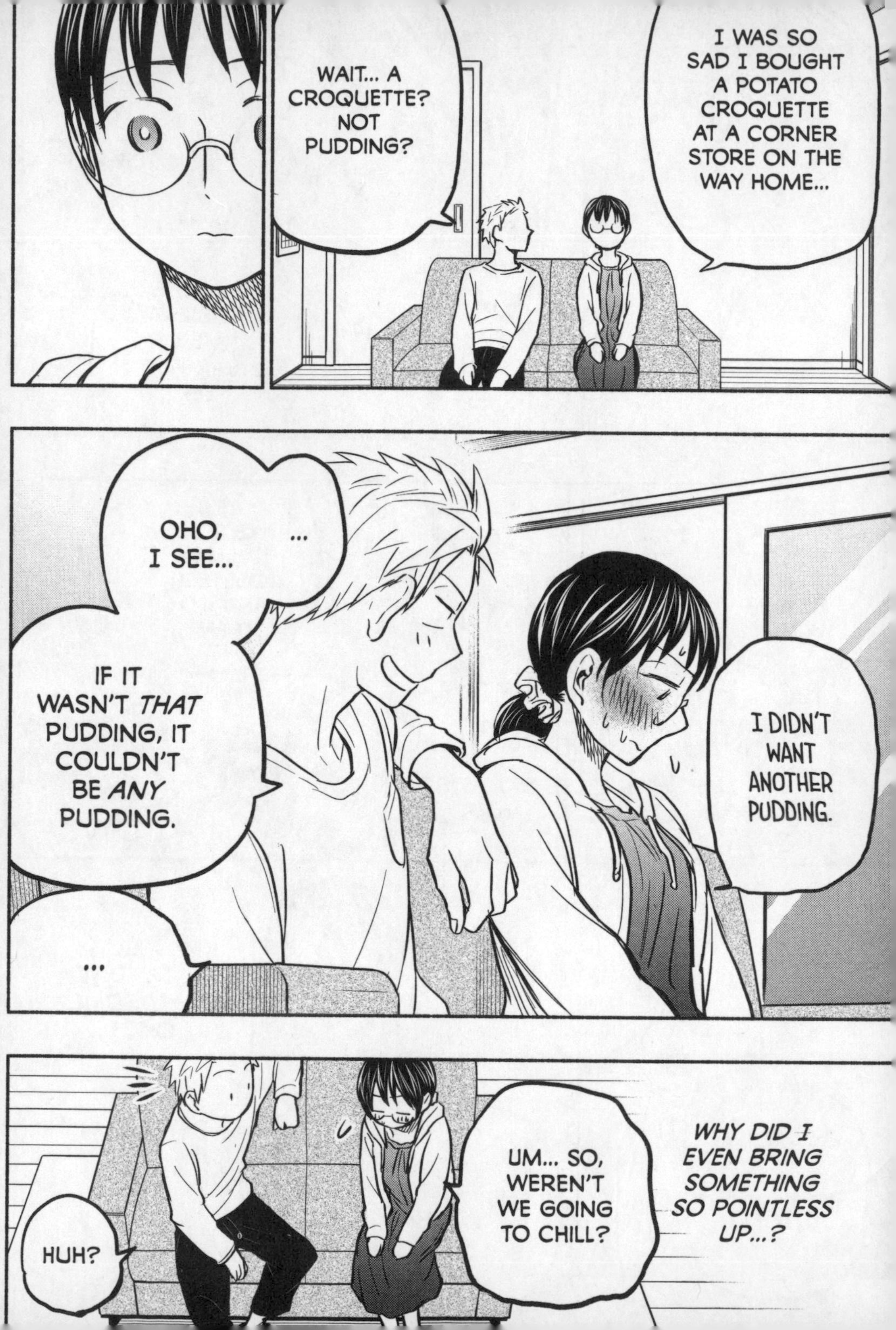
I WAS SO SAD I BOUGHT A POTATO CROQUETTE AT A CORNER STORE ON THE WAY HOME...
WAIT... A CROQUETTE? NOT PUDDING?
I DIDN'T WANT ANOTHER PUDDING.
...
OHO, I SEE...
IF IT WASN'T *THAT* PUDDING, IT COULDN'T BE *ANY* PUDDING.
...
WHY DID I EVEN BRING SOMETHING SO POINTLESS UP...?
UM... SO, WEREN'T WE GOING TO CHILL?
HUH?

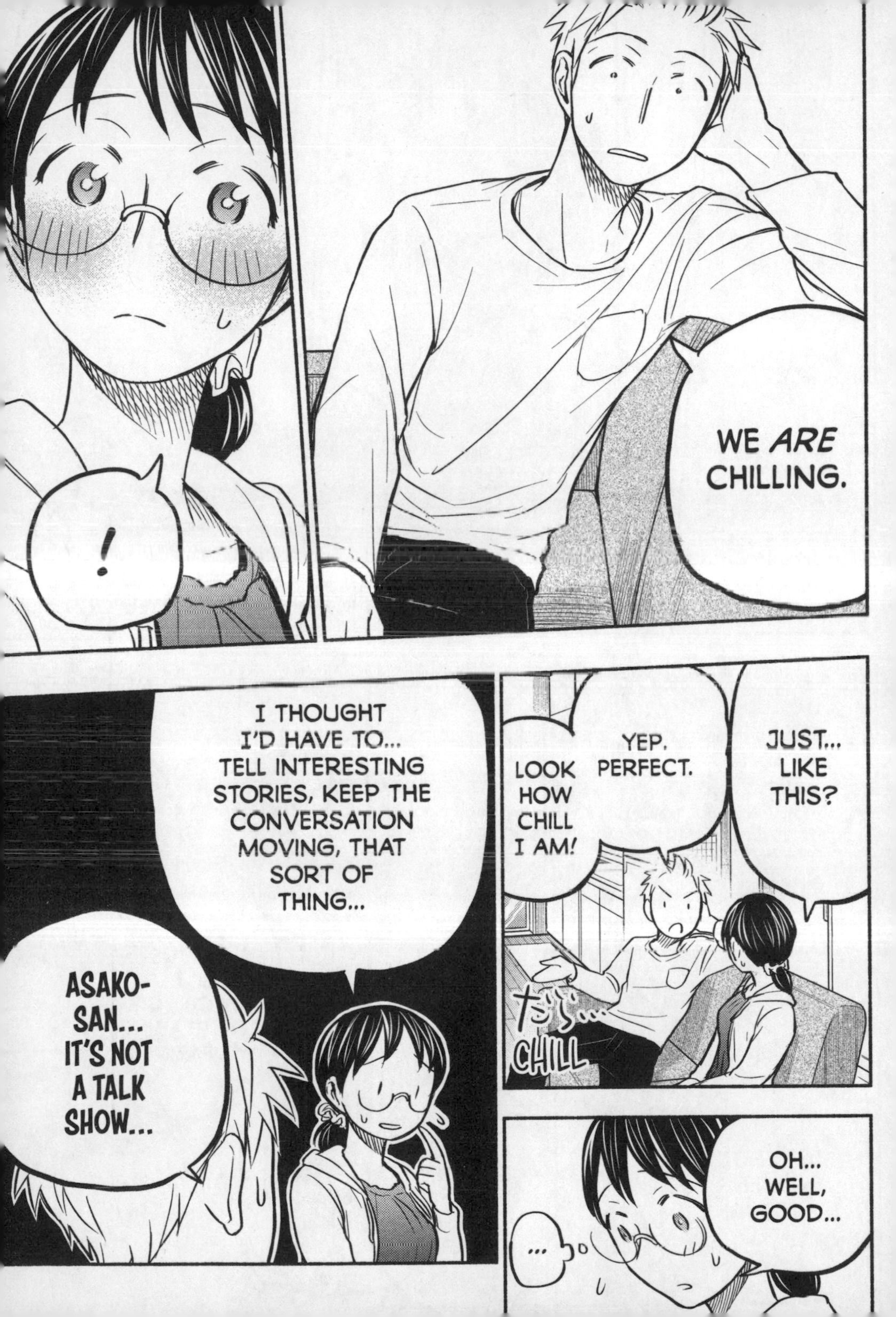
WE *ARE* CHILLING.
!
JUST... LIKE THIS?
YEP. PERFECT.
LOOK HOW CHILL I AM!
CHILL
OH... WELL, GOOD...
...
I THOUGHT I'D HAVE TO... TELL INTERESTING STORIES, KEEP THE CONVERSATION MOVING, THAT SORT OF THING...
ASAKO-SAN... IT'S NOT A TALK SHOW...

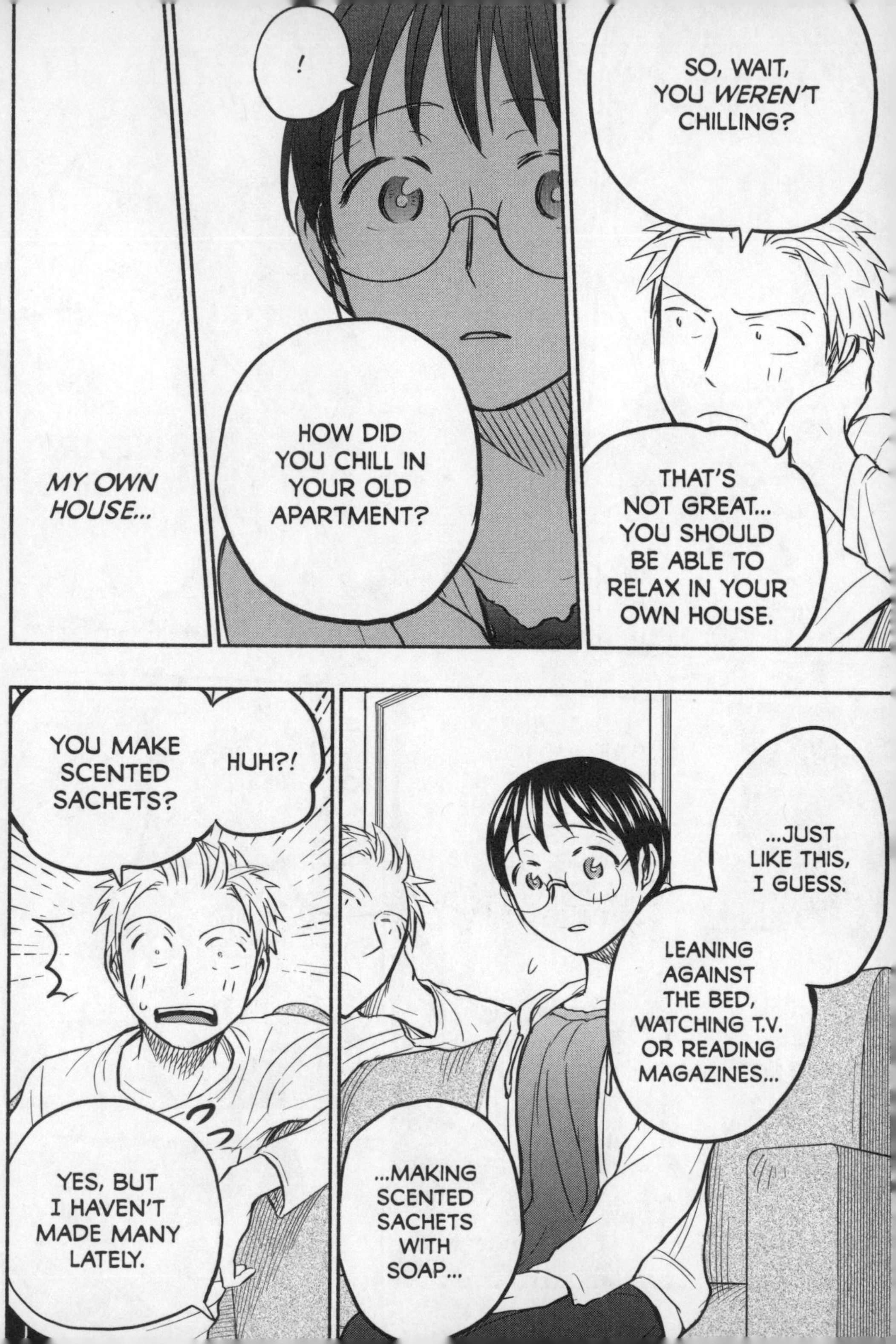
SO, WAIT, YOU *WEREN'T* CHILLING?
THAT'S NOT GREAT... YOU SHOULD BE ABLE TO RELAX IN YOUR OWN HOUSE.
!
HOW DID YOU CHILL IN YOUR OLD APARTMENT?
MY OWN HOUSE...
...JUST LIKE THIS, I GUESS.
LEANING AGAINST THE BED, WATCHING T.V. OR READING MAGAZINES...
...MAKING SCENTED SACHETS WITH SOAP...
HUH?!
YOU MAKE SCENTED SACHETS?
YES, BUT I HAVEN'T MADE MANY LATELY.

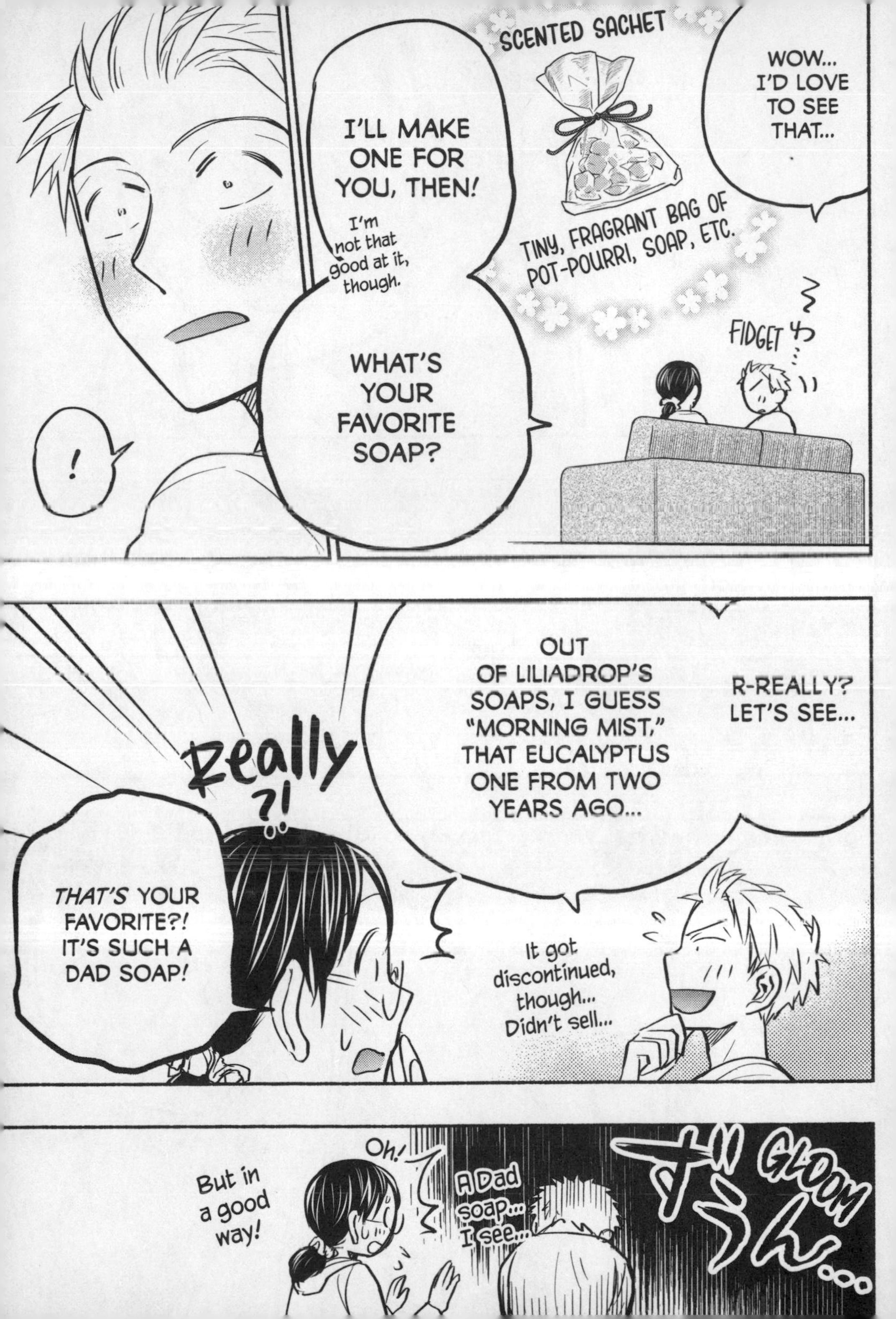
WOW... I'D LOVE TO SEE THAT...
SCENTED SACHET
TINY, FRAGRANT BAG OF POT-POURRI, SOAP, ETC.
FIDGET
I'LL MAKE ONE FOR YOU, THEN!
I'm not that good at it, though.
WHAT'S YOUR FAVORITE SOAP?
!
R-REALLY? LET'S SEE...
OUT OF LILIADROP'S SOAPS, I GUESS "MORNING MIST," THAT EUCALYPTUS ONE FROM TWO YEARS AGO...
It got discontinued, though... Didn't sell...
Really?!
THAT'S YOUR FAVORITE?! IT'S SUCH A DAD SOAP!
GLOOM
A Dad soap... I see...
Oh!
But in a good way!

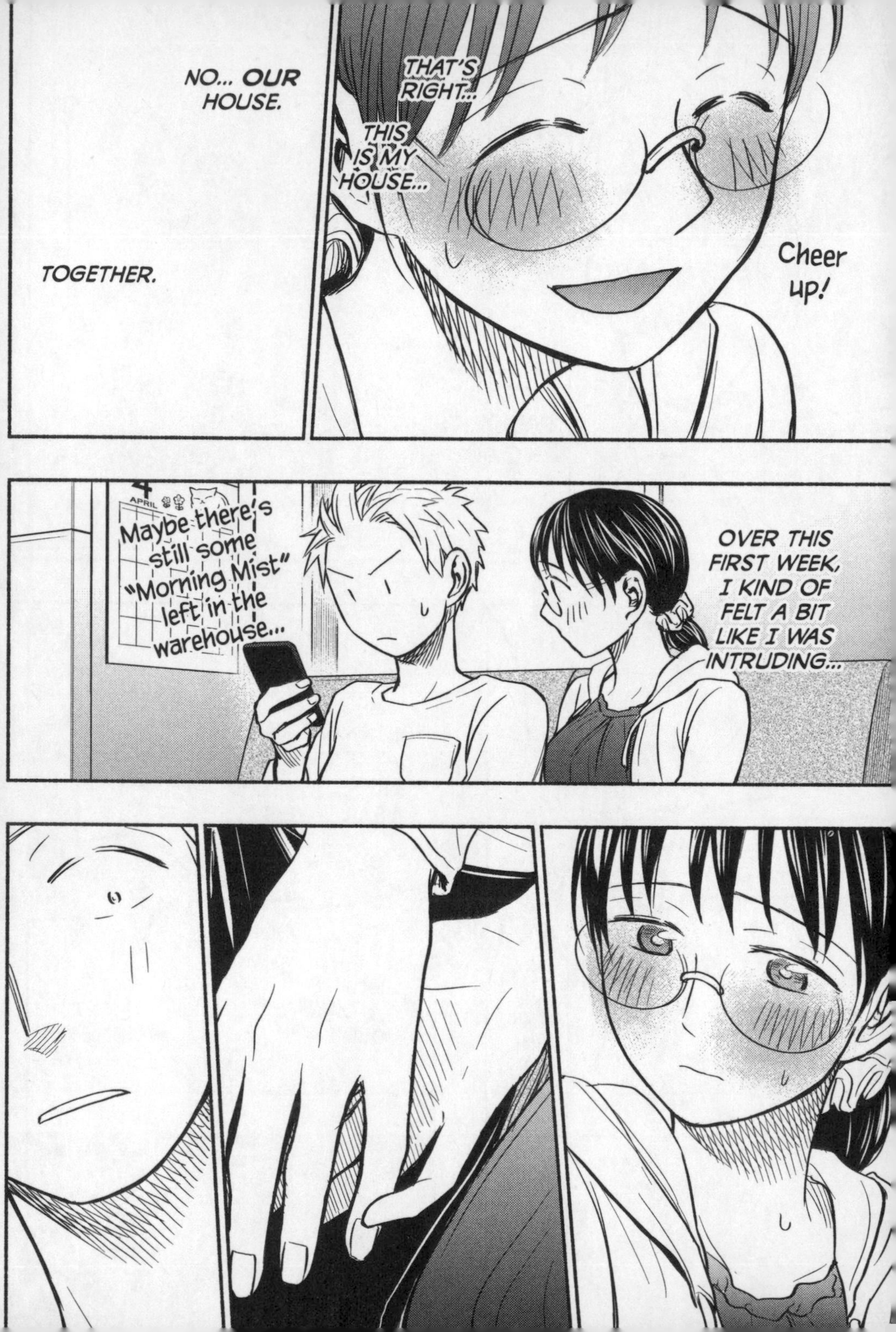
THAT'S RIGHT...
THIS IS MY HOUSE...
Cheer up!
NO... OUR HOUSE.
TOGETHER.
OVER THIS FIRST WEEK, I KIND OF FELT A BIT LIKE I WAS INTRUDING...
4 APRIL
Maybe there's still some "Morning Mist" left in the warehouse...

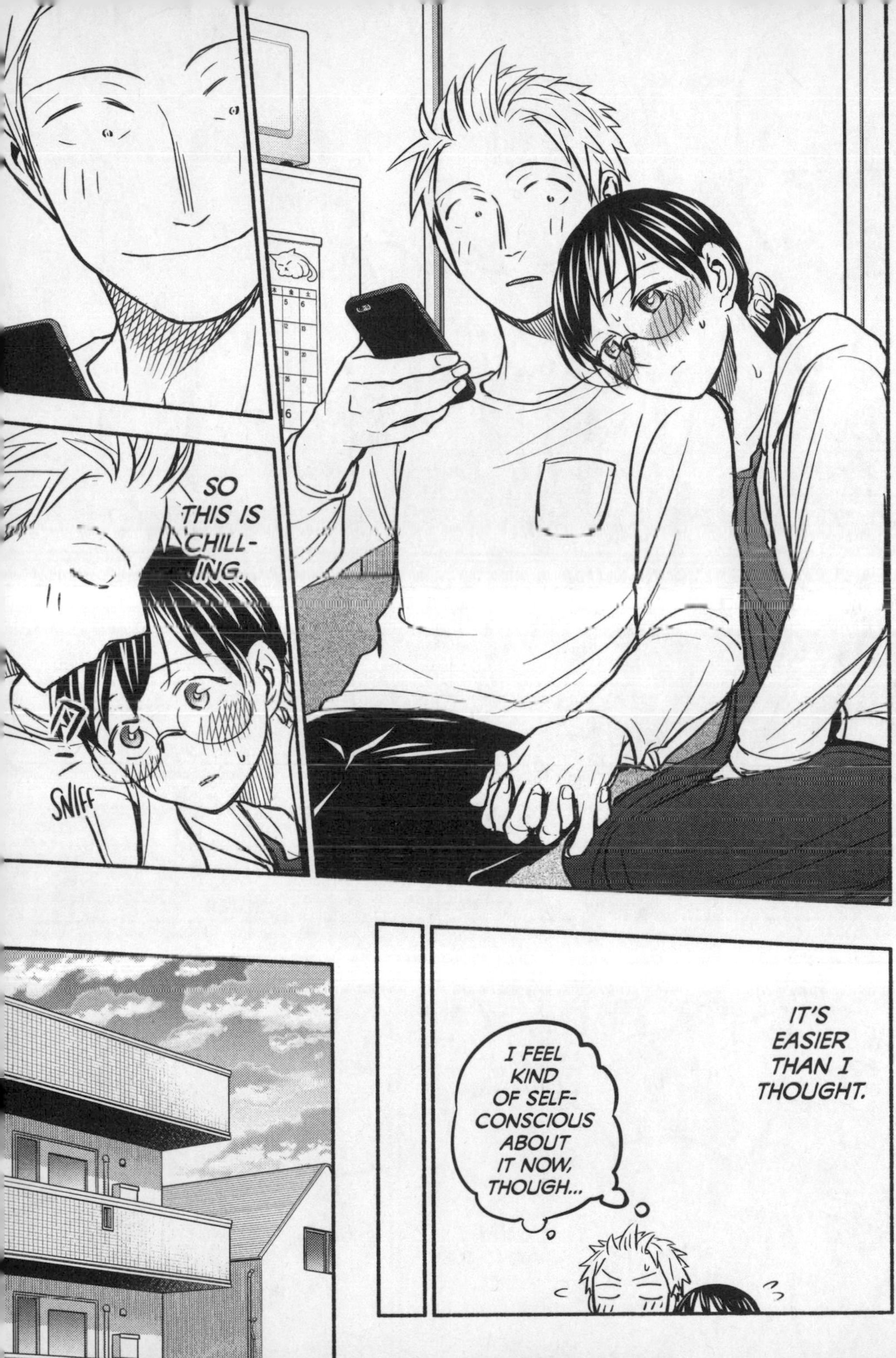
SO THIS IS CHILLING.
SNIFF
IT'S EASIER THAN I THOUGHT.
I FEEL KIND OF SELF-CONSCIOUS ABOUT IT NOW, THOUGH...

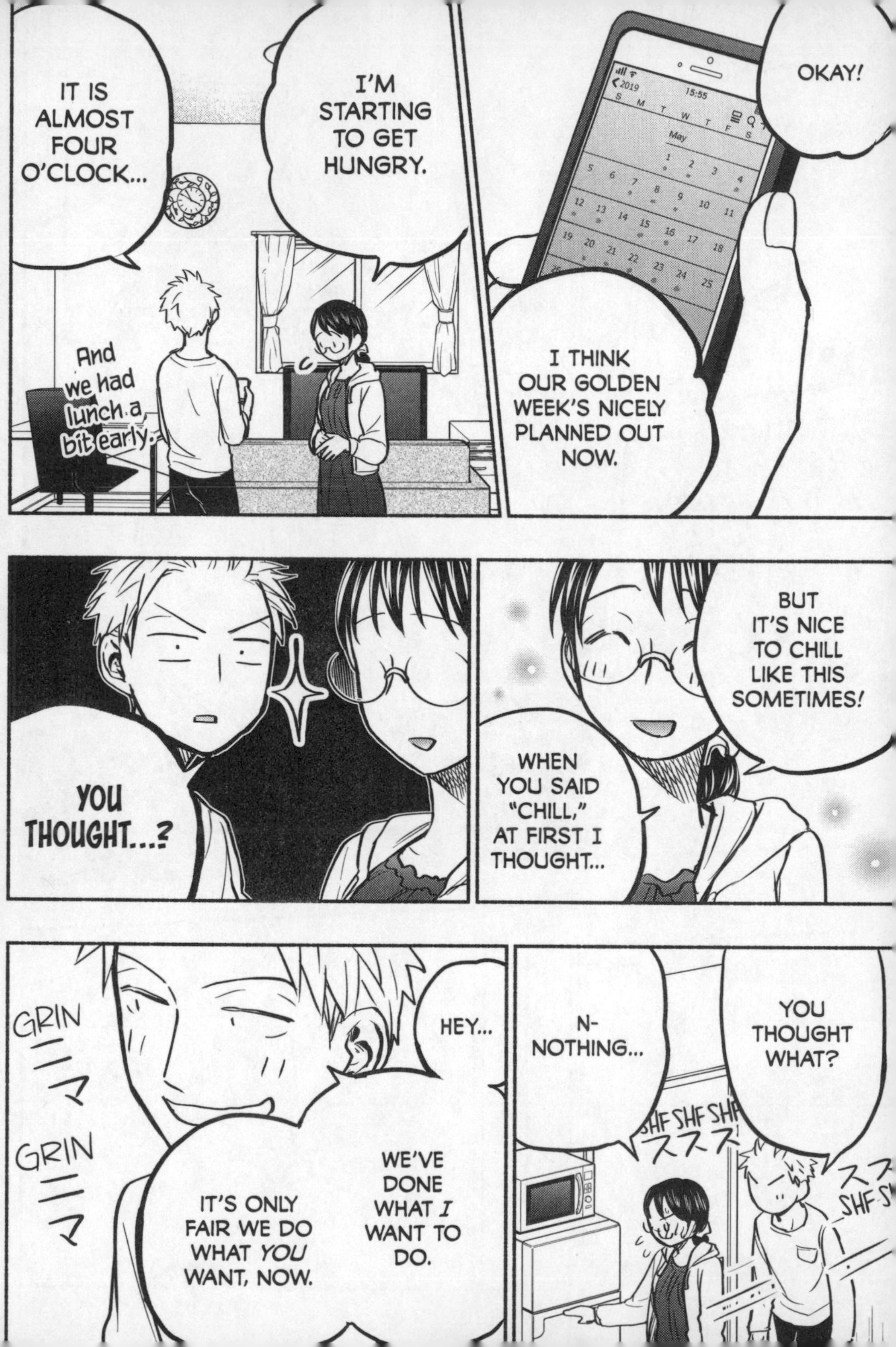

OKAY!
2019
15:55
May
I THINK OUR GOLDEN WEEK'S NICELY PLANNED OUT NOW.
I'M STARTING TO GET HUNGRY.
IT IS ALMOST FOUR O'CLOCK...
And we had lunch a bit early.
BUT IT'S NICE TO CHILL LIKE THIS SOMETIMES!
WHEN YOU SAID "CHILL," AT FIRST I THOUGHT...
YOU THOUGHT...?
YOU THOUGHT WHAT?
N- NOTHING...
SHF SHF SHF スススッ
HEY...
WE'VE DONE WHAT *I* WANT TO DO.
IT'S ONLY FAIR WE DO WHAT *YOU* WANT, NOW.
GRIN ニマ
GRIN ニマ

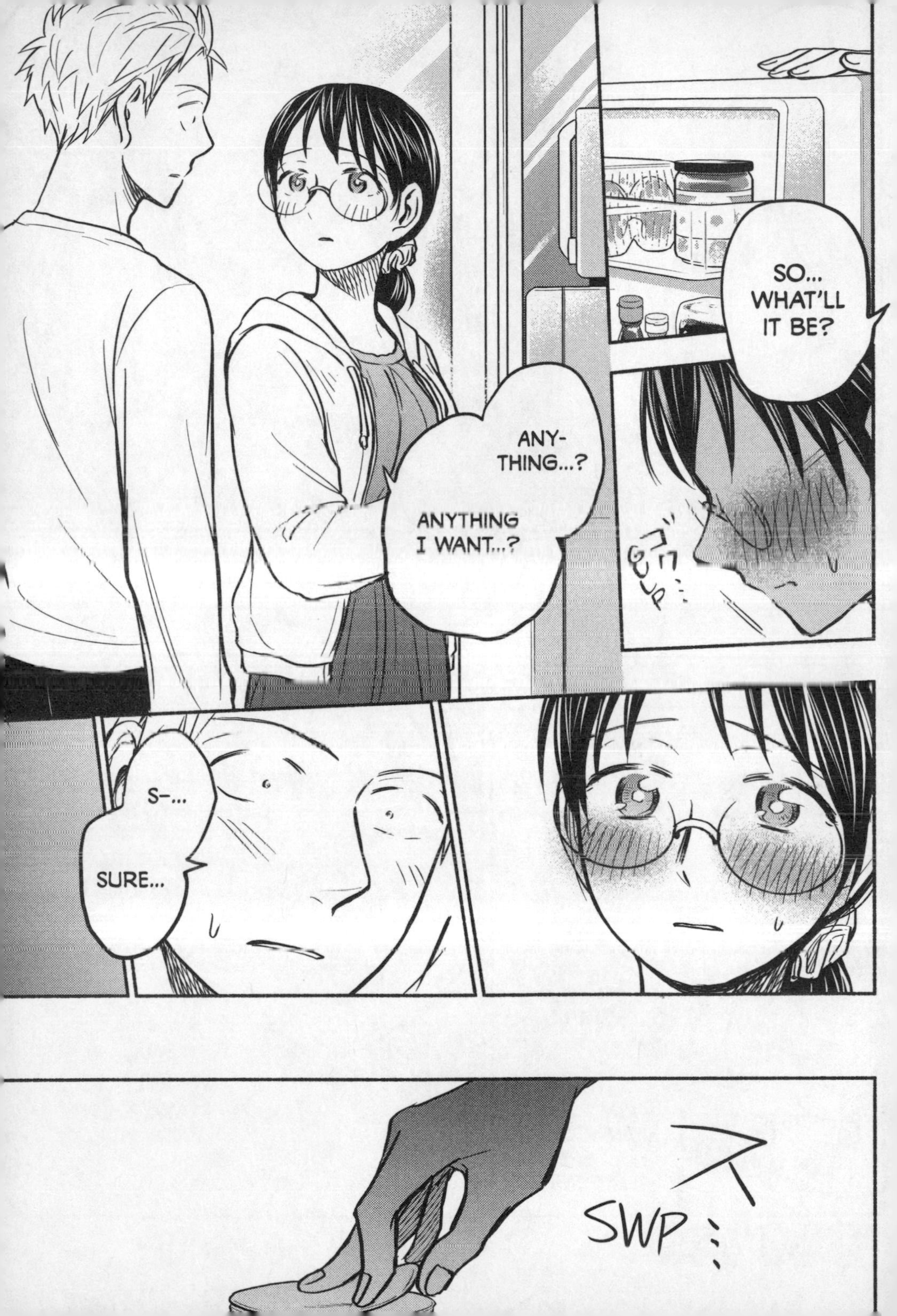
SO... WHAT'LL IT BE?
GULP
ANY-THING...?
ANYTHING I WANT...?
S-...
SURE...
SWP

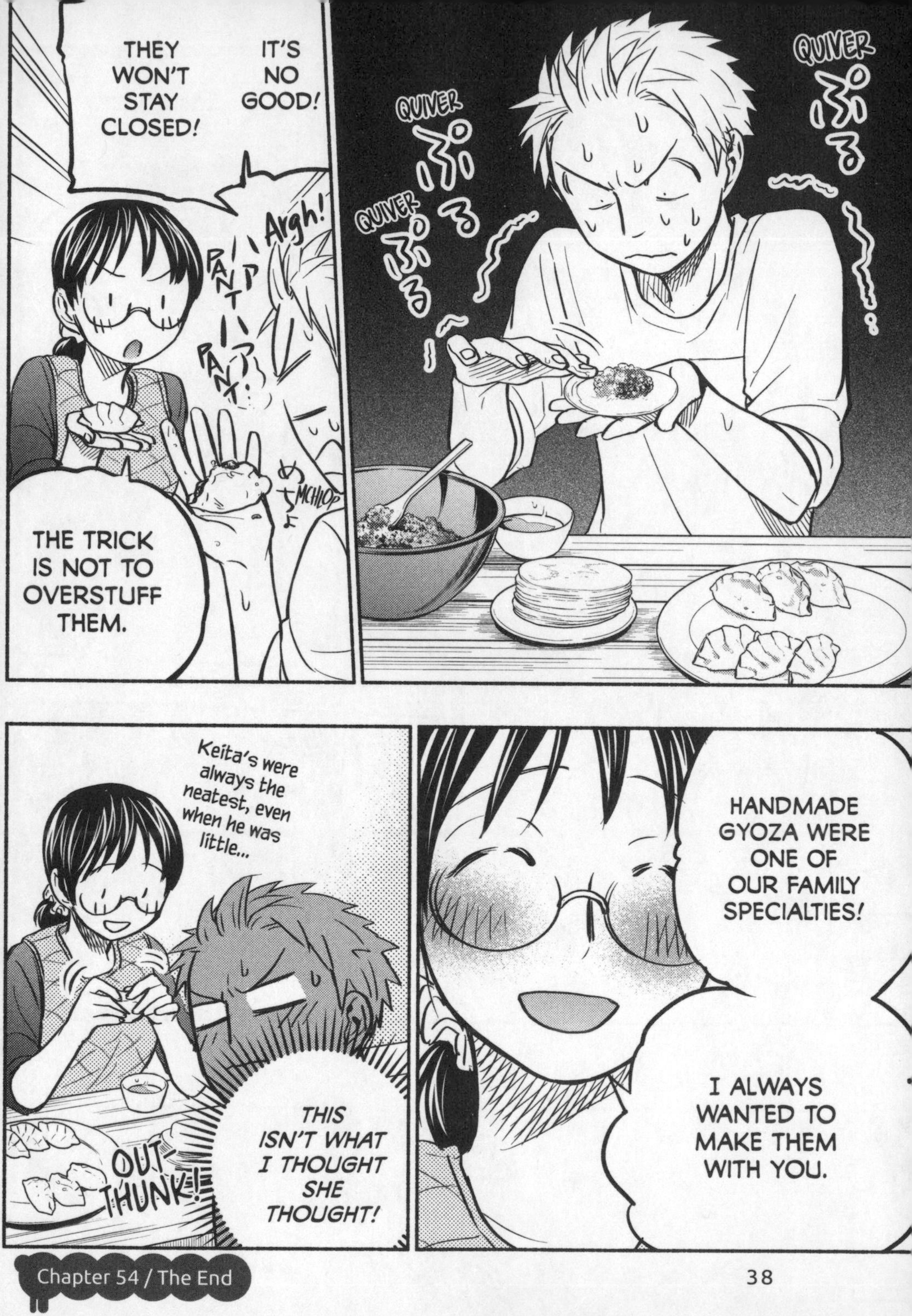
QUIVER
QUIVER
QUIVER
IT'S NO GOOD!
THEY WON'T STAY CLOSED!
Argh!
PANT PANT
MCHLOP
THE TRICK IS NOT TO OVERSTUFF THEM.
HANDMADE GYOZA WERE ONE OF OUR FAMILY SPECIALTIES!
I ALWAYS WANTED TO MAKE THEM WITH YOU.
Keita's were always the neatest, even when he was little...
THIS ISN'T WHAT I THOUGHT SHE THOUGHT!
OUT-THUNK!

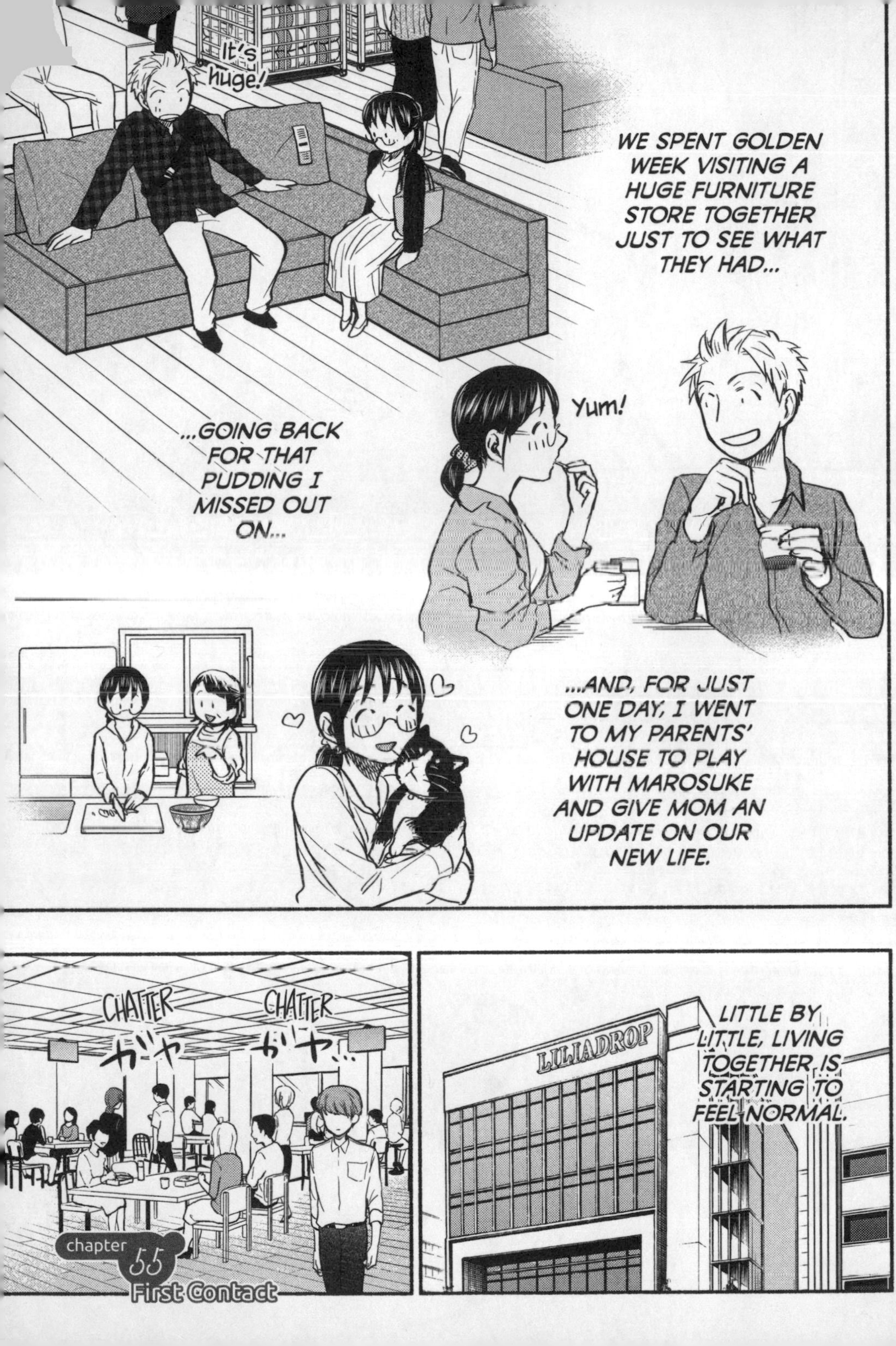
WE SPENT GOLDEN WEEK VISITING A HUGE FURNITURE STORE TOGETHER JUST TO SEE WHAT THEY HAD...
It's huge!
Yum!
...GOING BACK FOR THAT PUDDING I MISSED OUT ON...
...AND, FOR JUST ONE DAY, I WENT TO MY PARENTS' HOUSE TO PLAY WITH MAROSUKE AND GIVE MOM AN UPDATE ON OUR NEW LIFE.
LITTLE BY LITTLE, LIVING TOGETHER IS STARTING TO FEEL NORMAL.
LULIADROP
CHATTER ガヤ
CHATTER ガヤ...
chapter 55
First Contact

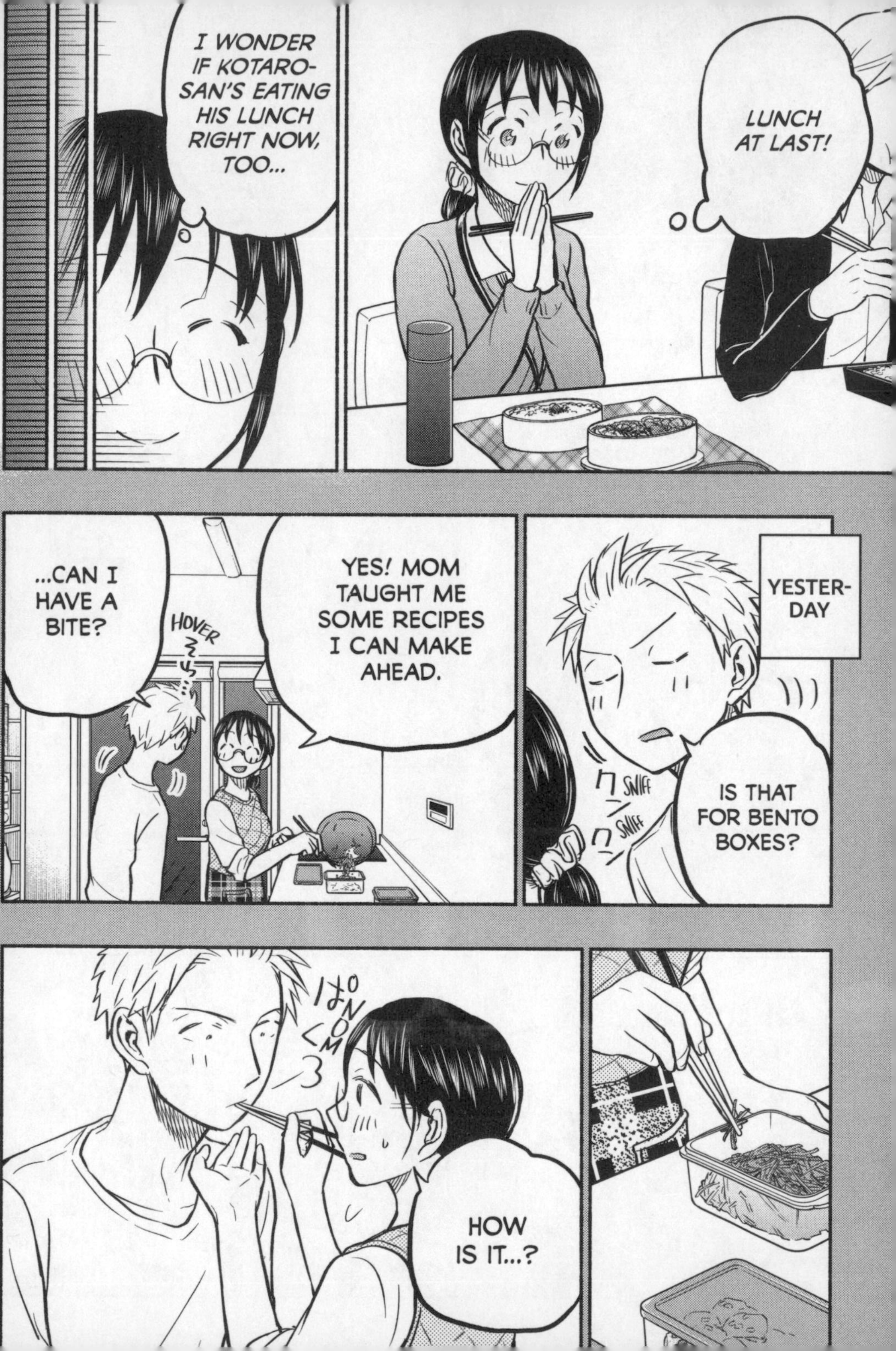
LUNCH AT LAST!
I WONDER IF KOTARO-SAN'S EATING HIS LUNCH RIGHT NOW, TOO...
YESTERDAY
SNIFF
SNIFF
IS THAT FOR BENTO BOXES?
YES! MOM TAUGHT ME SOME RECIPES I CAN MAKE AHEAD.
HOVER
...CAN I HAVE A BITE?
NOM
NOM
HOW IS IT...?

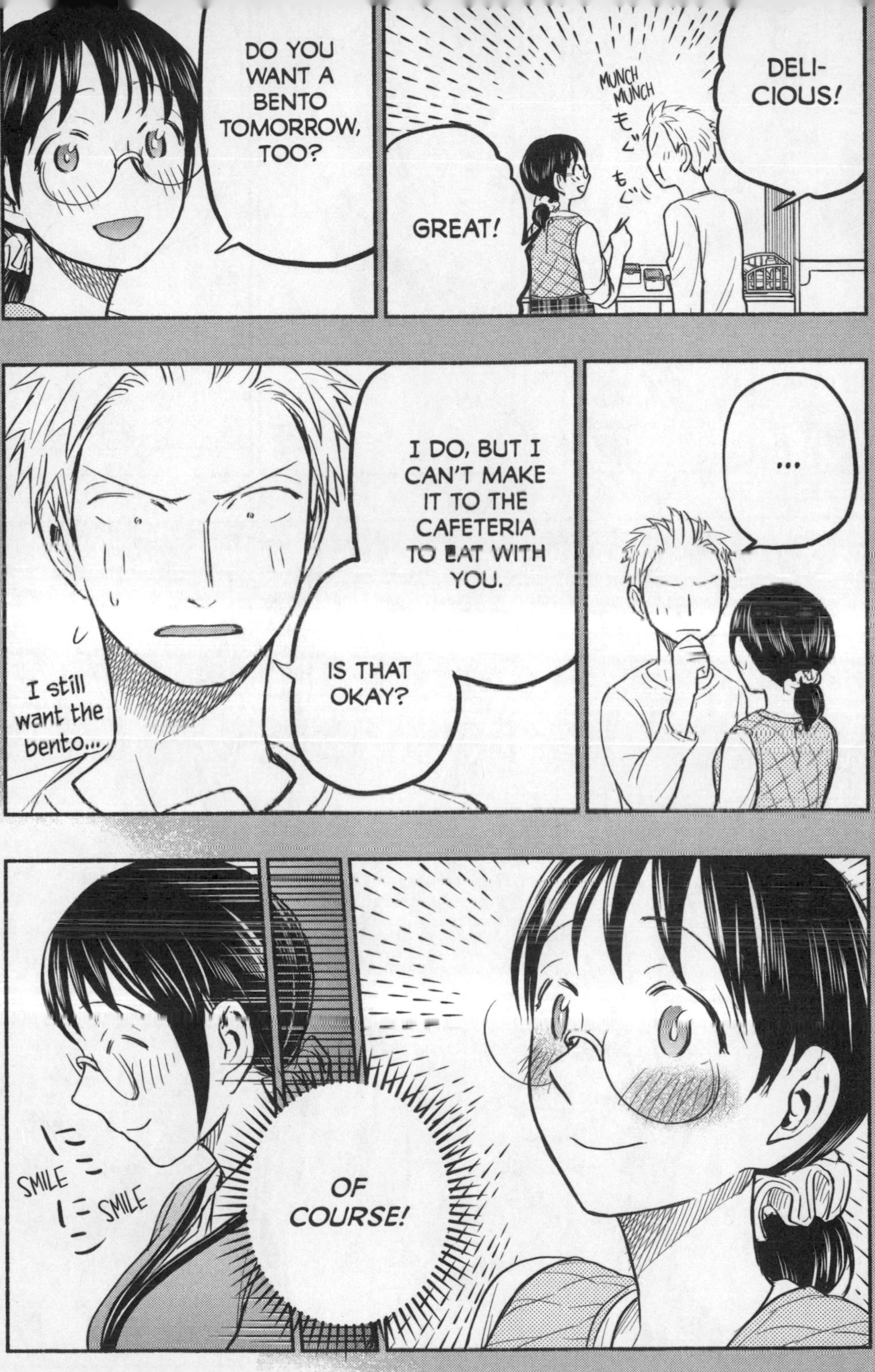
DELI-CIOUS!
MUNCH MUNCH
もぐもぐ
GREAT!
DO YOU WANT A BENTO TOMORROW, TOO?
...
I DO, BUT I CAN'T MAKE IT TO THE CAFETERIA TO EAT WITH YOU.
IS THAT OKAY?
I still want the bento...
OF COURSE!
SMILE SMILE

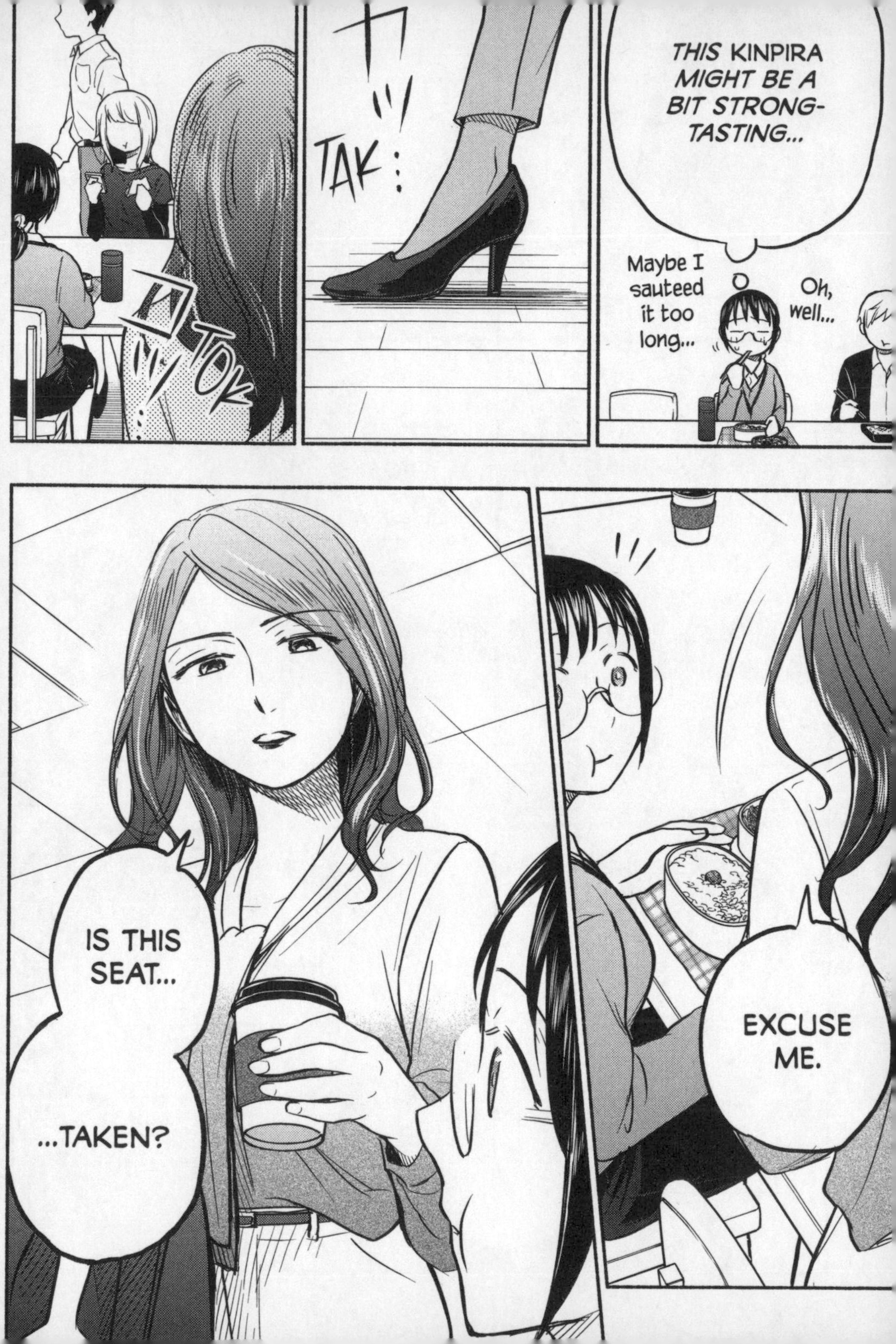
THIS KINPIRA MIGHT BE A BIT STRONG-TASTING...
Maybe I sauteed it too long...
Oh, well...
TAK...
TOK
EXCUSE ME.
IS THIS SEAT...
...TAKEN?

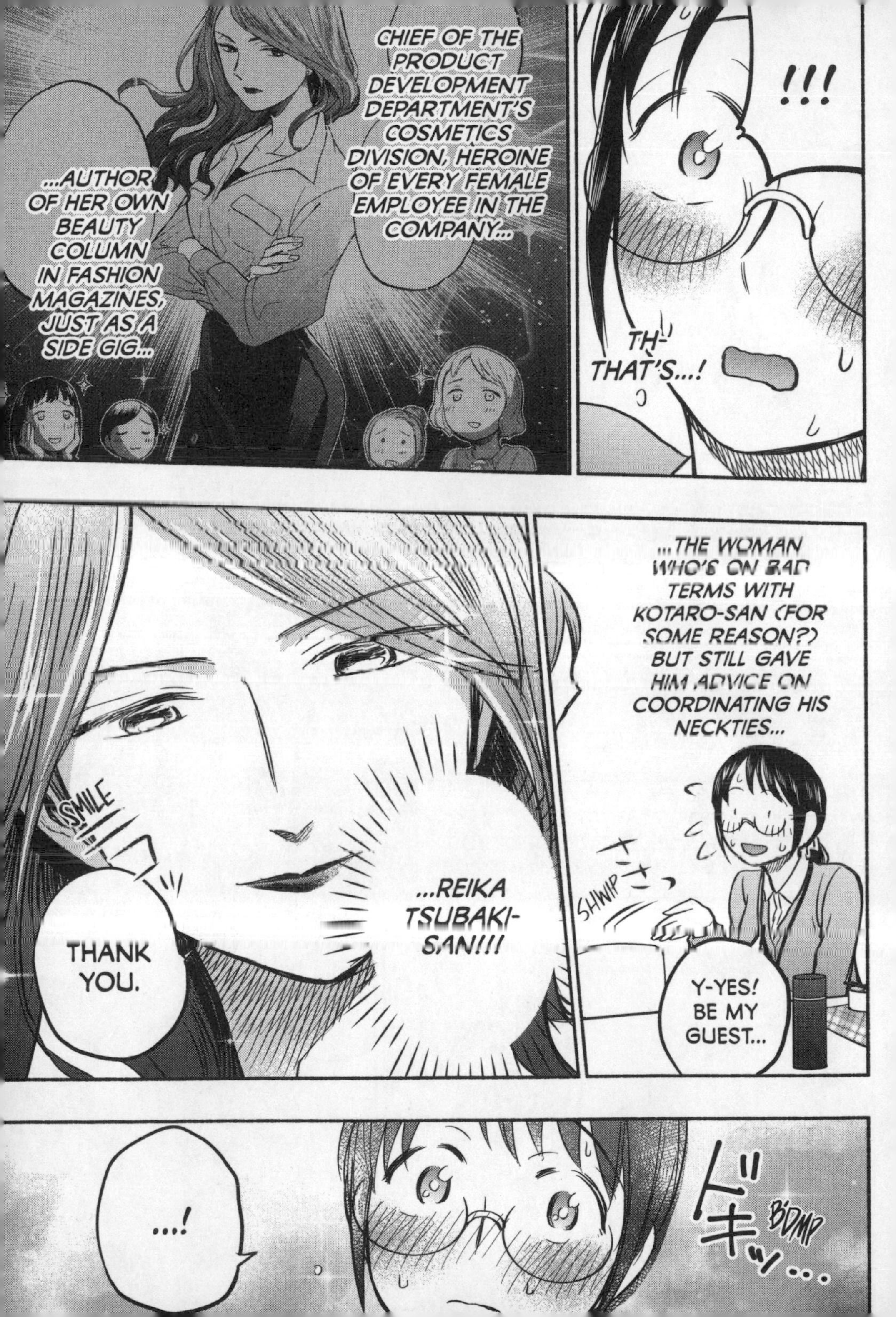
!!!
TH-THAT'S...!
CHIEF OF THE PRODUCT DEVELOPMENT DEPARTMENT'S COSMETICS DIVISION, HEROINE OF EVERY FEMALE EMPLOYEE IN THE COMPANY...
...AUTHOR OF HER OWN BEAUTY COLUMN IN FASHION MAGAZINES, JUST AS A SIDE GIG...
...THE WOMAN WHO'S ON BAD TERMS WITH KOTARO-SAN (FOR SOME REASON?) BUT STILL GAVE HIM ADVICE ON COORDINATING HIS NECKTIES...
SHWIP
Y-YES! BE MY GUEST...
...REIKA TSUBAKI-SAN!!!
SMILE
THANK YOU.
B'DMP
...!

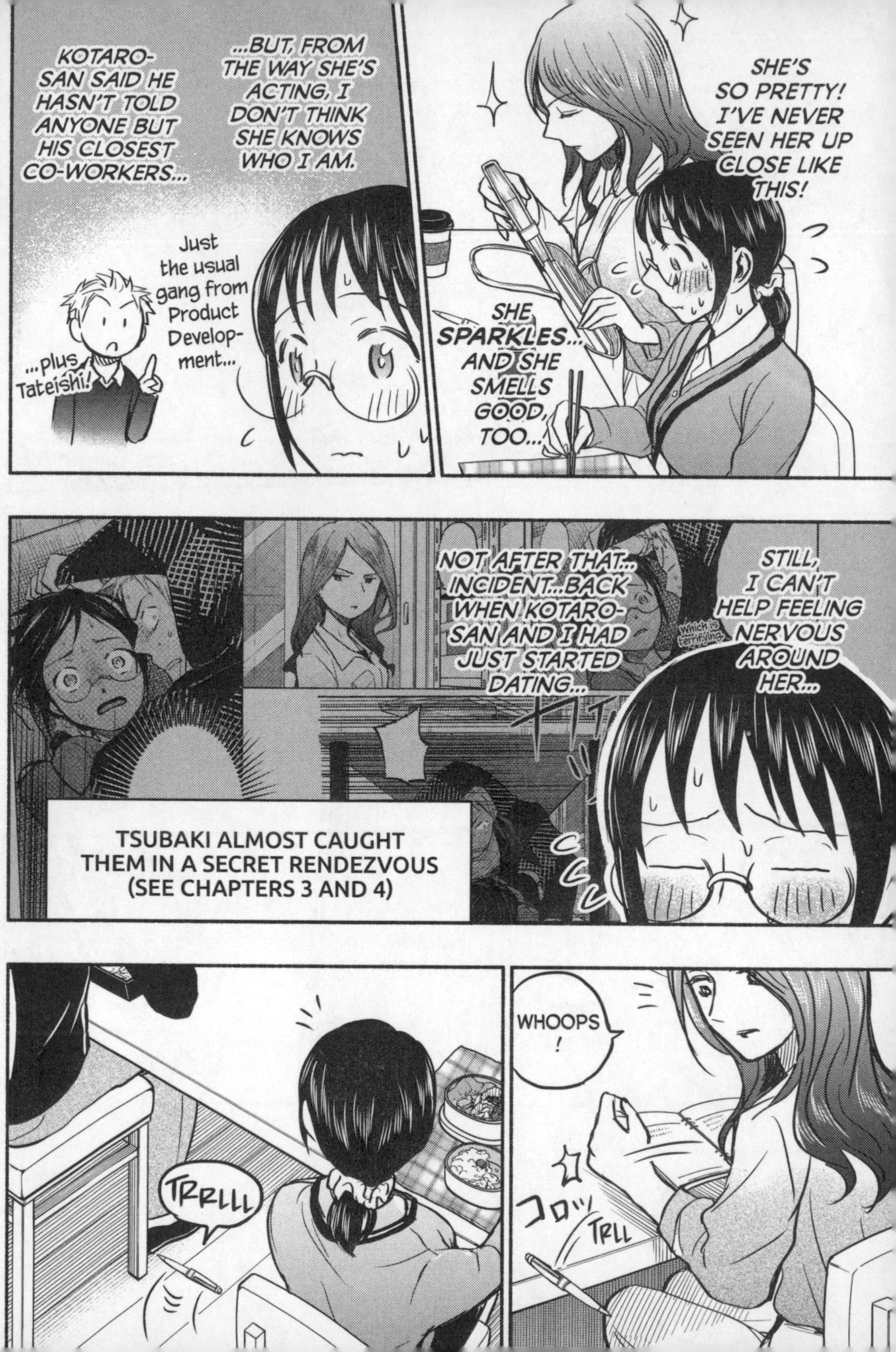
SHE'S SO PRETTY! I'VE NEVER SEEN HER UP CLOSE LIKE THIS!
SHE SPARKLES... AND SHE SMELLS GOOD, TOO...
KOTARO-SAN SAID HE HASN'T TOLD ANYONE BUT HIS CLOSEST CO-WORKERS...
...BUT, FROM THE WAY SHE'S ACTING, I DON'T THINK SHE KNOWS WHO I AM.
Just the usual gang from Product Development...
...plus Tateishi!
STILL, I CAN'T HELP FEELING NERVOUS AROUND HER...
Which is terrifying.
NOT AFTER THAT... INCIDENT...BACK WHEN KOTARO-SAN AND I HAD JUST STARTED DATING...
TSUBAKI ALMOST CAUGHT THEM IN A SECRET RENDEZVOUS (SEE CHAPTERS 3 AND 4)
WHOOPS!
コロッ
TRLL
TRRLLL

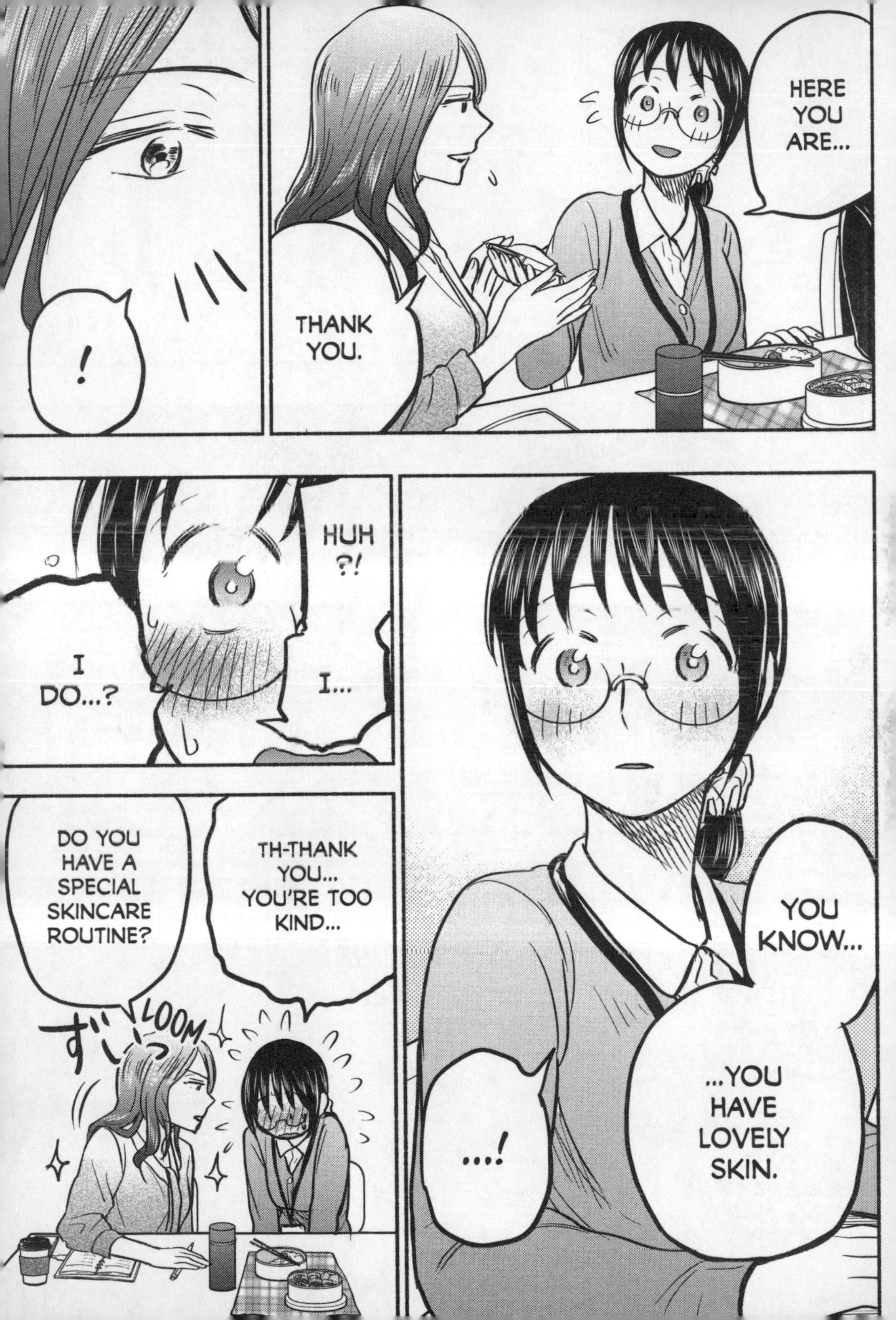
HERE YOU ARE...
THANK YOU.
!
YOU KNOW...
...YOU HAVE LOVELY SKIN.
...!
HUH ?!
I...
I DO...?
TH-THANK YOU... YOU'RE TOO KIND...
DO YOU HAVE A SPECIAL SKINCARE ROUTINE?
ずい
LOOM

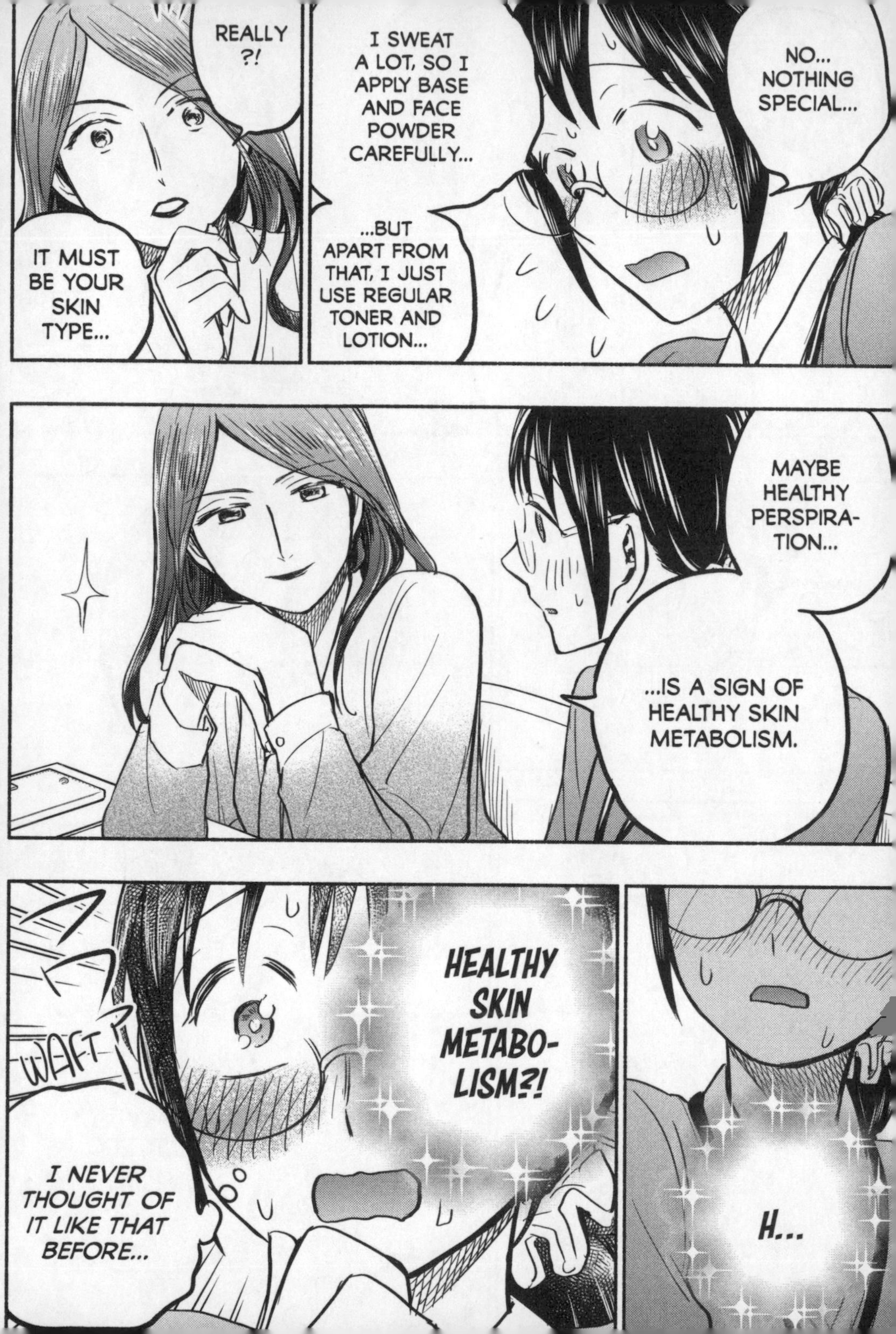
NO... NOTHING SPECIAL...
I SWEAT A LOT, SO I APPLY BASE AND FACE POWDER CAREFULLY...
...BUT APART FROM THAT, I JUST USE REGULAR TONER AND LOTION...
REALLY ?!
IT MUST BE YOUR SKIN TYPE...
MAYBE HEALTHY PERSPIRATION...
...IS A SIGN OF HEALTHY SKIN METABOLISM.
H...
HEALTHY SKIN METABOLISM?!
WAFT
I NEVER THOUGHT OF IT LIKE THAT BEFORE...

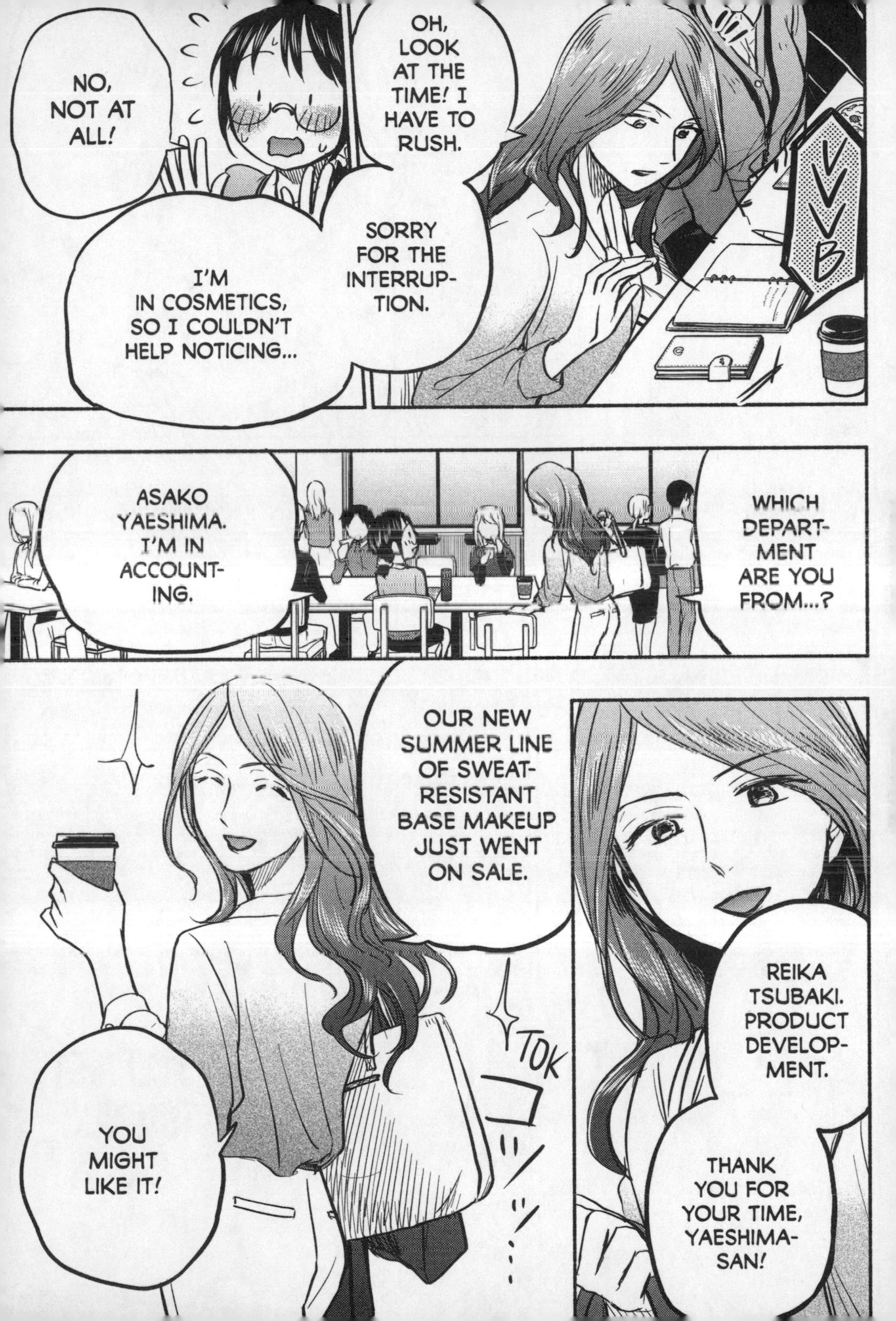
SORRY FOR THE INTERRUP-TION.
I'M IN COSMETICS, SO I COULDN'T HELP NOTICING...
NO, NOT AT ALL!
VVVB
OH, LOOK AT THE TIME! I HAVE TO RUSH.
WHICH DEPART-MENT ARE YOU FROM...?
ASAKO YAESHIMA. I'M IN ACCOUNT-ING.
REIKA TSUBAKI. PRODUCT DEVELOP-MENT.
THANK YOU FOR YOUR TIME, YAESHIMA-SAN!
OUR NEW SUMMER LINE OF SWEAT-RESISTANT BASE MAKEUP JUST WENT ON SALE.
YOU MIGHT LIKE IT!
TOK

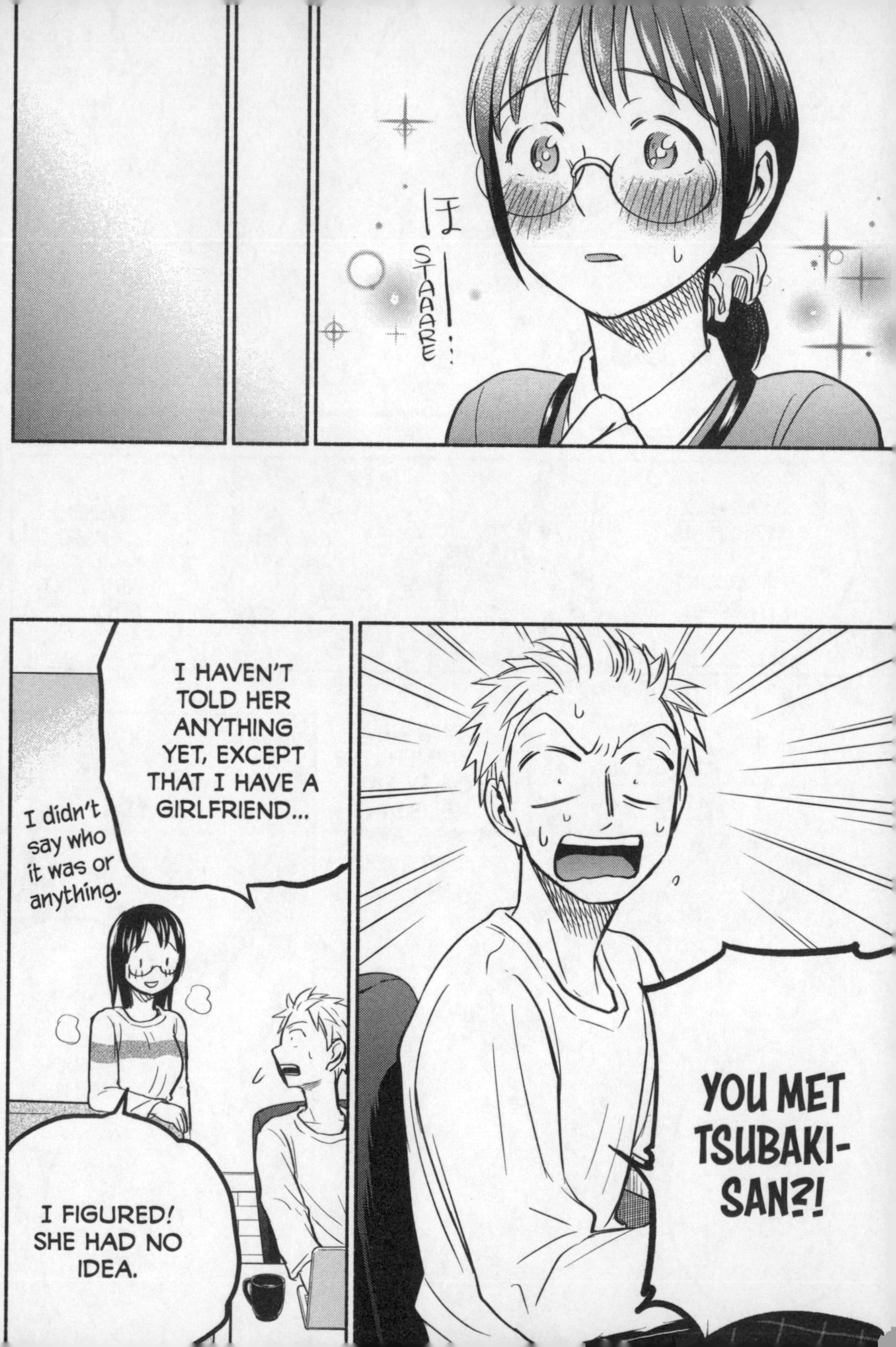
ほ
STAAARE
YOU MET TSUBAKI-SAN?!
I HAVEN'T TOLD HER ANYTHING YET, EXCEPT THAT I HAVE A GIRLFRIEND...
I didn't say who it was or anything.
I FIGURED! SHE HAD NO IDEA.

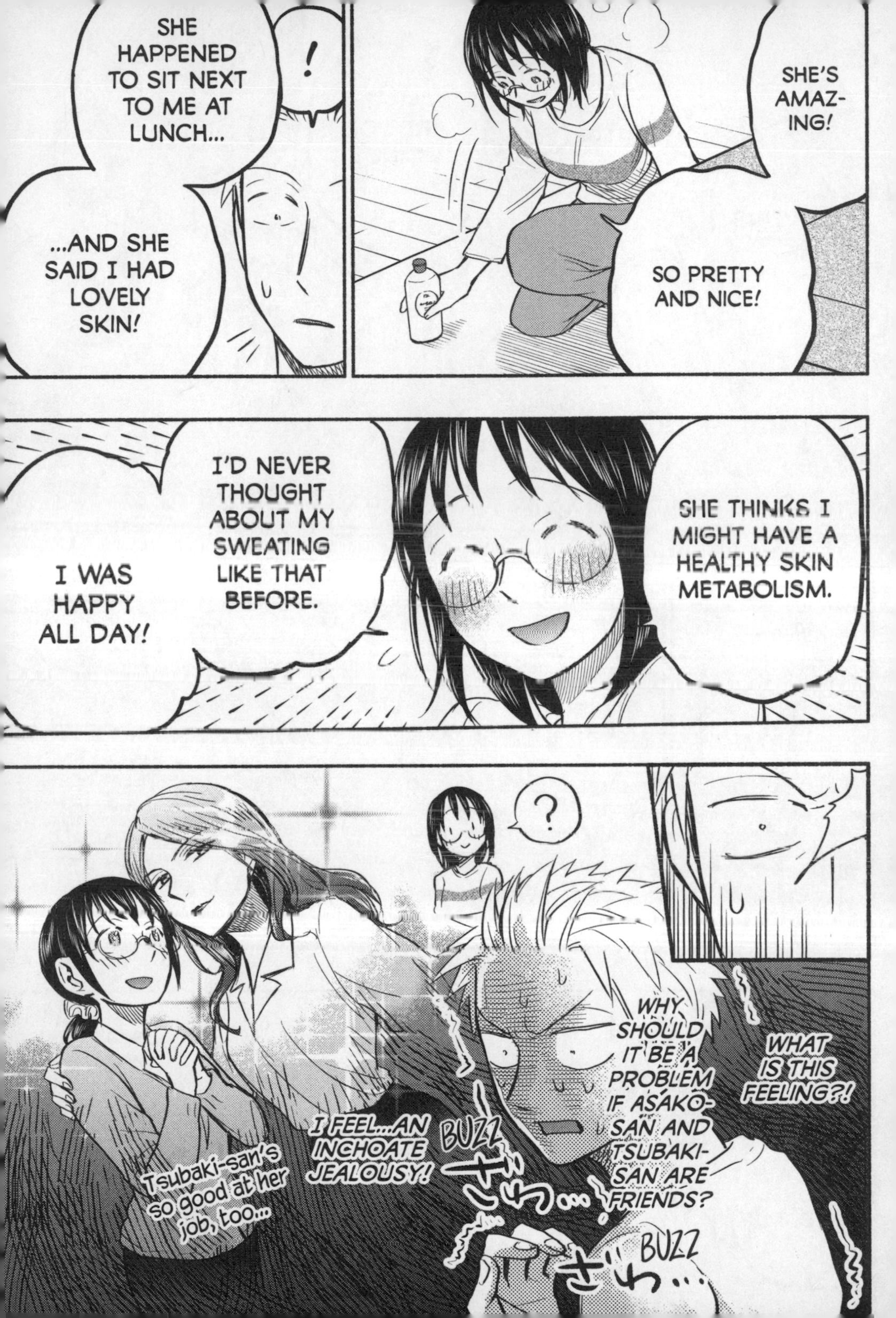
SHE'S AMAZ-ING!
SO PRETTY AND NICE!
!
SHE HAPPENED TO SIT NEXT TO ME AT LUNCH...
...AND SHE SAID I HAD LOVELY SKIN!
SHE THINKS I MIGHT HAVE A HEALTHY SKIN METABOLISM.
I'D NEVER THOUGHT ABOUT MY SWEATING LIKE THAT BEFORE.
I WAS HAPPY ALL DAY!
?
WHAT IS THIS FEELING?!
WHY SHOULD IT BE A PROBLEM IF ASAKO-SAN AND TSUBAKI-SAN ARE FRIENDS?
BUZZ
ざわ…
BUZZ
ざわ…
I FEEL...AN INCHOATE JEALOUSY!
Tsubaki-san's so good at her job, too...

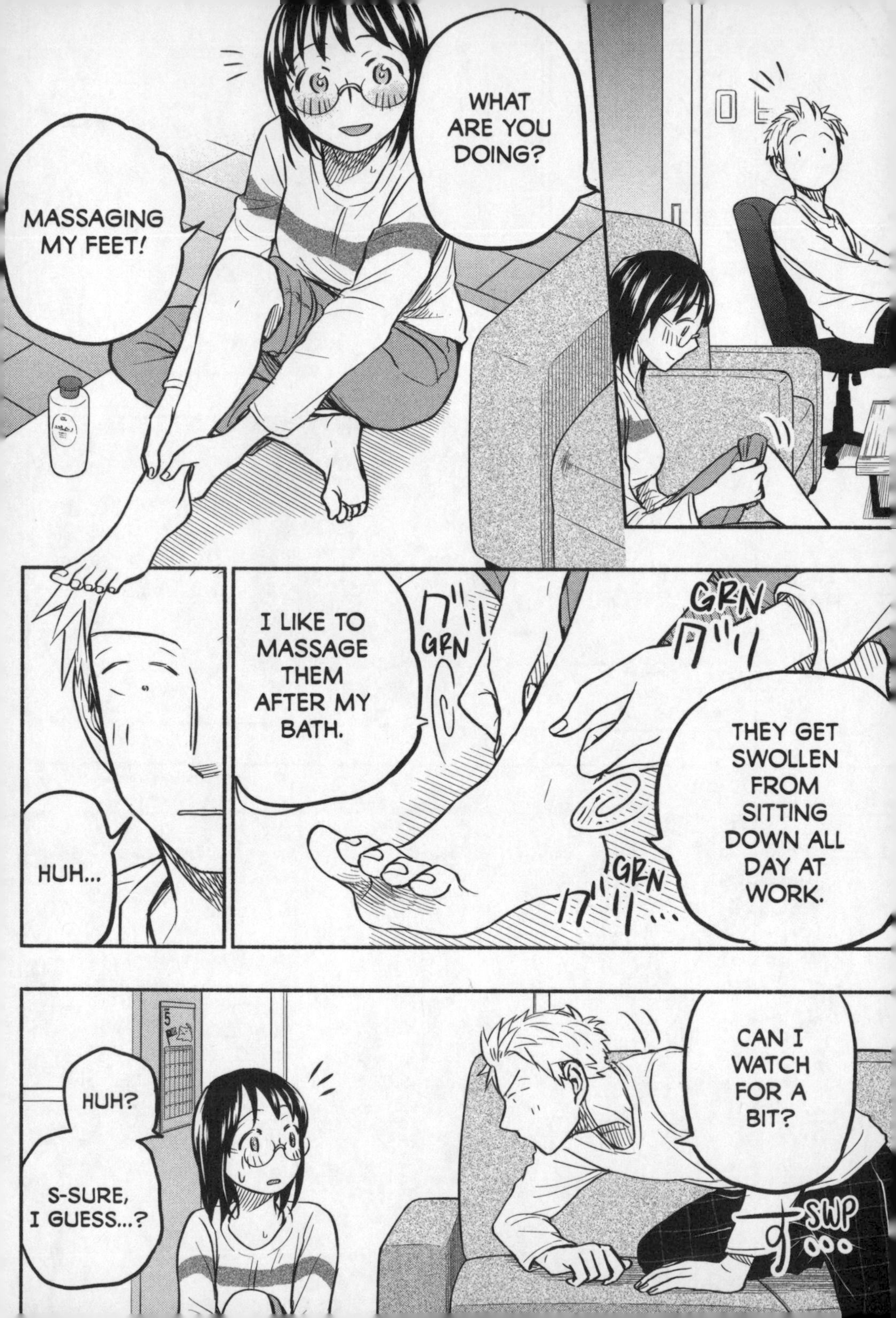
WHAT ARE YOU DOING?
MASSAGING MY FEET!
GRN
GRN
I LIKE TO MASSAGE THEM AFTER MY BATH.
THEY GET SWOLLEN FROM SITTING DOWN ALL DAY AT WORK.
GRN
HUH...
CAN I WATCH FOR A BIT?
SWP
HUH?
S-SURE, I GUESS...?

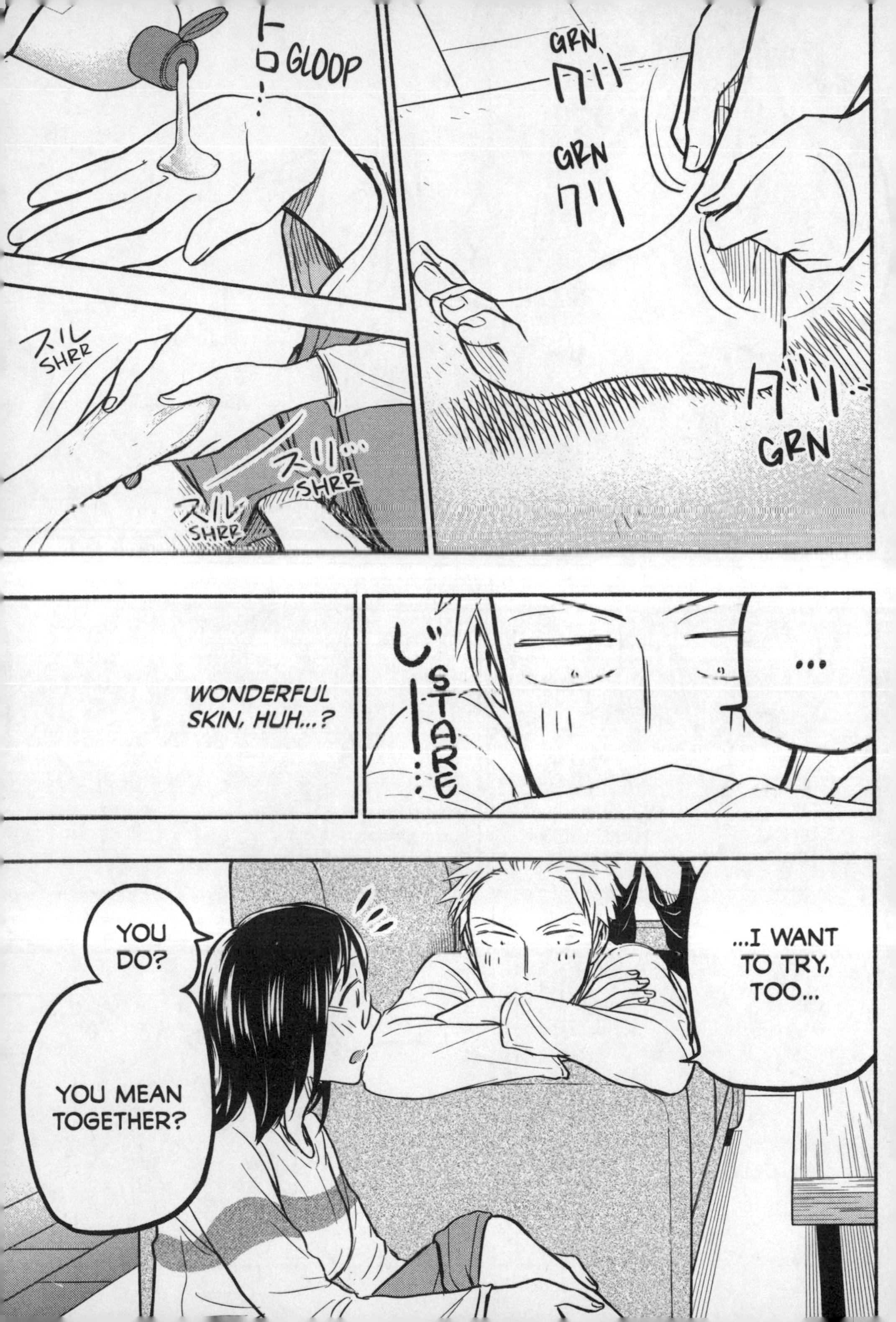
GRN
グリ
GRN
グリ
グリ…
GRN
トロ…
GLOOP
スル
SHRR
スリ…
SHRR
スル
SHRR
…
じーー…
STARE
WONDERFUL SKIN, HUH...?
...I WANT TO TRY, TOO...
YOU DO?
YOU MEAN TOGETHER?

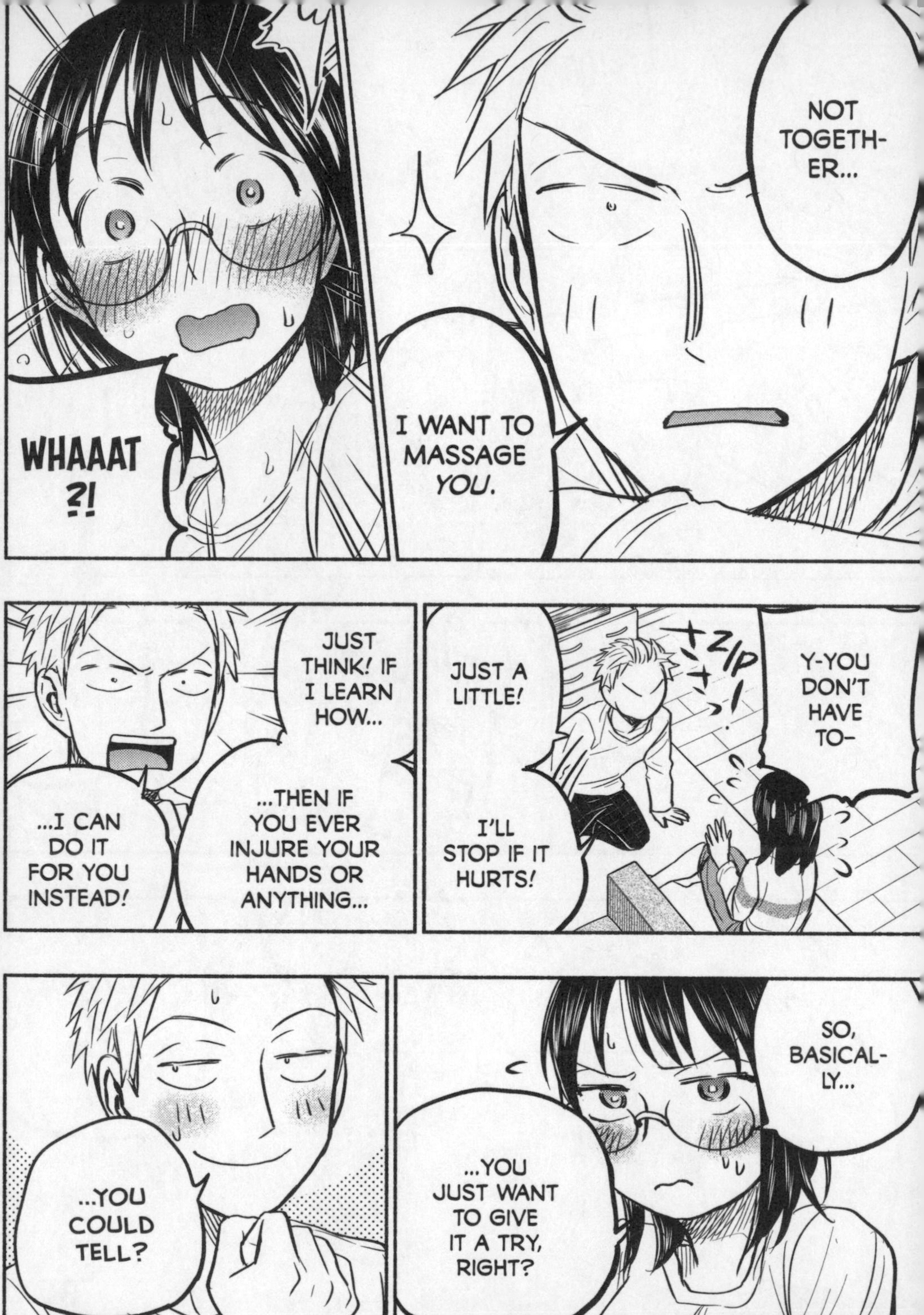
NOT TOGETH-ER...
I WANT TO MASSAGE YOU.
WHAAAT ?!
Y-YOU DON'T HAVE TO-
ZIP
JUST A LITTLE!
I'LL STOP IF IT HURTS!
JUST THINK! IF I LEARN HOW...
...THEN IF YOU EVER INJURE YOUR HANDS OR ANYTHING...
...I CAN DO IT FOR YOU INSTEAD!
SO, BASICAL-LY...
...YOU JUST WANT TO GIVE IT A TRY, RIGHT?
...YOU COULD TELL?

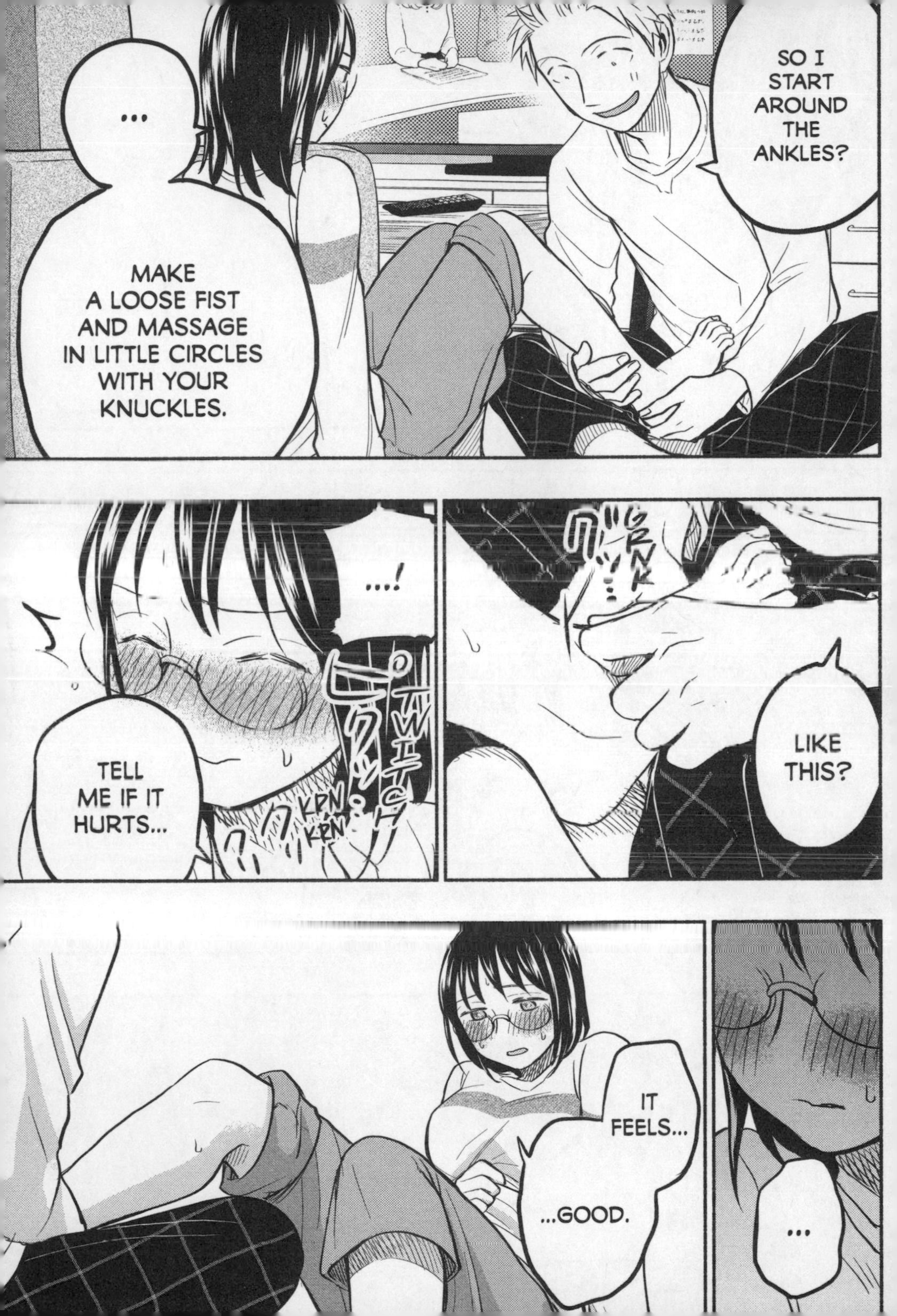
SO I START AROUND THE ANKLES?
...
MAKE A LOOSE FIST AND MASSAGE IN LITTLE CIRCLES WITH YOUR KNUCKLES.
GRNK
LIKE THIS?
...!
TWITCH
KRN KRN
TELL ME IF IT HURTS...
...
IT FEELS...
...GOOD.

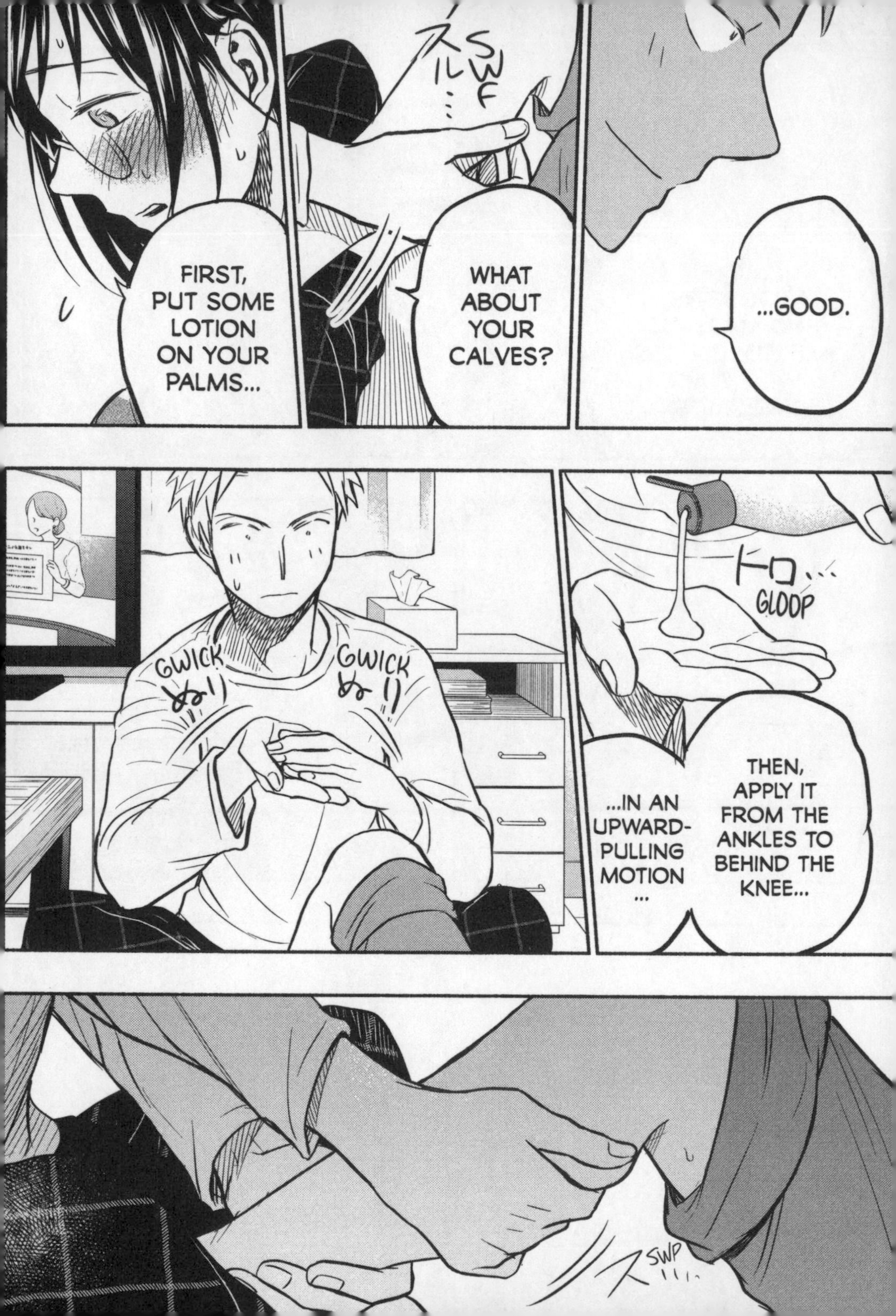
...GOOD.
スル…
SWF
WHAT ABOUT YOUR CALVES?
FIRST, PUT SOME LOTION ON YOUR PALMS...
トロ…
GLOOP
THEN, APPLY IT FROM THE ANKLES TO BEHIND THE KNEE...
...IN AN UPWARD-PULLING MOTION ...
GWICK
ぬり
GWICK
ぬり
ス
SWP

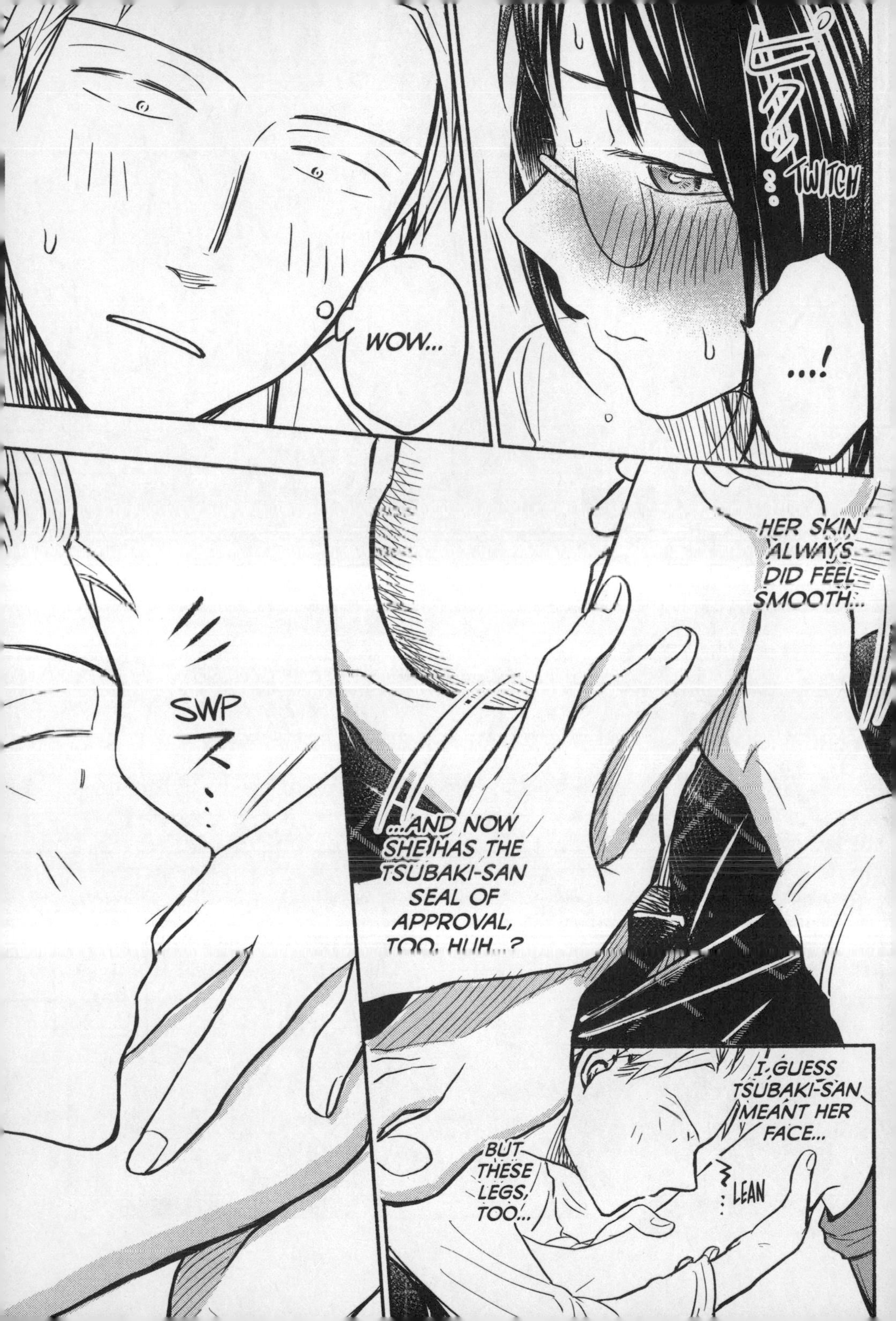
TWITCH
...!
WOW...
HER SKIN ALWAYS DID FEEL SMOOTH...
...AND NOW SHE HAS THE TSUBAKI-SAN SEAL OF APPROVAL, TOO, HUH...?
I GUESS TSUBAKI-SAN MEANT HER FACE...
BUT THESE LEGS, TOO...
LEAN
SWP
ス

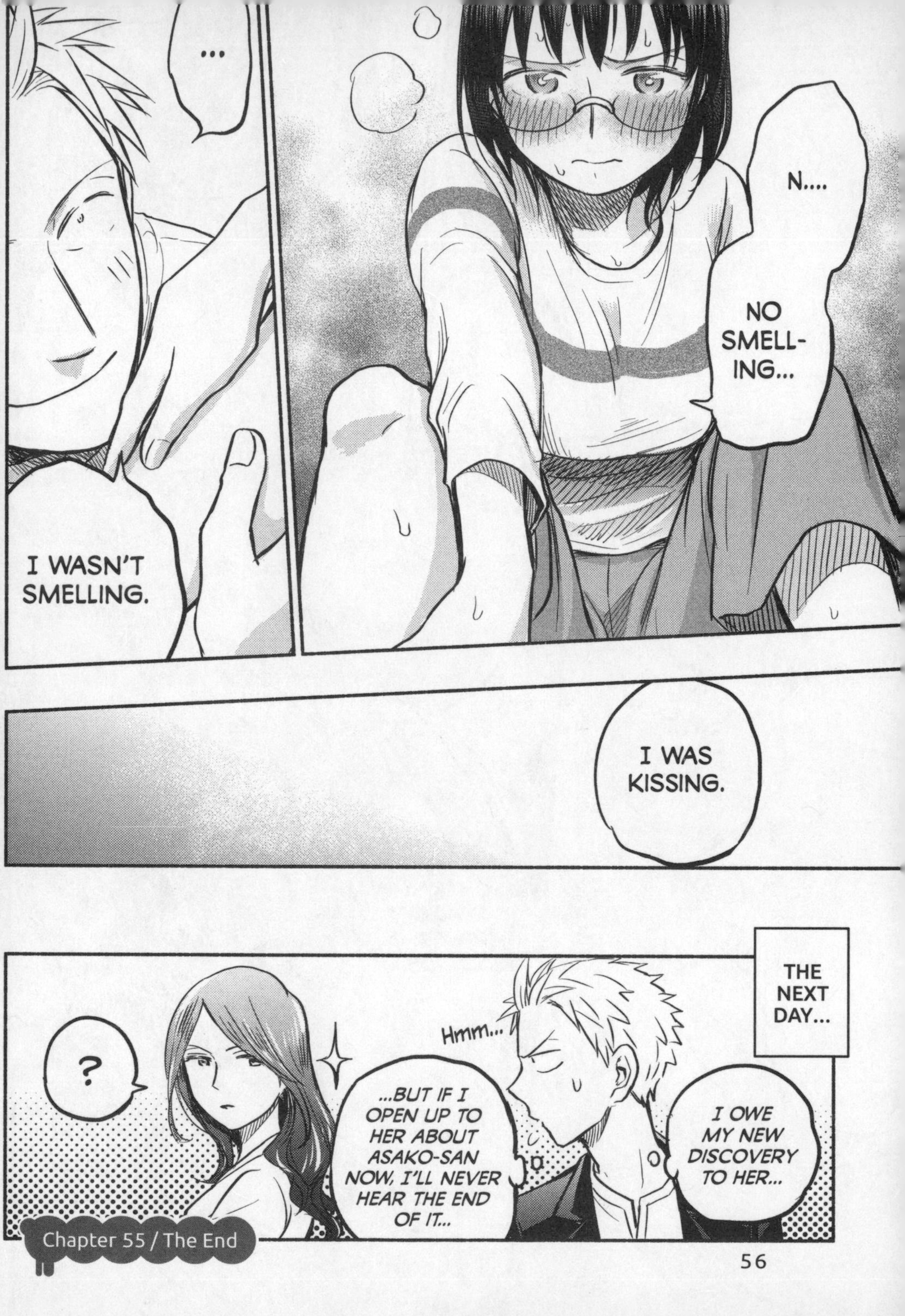
N....
NO SMELL-ING...
...
I WASN'T SMELLING.
I WAS KISSING.
THE NEXT DAY...
I OWE MY NEW DISCOVERY TO HER...
Hmm...
...BUT IF I OPEN UP TO HER ABOUT ASAKO-SAN NOW, I'LL NEVER HEAR THE END OF IT...
?
Chapter 55 / The End

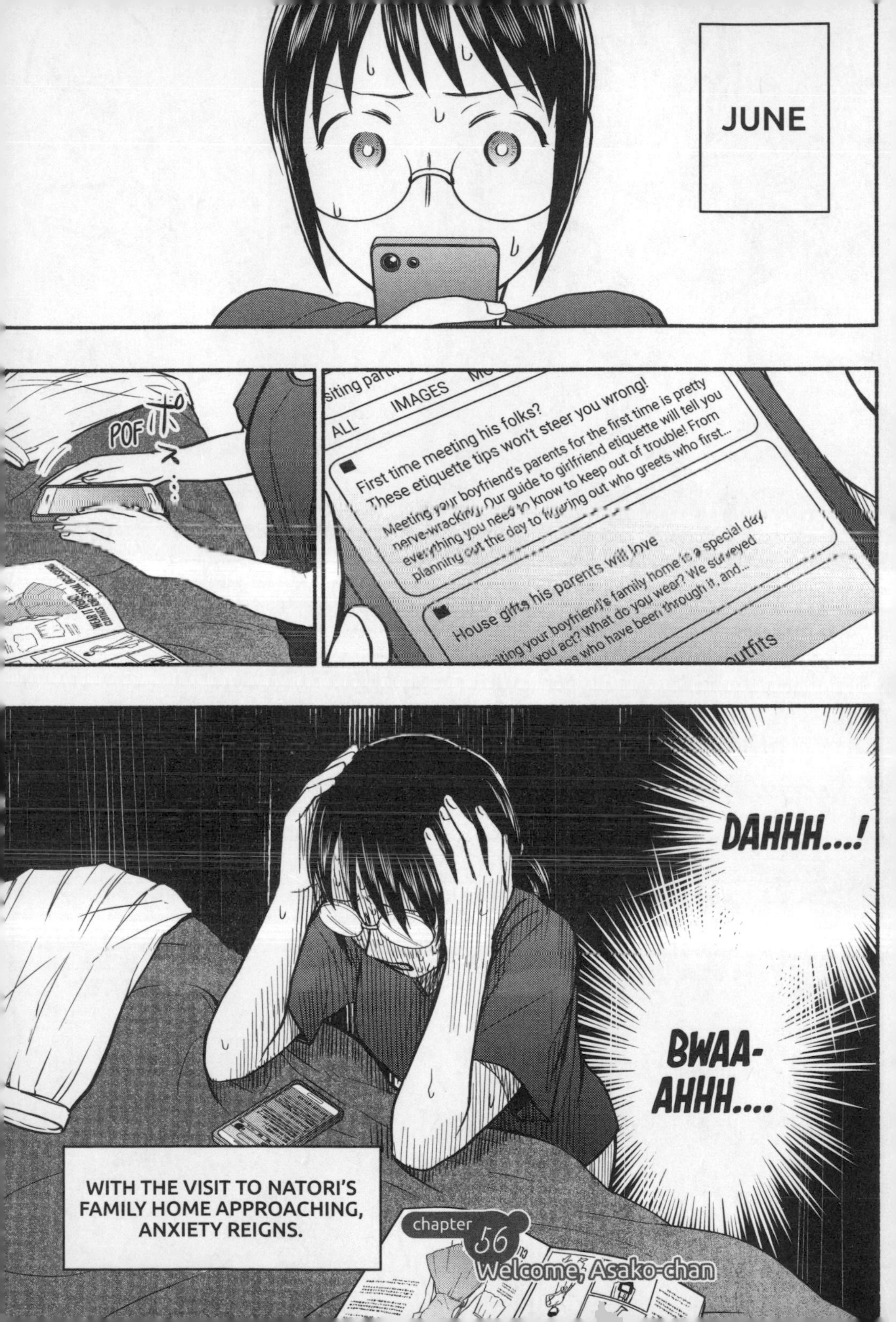
JUNE
ALL
IMAGES
First time meeting his folks?
These etiquette tips won't steer you wrong!
Meeting your boyfriend's parents for the first time is pretty nerve-wracking. Our guide to girlfriend etiquette will tell you everything you need to know to keep out of trouble! From planning out the day to figuring out who greets who first...
House gifts his parents will love
is a special day
you act? What do you wear? We surveyed
who have been through it, and...
outfits
POF
DAHHH...!
BWAA-AHHH....
WITH THE VISIT TO NATORI'S FAMILY HOME APPROACHING, ANXIETY REIGNS.
chapter 56
Welcome, Asako-chan

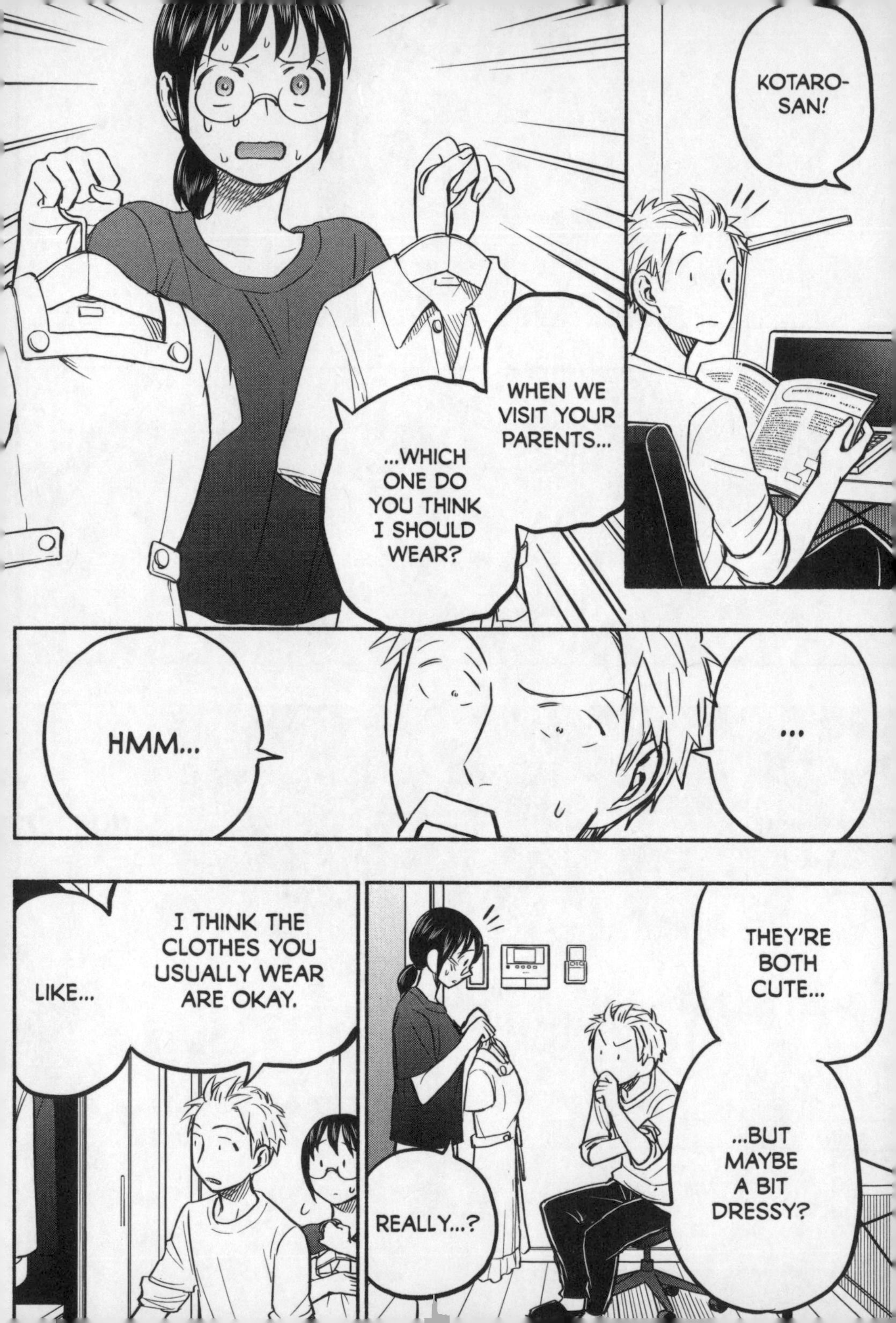
KOTARO-SAN!
WHEN WE VISIT YOUR PARENTS...
...WHICH ONE DO YOU THINK I SHOULD WEAR?
...
HMM...
THEY'RE BOTH CUTE...
...BUT MAYBE A BIT DRESSY?
REALLY...?
I THINK THE CLOTHES YOU USUALLY WEAR ARE OKAY.
LIKE...

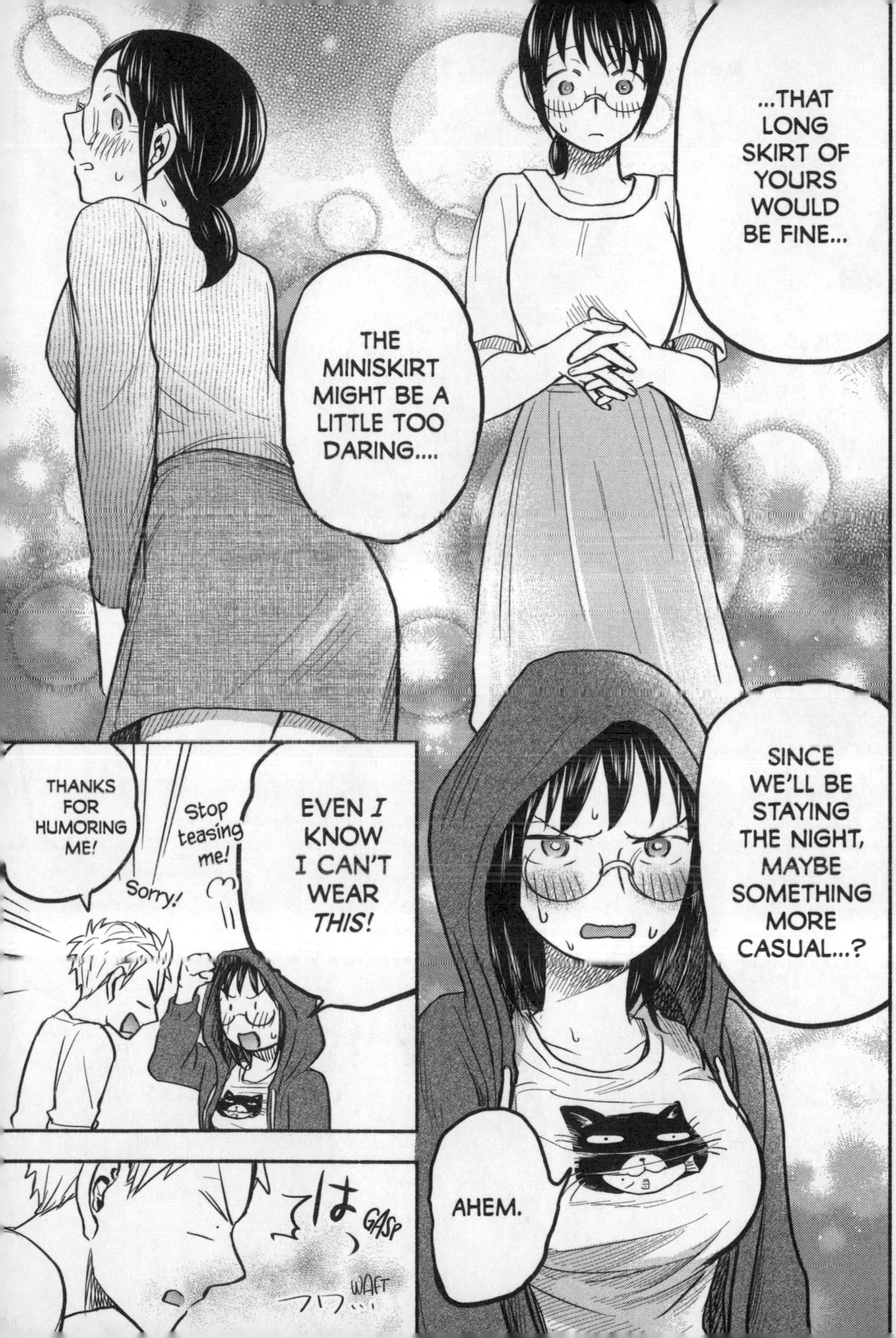
...THAT LONG SKIRT OF YOURS WOULD BE FINE...
THE MINISKIRT MIGHT BE A LITTLE TOO DARING....
SINCE WE'LL BE STAYING THE NIGHT, MAYBE SOMETHING MORE CASUAL...?
AHEM.
EVEN I KNOW I CAN'T WEAR THIS!
Stop teasing me!
Sorry!
THANKS FOR HUMORING ME!
GASP
WAFT

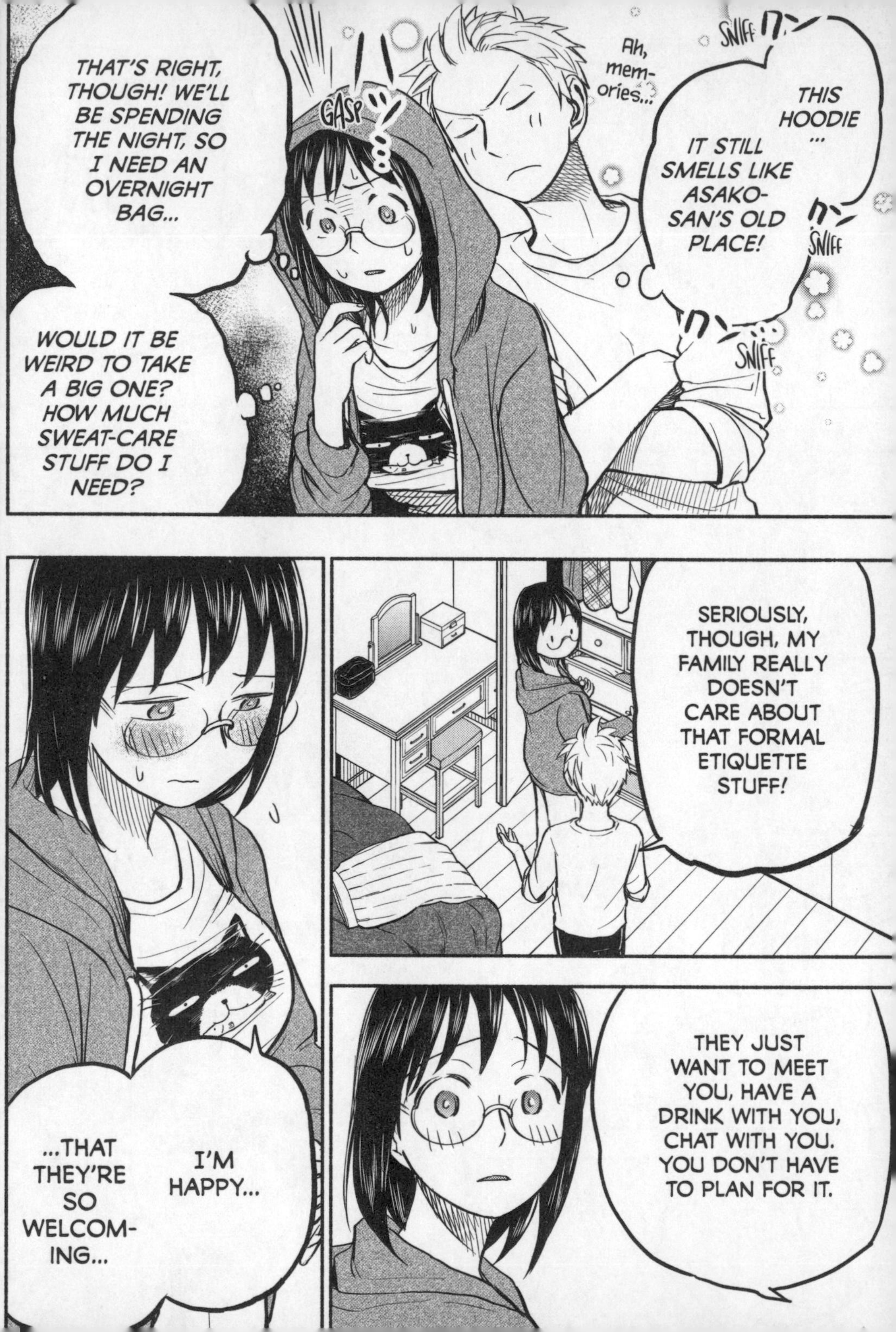
SNIFF
THIS HOODIE ...
IT STILL SMELLS LIKE ASAKO-SAN'S OLD PLACE!
SNIFF
SNIFF
Ah, mem-ories...
GASP
THAT'S RIGHT, THOUGH! WE'LL BE SPENDING THE NIGHT, SO I NEED AN OVERNIGHT BAG...
WOULD IT BE WEIRD TO TAKE A BIG ONE? HOW MUCH SWEAT-CARE STUFF DO I NEED?
SERIOUSLY, THOUGH, MY FAMILY REALLY DOESN'T CARE ABOUT THAT FORMAL ETIQUETTE STUFF!
THEY JUST WANT TO MEET YOU, HAVE A DRINK WITH YOU, CHAT WITH YOU. YOU DON'T HAVE TO PLAN FOR IT.
I'M HAPPY...
...THAT THEY'RE SO WELCOM-ING...

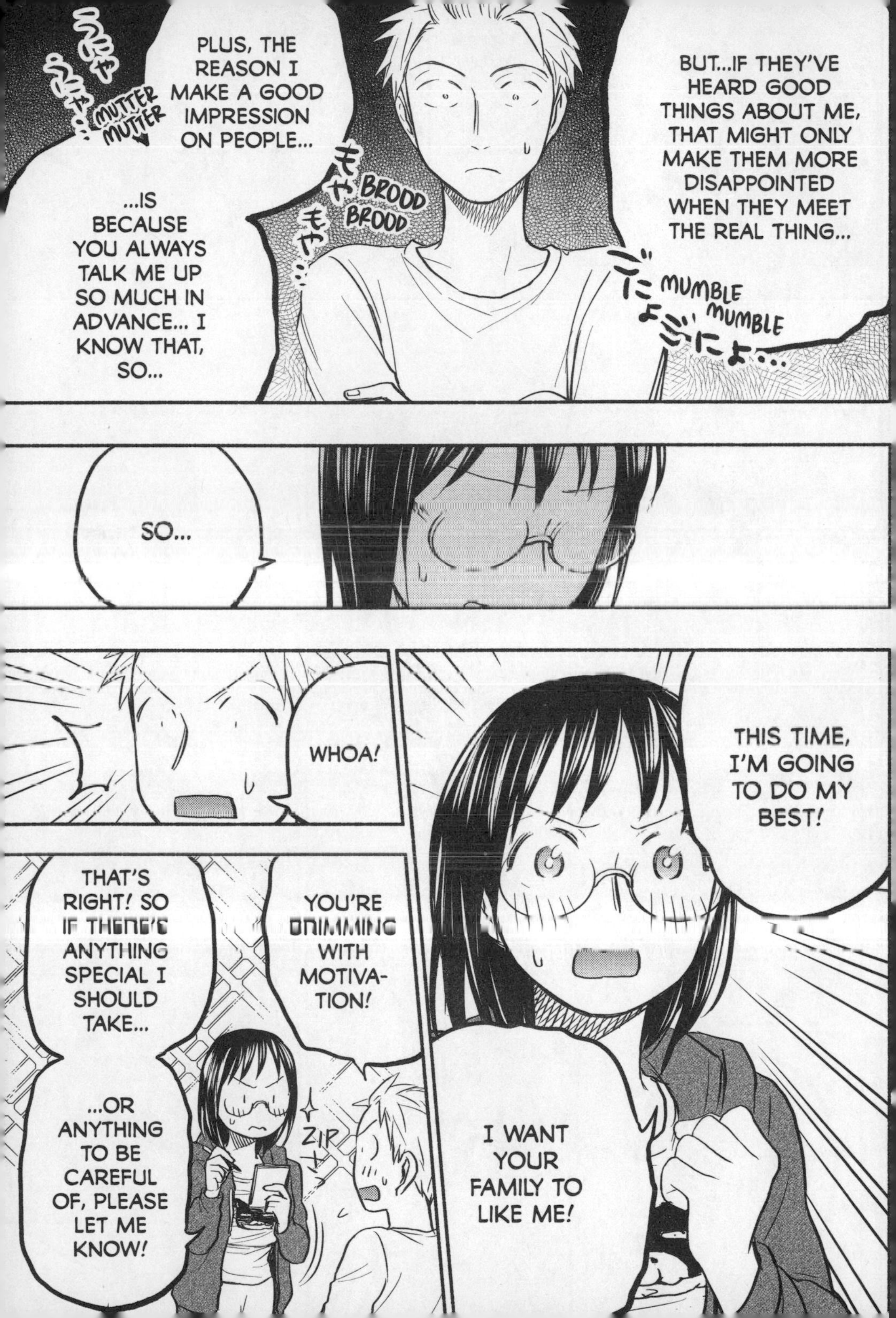
BUT...IF THEY'VE HEARD GOOD THINGS ABOUT ME, THAT MIGHT ONLY MAKE THEM MORE DISAPPOINTED WHEN THEY MEET THE REAL THING...
MUMBLE MUMBLE
BROOD BROOD
PLUS, THE REASON I MAKE A GOOD IMPRESSION ON PEOPLE...
MUTTER MUTTER
...IS BECAUSE YOU ALWAYS TALK ME UP SO MUCH IN ADVANCE... I KNOW THAT, SO...
SO...
THIS TIME, I'M GOING TO DO MY BEST!
I WANT YOUR FAMILY TO LIKE ME!
WHOA!
YOU'RE BRIMMING WITH MOTIVATION!
THAT'S RIGHT! SO IF THERE'S ANYTHING SPECIAL I SHOULD TAKE...
...OR ANYTHING TO BE CAREFUL OF, PLEASE LET ME KNOW!
ZIP

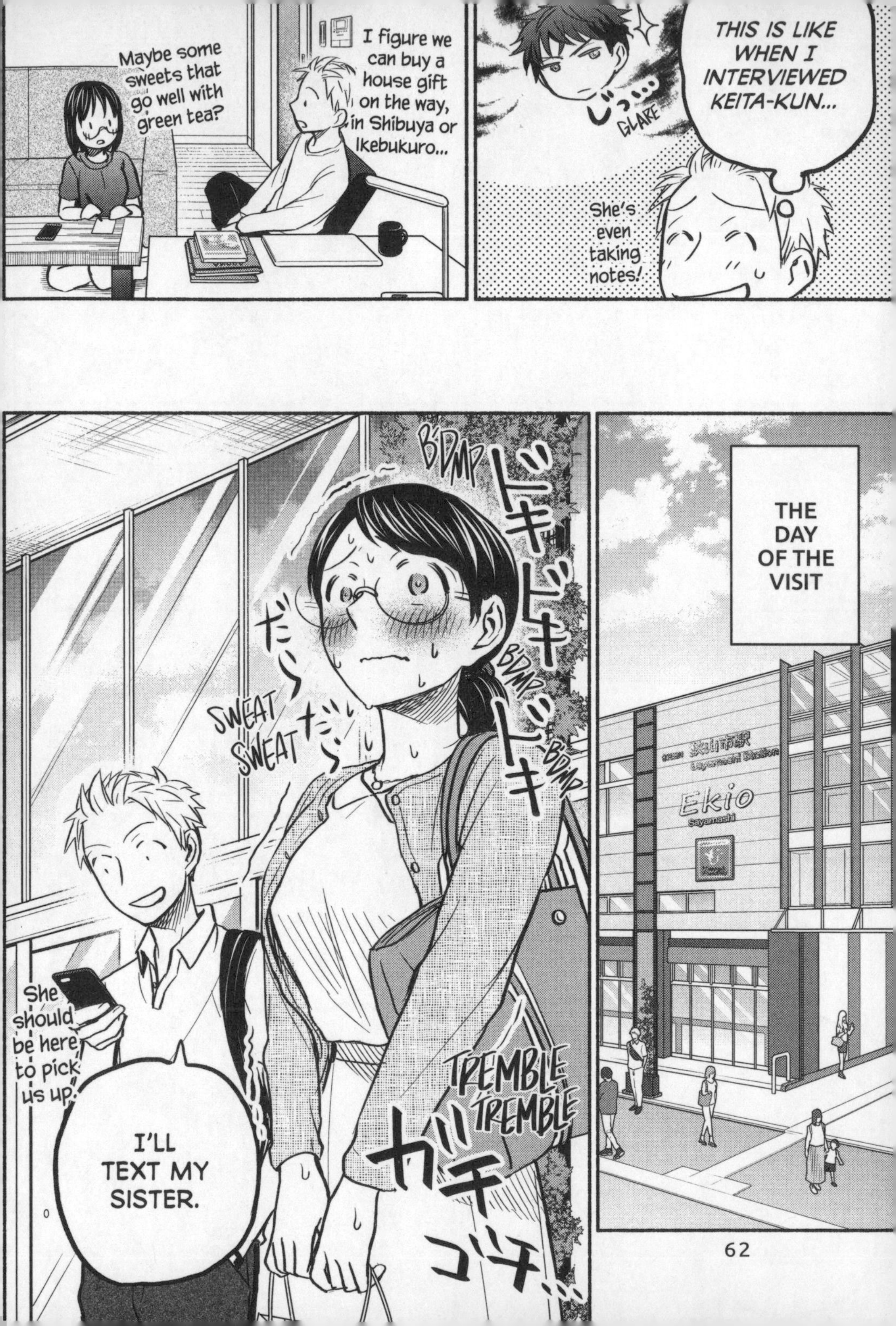
THIS IS LIKE WHEN I INTERVIEWED KEITA-KUN...
GLARE
She's even taking notes!
I figure we can buy a house gift on the way, in Shibuya or Ikebukuro...
Maybe some sweets that go well with green tea?
THE DAY OF THE VISIT
Ekio
Sayamashi
BDMP
BDMP
BDMP
SWEAT SWEAT
She should be here to pick us up.
I'LL TEXT MY SISTER.
TREMBLE TREMBLE

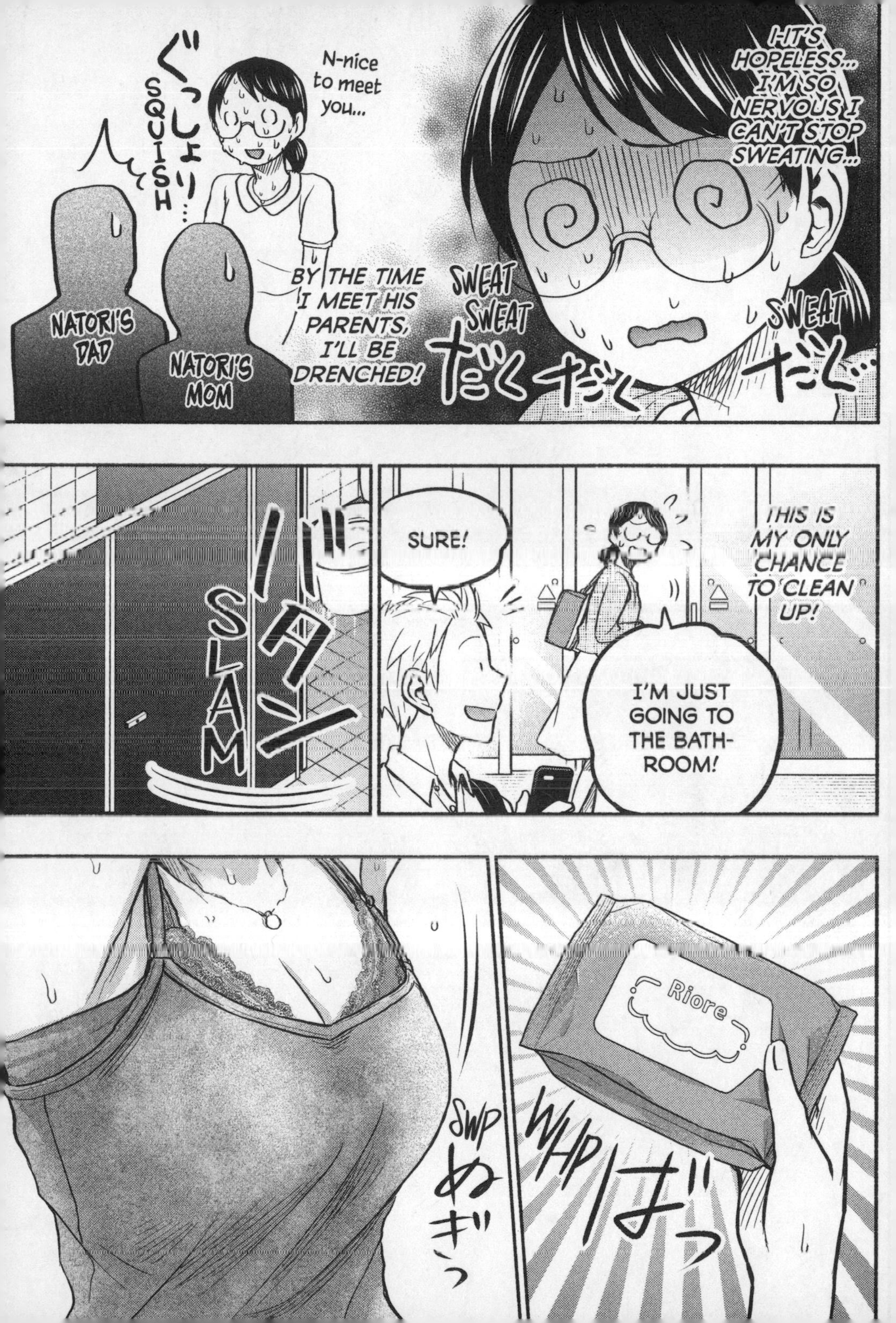
I-IT'S HOPELESS... I'M SO NERVOUS I CAN'T STOP SWEATING...
SWEAT SWEAT
SWEAT
だくだく だく…
BY THE TIME I MEET HIS PARENTS, I'LL BE DRENCHED!
N-nice to meet you...
ぐっしょり…
SQUISH
NATORI'S MOM
NATORI'S DAD
THIS IS MY ONLY CHANCE TO 'CLEAN UP'!
I'M JUST GOING TO THE BATH-ROOM!
SURE!
バターン
SLAM
Riore
ぱっ
WHP
ぬぎっ
SWP

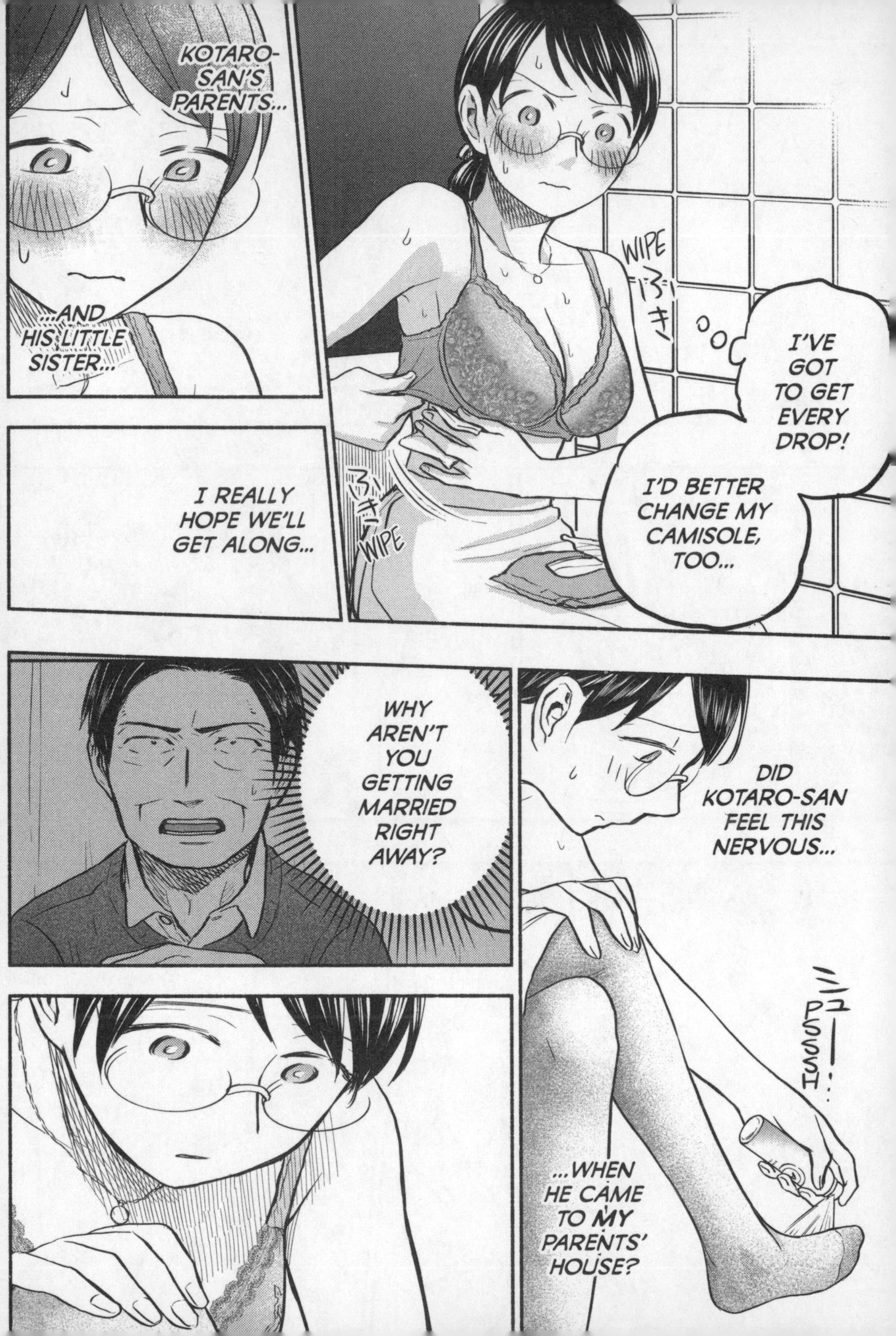
WIPE
ふき
I'VE GOT TO GET EVERY DROP!
I'D BETTER CHANGE MY CAMISOLE, TOO...
ふき
WIPE
KOTARO-SAN'S PARENTS...
...AND HIS LITTLE SISTER...
I REALLY HOPE WE'LL GET ALONG...
DID KOTARO-SAN FEEL THIS NERVOUS...
シュー
PSSSH
...WHEN HE CAME TO MY PARENTS' HOUSE?
WHY AREN'T YOU GETTING MARRIED RIGHT AWAY?

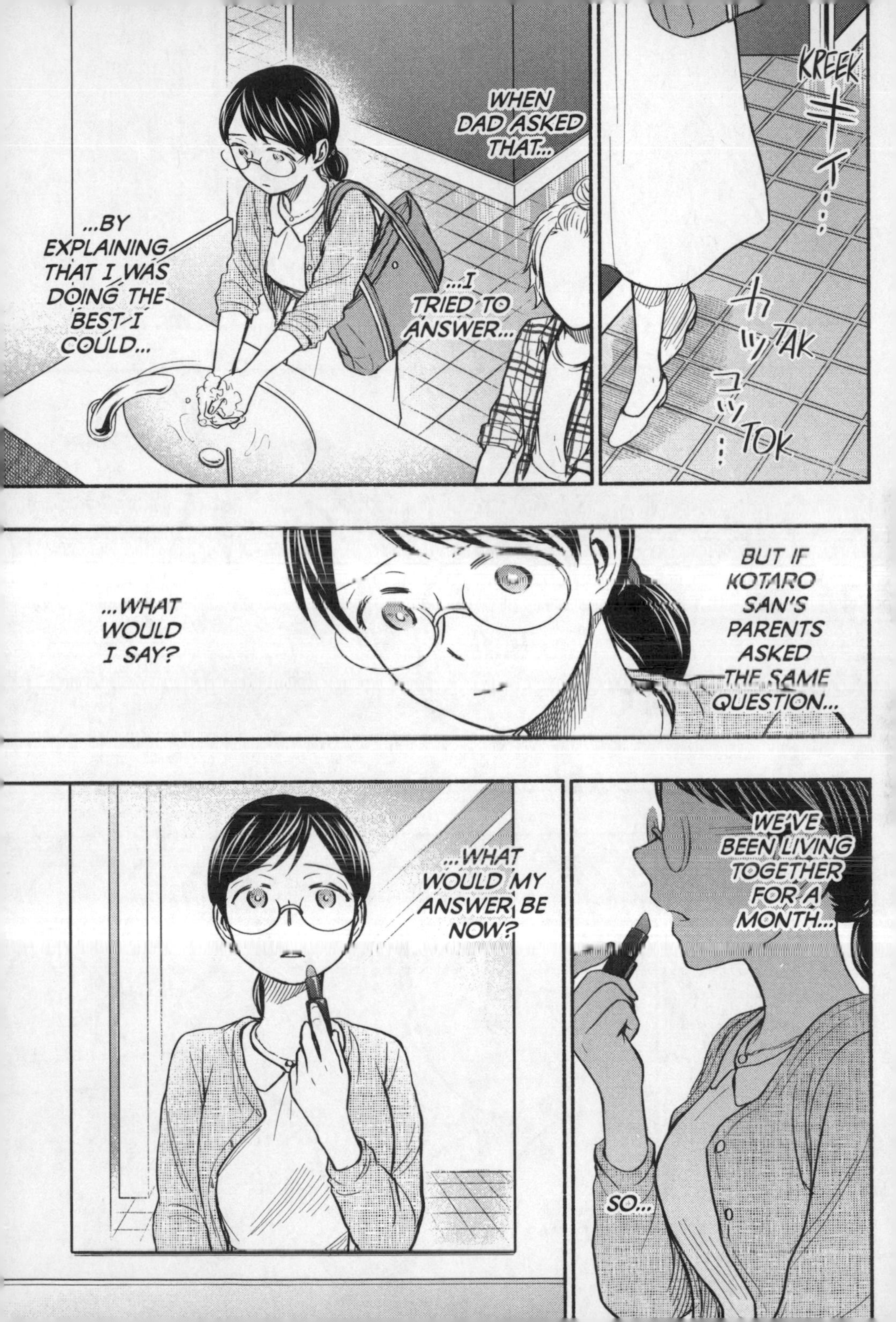
KREEK
キイ…
カッ TAK
コッ TOK…
WHEN DAD ASKED THAT...
...I TRIED TO ANSWER...
...BY EXPLAINING THAT I WAS DOING THE BEST I COULD...
BUT IF KOTARO SAN'S PARENTS ASKED THE SAME QUESTION...
...WHAT WOULD I SAY?
WE'VE BEEN LIVING TOGETHER FOR A MONTH...
SO...
...WHAT WOULD MY ANSWER BE NOW?

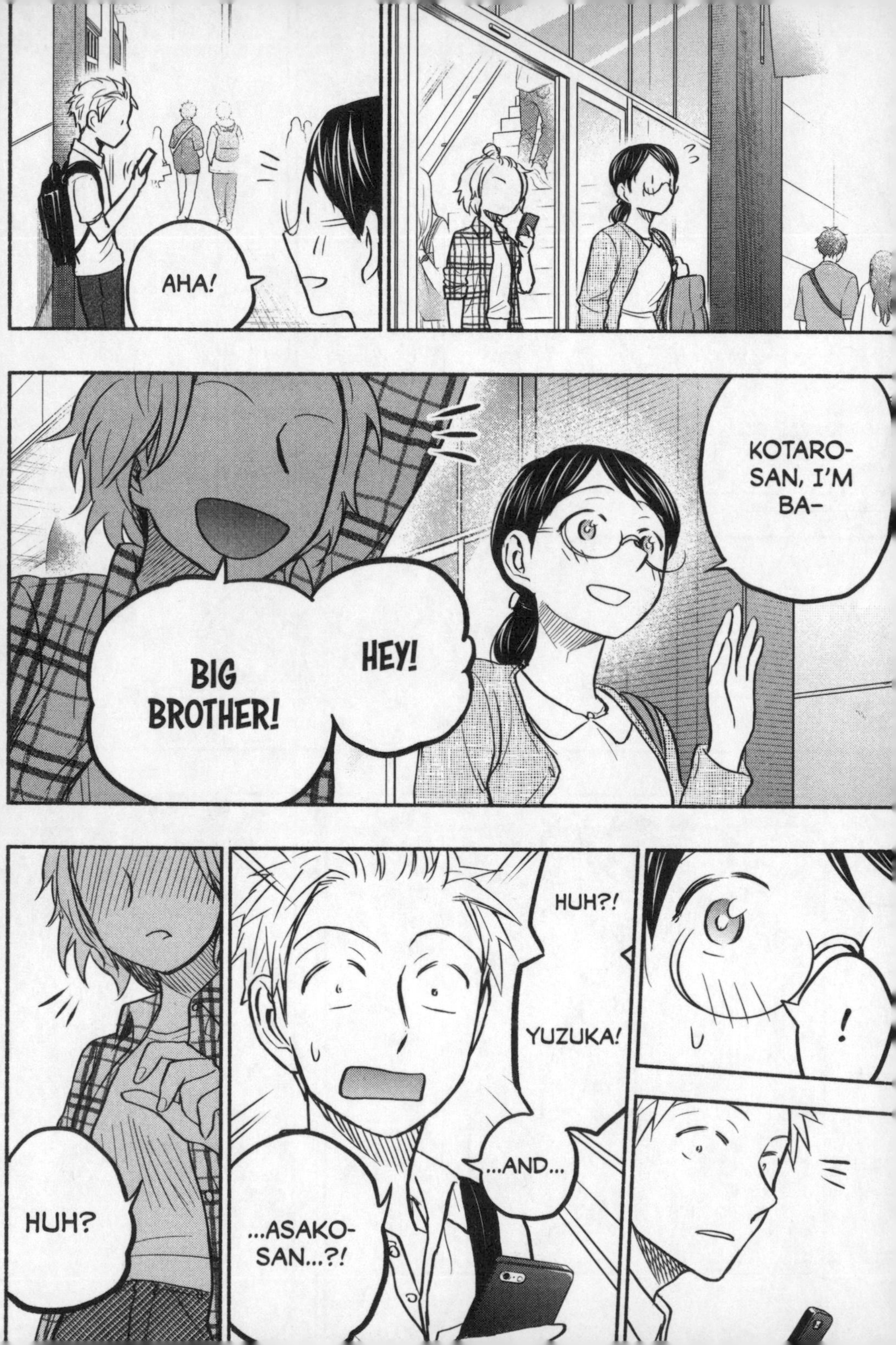
AHA!
KOTARO-SAN, I'M BA–
HEY! BIG BROTHER!
!
HUH?! YUZUKA!
...AND...
...ASAKO-SAN...?!
HUH?

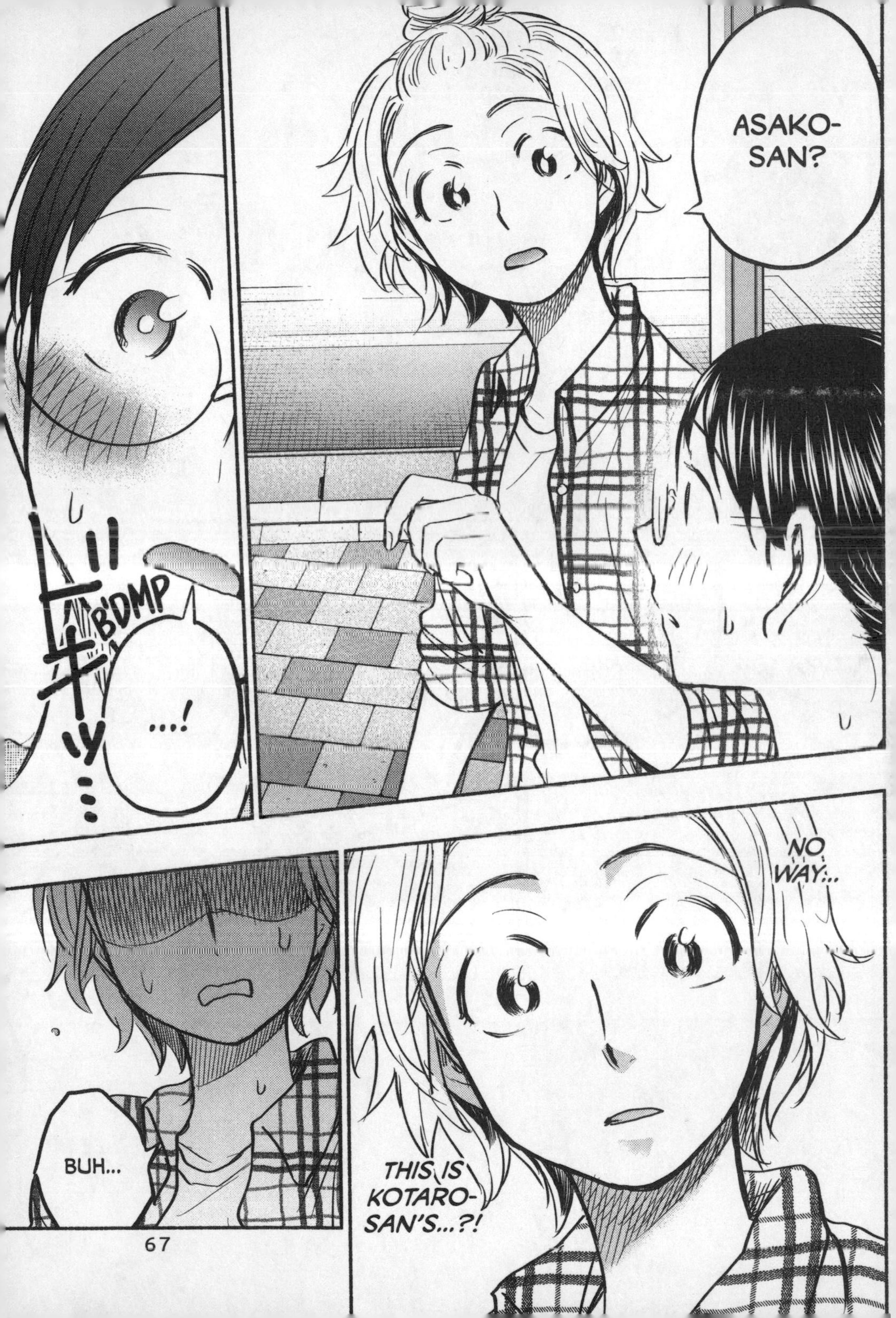
ASAKO-SAN?
B'DMP
...!
NO WAY...
THIS IS KOTARO-SAN'S...?!
BUH...

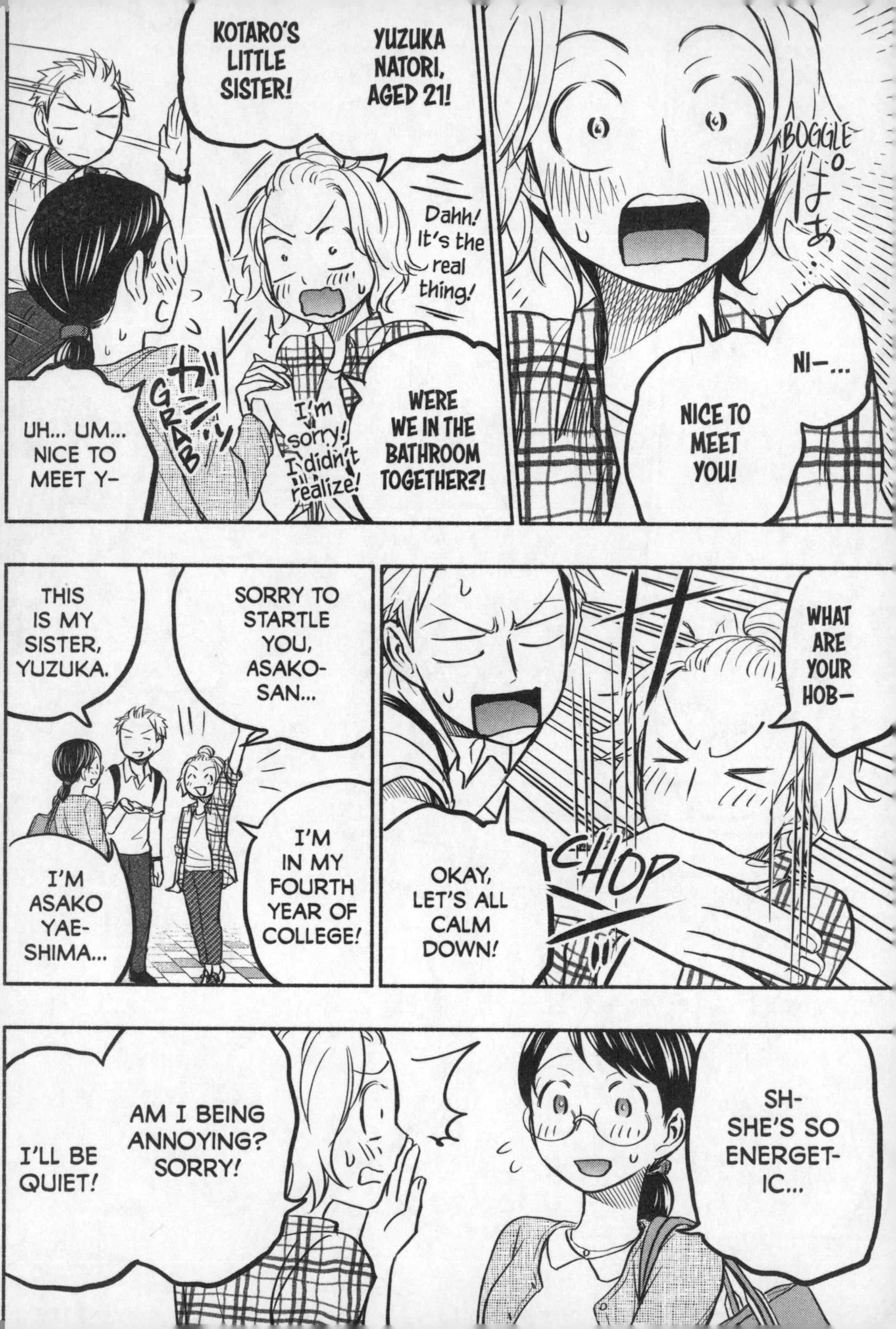
BOGGLE
ぱあ
NI—...
NICE TO MEET YOU!
YUZUKA NATORI, AGED 21!
KOTARO'S LITTLE SISTER!
Dahh! It's the real thing!
WERE WE IN THE BATHROOM TOGETHER?!
I'm sorry! I didn't realize!
GRAB
UH... UM... NICE TO MEET Y-
WHAT ARE YOUR HOB—
CHOP
OKAY, LET'S ALL CALM DOWN!
SORRY TO STARTLE YOU, ASAKO-SAN...
THIS IS MY SISTER, YUZUKA.
I'M IN MY FOURTH YEAR OF COLLEGE!
I'M ASAKO YAE-SHIMA...
SH- SHE'S SO ENERGET-IC...
AM I BEING ANNOYING? SORRY!
I'LL BE QUIET!

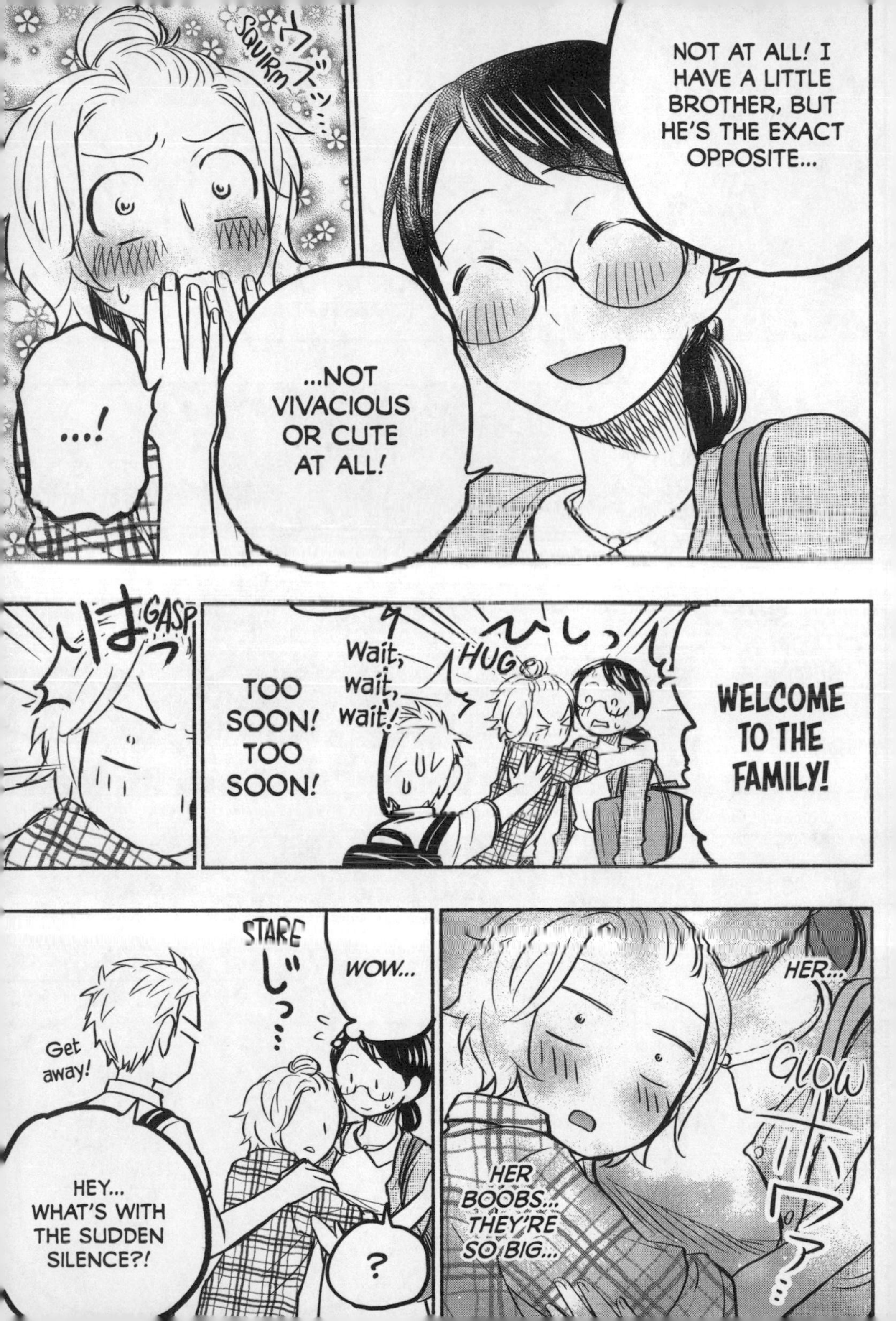

NOT AT ALL! I HAVE A LITTLE BROTHER, BUT HE'S THE EXACT OPPOSITE...
...NOT VIVACIOUS OR CUTE AT ALL!
SQUIRM
...!
WELCOME TO THE FAMILY!
HUG
Wait, wait, wait!
TOO SOON! TOO SOON!
GASP
HER...
GLOW
HER BOOBS... THEY'RE SO BIG...
WOW...
STARE
Get away!
HEY... WHAT'S WITH THE SUDDEN SILENCE?!
?

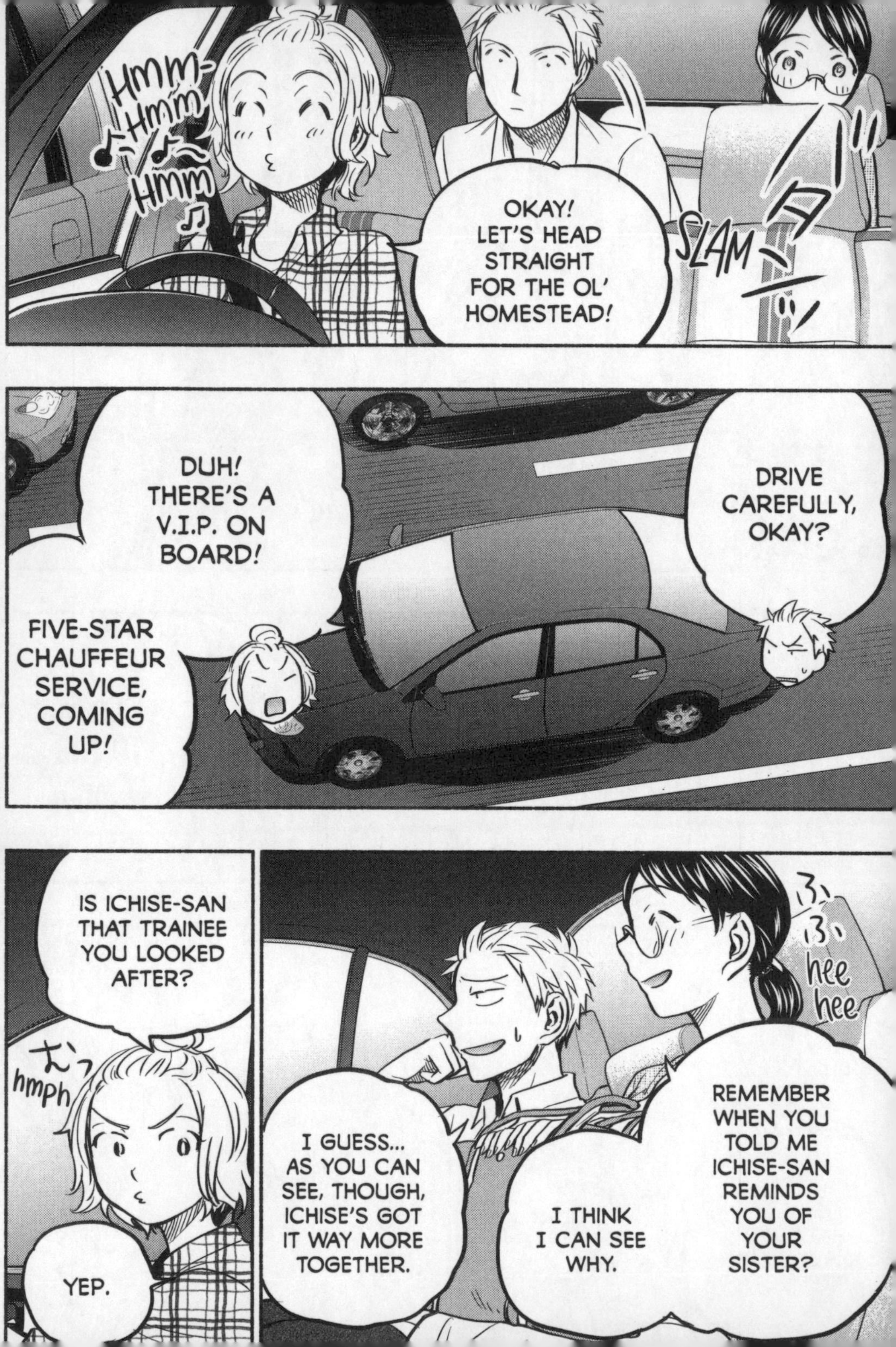
SLAM
OKAY! LET'S HEAD STRAIGHT FOR THE OL' HOMESTEAD!
Hmm-Hmm Hmm
DRIVE CAREFULLY, OKAY?
DUH! THERE'S A V.I.P. ON BOARD!
FIVE-STAR CHAUFFEUR SERVICE, COMING UP!
ふふ
hee hee
REMEMBER WHEN YOU TOLD ME ICHISE-SAN REMINDS YOU OF YOUR SISTER?
I THINK I CAN SEE WHY.
I GUESS... AS YOU CAN SEE, THOUGH, ICHISE'S GOT IT WAY MORE TOGETHER.
IS ICHISE-SAN THAT TRAINEE YOU LOOKED AFTER?
hmph
YEP.

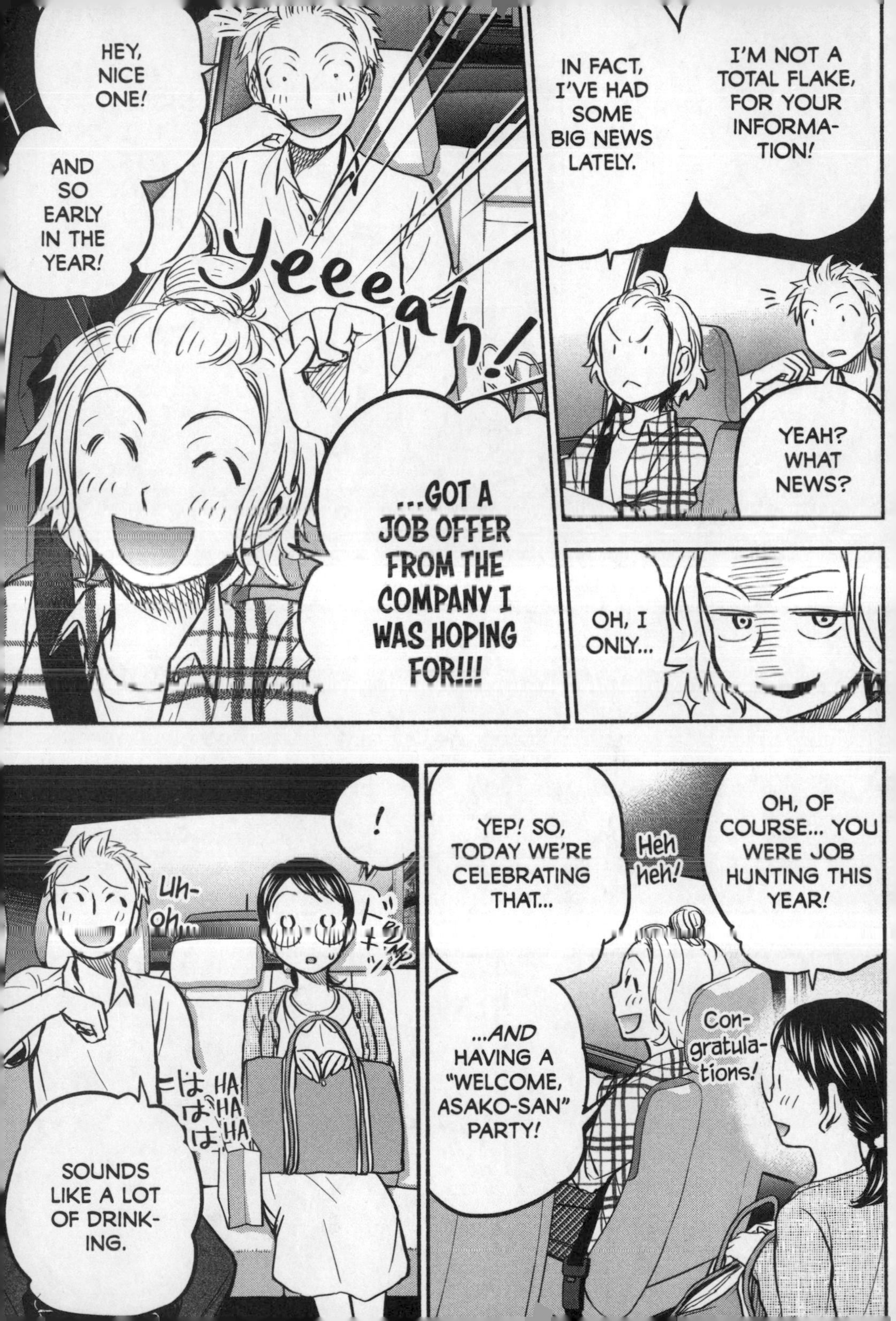
I'M NOT A TOTAL FLAKE, FOR YOUR INFORMATION!
IN FACT, I'VE HAD SOME BIG NEWS LATELY.
YEAH? WHAT NEWS?
OH, I ONLY...
...GOT A JOB OFFER FROM THE COMPANY I WAS HOPING FOR!!!
Yeeeah!
HEY, NICE ONE!
AND SO EARLY IN THE YEAR!
OH, OF COURSE... YOU WERE JOB HUNTING THIS YEAR!
Con-gratula-tions!
Heh heh!
YEP! SO, TODAY WE'RE CELEBRATING THAT...
...AND HAVING A "WELCOME, ASAKO-SAN" PARTY!
!
ドキッ
Uh-oh...
ははは HA HA HA
SOUNDS LIKE A LOT OF DRINKING.

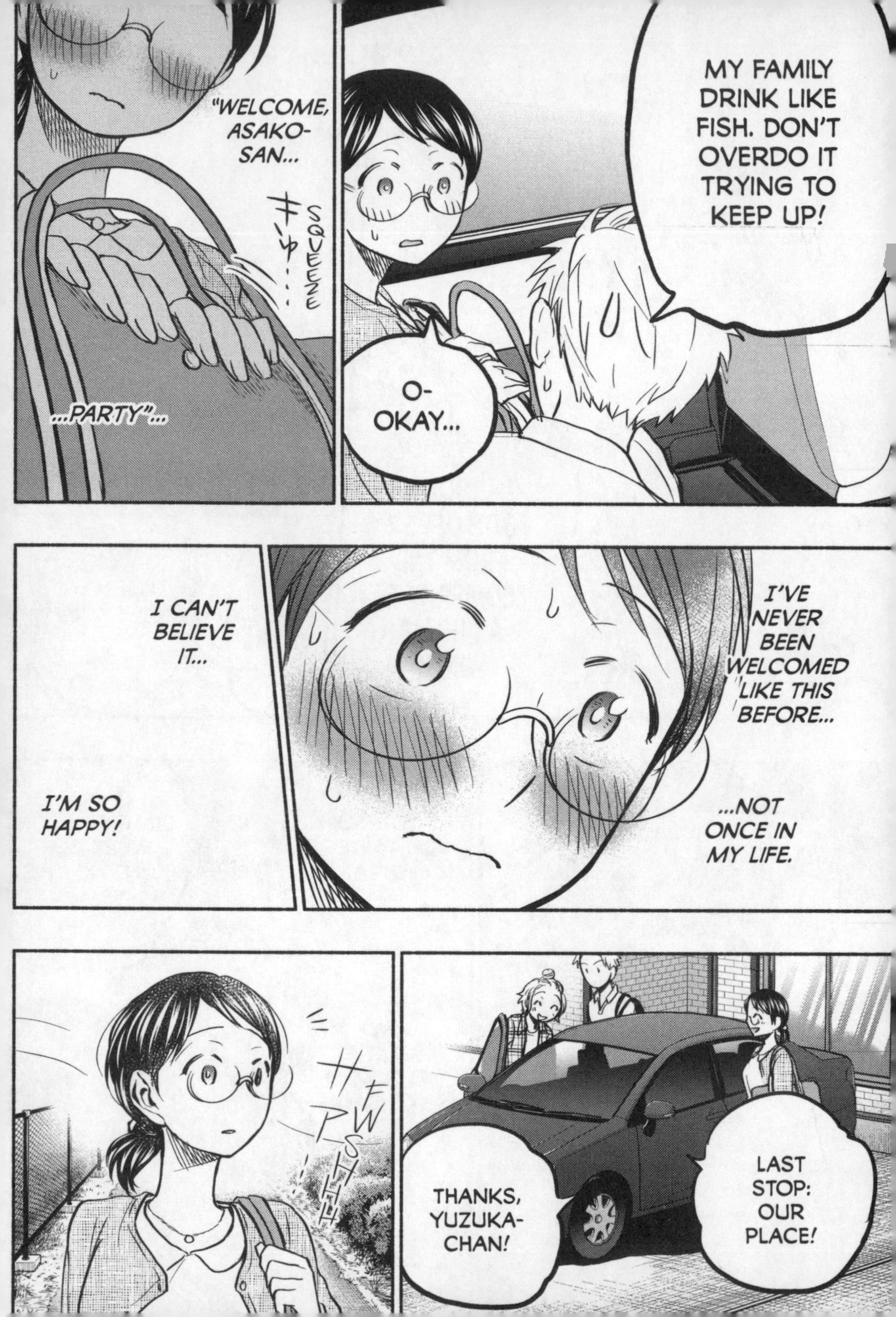
MY FAMILY DRINK LIKE FISH. DON'T OVERDO IT TRYING TO KEEP UP!
O- OKAY...
"WELCOME, ASAKO-SAN...
キュ… SQUEEZE
...PARTY"...
I'VE NEVER BEEN WELCOMED LIKE THIS BEFORE...
...NOT ONCE IN MY LIFE.
I CAN'T BELIEVE IT...
I'M SO HAPPY!
LAST STOP: OUR PLACE!
THANKS, YUZUKA-CHAN!
FWSHHH!

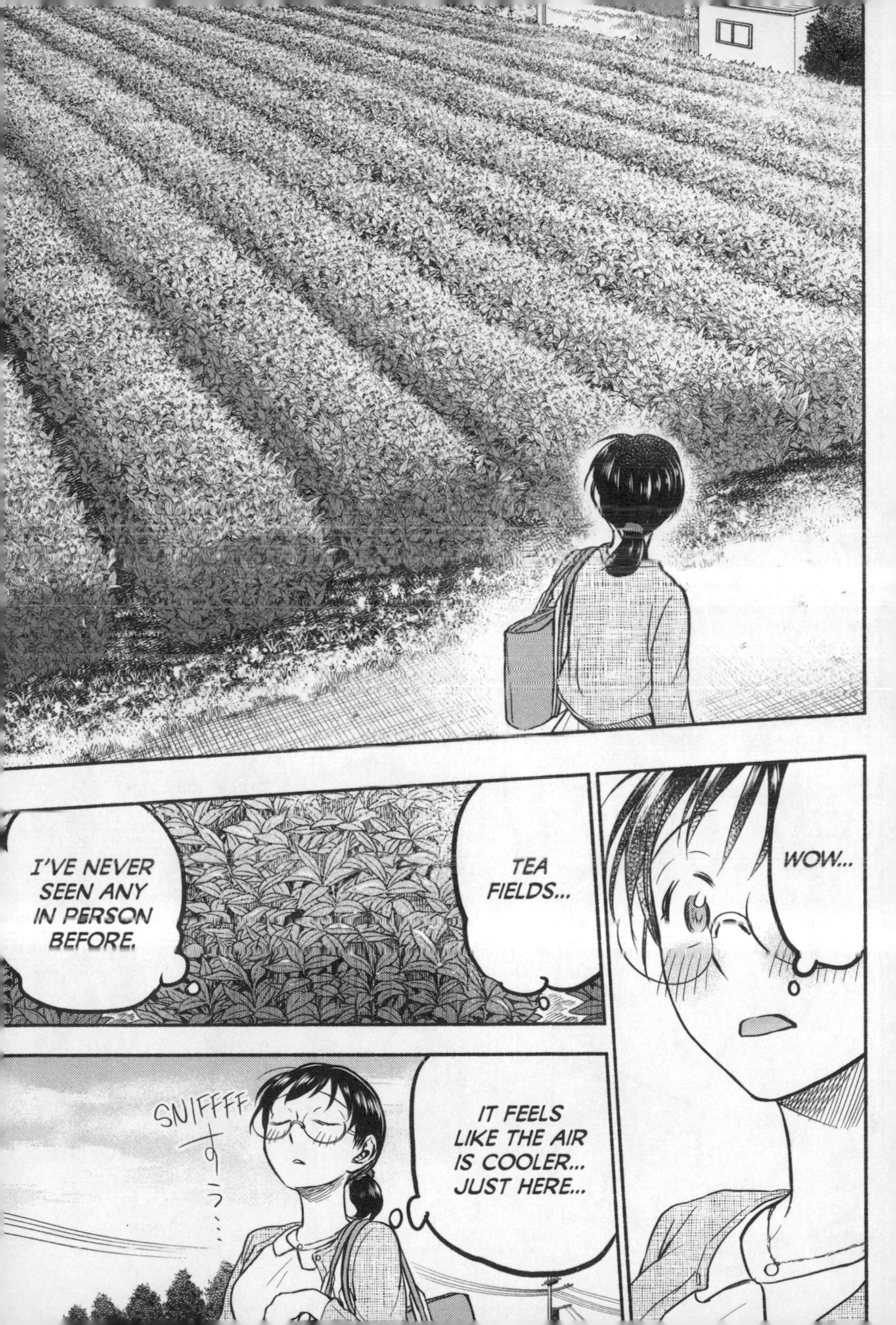
WOW...
TEA FIELDS...
I'VE NEVER SEEN ANY IN PERSON BEFORE.
IT FEELS LIKE THE AIR IS COOLER... JUST HERE...
SNIFFFF
すぅ…

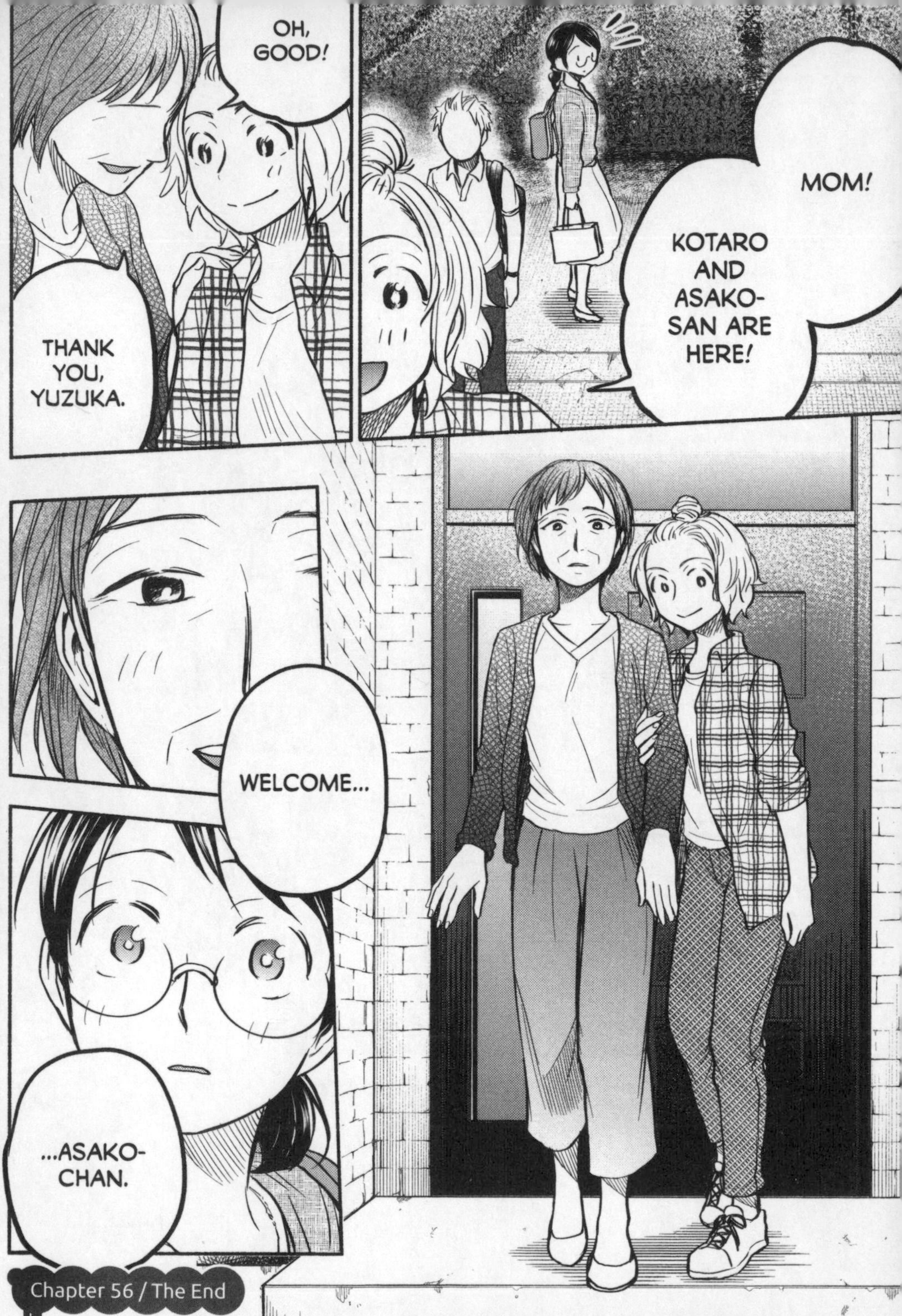
MOM!
KOTARO AND ASAKO-SAN ARE HERE!
OH, GOOD!
THANK YOU, YUZUKA.
WELCOME...
...ASAKO-CHAN.

Chapter 56 / The End

chapter 57 The Natori Family Feast

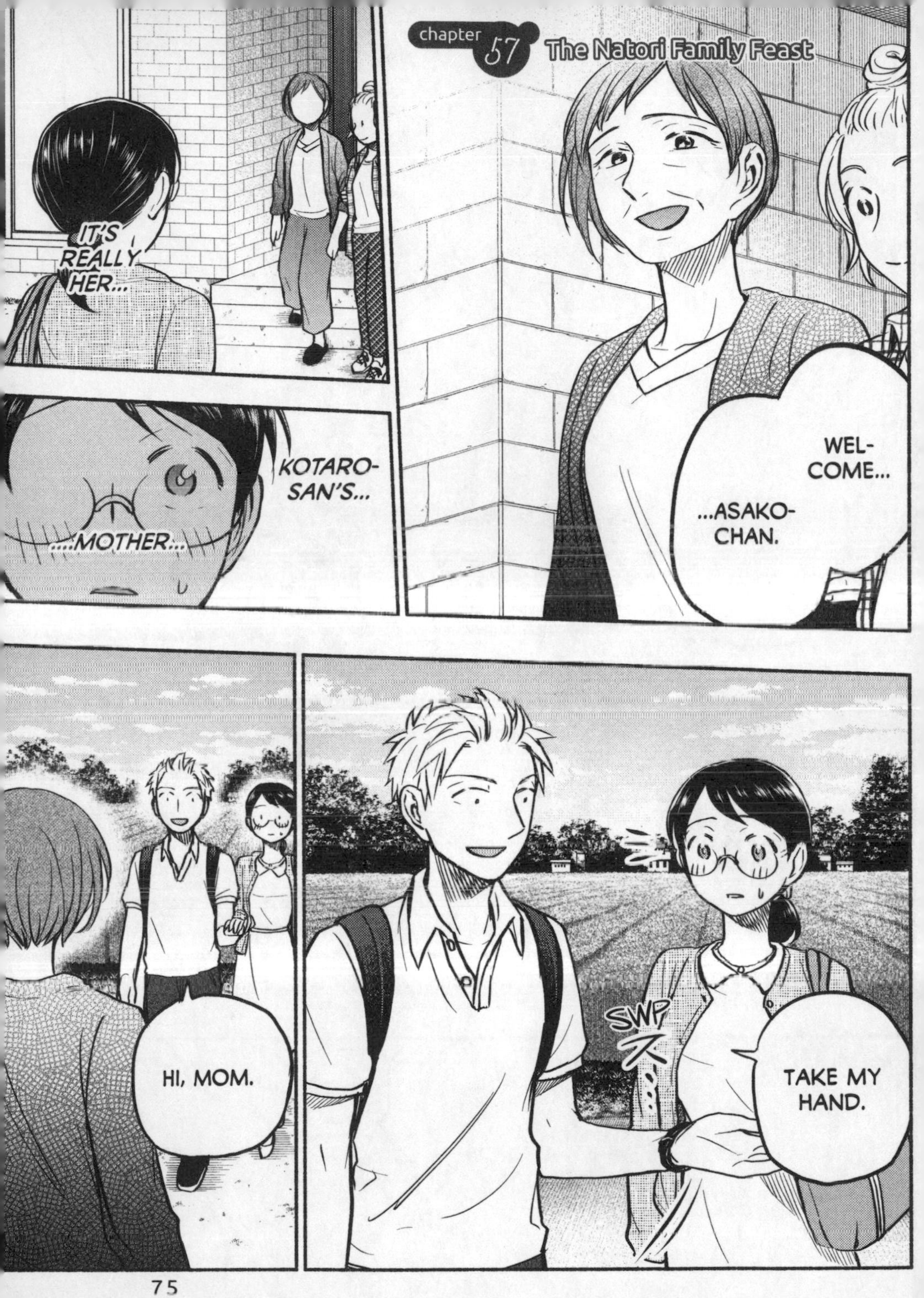
WEL-COME...
...ASAKO-CHAN.
IT'S REALLY HER...
KOTARO-SAN'S...
...MOTHER...
SWP
ス...
TAKE MY HAND.
HI, MOM.

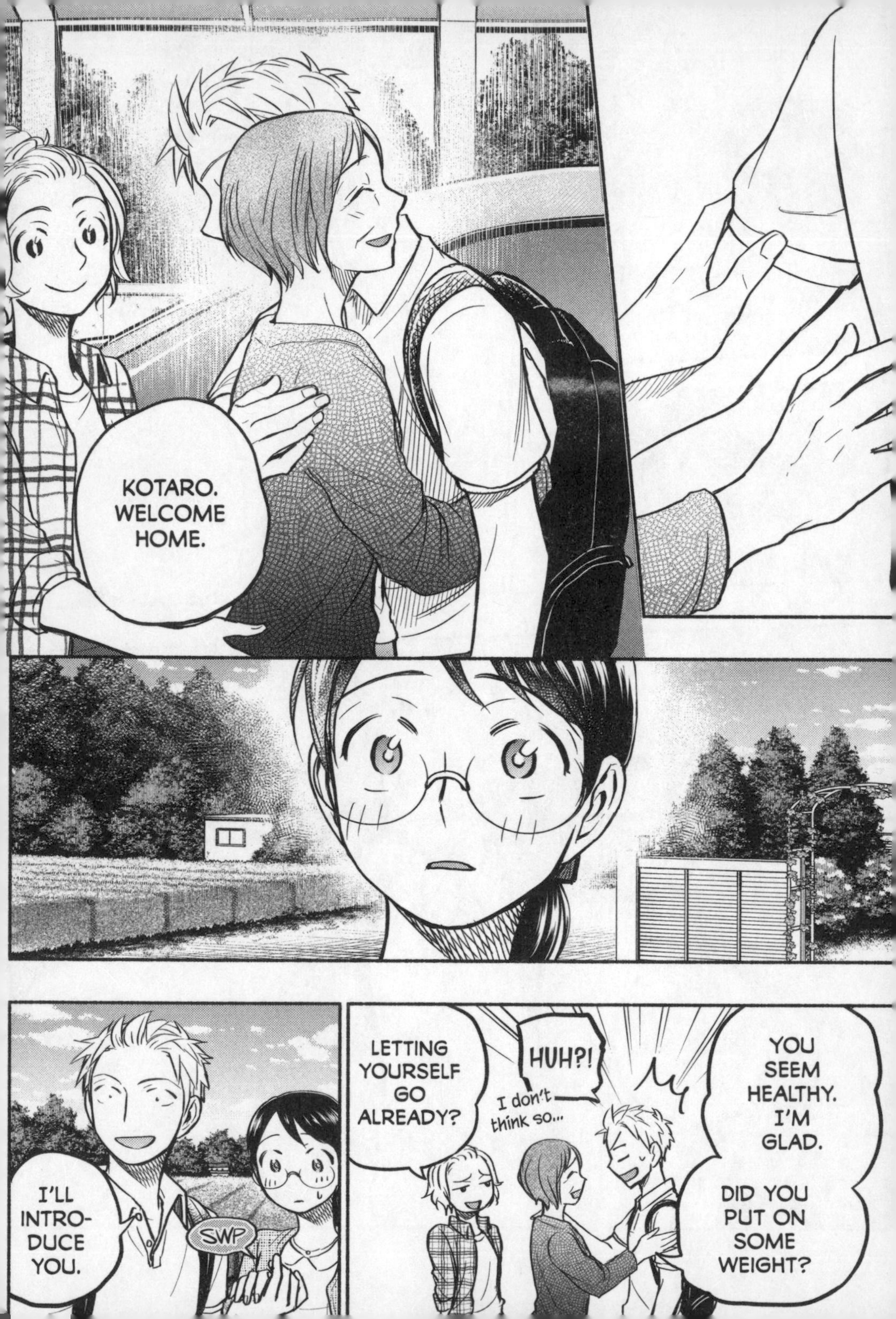
KOTARO. WELCOME HOME.
YOU SEEM HEALTHY. I'M GLAD.
DID YOU PUT ON SOME WEIGHT?
HUH?!
I don't think so...
LETTING YOURSELF GO ALREADY?
I'LL INTRO-DUCE YOU.
SWP

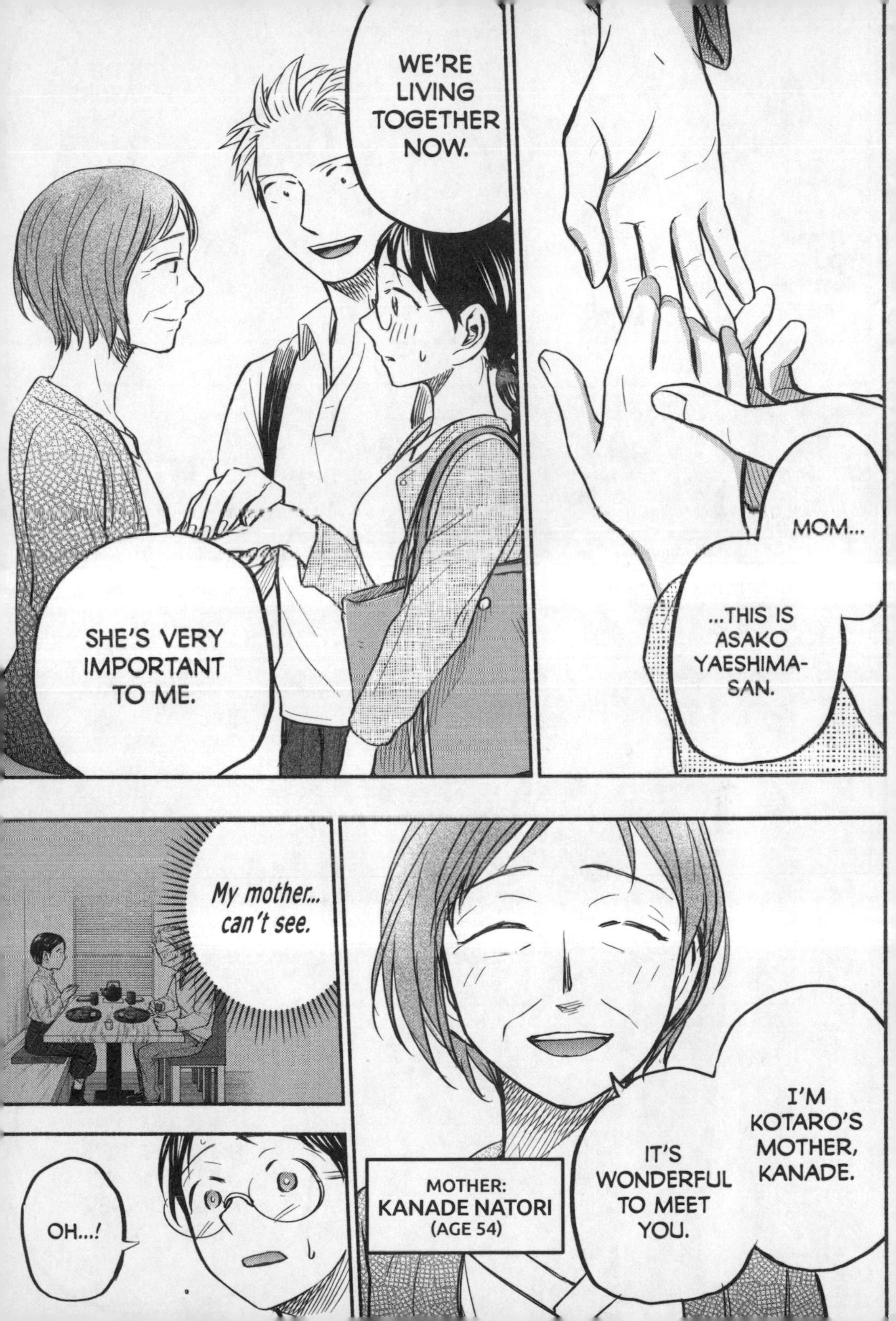
MOM...
...THIS IS ASAKO YAESHIMA-SAN.
WE'RE LIVING TOGETHER NOW.
SHE'S VERY IMPORTANT TO ME.
I'M KOTARO'S MOTHER, KANADE.
IT'S WONDERFUL TO MEET YOU.
MOTHER: KANADE NATORI (AGE 54)
My mother... can't see.
OH...!

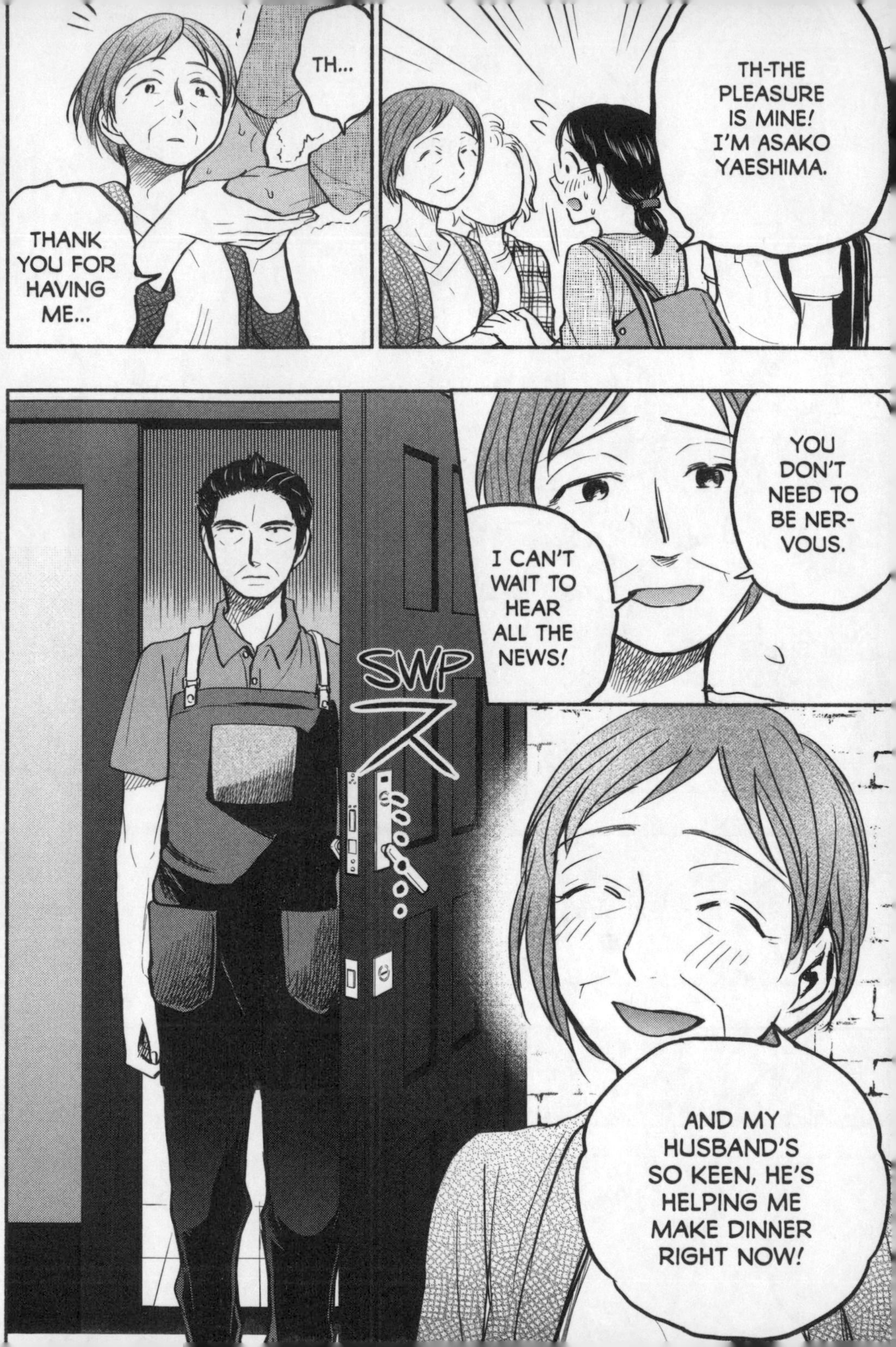
TH-THE PLEASURE IS MINE! I'M ASAKO YAESHIMA.
TH...
THANK YOU FOR HAVING ME...
YOU DON'T NEED TO BE NER-VOUS.
I CAN'T WAIT TO HEAR ALL THE NEWS!
AND MY HUSBAND'S SO KEEN, HE'S HELPING ME MAKE DINNER RIGHT NOW!
SWP
ス

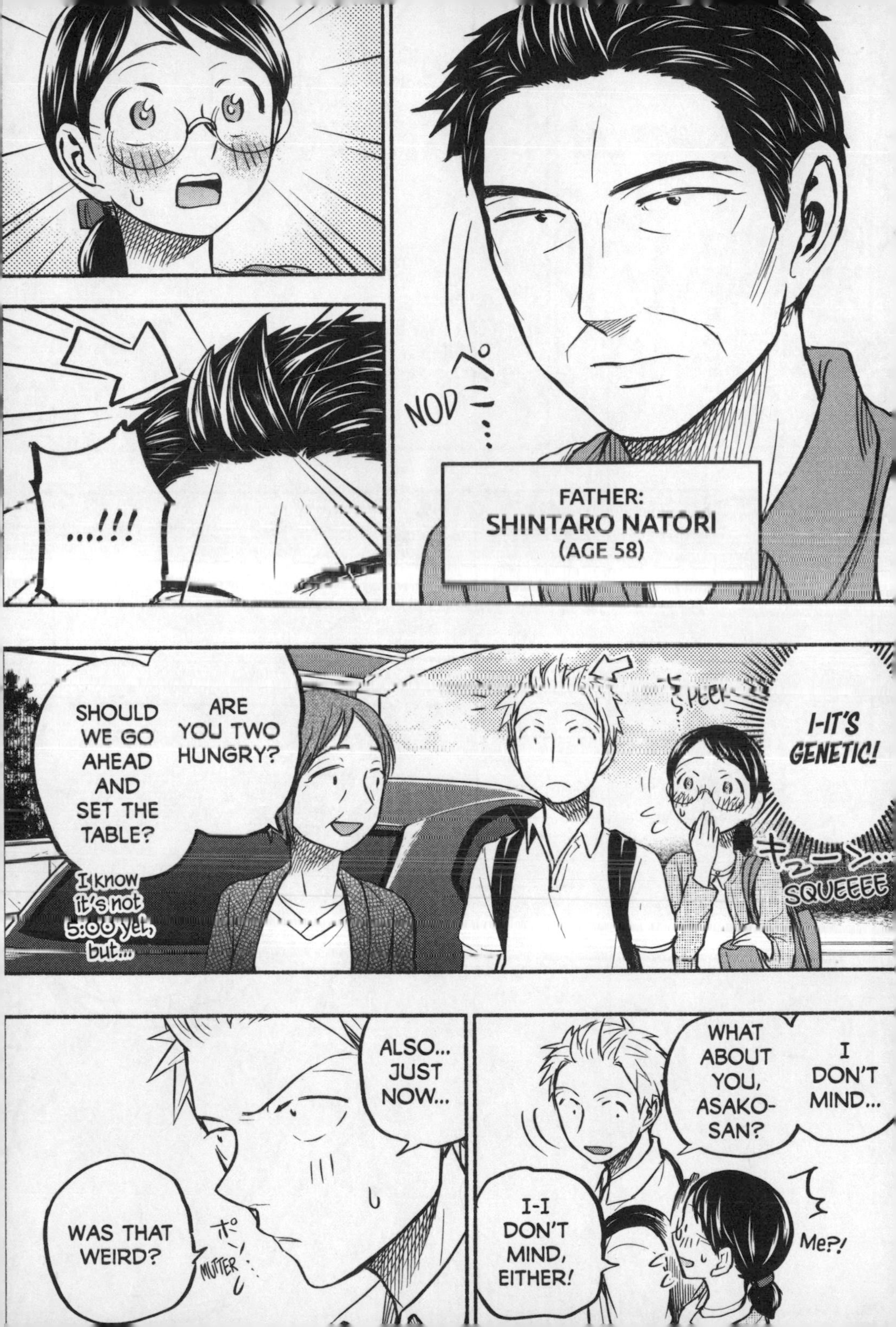
NOD
FATHER:
SHINTARO NATORI
(AGE 58)
...!!!
I-IT'S GENETIC!
SQUEEEE
PEEK
ARE YOU TWO HUNGRY?
SHOULD WE GO AHEAD AND SET THE TABLE?
I know it's not 5:00 yet, but...
I DON'T MIND...
WHAT ABOUT YOU, ASAKO-SAN?
Me?!
I-I DON'T MIND, EITHER!
ALSO... JUST NOW...
WAS THAT WEIRD?
MUTTER

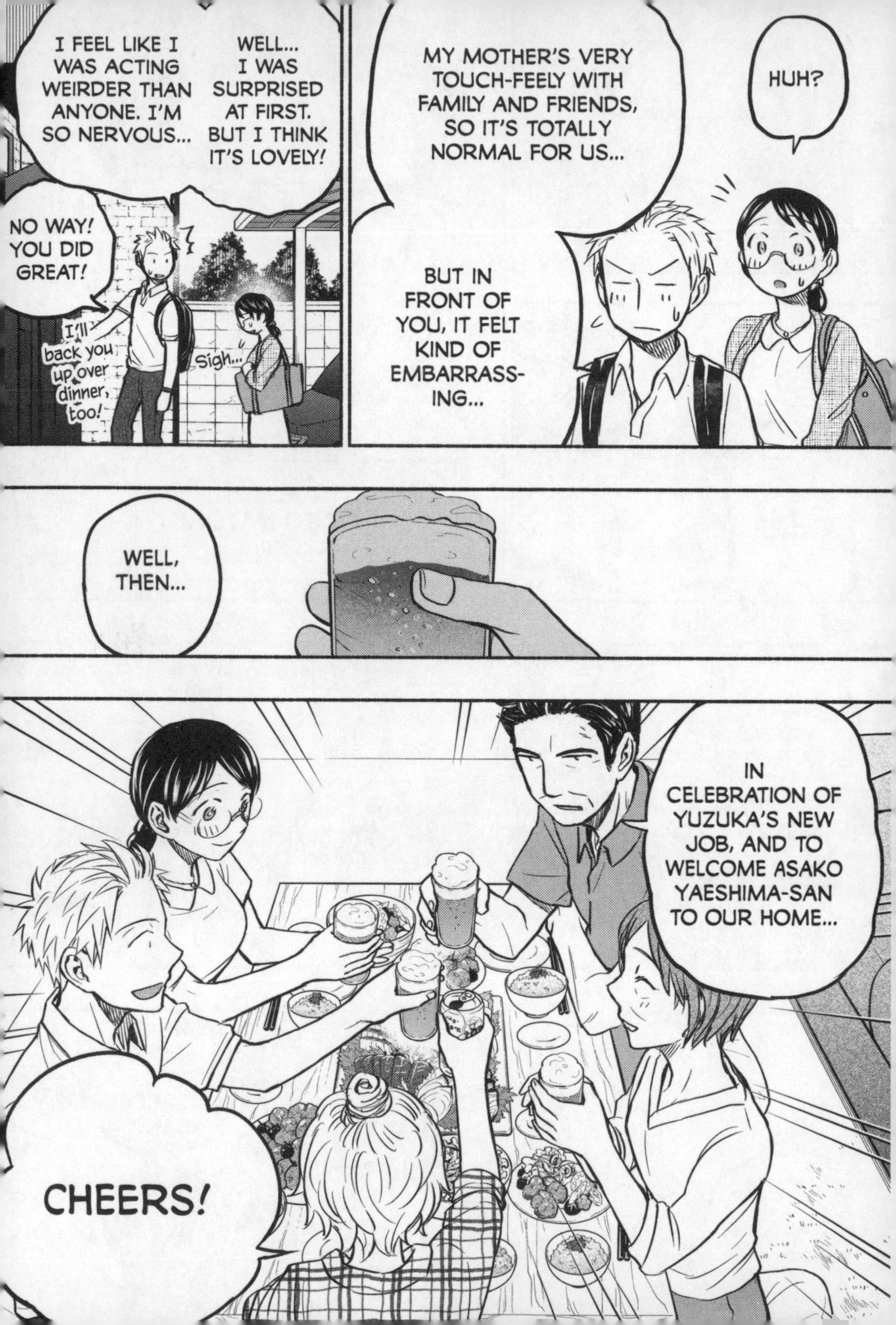
HUH?
MY MOTHER'S VERY TOUCH-FEELY WITH FAMILY AND FRIENDS, SO IT'S TOTALLY NORMAL FOR US...
BUT IN FRONT OF YOU, IT FELT KIND OF EMBARRASS-ING...
WELL... I WAS SURPRISED AT FIRST. BUT I THINK IT'S LOVELY!
I FEEL LIKE I WAS ACTING WEIRDER THAN ANYONE. I'M SO NERVOUS...
NO WAY! YOU DID GREAT!
Sigh...
I'll back you up over dinner, too!
WELL, THEN...
IN CELEBRATION OF YUZUKA'S NEW JOB, AND TO WELCOME ASAKO YAESHIMA-SAN TO OUR HOME...
CHEERS!

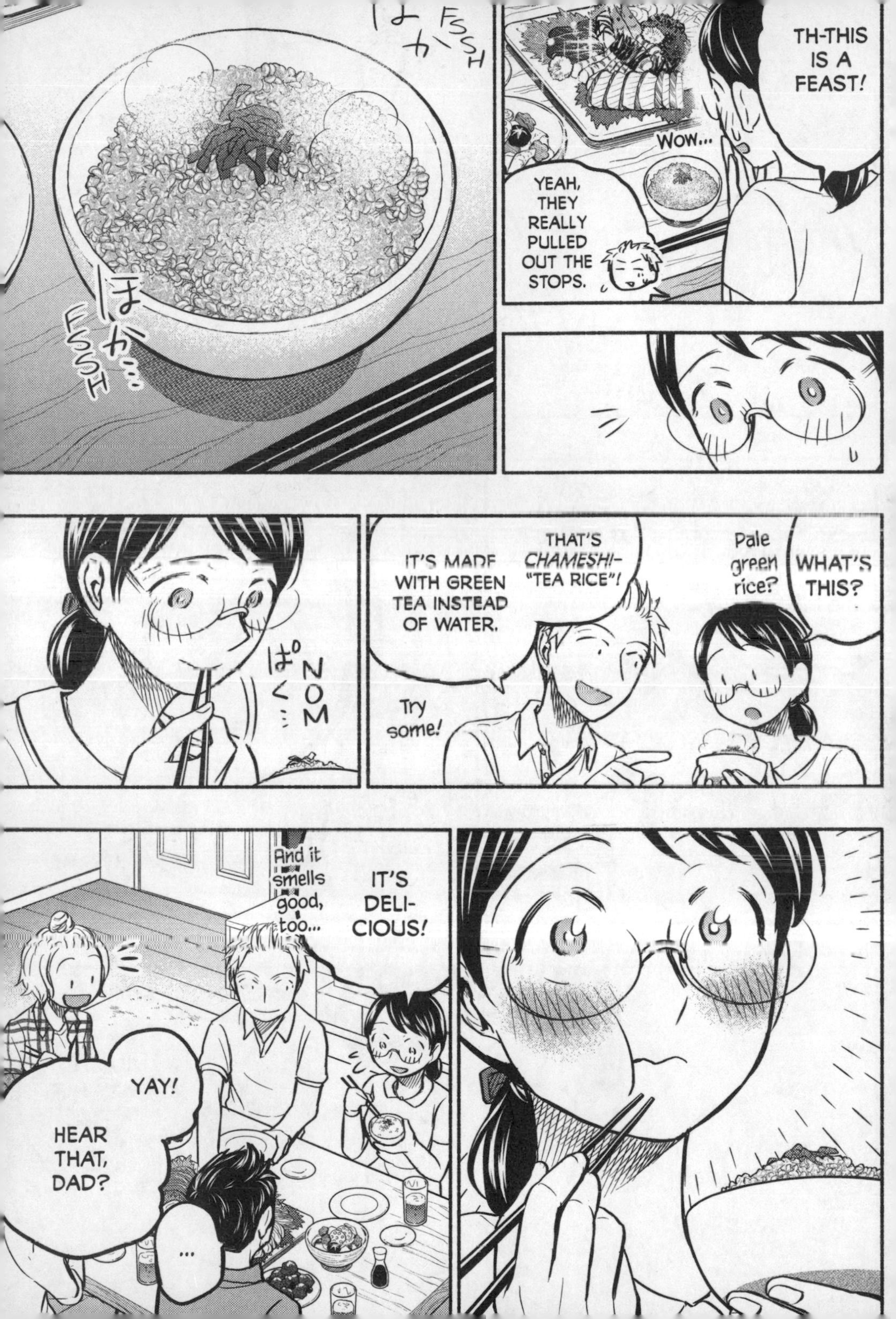

TH-THIS IS A FEAST!
WOW...
YEAH, THEY REALLY PULLED OUT THE STOPS.
はか FSSH
ほか… FSSH
WHAT'S THIS?
Pale green rice?
THAT'S *CHAMESHI*— "TEA RICE"!
IT'S MADE WITH GREEN TEA INSTEAD OF WATER.
Try some!
ぱく… NOM NOM
IT'S DELICIOUS!
And it smells good, too...
YAY!
HEAR THAT, DAD?
...

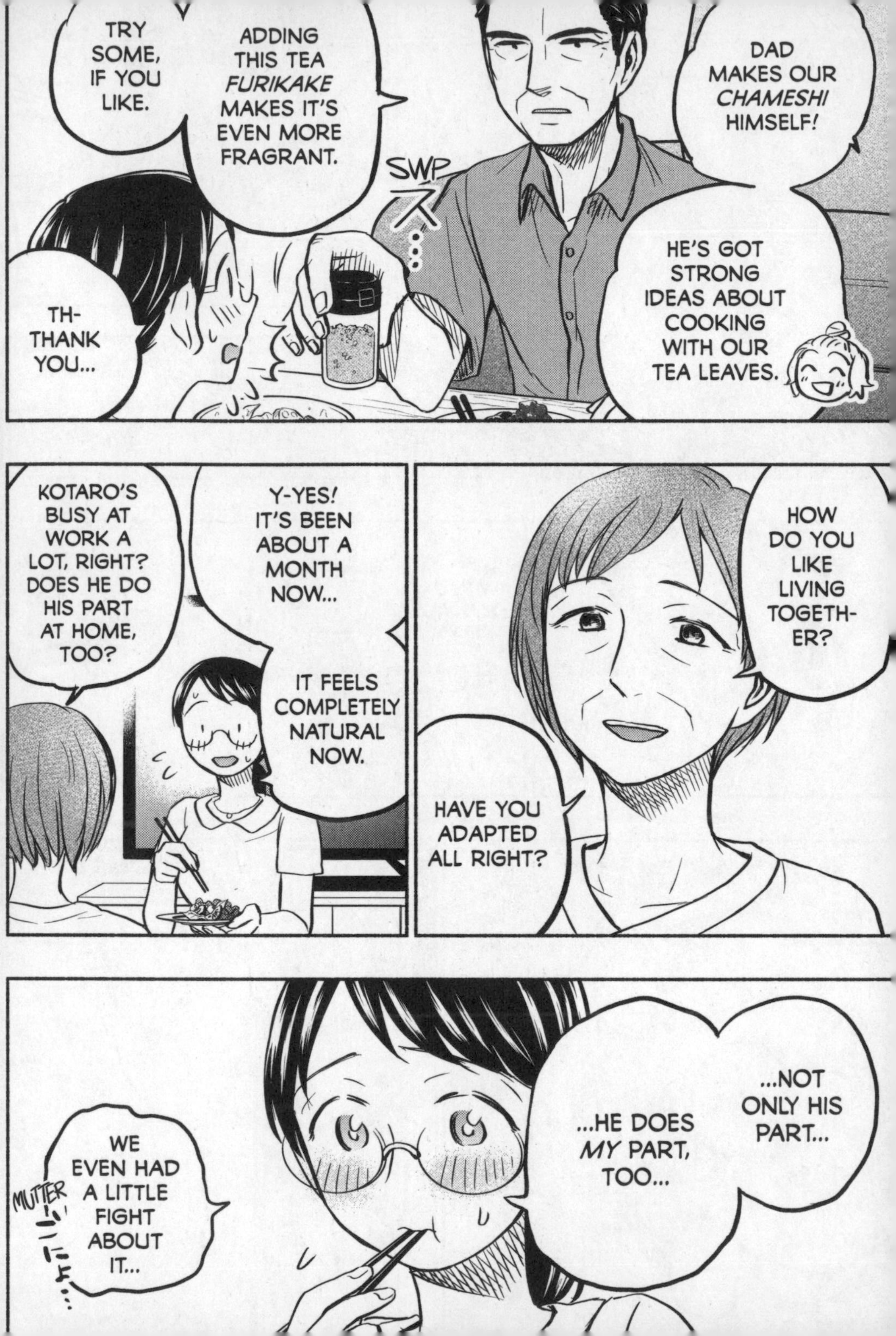
DAD MAKES OUR *CHAMESHI* HIMSELF!
HE'S GOT STRONG IDEAS ABOUT COOKING WITH OUR TEA LEAVES.
SWP
ADDING THIS TEA *FURIKAKE* MAKES IT'S EVEN MORE FRAGRANT.
TRY SOME, IF YOU LIKE.
TH- THANK YOU...
HOW DO YOU LIKE LIVING TOGETH-ER?
HAVE YOU ADAPTED ALL RIGHT?
Y-YES! IT'S BEEN ABOUT A MONTH NOW...
IT FEELS COMPLETELY NATURAL NOW.
KOTARO'S BUSY AT WORK A LOT, RIGHT? DOES HE DO HIS PART AT HOME, TOO?
...NOT ONLY HIS PART...
...HE DOES *MY* PART, TOO...
WE EVEN HAD A LITTLE FIGHT ABOUT IT...
MUTTER

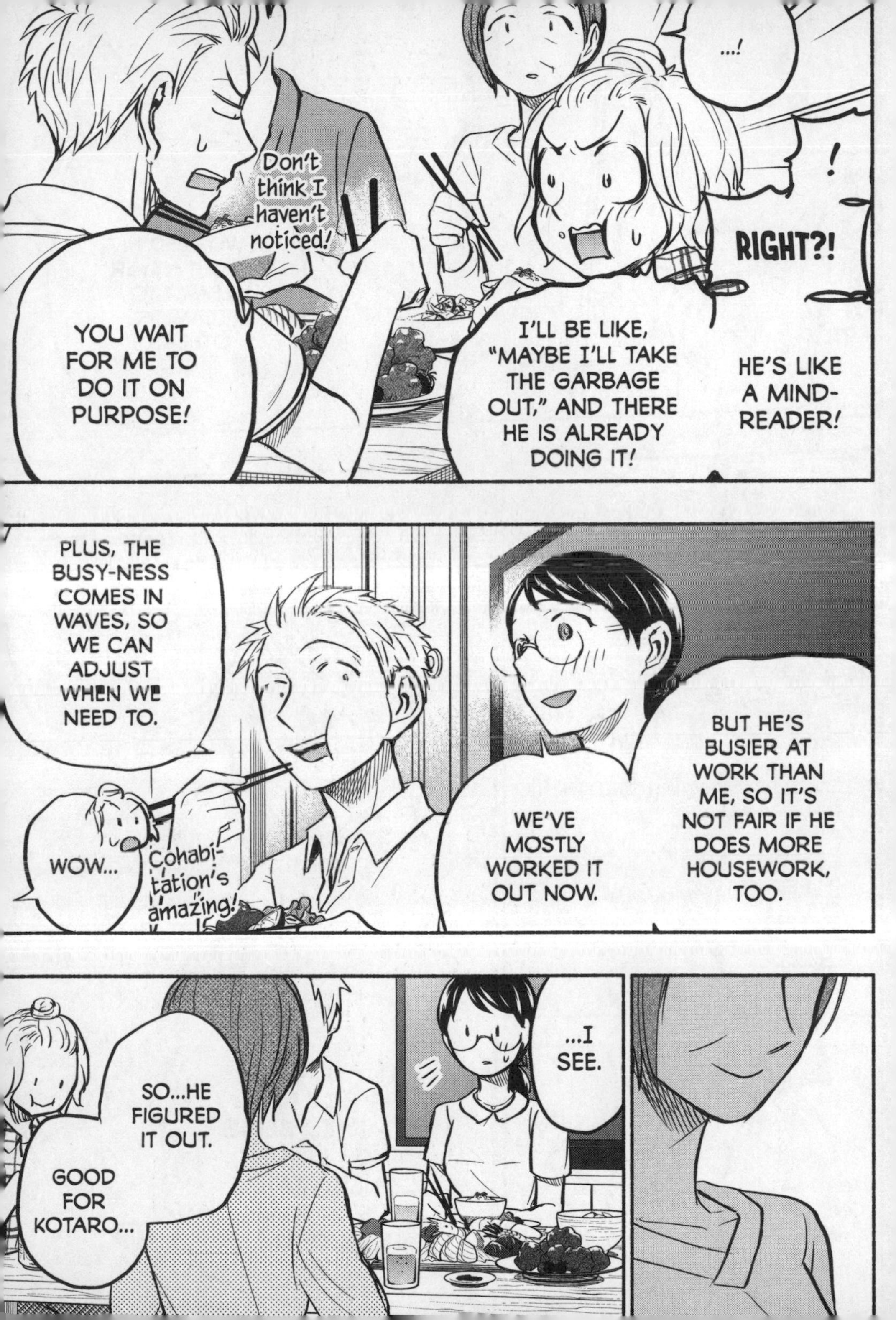
...!
!
RIGHT?!
HE'S LIKE A MIND-READER!
I'LL BE LIKE, "MAYBE I'LL TAKE THE GARBAGE OUT," AND THERE HE IS ALREADY DOING IT!
Don't think I haven't noticed!
YOU WAIT FOR ME TO DO IT ON PURPOSE!
BUT HE'S BUSIER AT WORK THAN ME, SO IT'S NOT FAIR IF HE DOES MORE HOUSEWORK, TOO.
WE'VE MOSTLY WORKED IT OUT NOW.
PLUS, THE BUSY-NESS COMES IN WAVES, SO WE CAN ADJUST WHEN WE NEED TO.
Cohabi-tation's amazing!
WOW...
...I SEE.
SO...HE FIGURED IT OUT.
GOOD FOR KOTARO...

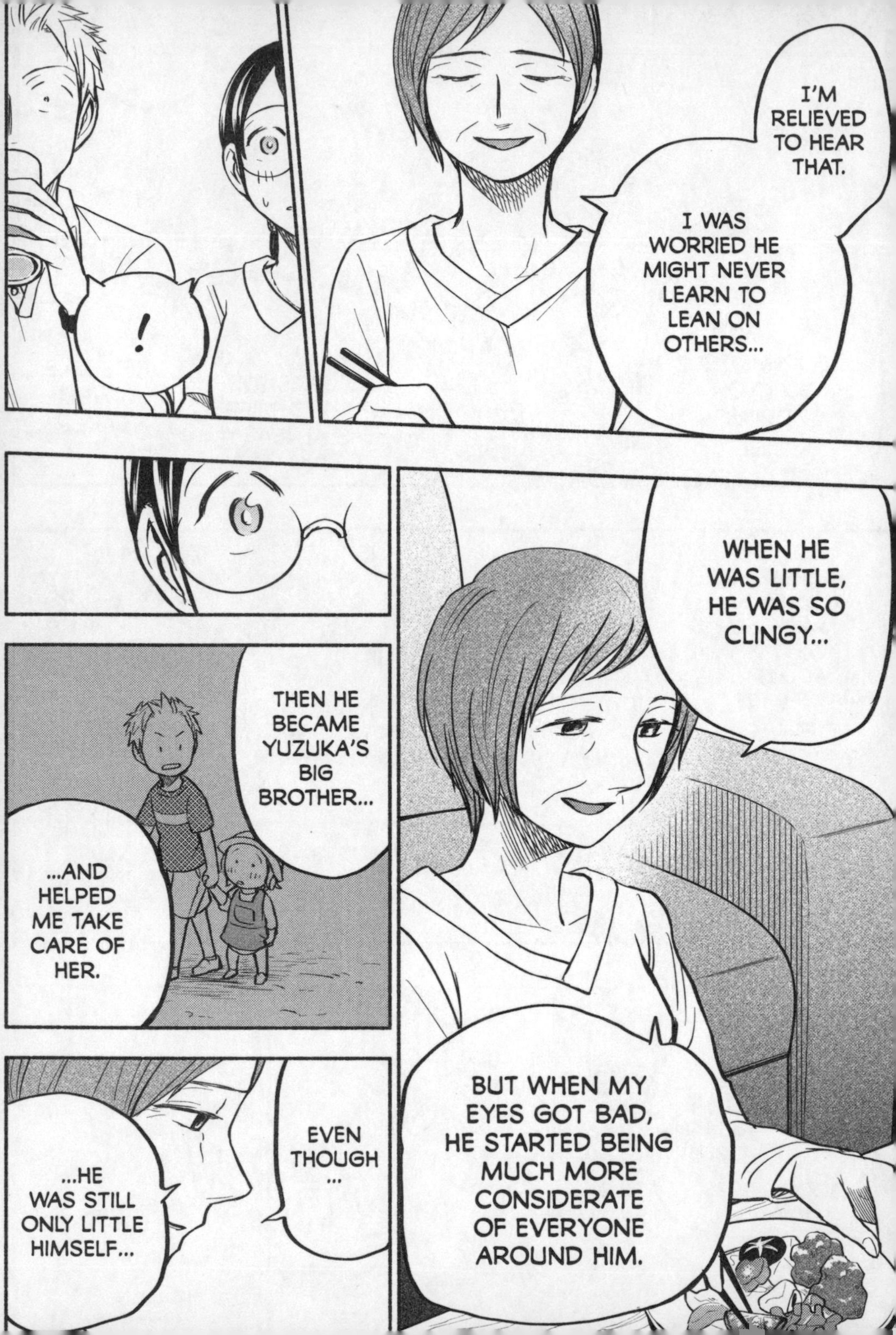
I'M RELIEVED TO HEAR THAT.
I WAS WORRIED HE MIGHT NEVER LEARN TO LEAN ON OTHERS...
!
WHEN HE WAS LITTLE, HE WAS SO CLINGY...
BUT WHEN MY EYES GOT BAD, HE STARTED BEING MUCH MORE CONSIDERATE OF EVERYONE AROUND HIM.
THEN HE BECAME YUZUKA'S BIG BROTHER...
...AND HELPED ME TAKE CARE OF HER.
EVEN THOUGH...
...HE WAS STILL ONLY LITTLE HIMSELF...

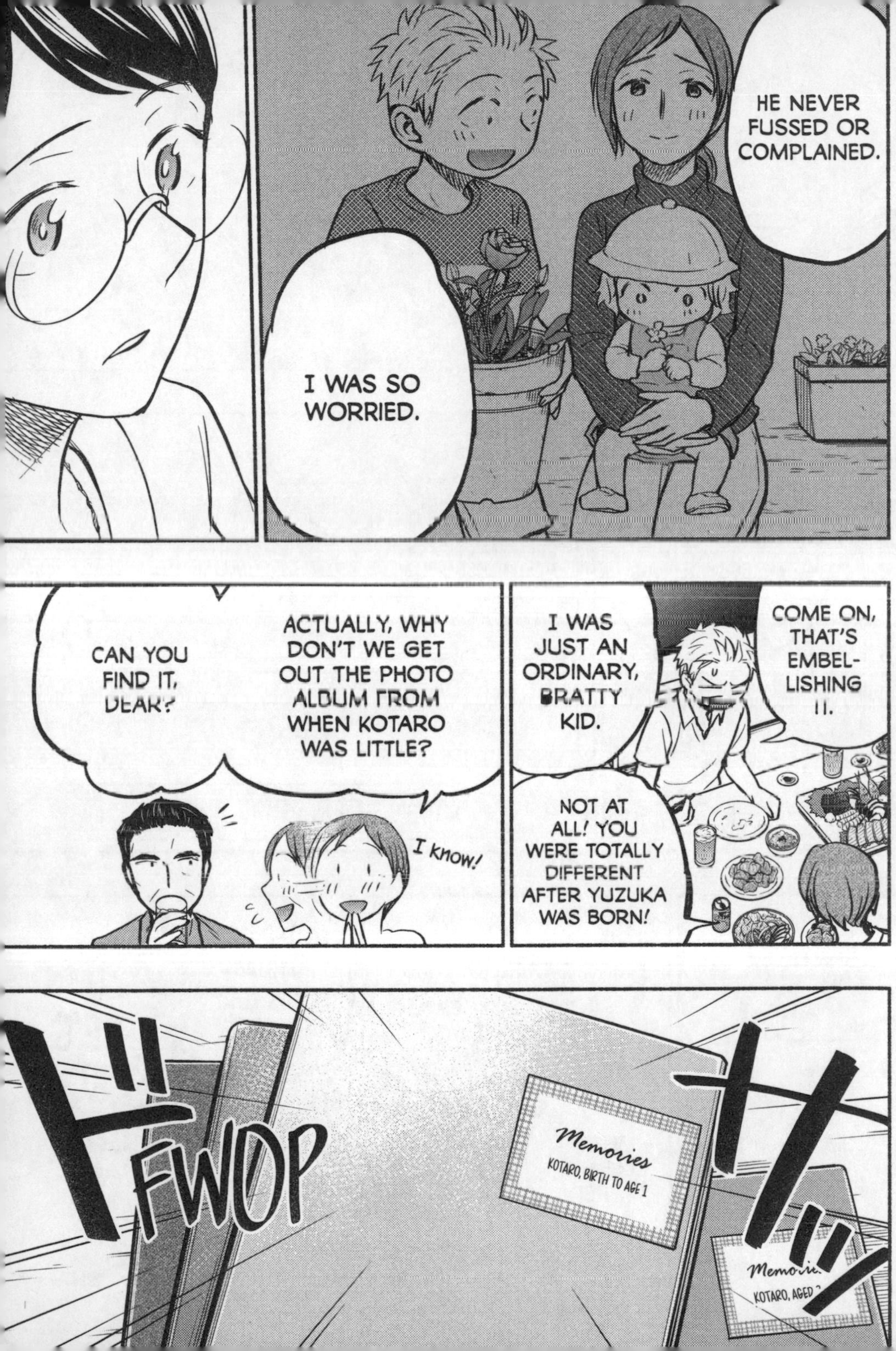
HE NEVER FUSSED OR COMPLAINED.
I WAS SO WORRIED.
COME ON, THAT'S EMBEL-LISHING IT.
I WAS JUST AN ORDINARY, BRATTY KID.
NOT AT ALL! YOU WERE TOTALLY DIFFERENT AFTER YUZUKA WAS BORN!
ACTUALLY, WHY DON'T WE GET OUT THE PHOTO ALBUM FROM WHEN KOTARO WAS LITTLE?
CAN YOU FIND IT, DEAR?
I know!
FWOP
Memories
KOTARO, BIRTH TO AGE 1

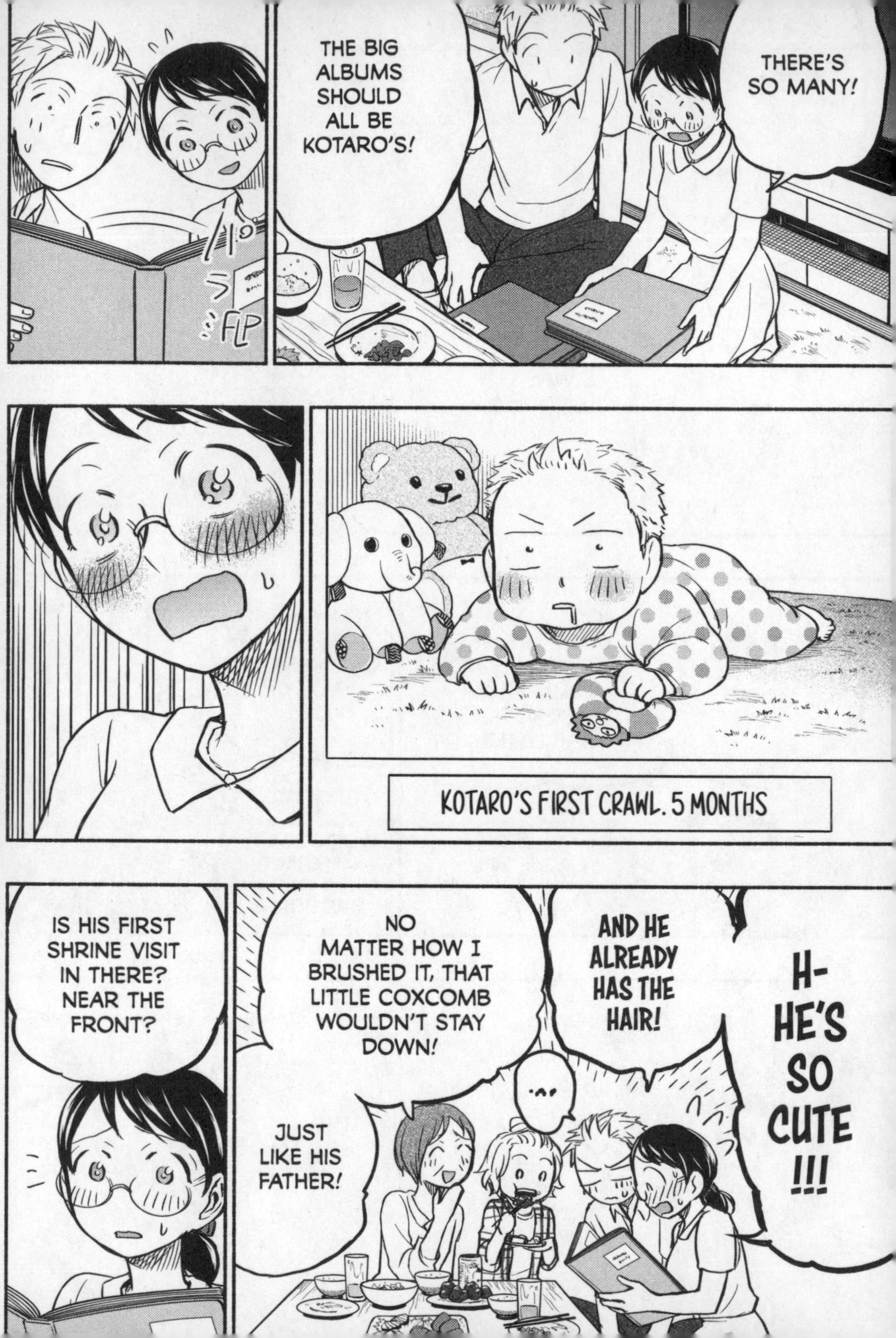
THERE'S SO MANY!
THE BIG ALBUMS SHOULD ALL BE KOTARO'S!
FLP
KOTARO'S FIRST CRAWL. 5 MONTHS
H- HE'S SO CUTE !!!
AND HE ALREADY HAS THE HAIR!
NO MATTER HOW I BRUSHED IT, THAT LITTLE COXCOMB WOULDN'T STAY DOWN!
JUST LIKE HIS FATHER!
IS HIS FIRST SHRINE VISIT IN THERE? NEAR THE FRONT?

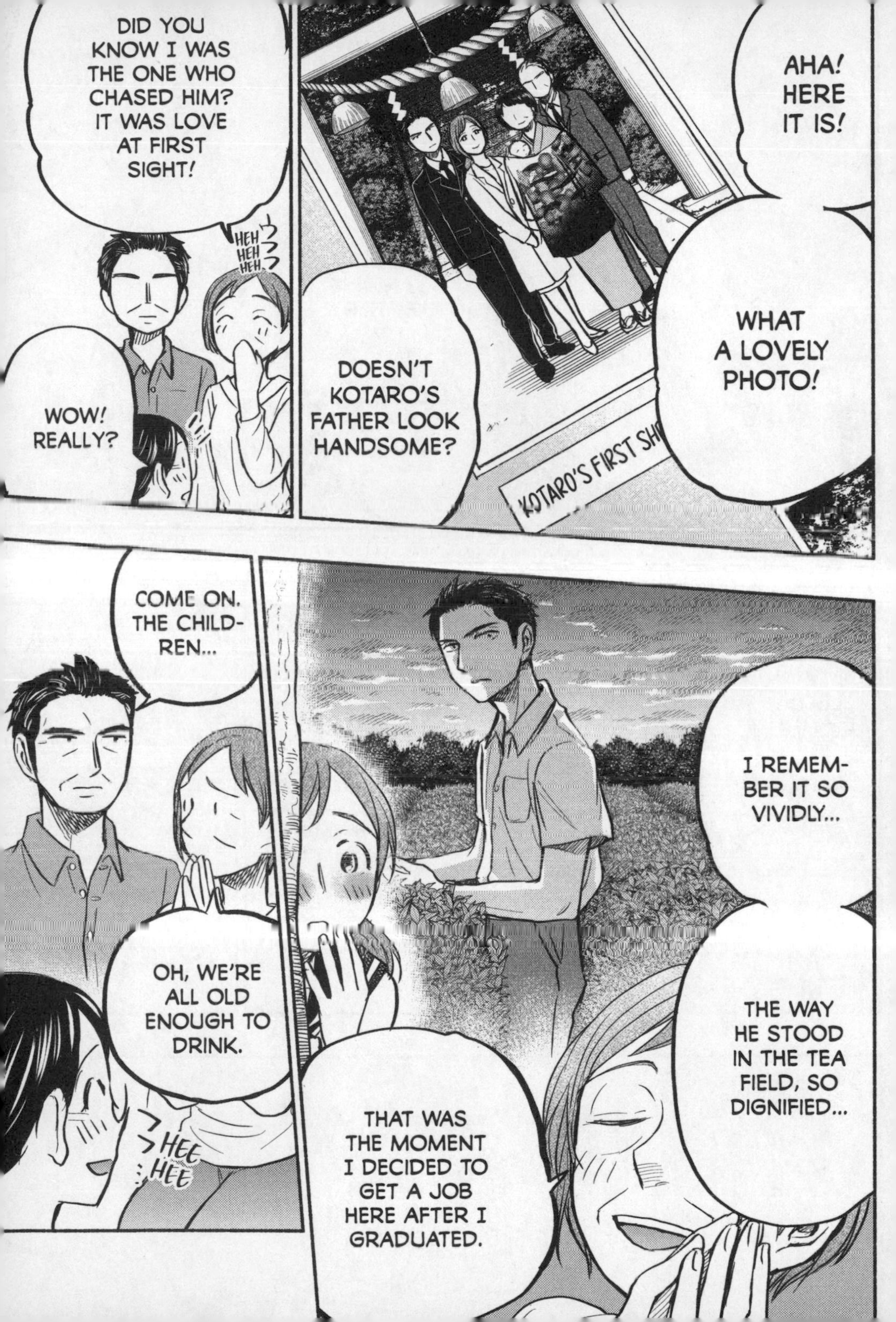
AHA! HERE IT IS!
WHAT A LOVELY PHOTO!
DOESN'T KOTARO'S FATHER LOOK HANDSOME?
KOTARO'S FIRST
DID YOU KNOW I WAS THE ONE WHO CHASED HIM? IT WAS LOVE AT FIRST SIGHT!
HEH HEH HEH
WOW! REALLY?
I REMEMBER IT SO VIVIDLY...
THE WAY HE STOOD IN THE TEA FIELD, SO DIGNIFIED...
THAT WAS THE MOMENT I DECIDED TO GET A JOB HERE AFTER I GRADUATED.
COME ON. THE CHILDREN...
OH, WE'RE ALL OLD ENOUGH TO DRINK.
HEE HEE

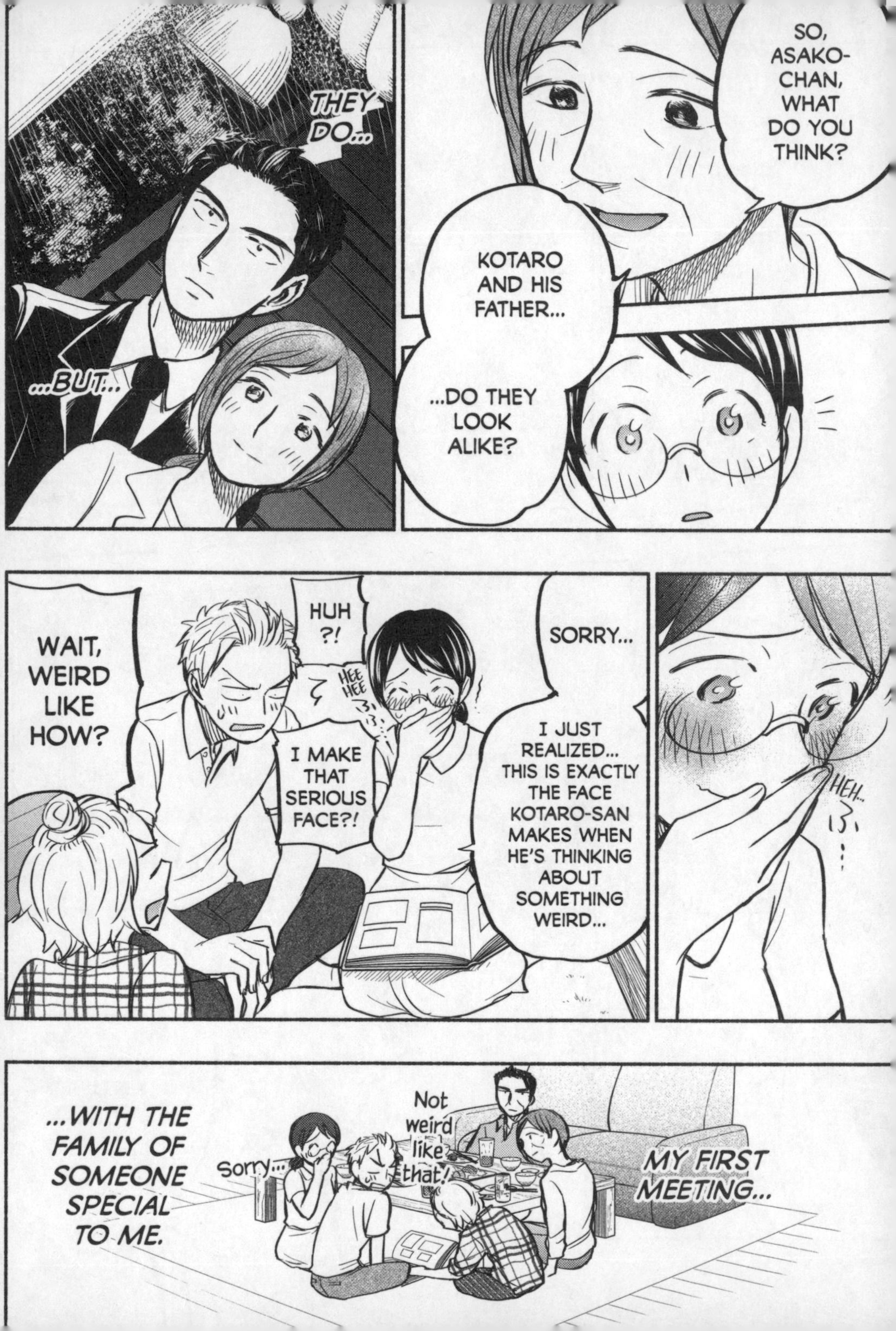
SO, ASAKO-CHAN, WHAT DO YOU THINK?
KOTARO AND HIS FATHER...
...DO THEY LOOK ALIKE?
THEY DO...
...BUT...
HEH...
SORRY...
I JUST REALIZED... THIS IS EXACTLY THE FACE KOTARO-SAN MAKES WHEN HE'S THINKING ABOUT SOMETHING WEIRD...
HUH ?!
HEE HEE
I MAKE THAT SERIOUS FACE?!
WAIT, WEIRD LIKE HOW?
MY FIRST MEETING...
Not weird like that!
Sorry...
...WITH THE FAMILY OF SOMEONE SPECIAL TO ME.

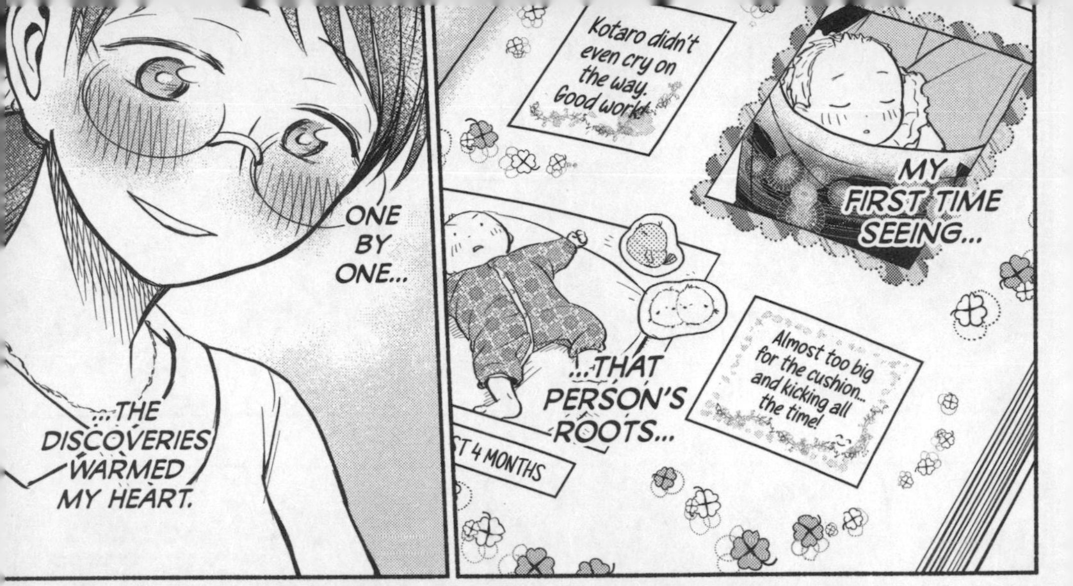
MY FIRST TIME SEEING...
Kotaro didn't even cry on the way. Good work!
Almost too big for the cushion... and kicking all the time!
...THAT PERSON'S ROOTS...
ST 4 MONTHS
ONE BY ONE...
...THE DISCOVERIES WARMED MY HEART.

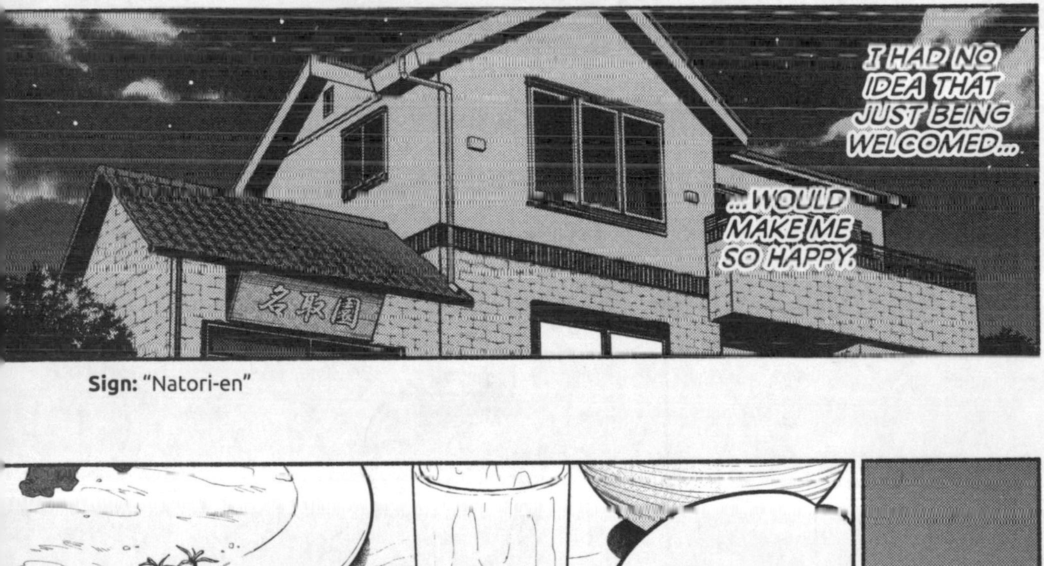
I HAD NO IDEA THAT JUST BEING WELCOMED...
...WOULD MAKE ME SO HAPPY.
名取園

Sign: "Natori-en"

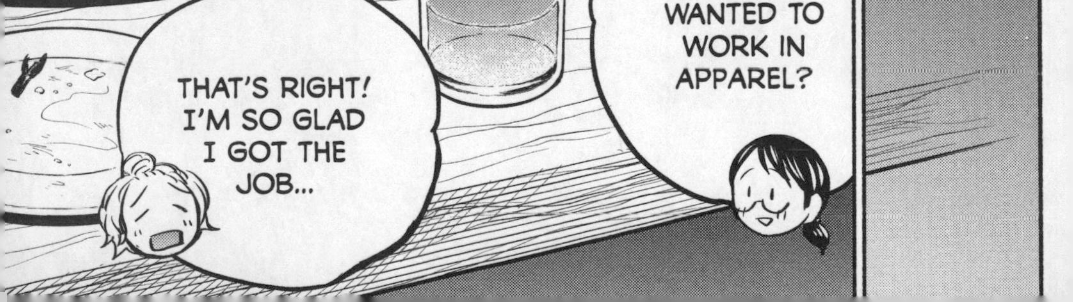
SO YOU ALWAYS WANTED TO WORK IN APPAREL?
THAT'S RIGHT! I'M SO GLAD I GOT THE JOB...

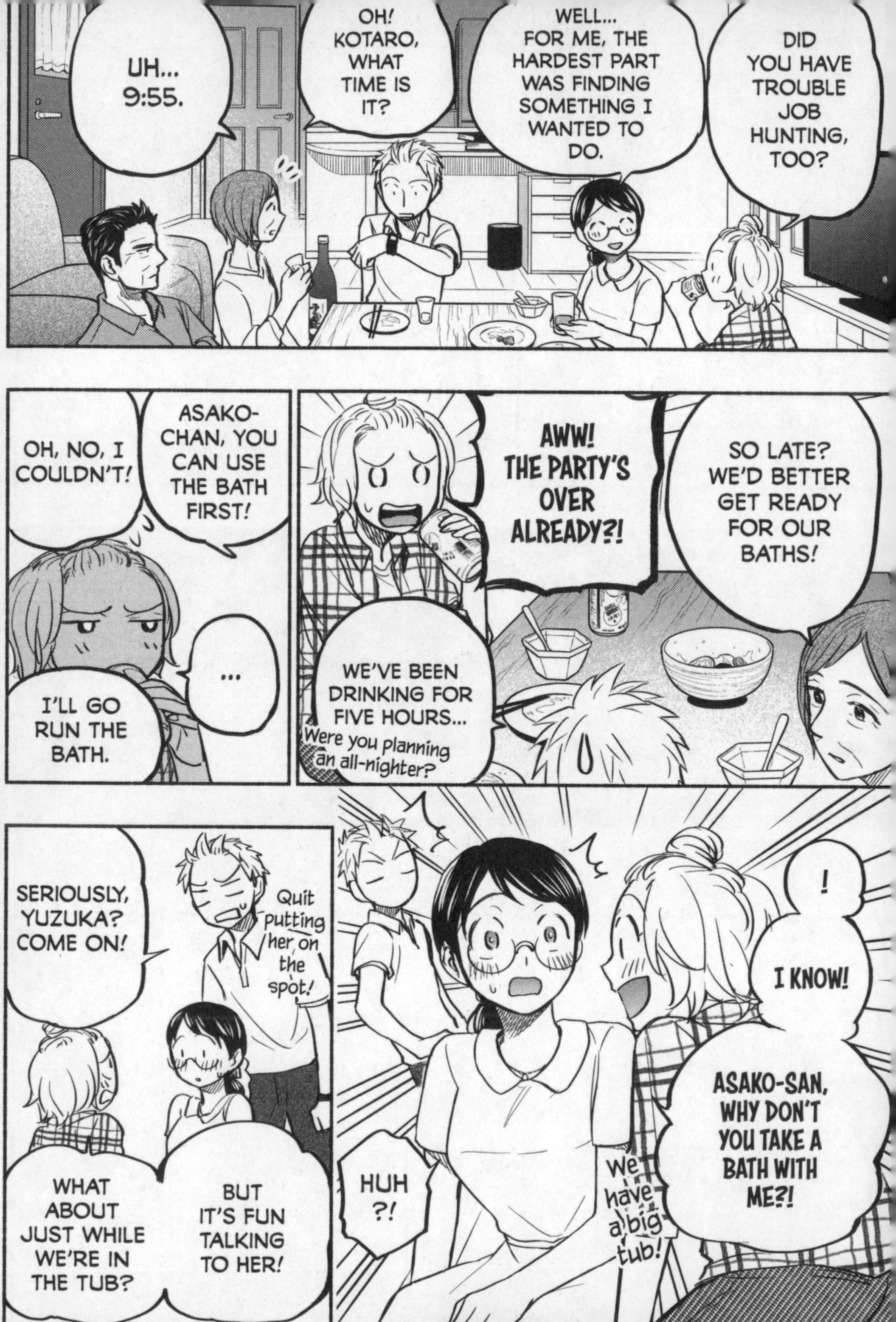
DID YOU HAVE TROUBLE JOB HUNTING, TOO?
WELL... FOR ME, THE HARDEST PART WAS FINDING SOMETHING I WANTED TO DO.
OH! KOTARO, WHAT TIME IS IT?
UH... 9:55.
SO LATE? WE'D BETTER GET READY FOR OUR BATHS!
AWW! THE PARTY'S OVER ALREADY?!
WE'VE BEEN DRINKING FOR FIVE HOURS...
Were you planning an all-nighter?
ASAKO-CHAN, YOU CAN USE THE BATH FIRST!
OH, NO, I COULDN'T!
...
I'LL GO RUN THE BATH.
!
I KNOW!
ASAKO-SAN, WHY DON'T YOU TAKE A BATH WITH ME?!
We have a big tub!
HUH ?!
SERIOUSLY, YUZUKA? COME ON!
Quit putting her on the spot!
BUT IT'S FUN TALKING TO HER!
WHAT ABOUT JUST WHILE WE'RE IN THE TUB?

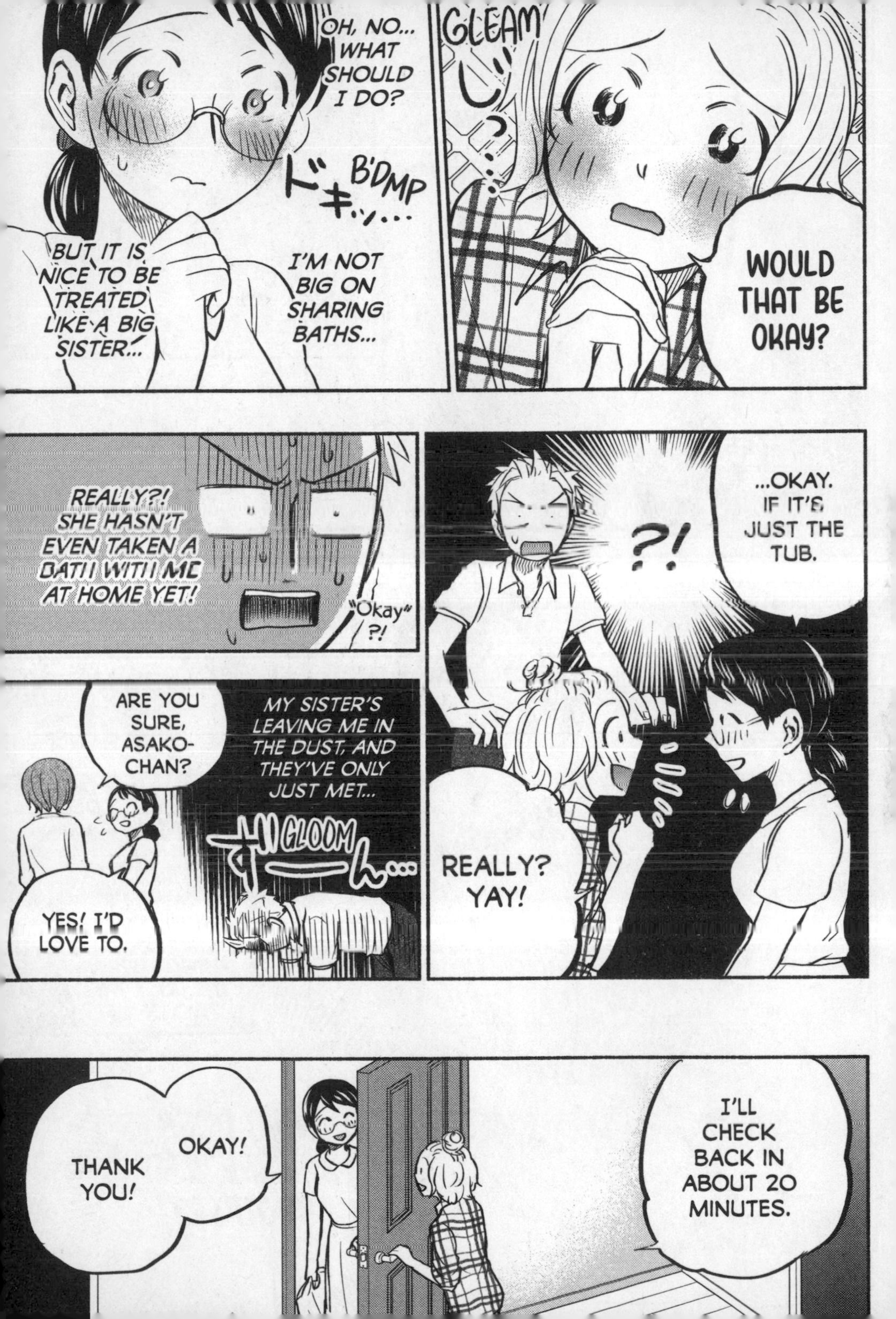
GLEAM
WOULD THAT BE OKAY?
OH, NO... WHAT SHOULD I DO?
B'DMP
I'M NOT BIG ON SHARING BATHS...
BUT IT IS NICE TO BE TREATED LIKE A BIG SISTER...
...OKAY. IF IT'S JUST THE TUB.
?!
REALLY? YAY!
REALLY?! SHE HASN'T EVEN TAKEN A BATH WITH ME AT HOME YET!
"Okay"?!
MY SISTER'S LEAVING ME IN THE DUST, AND THEY'VE ONLY JUST MET...
ARE YOU SURE, ASAKO-CHAN?
GLOOM
YES! I'D LOVE TO.
I'LL CHECK BACK IN ABOUT 20 MINUTES.
OKAY!
THANK YOU!

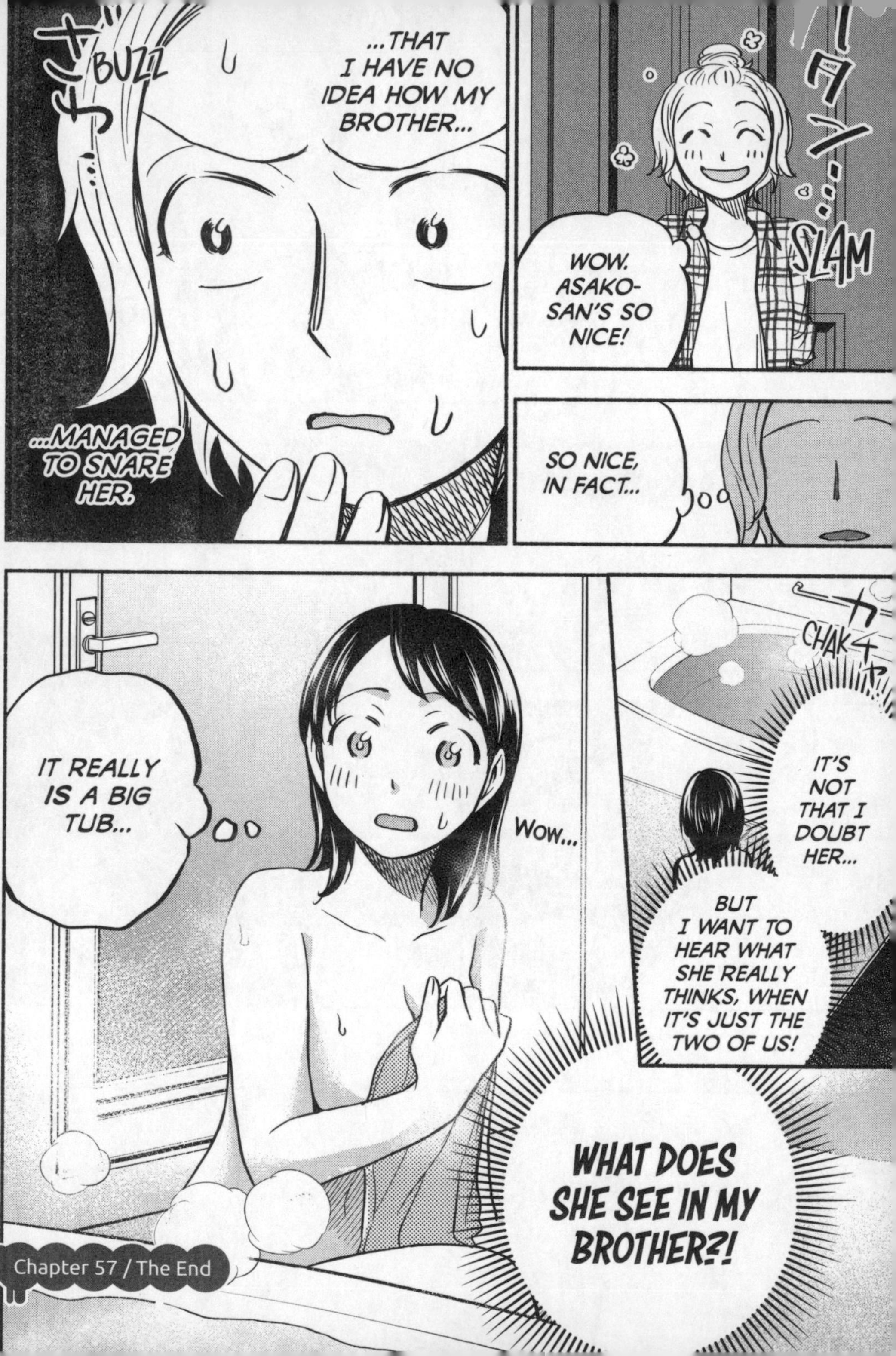
SLAM
WOW. ASAKO-SAN'S SO NICE!
SO NICE, IN FACT...
...THAT I HAVE NO IDEA HOW MY BROTHER...
BUZZ
...MANAGED TO SNARE HER.
CHAK
IT'S NOT THAT I DOUBT HER...
BUT I WANT TO HEAR WHAT SHE REALLY THINKS, WHEN IT'S JUST THE TWO OF US!
Wow...
IT REALLY IS A BIG TUB...
WHAT DOES SHE SEE IN MY BROTHER?!
Chapter 57 / The End

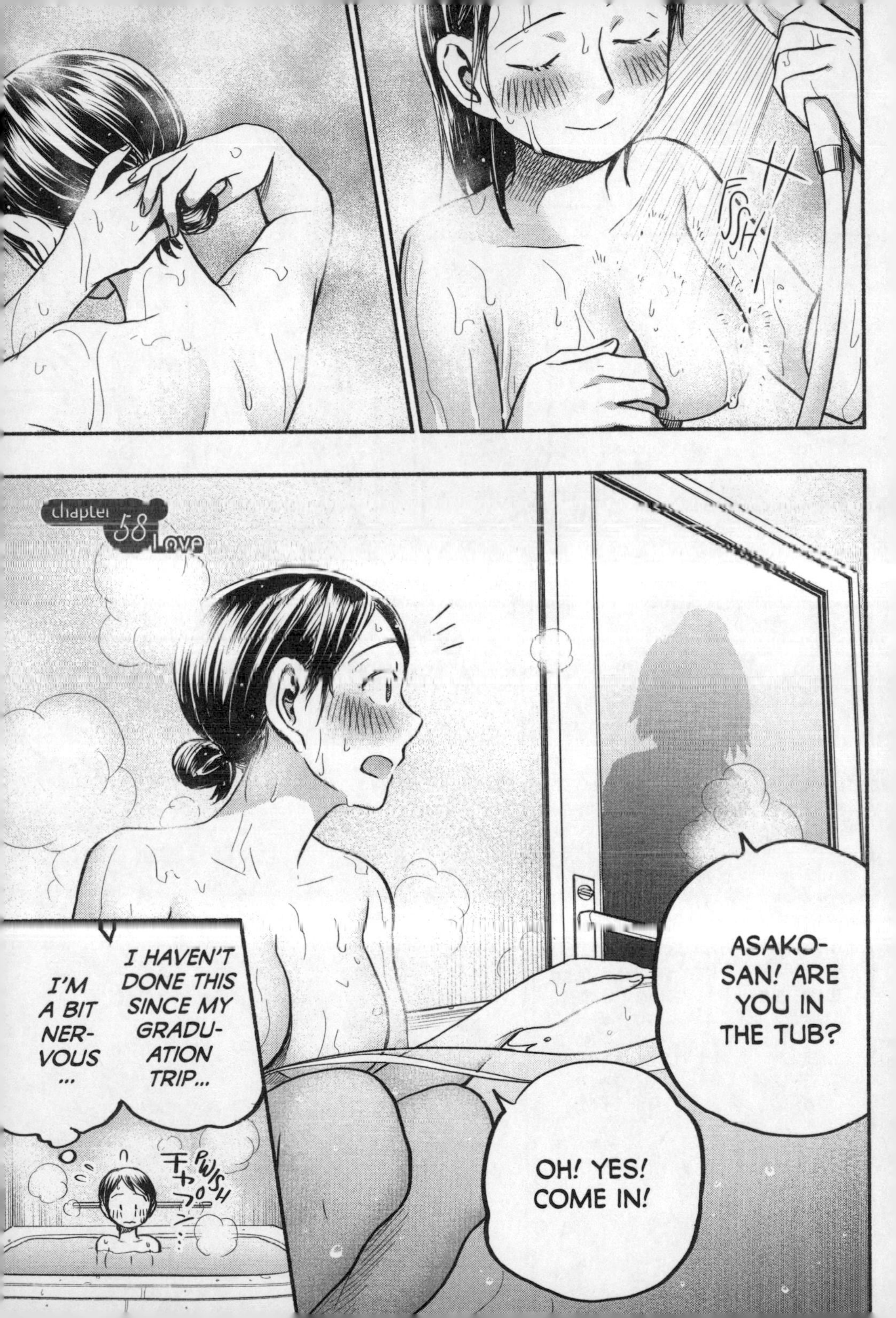
FSSH
chapter 58 Love
ASAKO-SAN! ARE YOU IN THE TUB?
I HAVEN'T DONE THIS SINCE MY GRADUATION TRIP...
I'M A BIT NERVOUS...
OH! YES! COME IN!
PWISH

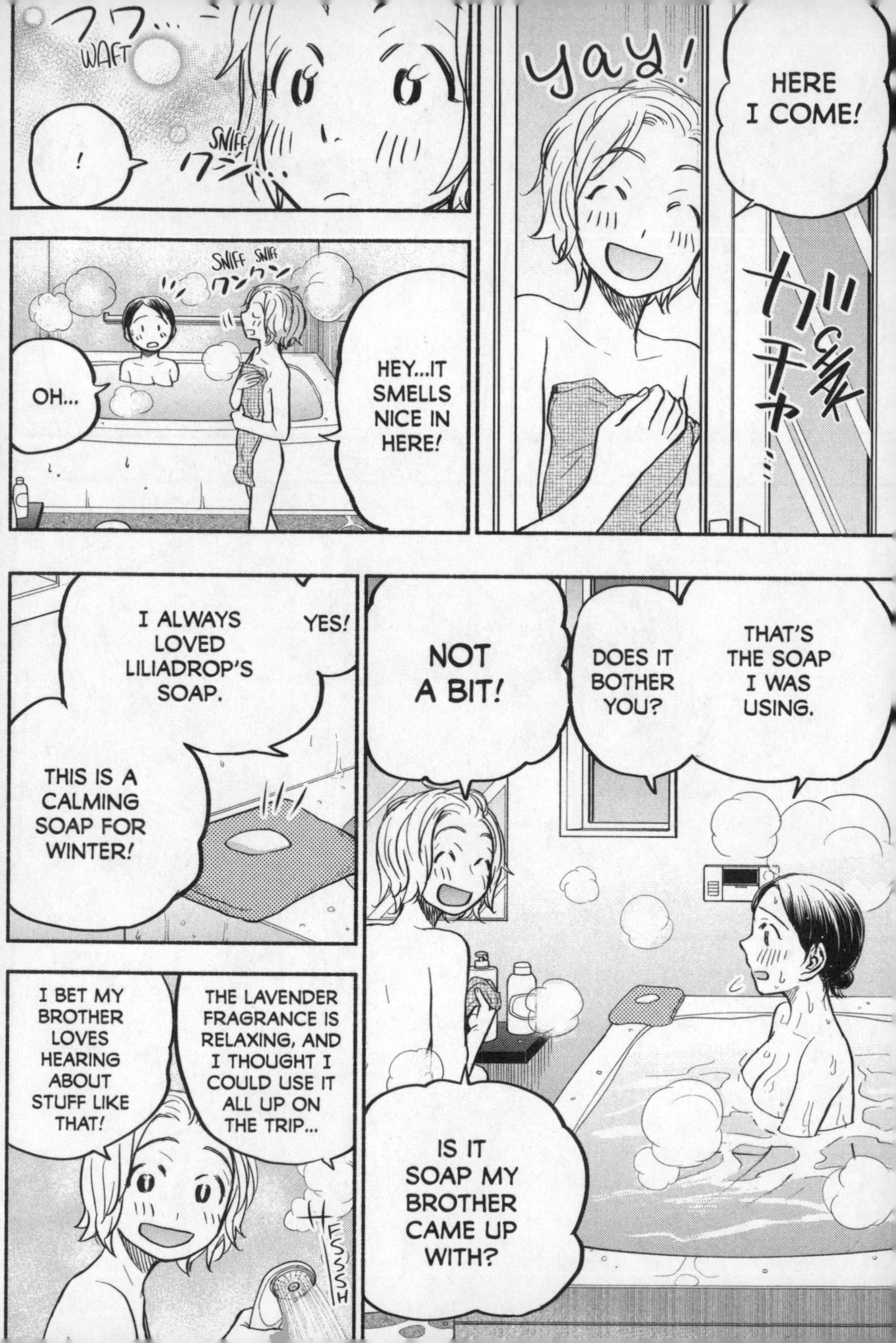
yay!
HERE I COME!
ガチャ…
フワ…
WAFT
SNIFF
クン
!
SNIFF SNIFF
クンクン
HEY...IT SMELLS NICE IN HERE!
OH...
THAT'S THE SOAP I WAS USING.
DOES IT BOTHER YOU?
NOT A BIT!
IS IT SOAP MY BROTHER CAME UP WITH?
YES!
I ALWAYS LOVED LILIADROP'S SOAP.
THIS IS A CALMING SOAP FOR WINTER!
THE LAVENDER FRAGRANCE IS RELAXING, AND I THOUGHT I COULD USE IT ALL UP ON THE TRIP...
I BET MY BROTHER LOVES HEARING ABOUT STUFF LIKE THAT!
FSSSH

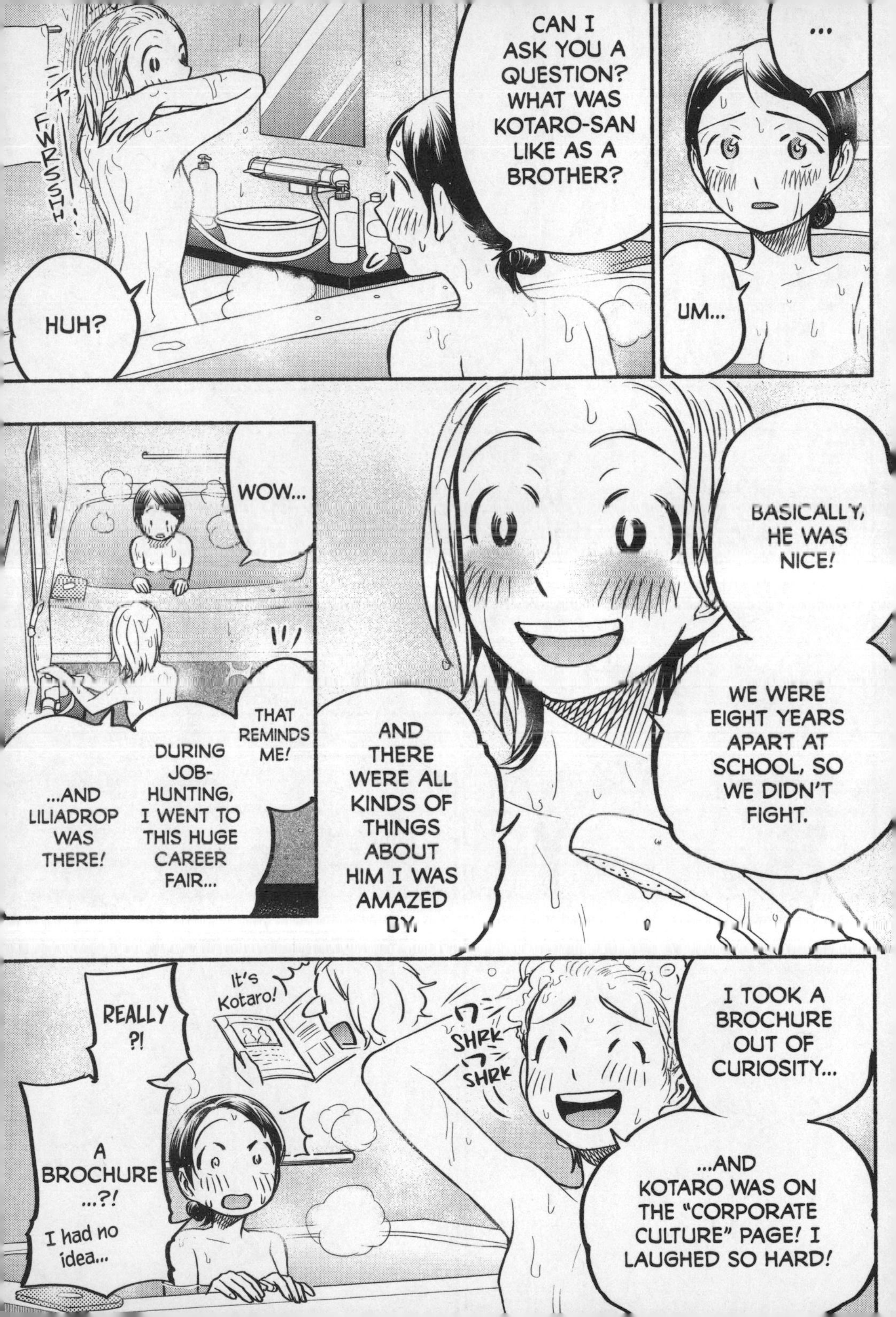
...
UM...
CAN I ASK YOU A QUESTION? WHAT WAS KOTARO-SAN LIKE AS A BROTHER?
FWRSSHH...
HUH?
BASICALLY, HE WAS NICE!
WE WERE EIGHT YEARS APART AT SCHOOL, SO WE DIDN'T FIGHT.
AND THERE WERE ALL KINDS OF THINGS ABOUT HIM I WAS AMAZED BY.
WOW...
THAT REMINDS ME!
DURING JOB-HUNTING, I WENT TO THIS HUGE CAREER FAIR...
...AND LILIADROP WAS THERE!
I TOOK A BROCHURE OUT OF CURIOSITY...
...AND KOTARO WAS ON THE "CORPORATE CULTURE" PAGE! I LAUGHED SO HARD!
SHRK SHRK
It's Kotaro!
REALLY?!
A BROCHURE...?!
I had no idea...

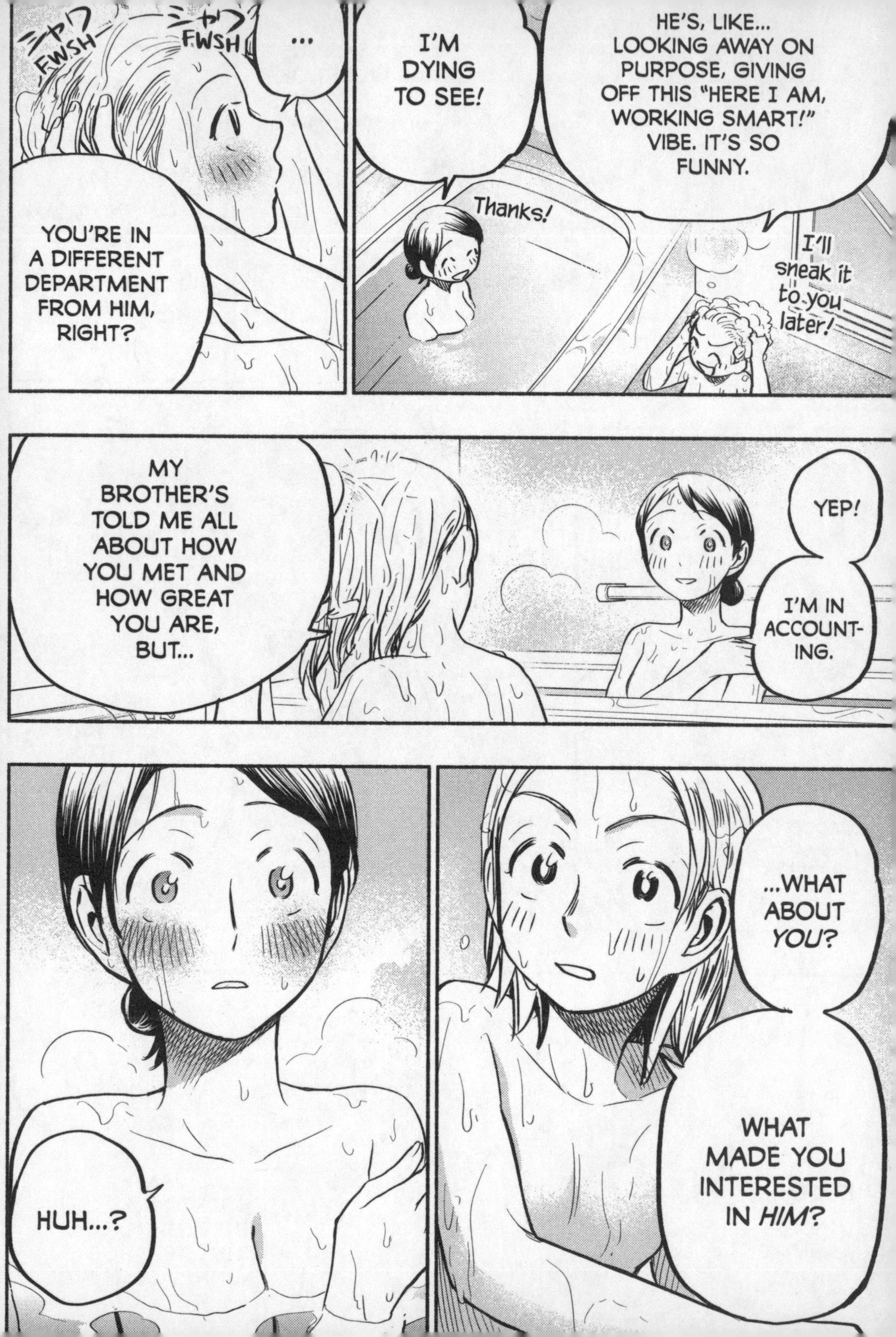
HE'S, LIKE... LOOKING AWAY ON PURPOSE, GIVING OFF THIS "HERE I AM, WORKING SMART!" VIBE. IT'S SO FUNNY.
I'M DYING TO SEE!
I'll sneak it to you later!
Thanks!
FWSH
FWSH
...
YOU'RE IN A DIFFERENT DEPARTMENT FROM HIM, RIGHT?
YEP!
I'M IN ACCOUNT-ING.
MY BROTHER'S TOLD ME ALL ABOUT HOW YOU MET AND HOW GREAT YOU ARE, BUT...
...WHAT ABOUT *YOU*?
WHAT MADE YOU INTERESTED IN *HIM*?
HUH...?

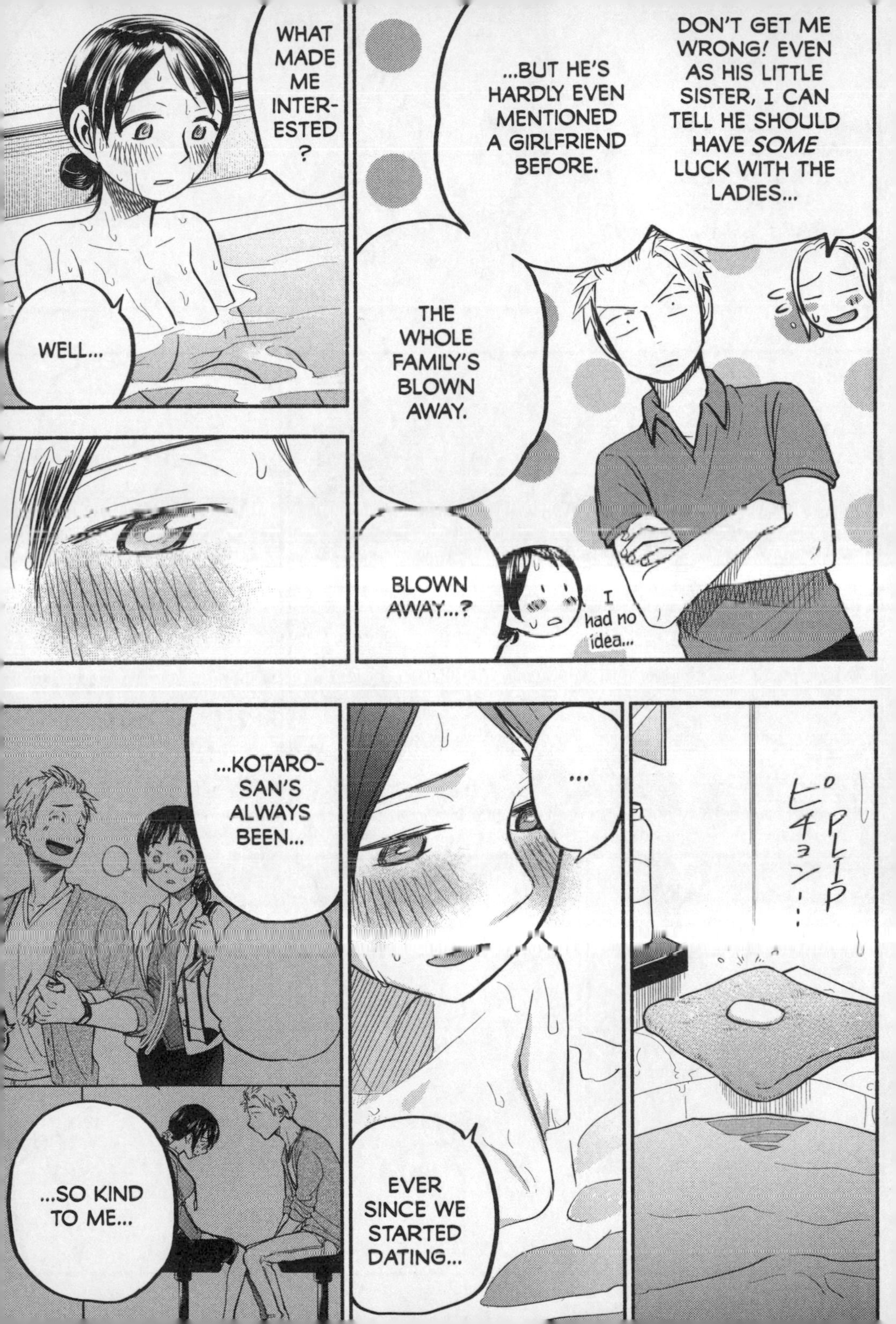
DON'T GET ME WRONG! EVEN AS HIS LITTLE SISTER, I CAN TELL HE SHOULD HAVE *SOME* LUCK WITH THE LADIES...
...BUT HE'S HARDLY EVEN MENTIONED A GIRLFRIEND BEFORE.
THE WHOLE FAMILY'S BLOWN AWAY.
BLOWN AWAY...?
I had no idea...
WHAT MADE ME INTER-ESTED?
WELL...
ピチョン...
PLIP
...
EVER SINCE WE STARTED DATING...
...KOTARO-SAN'S ALWAYS BEEN...
...SO KIND TO ME...

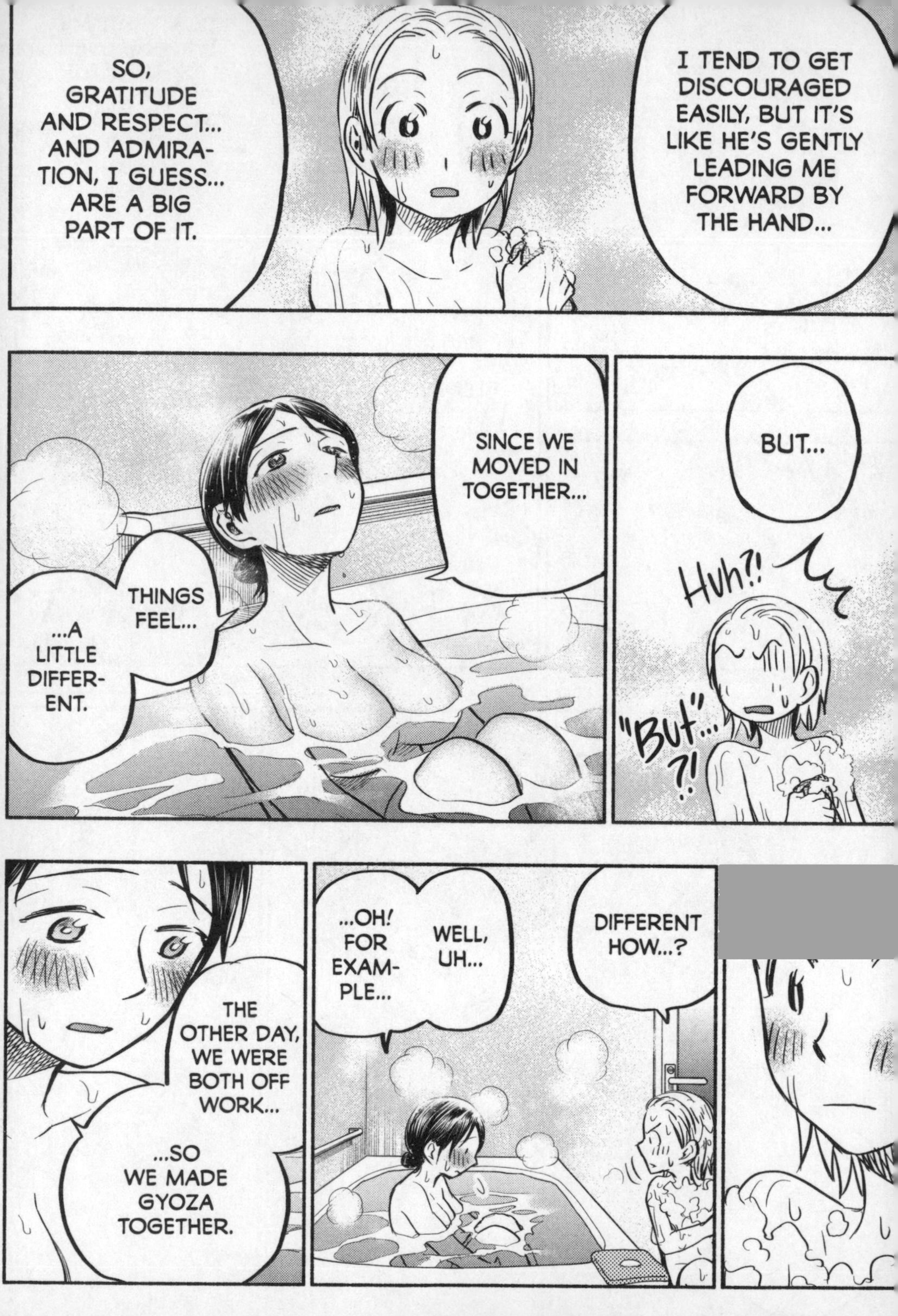
I TEND TO GET DISCOURAGED EASILY, BUT IT'S LIKE HE'S GENTLY LEADING ME FORWARD BY THE HAND...
SO, GRATITUDE AND RESPECT... AND ADMIRATION, I GUESS... ARE A BIG PART OF IT.
BUT...
Huh?!
"But"...?!
SINCE WE MOVED IN TOGETHER...
THINGS FEEL...
...A LITTLE DIFFERENT.
DIFFERENT HOW...?
WELL, UH...
...OH! FOR EXAMPLE...
THE OTHER DAY, WE WERE BOTH OFF WORK...
...SO WE MADE GYOZA TOGETHER.

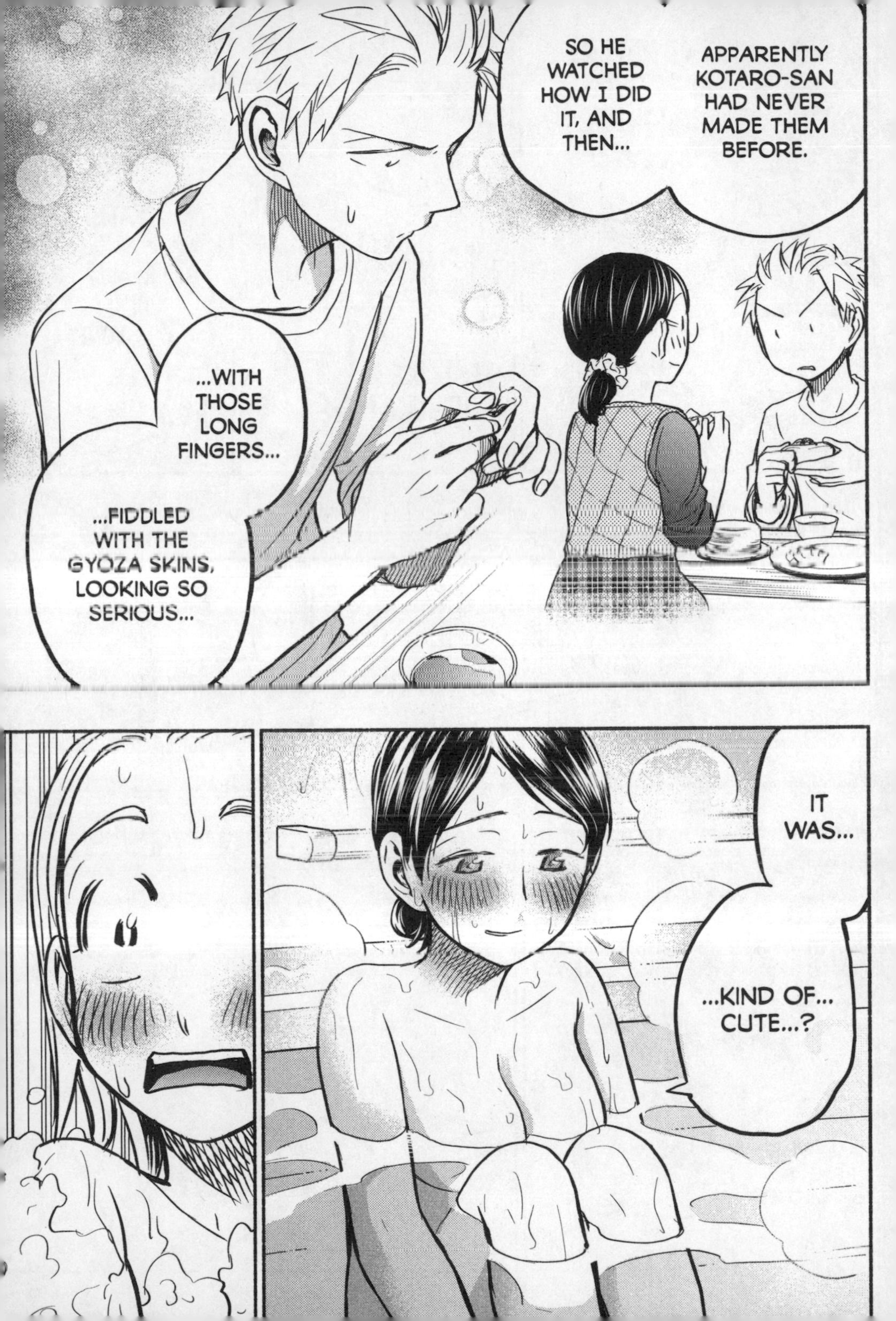
APPARENTLY KOTARO-SAN HAD NEVER MADE THEM BEFORE.
SO HE WATCHED HOW I DID IT, AND THEN...
...WITH THOSE LONG FINGERS...
...FIDDLED WITH THE GYOZA SKINS, LOOKING SO SERIOUS...
IT WAS...
...KIND OF... CUTE...?

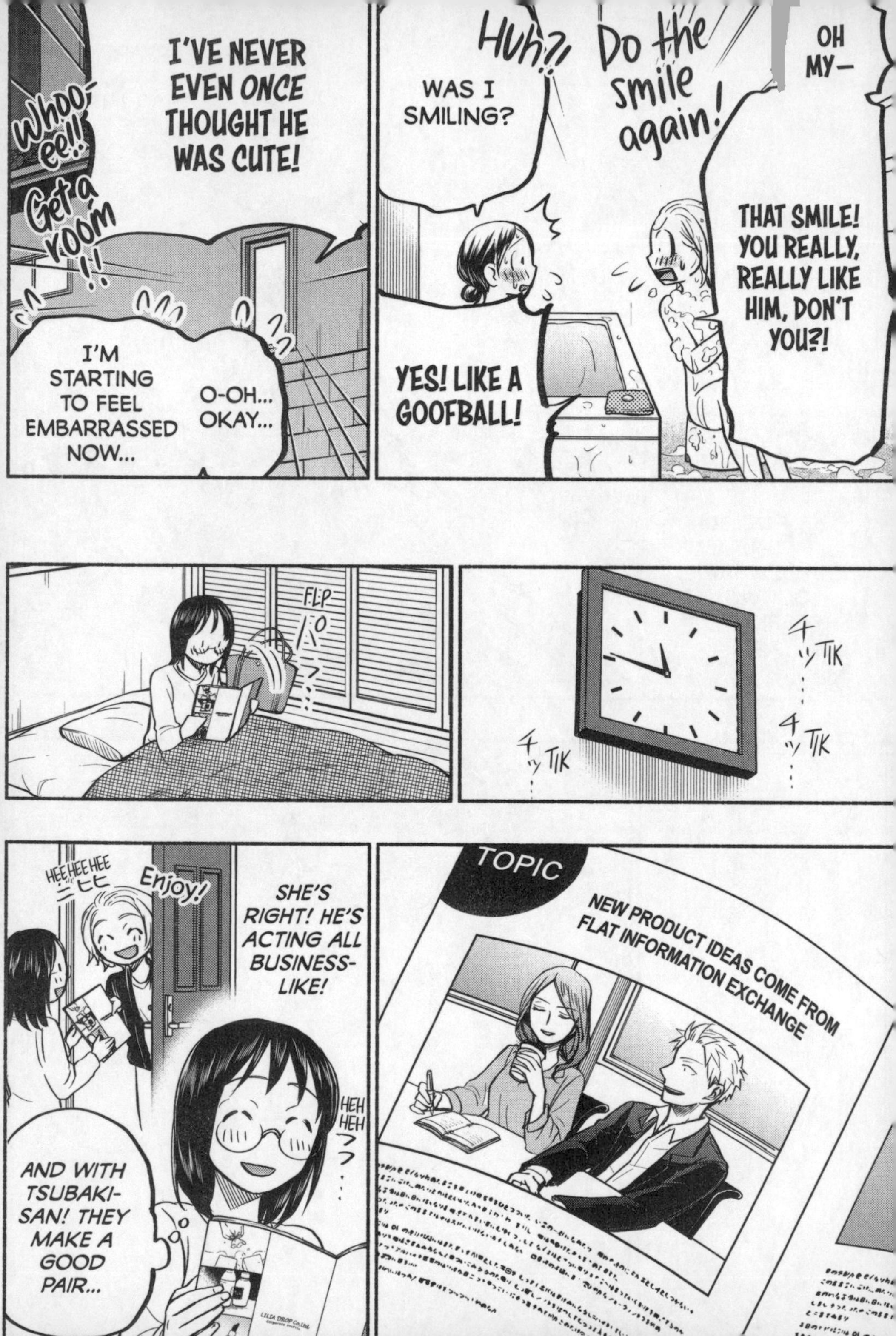
OH MY—
Do the smile again!
Huh?!
WAS I SMILING?
THAT SMILE! YOU REALLY, REALLY LIKE HIM, DON'T YOU?!
YES! LIKE A GOOFBALL!
I'VE NEVER EVEN ONCE THOUGHT HE WAS CUTE!
Whoo-ee!!
Get a room!!
O-OH... OKAY...
I'M STARTING TO FEEL EMBARRASSED NOW...
チッ TIK
チッ TIK
チッ TIK
FLIP
パ
TOPIC
NEW PRODUCT IDEAS COME FROM FLAT INFORMATION EXCHANGE
HEEHEEHEE
ニヒヒ
Enjoy!
SHE'S RIGHT! HE'S ACTING ALL BUSINESS-LIKE!
HEH HEH
フフ
AND WITH TSUBAKI-SAN! THEY MAKE A GOOD PAIR...

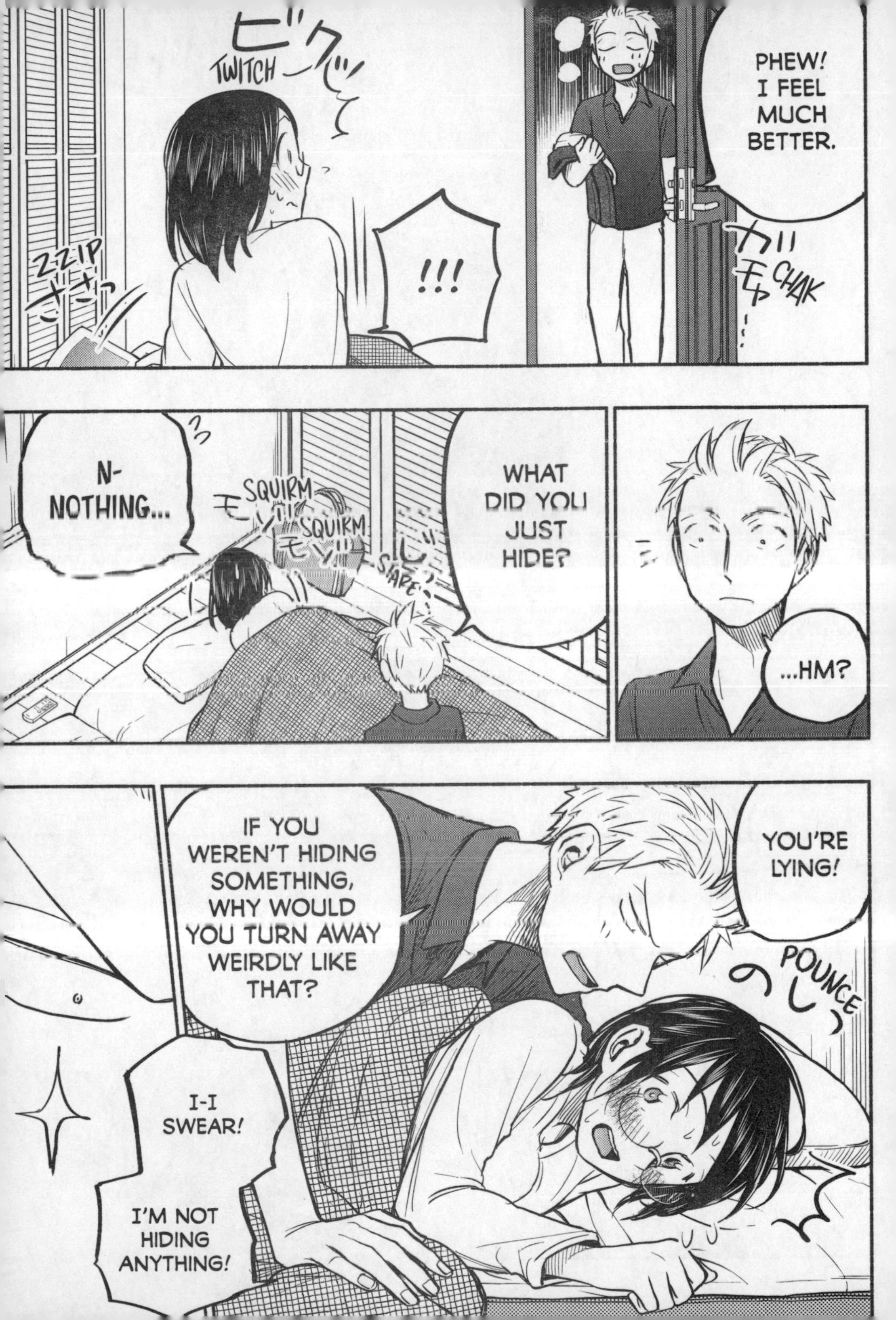
PHEW! I FEEL MUCH BETTER.
CHAK
TWITCH
!!!
ZZIP
...HM?
WHAT DID YOU JUST HIDE?
STARE
SQUIRM
SQUIRM
N-NOTHING...
YOU'RE LYING!
POUNCE
IF YOU WEREN'T HIDING SOMETHING, WHY WOULD YOU TURN AWAY WEIRDLY LIKE THAT?
I-I SWEAR!
I'M NOT HIDING ANYTHING!

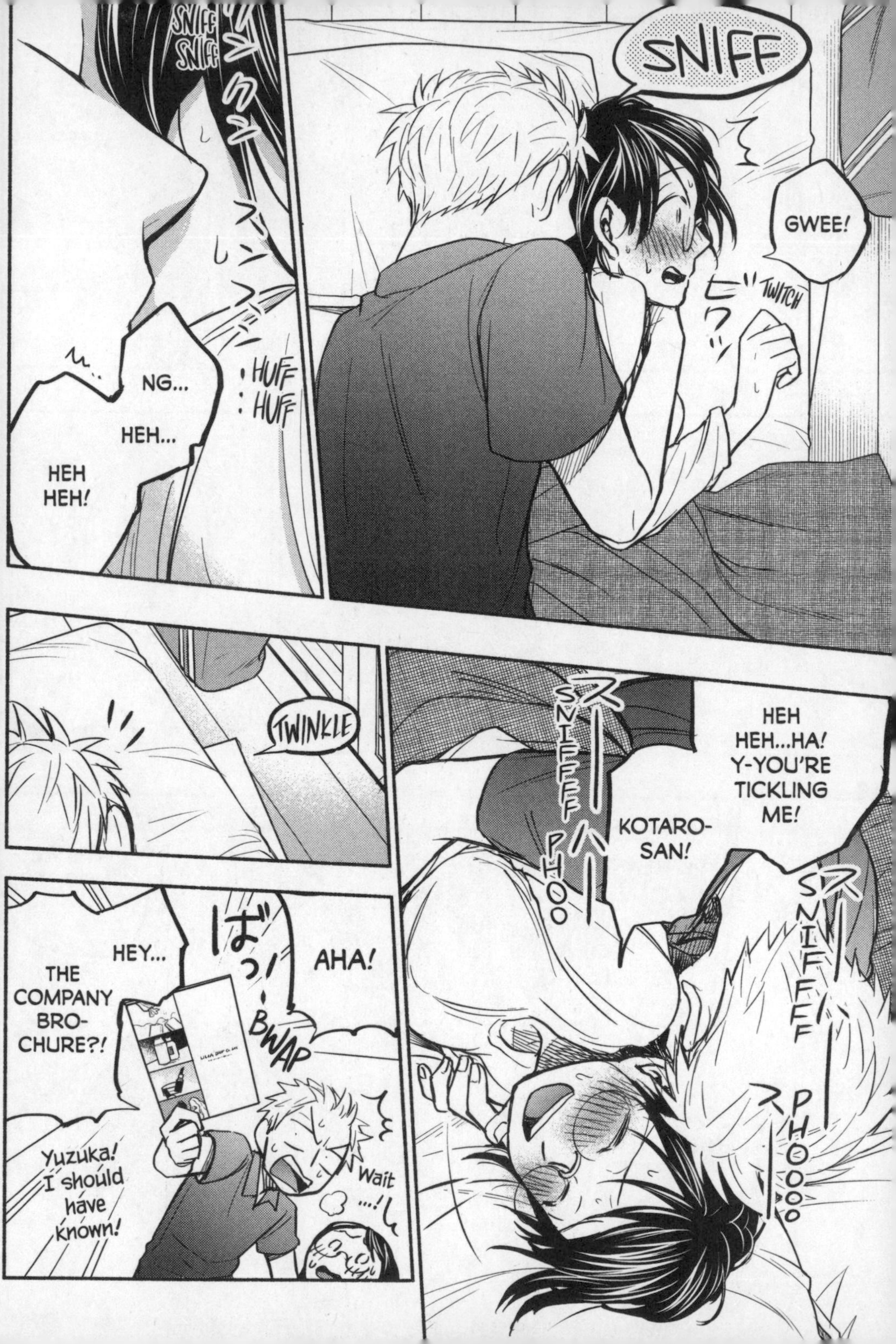
SNIFF
GWEE!
TWITCH
SNIFF SNIFF
HUFF HUFF
NG...
HEH...
HEH HEH!
HEH HEH...HA! Y-YOU'RE TICKLING ME!
SNIFFF PHOO
KOTARO-SAN!
SNIFFFF PHOOOOO
TWINKLE
AHA!
BWAP
HEY...
THE COMPANY BRO-CHURE?!
Wait ...!
Yuzuka! I should have known!

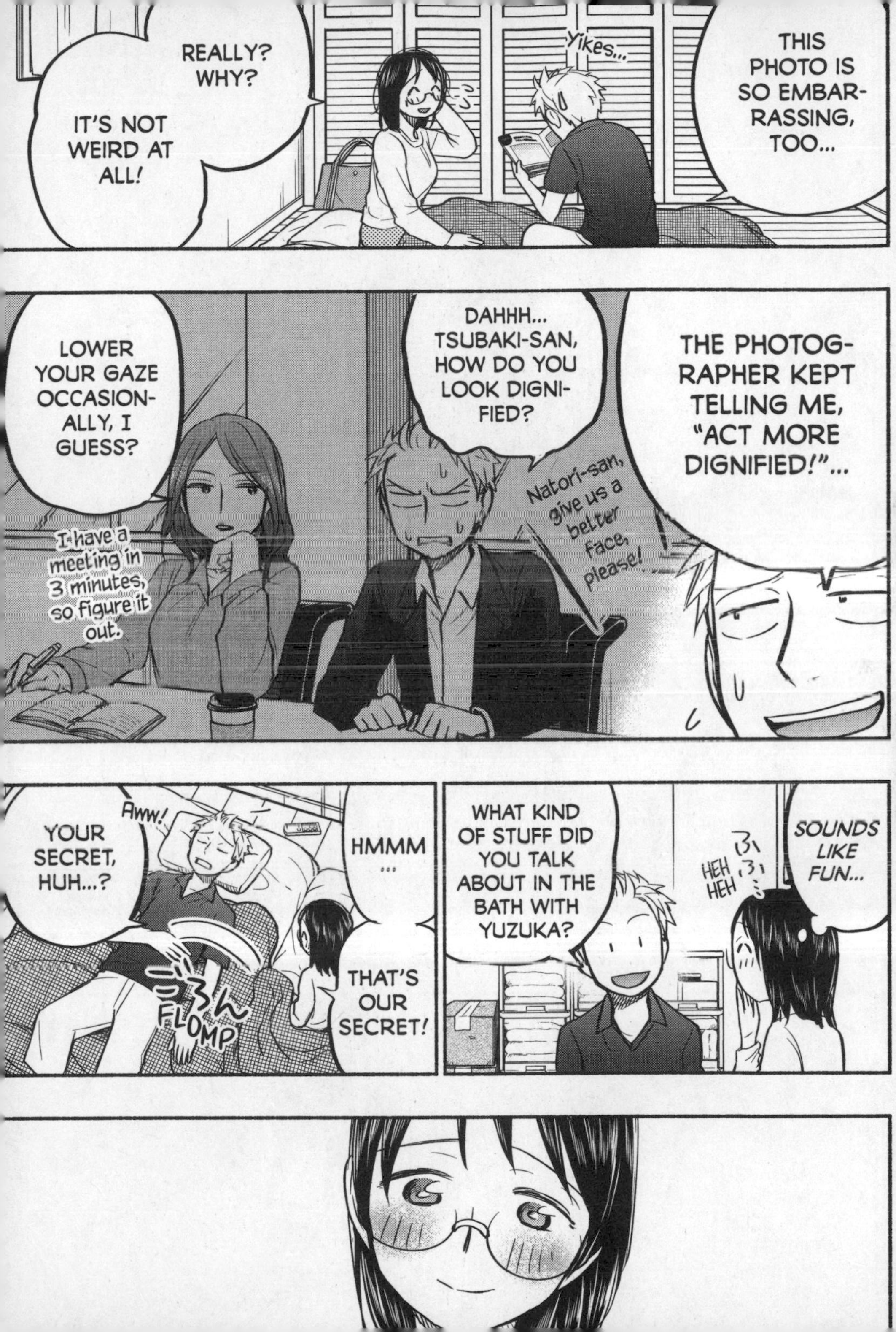
THIS PHOTO IS SO EMBARRASSING, TOO...
Yikes...
REALLY? WHY?
IT'S NOT WEIRD AT ALL!
THE PHOTOGRAPHER KEPT TELLING ME, "ACT MORE DIGNIFIED!"...
Natori-san, give us a better face, please!
DAHHH... TSUBAKI-SAN, HOW DO YOU LOOK DIGNIFIED?
LOWER YOUR GAZE OCCASIONALLY, I GUESS?
I have a meeting in 3 minutes, so figure it out.
SOUNDS LIKE FUN...
HEH HEH
WHAT KIND OF STUFF DID YOU TALK ABOUT IN THE BATH WITH YUZUKA?
HMMM ...
THAT'S OUR SECRET!
Aww!
YOUR SECRET, HUH...?
FLOMP

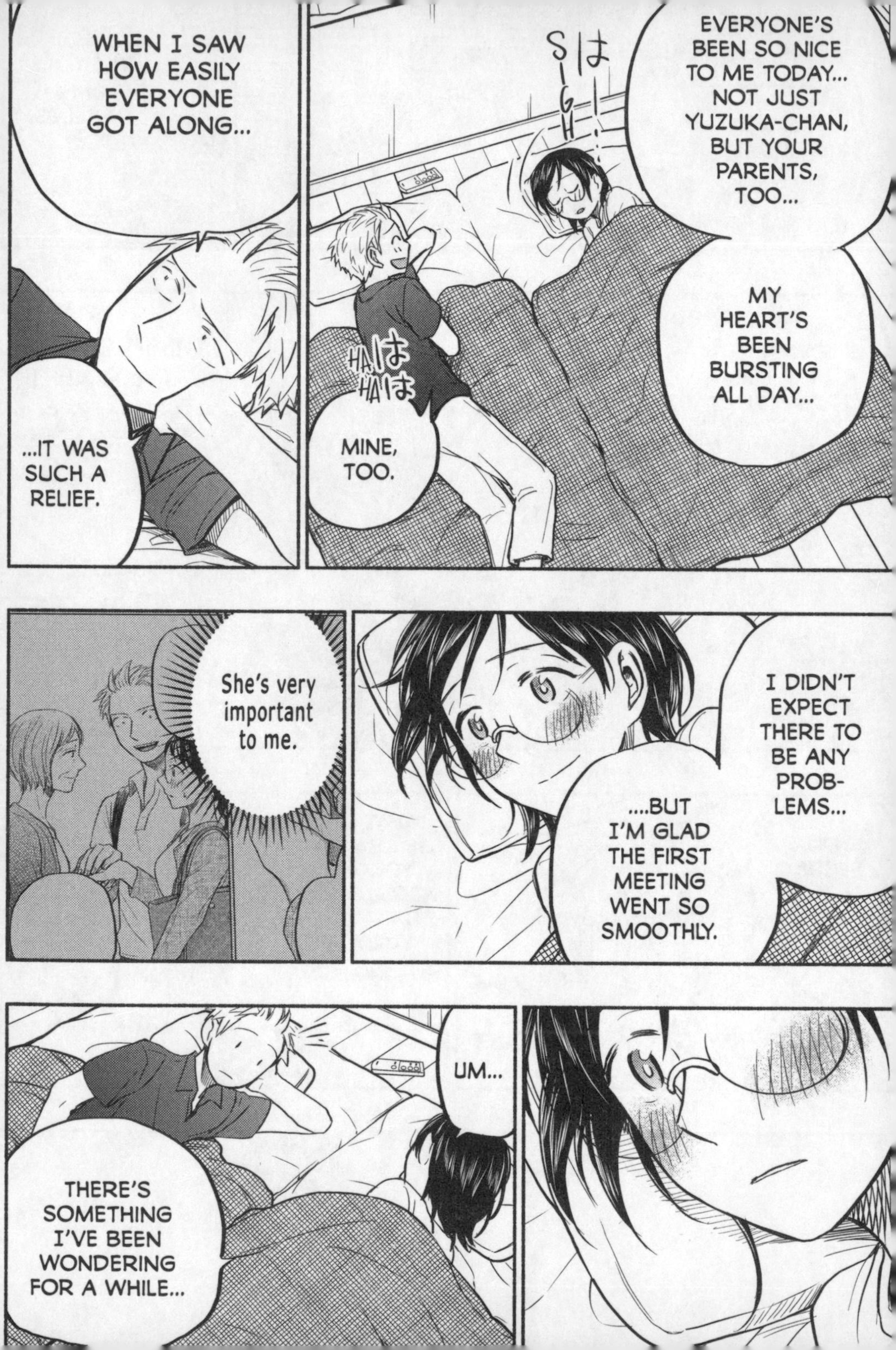
EVERYONE'S BEEN SO NICE TO ME TODAY... NOT JUST YUZUKA-CHAN, BUT YOUR PARENTS, TOO...
SIGH はーー...
MY HEART'S BEEN BURSTING ALL DAY...
HA HA はは
MINE, TOO.
WHEN I SAW HOW EASILY EVERYONE GOT ALONG...
...IT WAS SUCH A RELIEF.
I DIDN'T EXPECT THERE TO BE ANY PROB-LEMS...
....BUT I'M GLAD THE FIRST MEETING WENT SO SMOOTHLY.
She's very important to me.
UM...
THERE'S SOMETHING I'VE BEEN WONDERING FOR A WHILE...

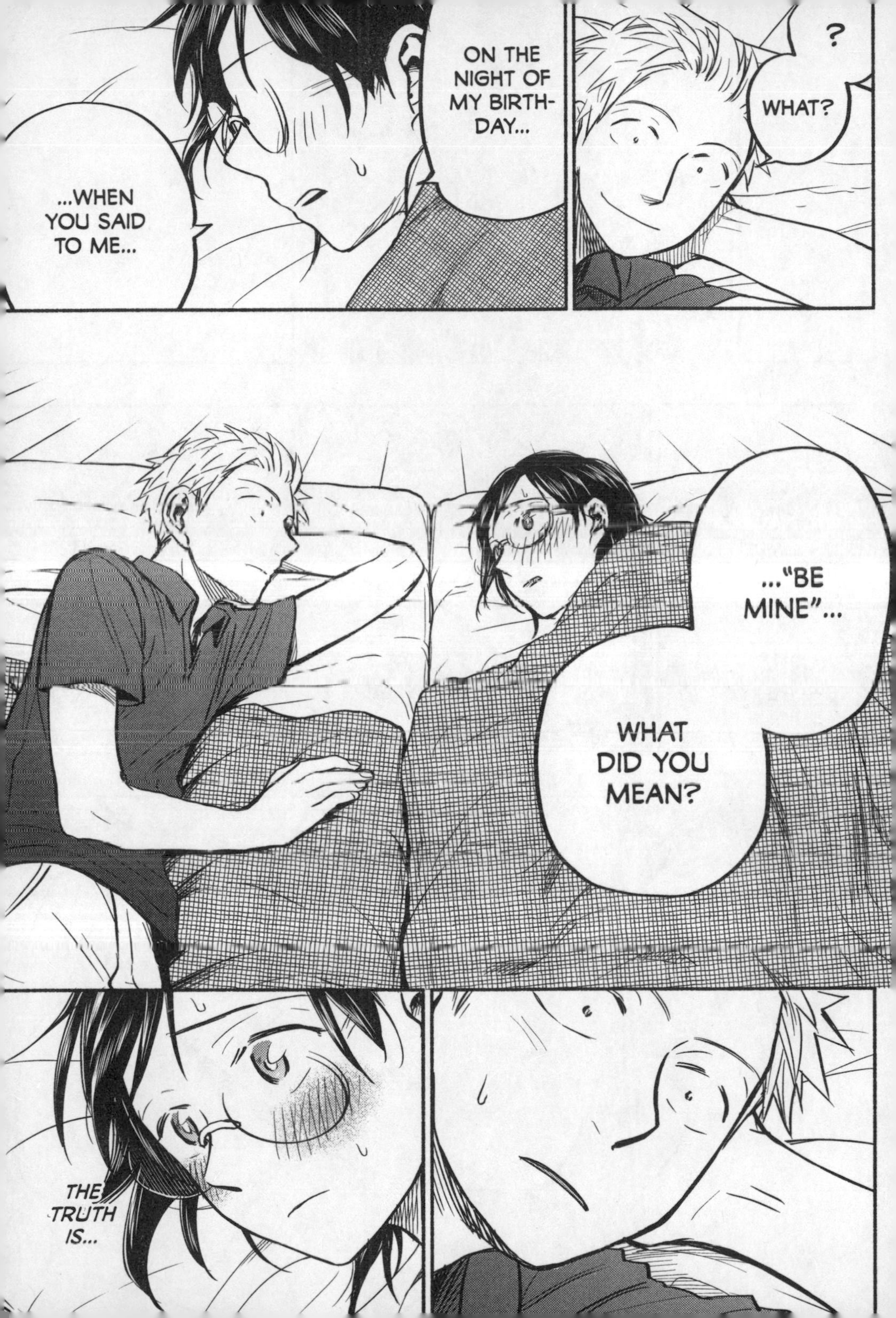
?
WHAT?
ON THE NIGHT OF MY BIRTH-DAY...
...WHEN YOU SAID TO ME...
..."BE MINE"...
WHAT DID YOU MEAN?
THE TRUTH IS...

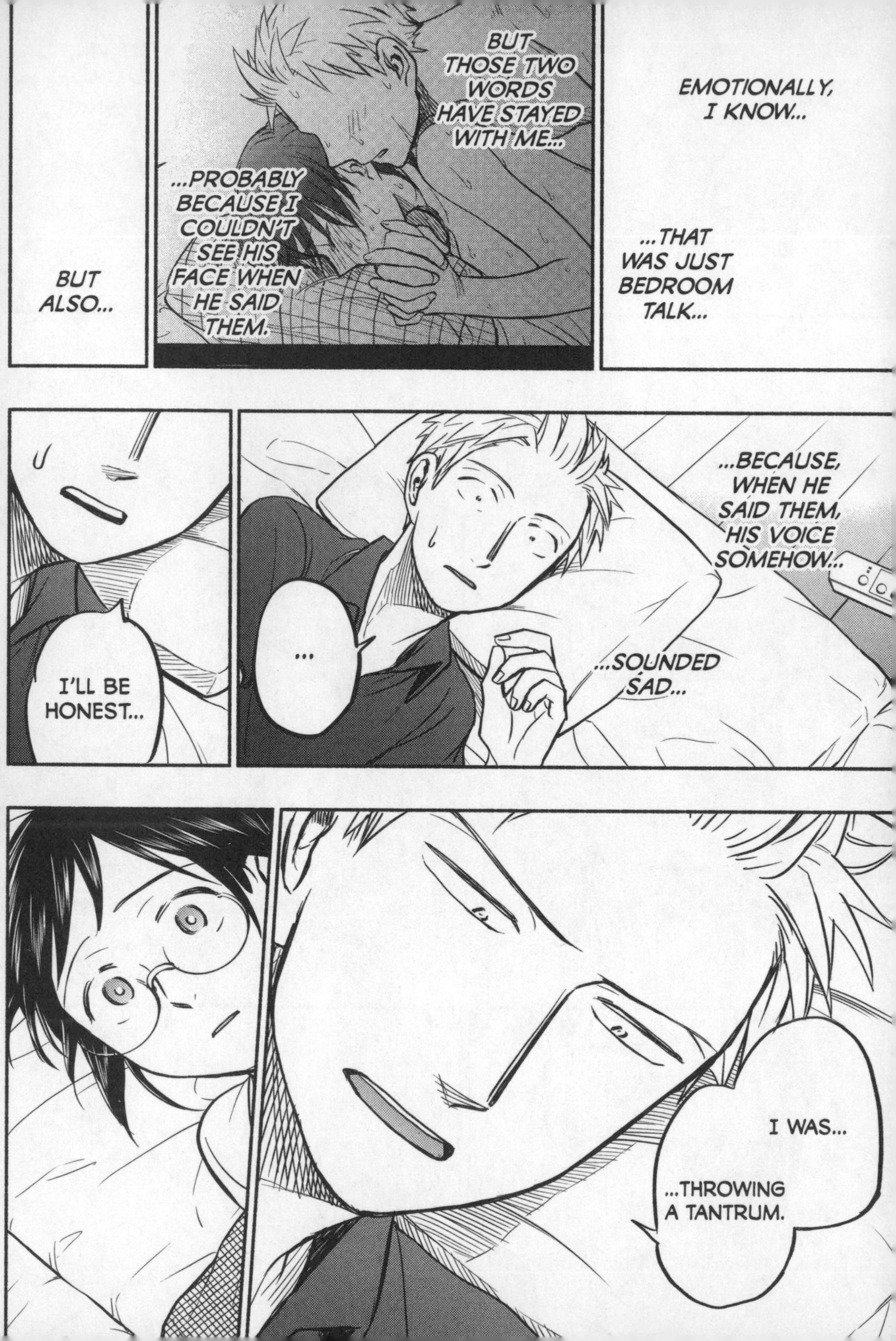
EMOTIONALLY, I KNOW...
...THAT WAS JUST BEDROOM TALK...
BUT THOSE TWO WORDS HAVE STAYED WITH ME...
...PROBABLY BECAUSE I COULDN'T SEE HIS FACE WHEN HE SAID THEM.
BUT ALSO...
...BECAUSE, WHEN HE SAID THEM, HIS VOICE SOMEHOW...
...SOUNDED SAD...
...
I'LL BE HONEST...
I WAS...
...THROWING A TANTRUM.

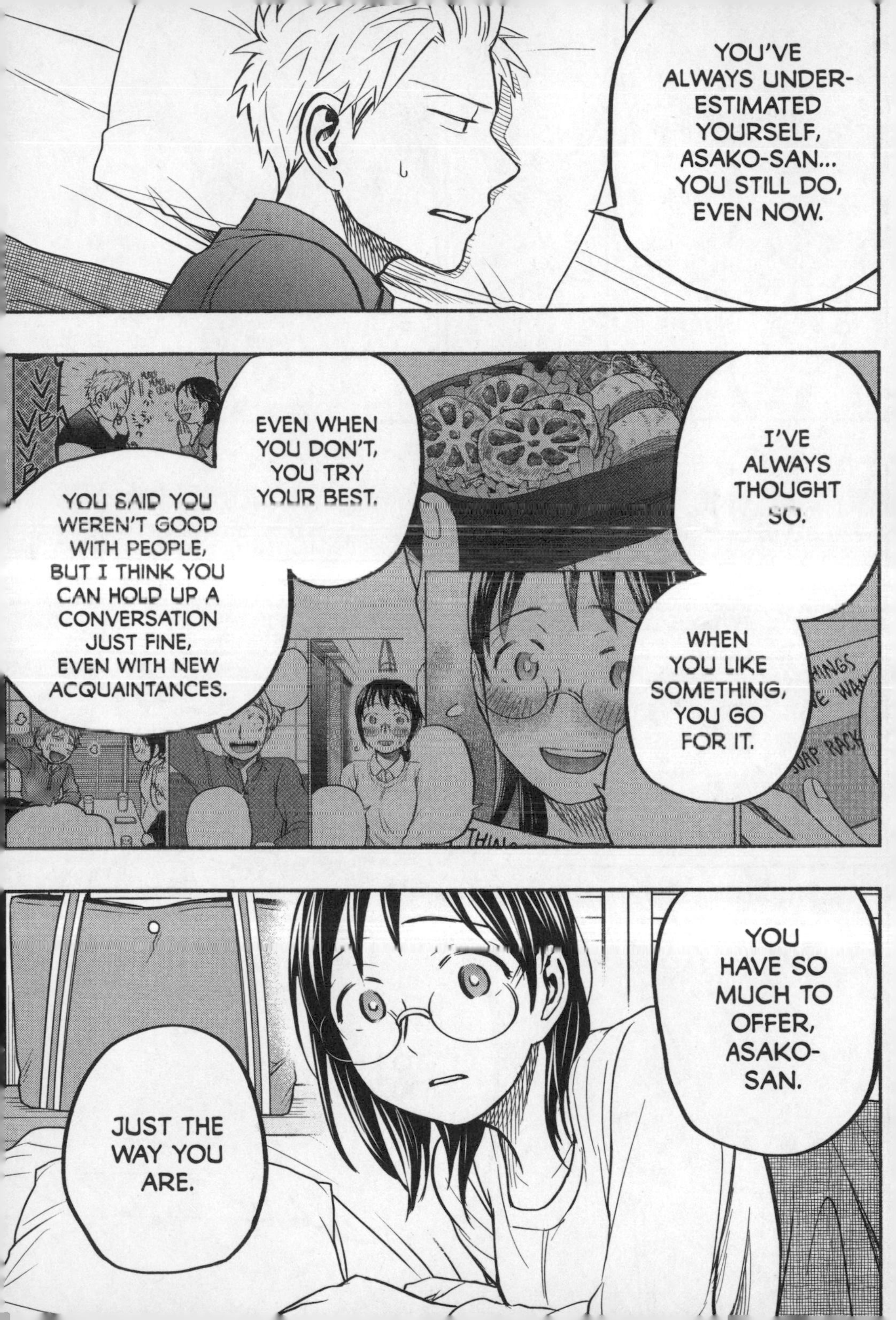
YOU'VE ALWAYS UNDER-ESTIMATED YOURSELF, ASAKO-SAN... YOU STILL DO, EVEN NOW.
I'VE ALWAYS THOUGHT SO.
WHEN YOU LIKE SOMETHING, YOU GO FOR IT.
EVEN WHEN YOU DON'T, YOU TRY YOUR BEST.
YOU SAID YOU WEREN'T GOOD WITH PEOPLE, BUT I THINK YOU CAN HOLD UP A CONVERSATION JUST FINE, EVEN WITH NEW ACQUAINTANCES.
YOU HAVE SO MUCH TO OFFER, ASAKO-SAN.
JUST THE WAY YOU ARE.

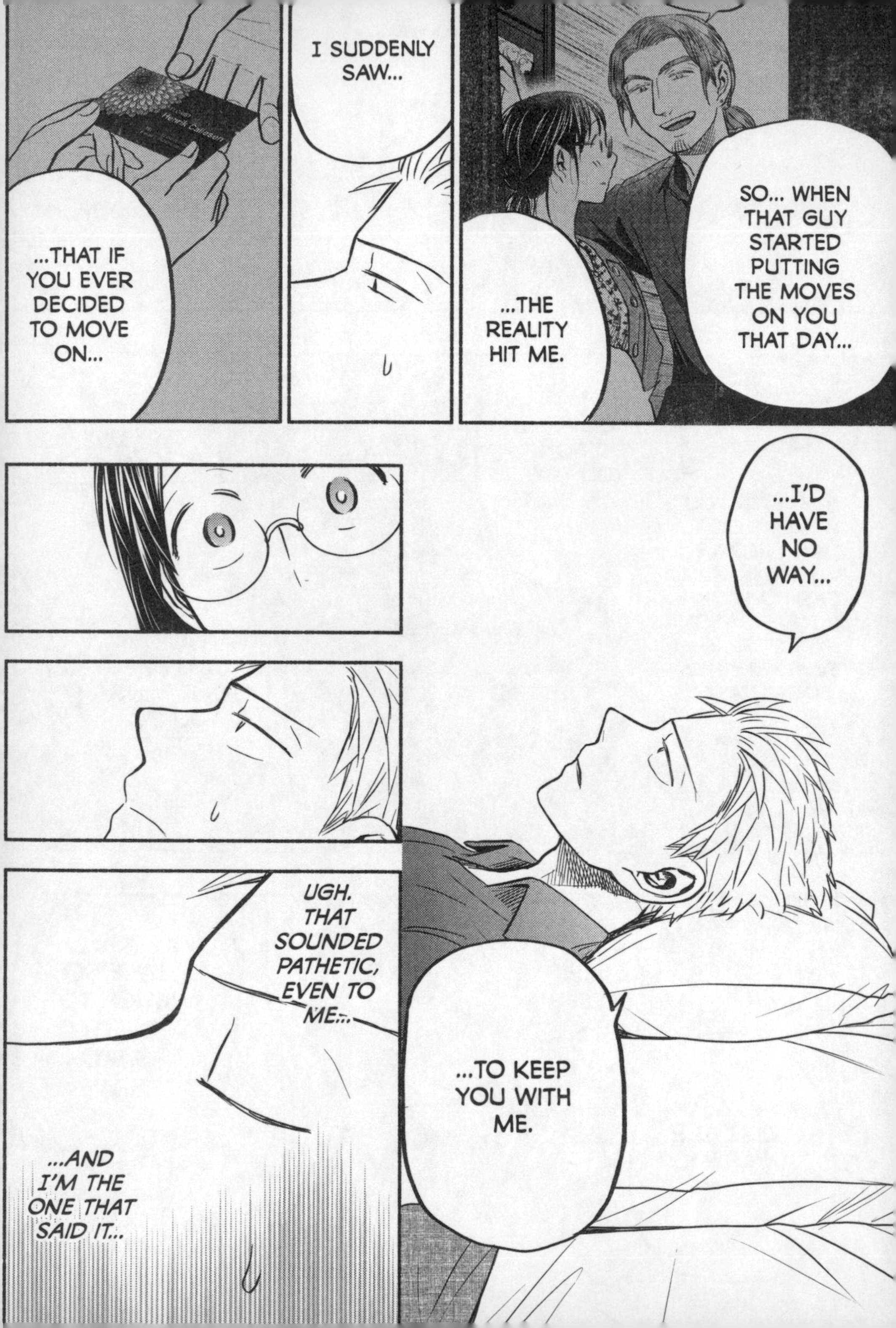
SO... WHEN THAT GUY STARTED PUTTING THE MOVES ON YOU THAT DAY...
...THE REALITY HIT ME.
I SUDDENLY SAW...
...THAT IF YOU EVER DECIDED TO MOVE ON...
...I'D HAVE NO WAY...
...TO KEEP YOU WITH ME.
UGH. THAT SOUNDED PATHETIC, EVEN TO ME...
...AND I'M THE ONE THAT SAID IT...

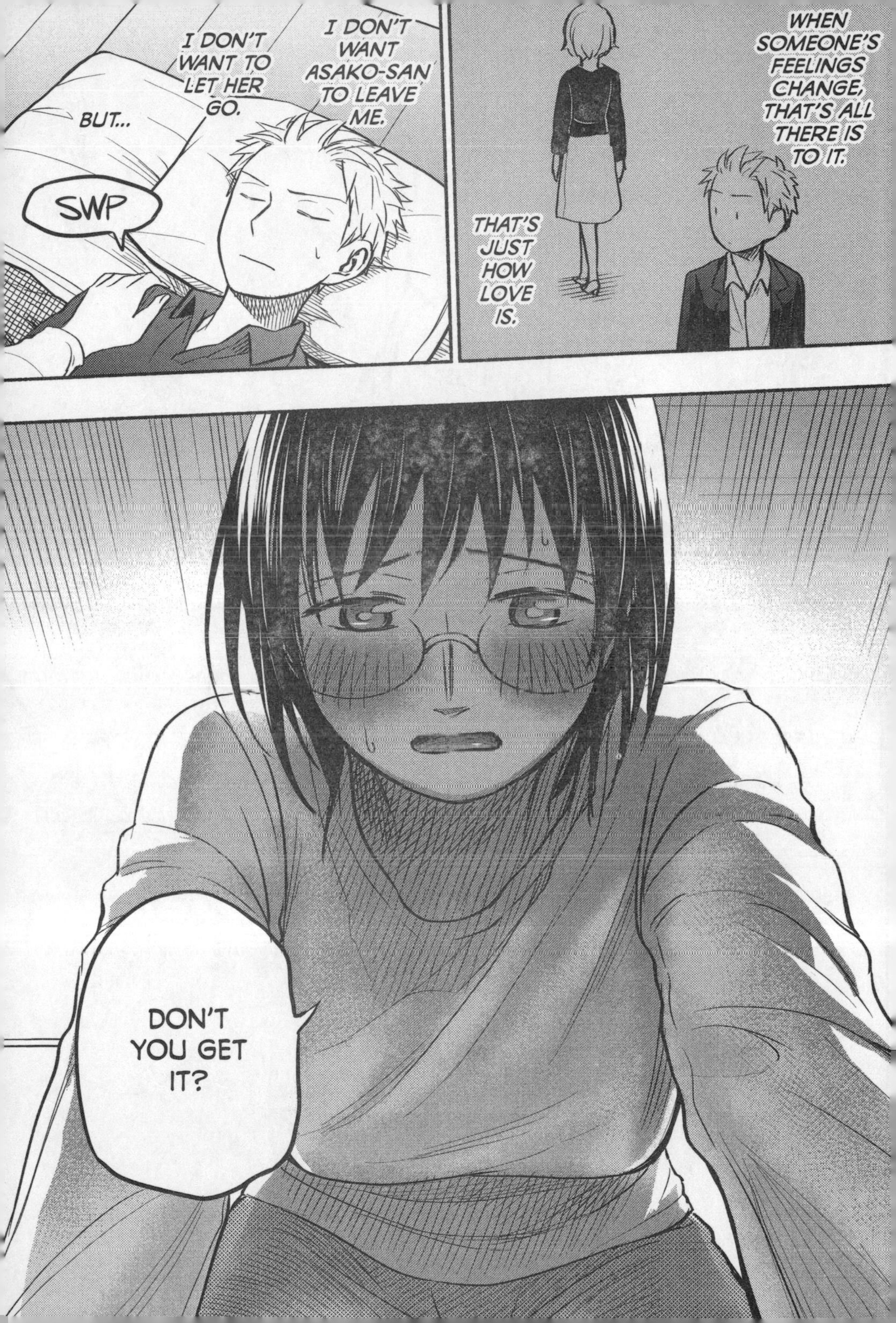
WHEN SOMEONE'S FEELINGS CHANGE, THAT'S ALL THERE IS TO IT.
THAT'S JUST HOW LOVE IS.
I DON'T WANT ASAKO-SAN TO LEAVE ME.
I DON'T WANT TO LET HER GO.
BUT...
SWP
DON'T YOU GET IT?

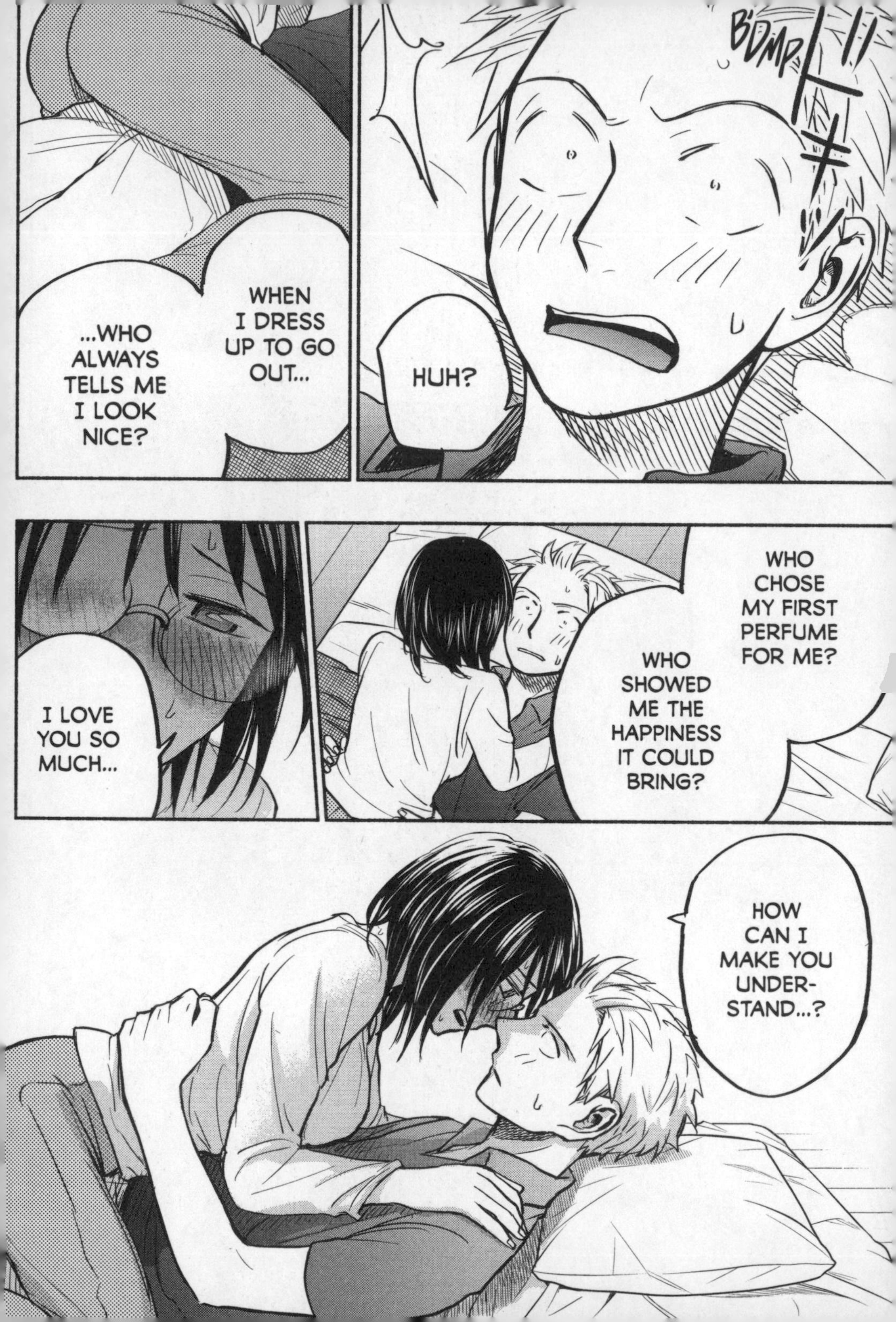
B'DMP!!
HUH?
WHEN I DRESS UP TO GO OUT...
...WHO ALWAYS TELLS ME I LOOK NICE?
WHO CHOSE MY FIRST PERFUME FOR ME?
WHO SHOWED ME THE HAPPINESS IT COULD BRING?
I LOVE YOU SO MUCH...
HOW CAN I MAKE YOU UNDER-STAND...?

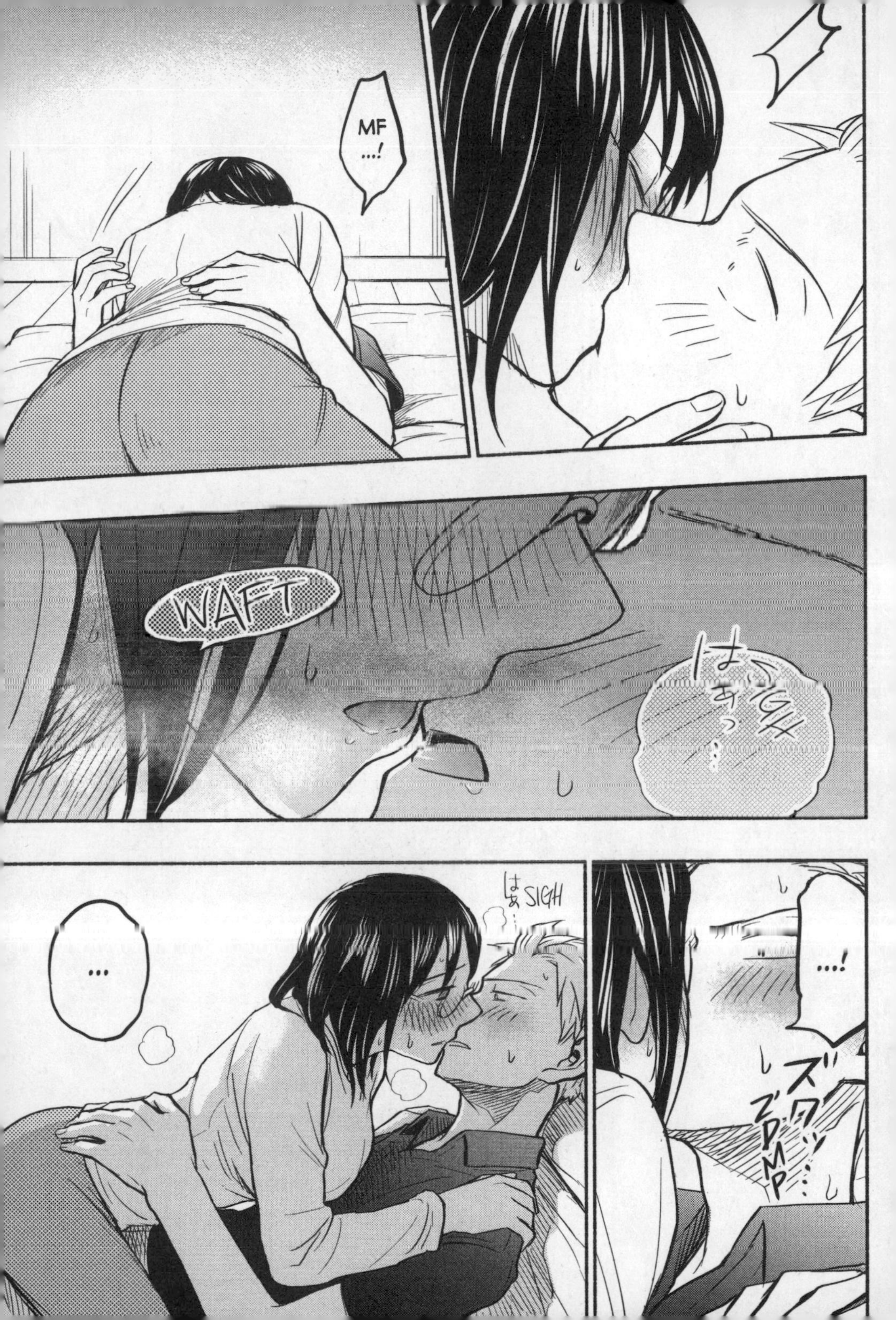
MF ....!
WAFT
はぁっ…
SIGH
....!
ズダッ…
DMP
はぁ
SIGH
...

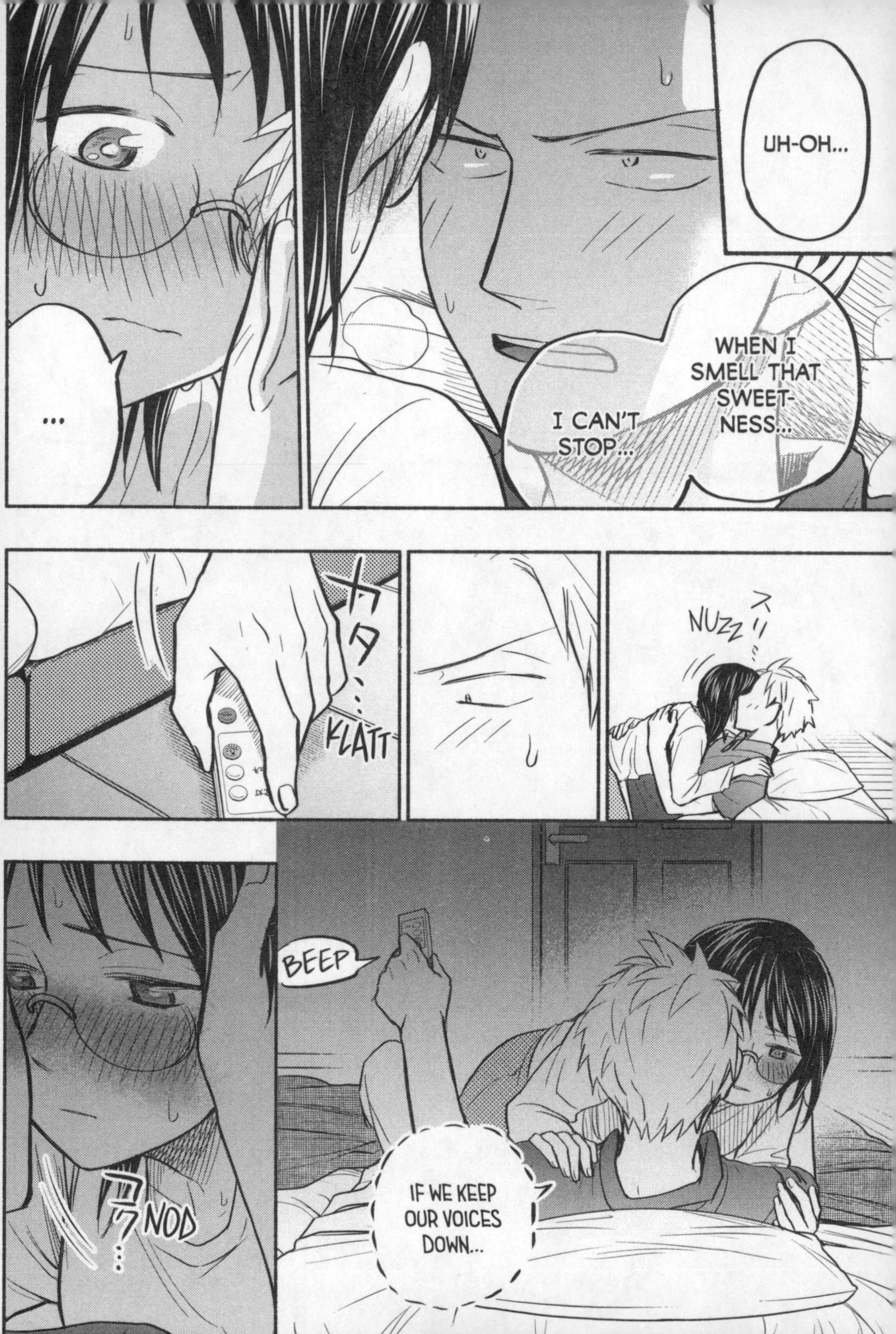
UH-OH...
WHEN I SMELL THAT SWEET-NESS...
I CAN'T STOP...
...
NUZZ
KLATT
BEEP
IF WE KEEP OUR VOICES DOWN...
NOD

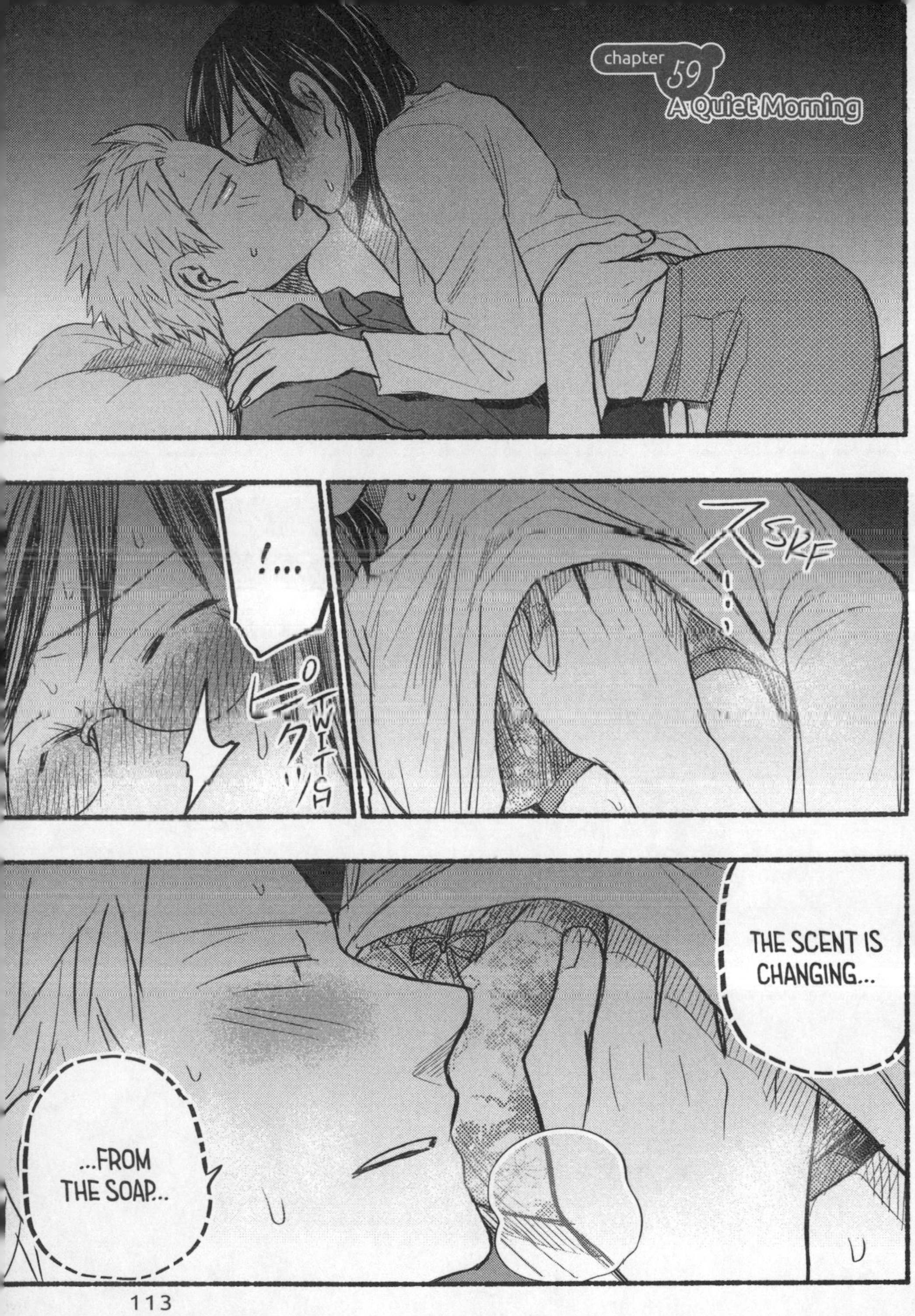
chapter 59
A Quiet Morning
SKF
!...
TWITCH
THE SCENT IS CHANGING...
...FROM THE SOAP...

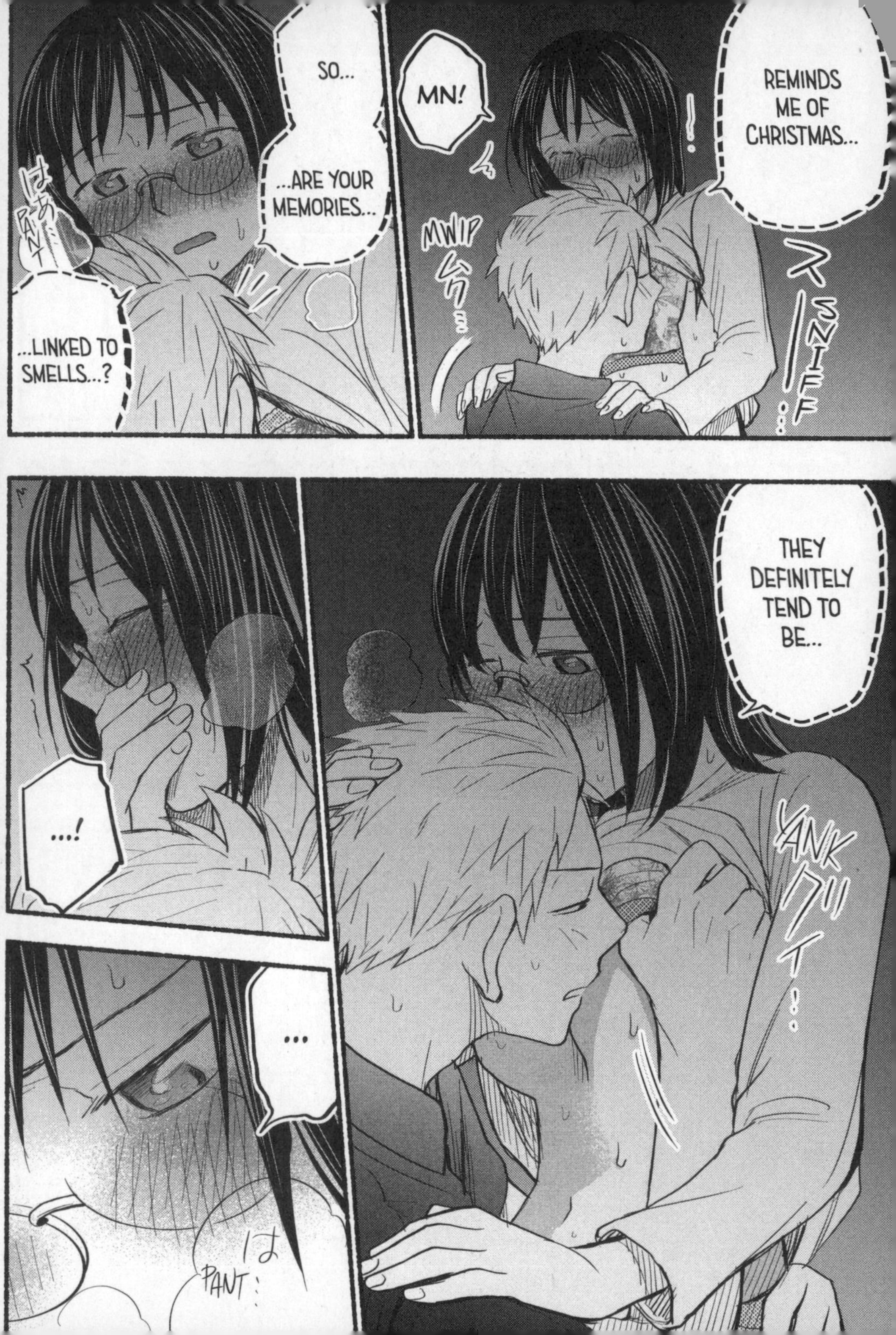
REMINDS ME OF CHRISTMAS...
!
SNIFF...
MN!
MWIP
SO...
...ARE YOUR MEMORIES...
PANT
...LINKED TO SMELLS...?
THEY DEFINITELY TEND TO BE...
YANK
...!
...
は
PANT

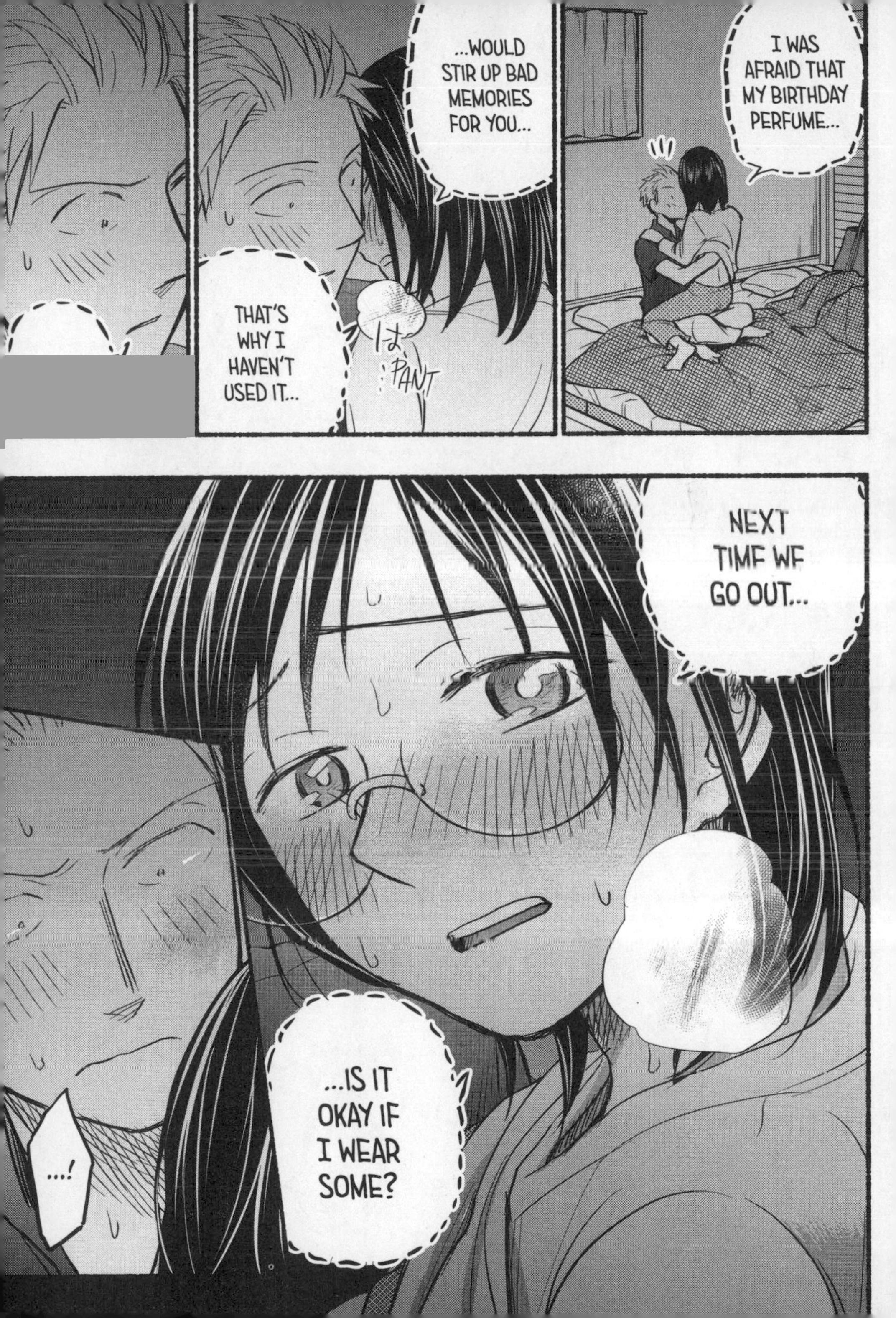
I WAS AFRAID THAT MY BIRTHDAY PERFUME...
...WOULD STIR UP BAD MEMORIES FOR YOU...
THAT'S WHY I HAVEN'T USED IT...
は PANT
NEXT TIME WE GO OUT...
...IS IT OKAY IF I WEAR SOME?
...!

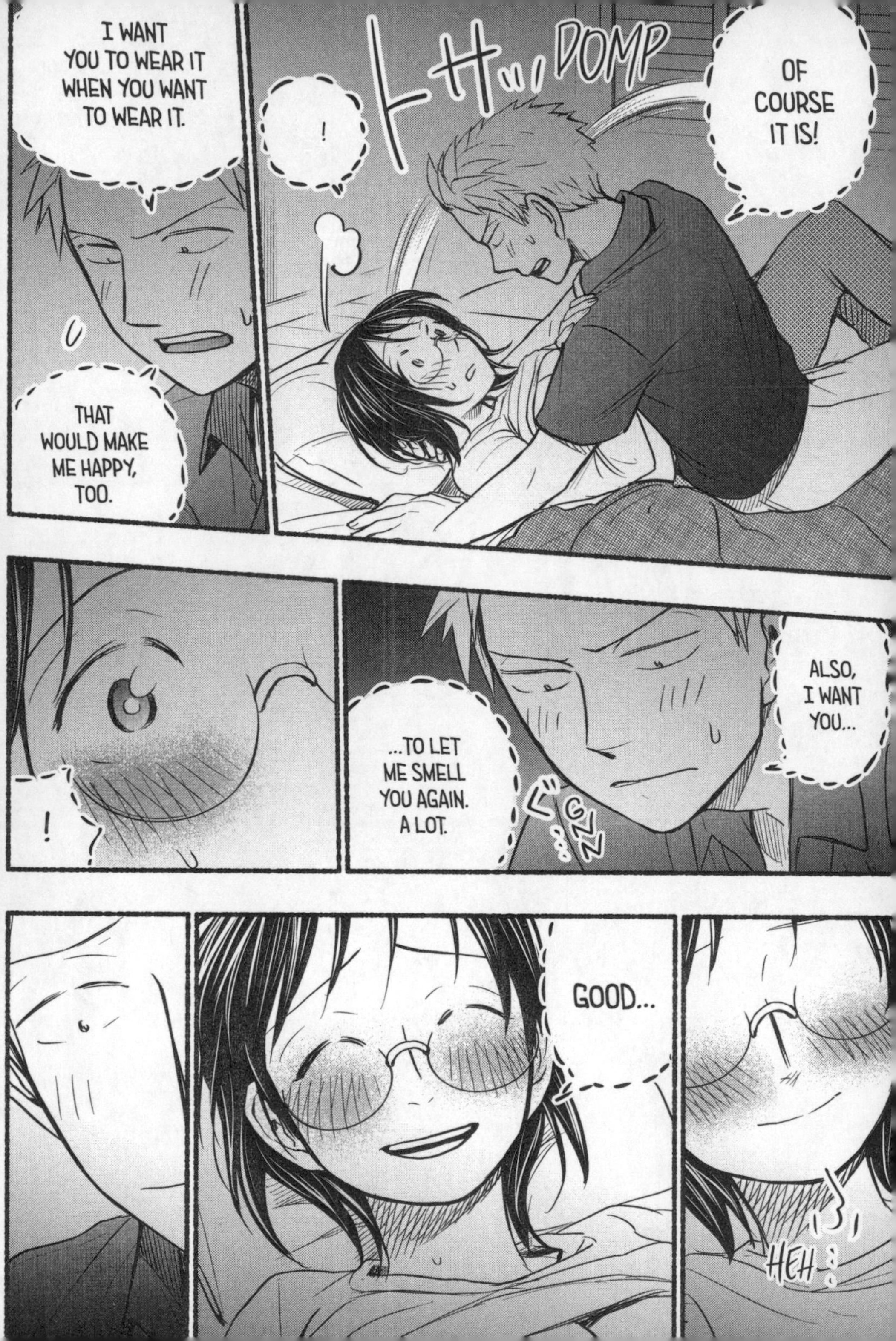
OF COURSE IT IS!
DOMP
!
I WANT YOU TO WEAR IT WHEN YOU WANT TO WEAR IT.
THAT WOULD MAKE ME HAPPY, TOO.
ALSO, I WANT YOU...
GNN
...TO LET ME SMELL YOU AGAIN. A LOT.
!
HEH
GOOD...

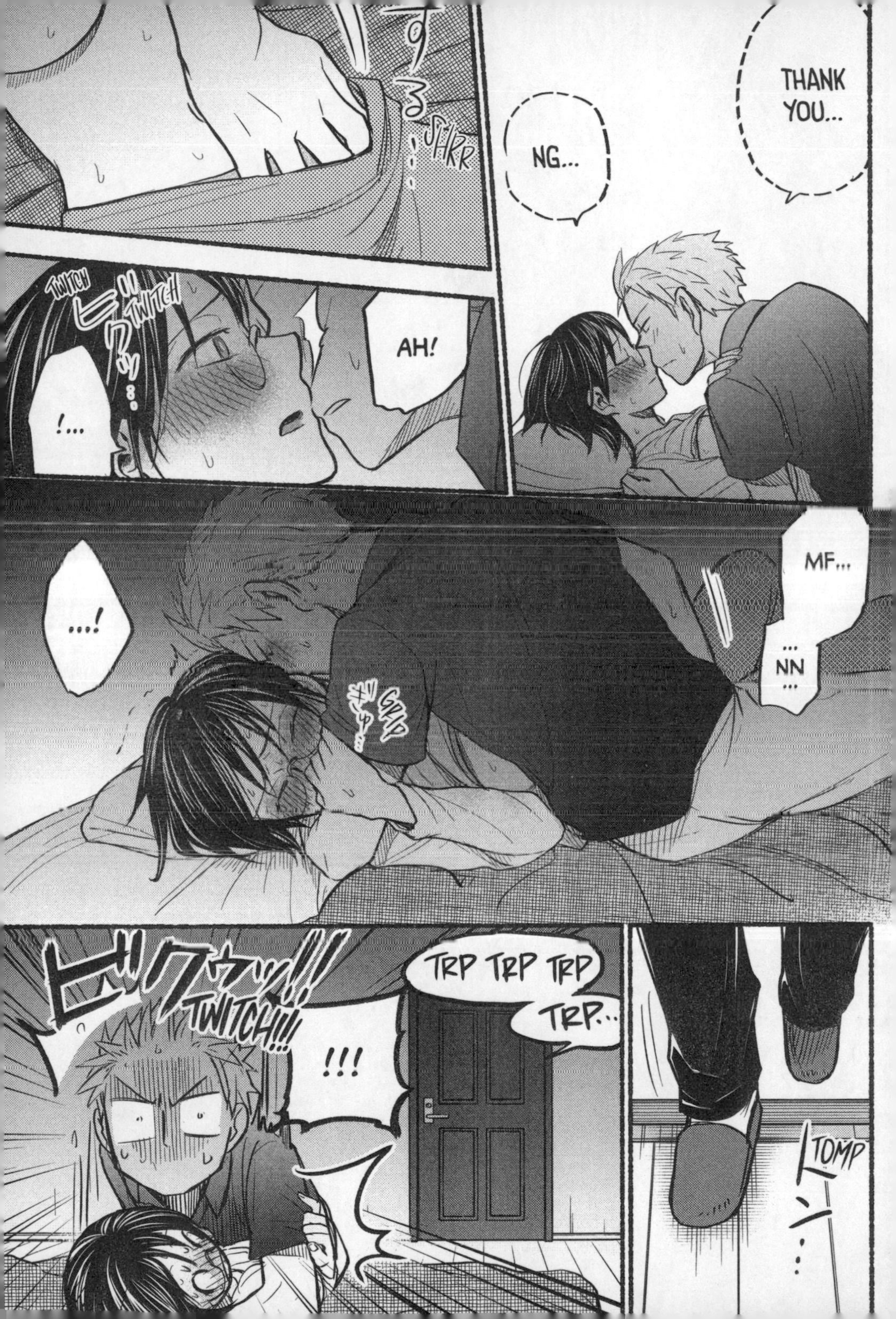
THANK YOU...
NG...
SHRR
AH!
TWITCH TWITCH
!...
MF...
...NN...
GRIP
...!
TOMP
TRP TRP TRP TRP...
!!!
TWITCH!!!

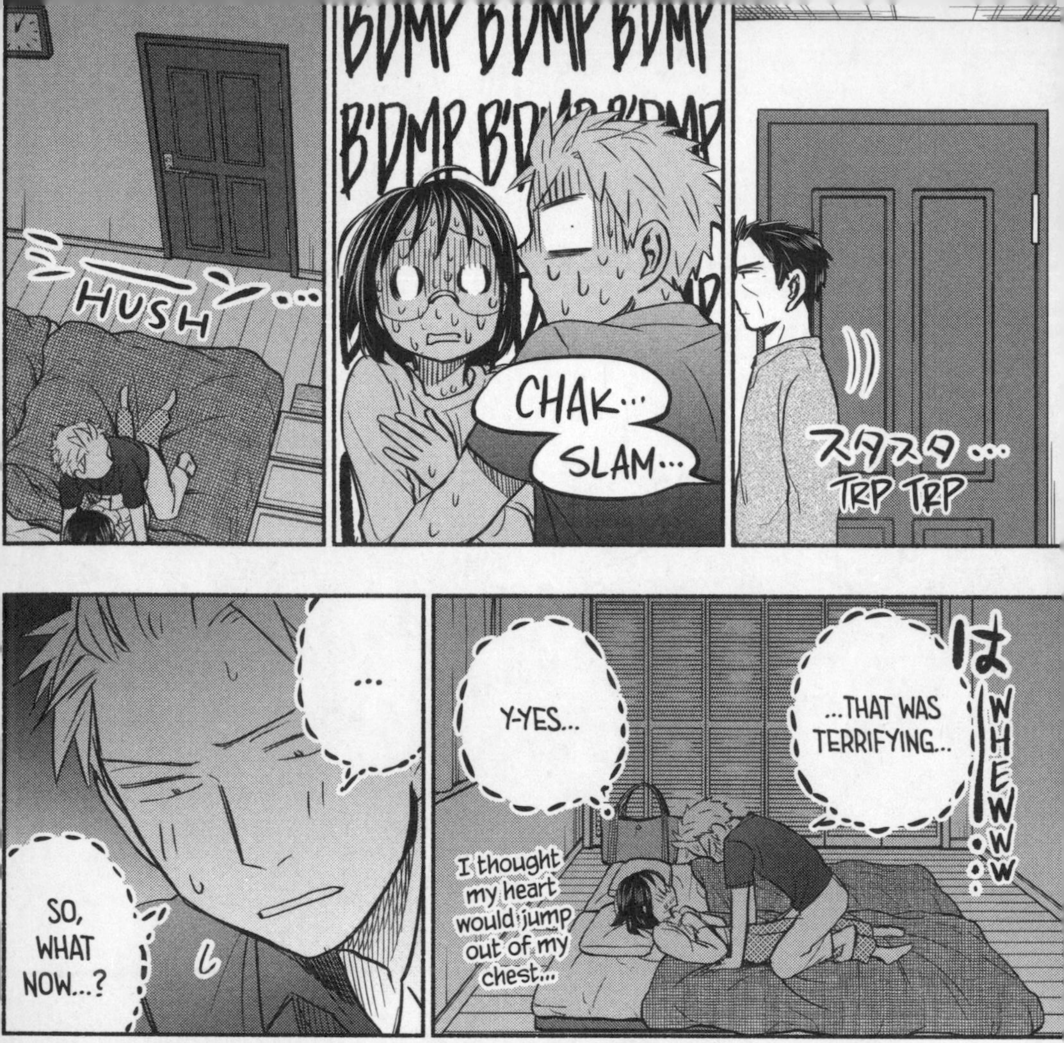
スタスタ…
TRP TRP
B'DMP B'DMP B'DMP
B'DMP B'DMP B'DMP
CHAK…
SLAM…
HUSH…
は
WHEEWWW…
…THAT WAS TERRIFYING…
Y-YES…
I thought my heart would jump out of my chest…
…
SO, WHAT NOW…?

Sign: "Natori-en"

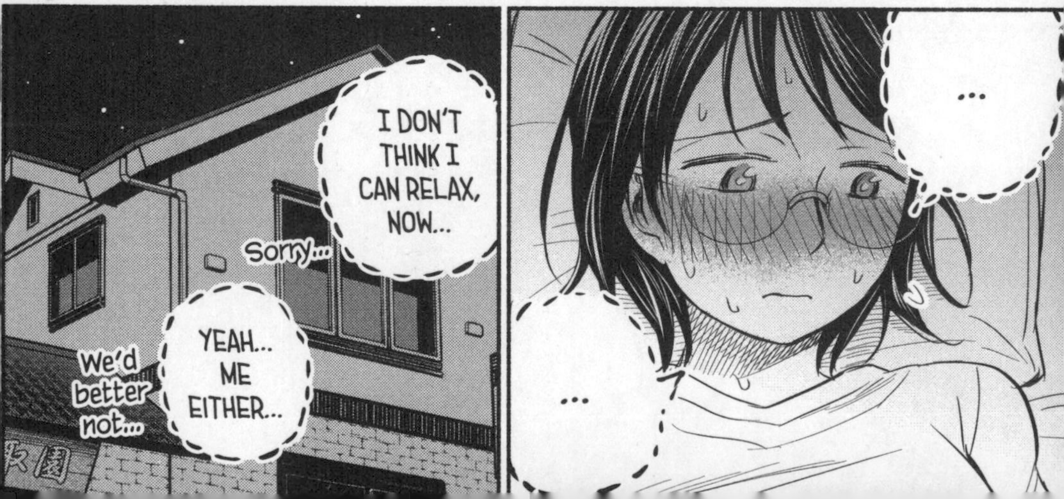
…
…
I DON'T THINK I CAN RELAX, NOW…
Sorry…
YEAH… ME EITHER…
We'd better not…

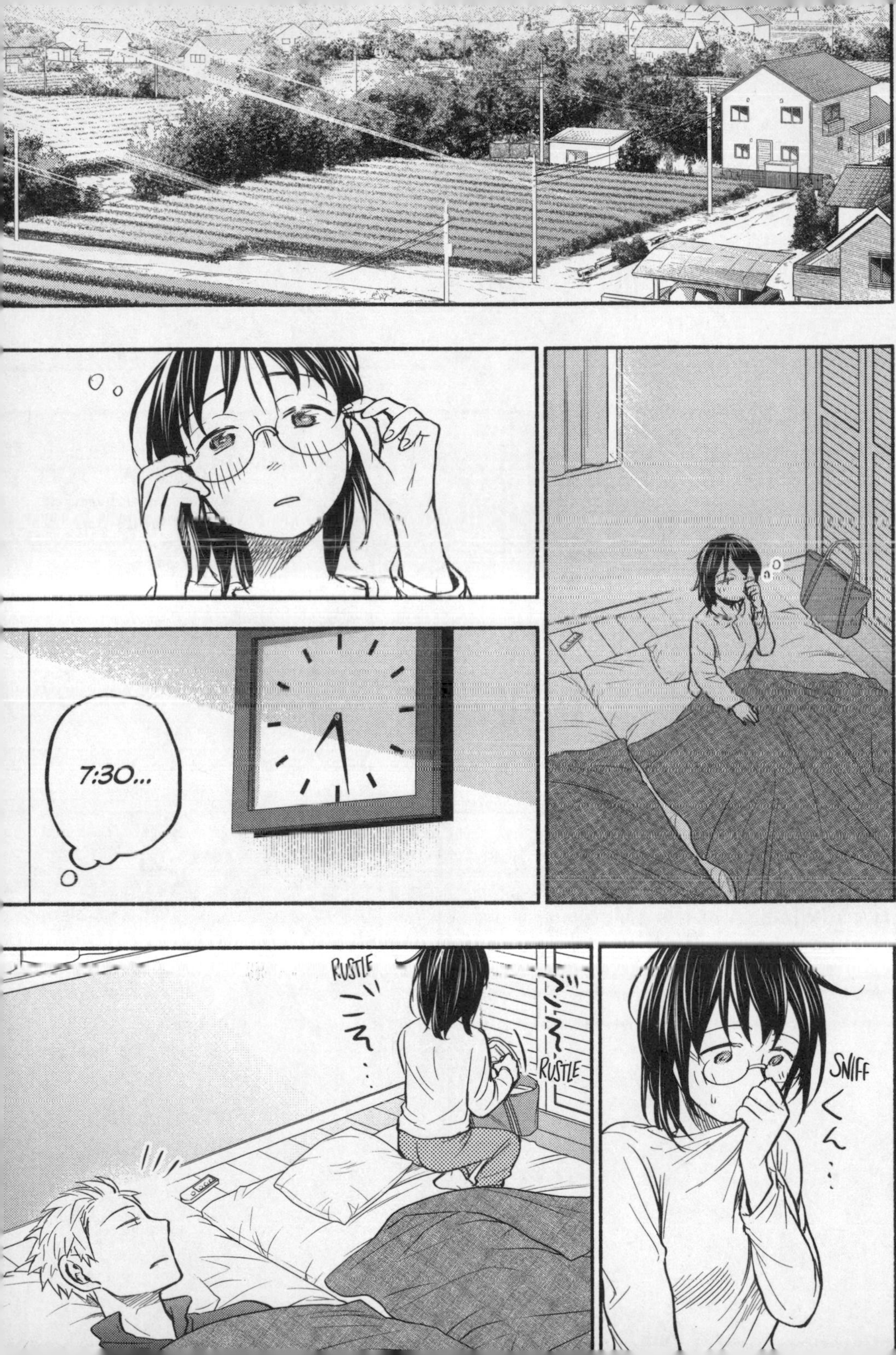
7:30...
SNIFF
くん...
RUSTLE
RUSTLE

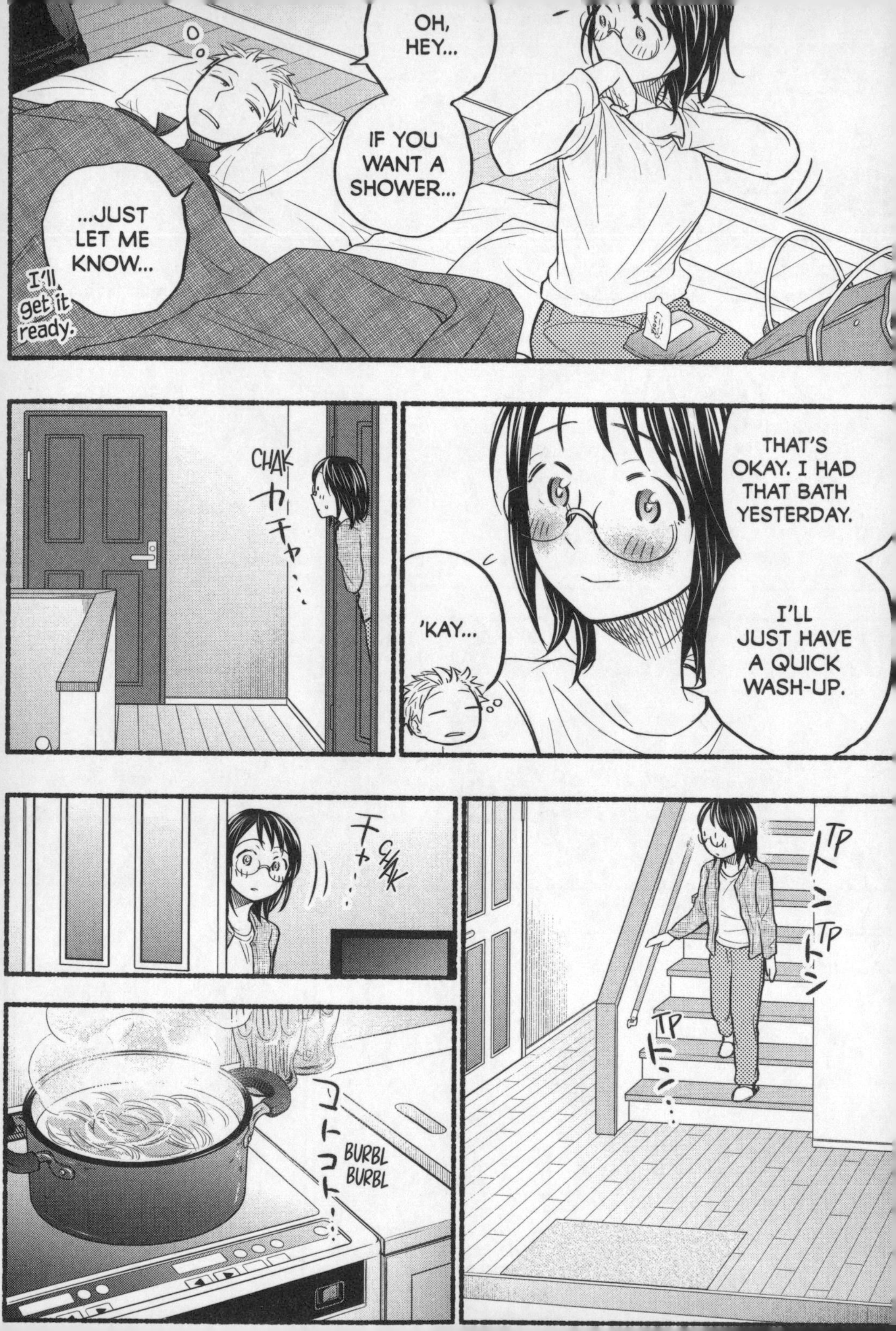
OH, HEY...
IF YOU WANT A SHOWER...
...JUST LET ME KNOW...
I'll get it ready.
THAT'S OKAY. I HAD THAT BATH YESTERDAY.
I'LL JUST HAVE A QUICK WASH-UP.
'KAY...
カチャ...
CHAK
トン TP
トン TP
トン... TP
チャ...
CHAK
コトコト...
BURBL BURBL

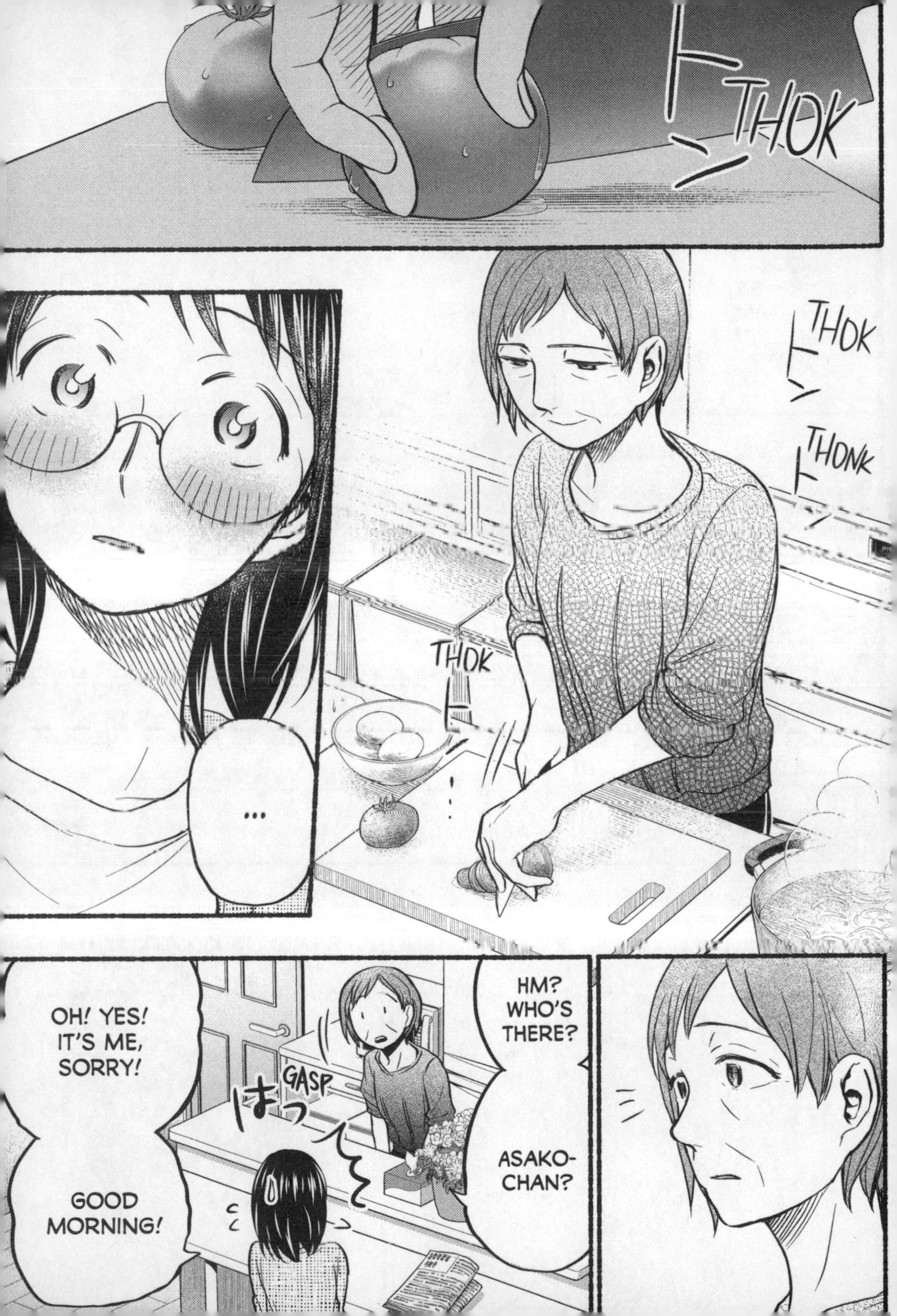
THOK
THOK
THONK
THOK
...
HM? WHO'S THERE?
ASAKO-CHAN?
OH! YES! IT'S ME, SORRY!
GASP
GOOD MORNING!

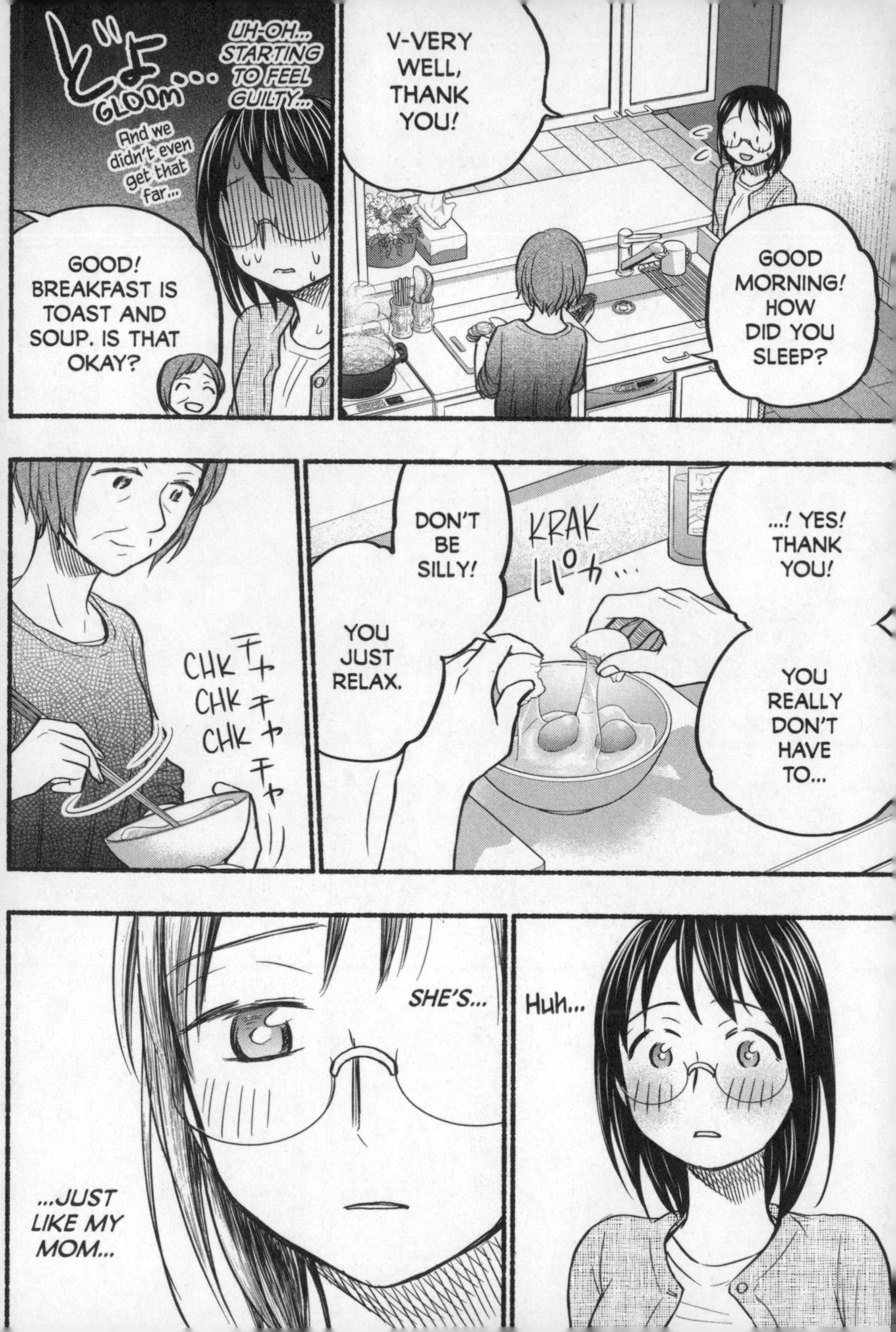
GOOD MORNING! HOW DID YOU SLEEP?
V-VERY WELL, THANK YOU!
UH-OH... STARTING TO FEEL GUILTY...
どよ... GLOOM
And we didn't even get that far...
GOOD! BREAKFAST IS TOAST AND SOUP. IS THAT OKAY?
...! YES! THANK YOU!
YOU REALLY DON'T HAVE TO...
DON'T BE SILLY!
KRAK パカ...
YOU JUST RELAX.
CHK チャ CHK チャ CHK チャ チャ
Huh...
SHE'S...
...JUST LIKE MY MOM...

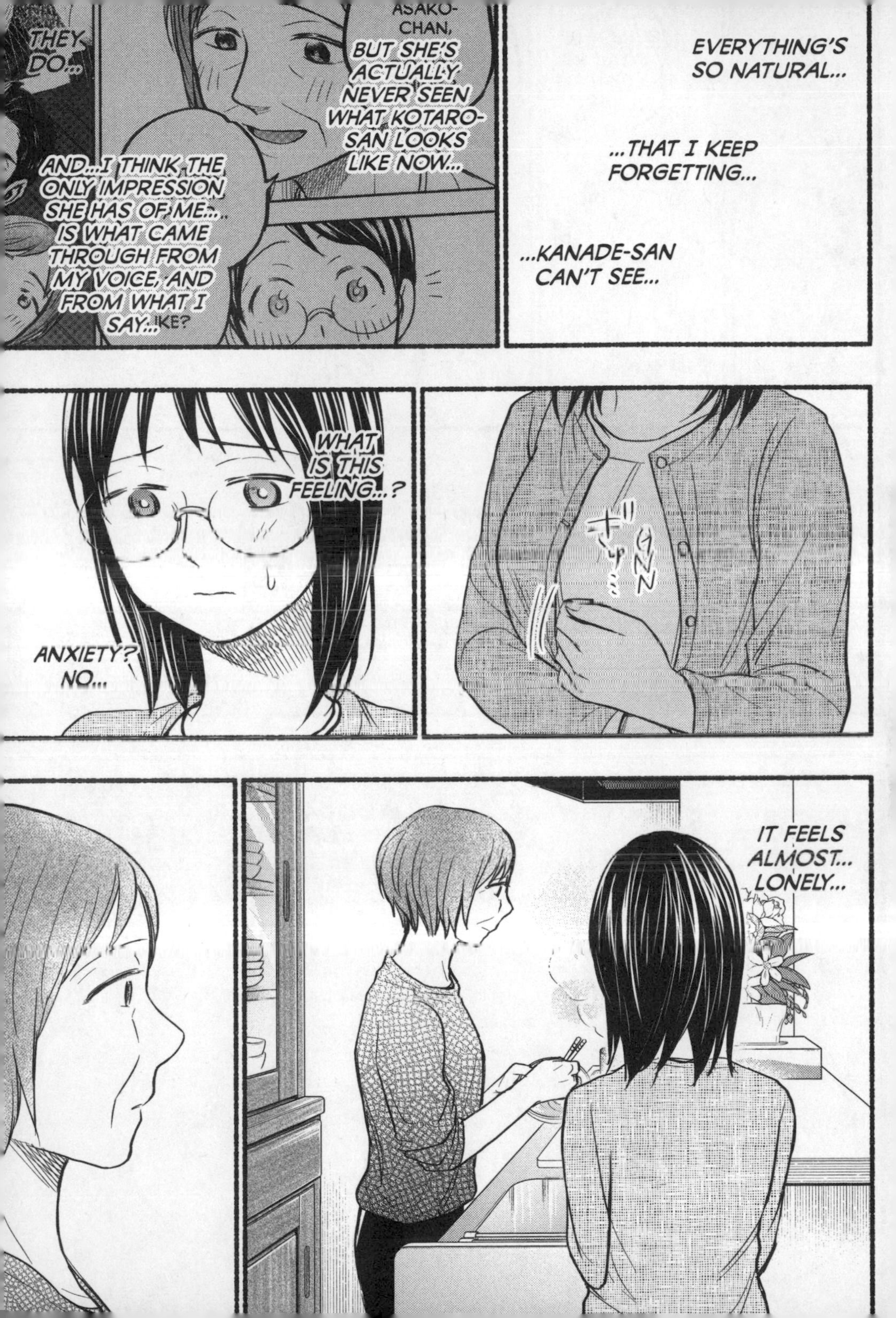
EVERYTHING'S SO NATURAL...
...THAT I KEEP FORGETTING...
...KANADE-SAN CAN'T SEE...
ASAKO-CHAN, BUT SHE'S ACTUALLY NEVER SEEN WHAT KOTARO-SAN LOOKS LIKE NOW...
AND...I THINK THE ONLY IMPRESSION SHE HAS OF ME... IS WHAT CAME THROUGH FROM MY VOICE, AND FROM WHAT I SAY...
THEY DO...
GNN
WHAT IS THIS FEELING...?
ANXIETY? NO...
IT FEELS ALMOST... LONELY...

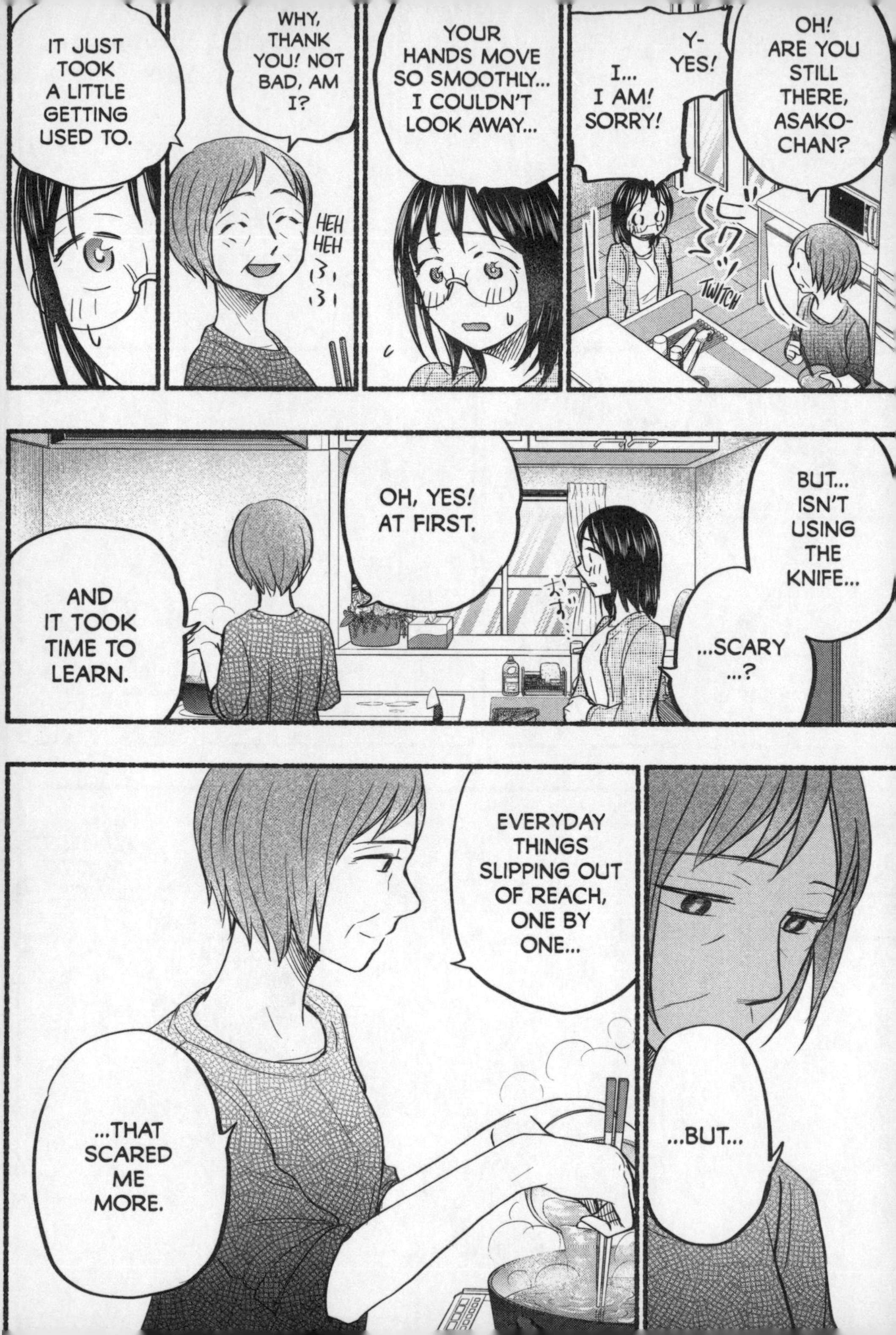
OH! ARE YOU STILL THERE, ASAKO-CHAN?
Y- YES!
I... I AM! SORRY!
TWITCH
YOUR HANDS MOVE SO SMOOTHLY... I COULDN'T LOOK AWAY...
WHY, THANK YOU! NOT BAD, AM I?
HEH HEH
IT JUST TOOK A LITTLE GETTING USED TO.
BUT... ISN'T USING THE KNIFE...
...SCARY ...?
OH, YES! AT FIRST.
AND IT TOOK TIME TO LEARN.
...BUT...
EVERYDAY THINGS SLIPPING OUT OF REACH, ONE BY ONE...
...THAT SCARED ME MORE.

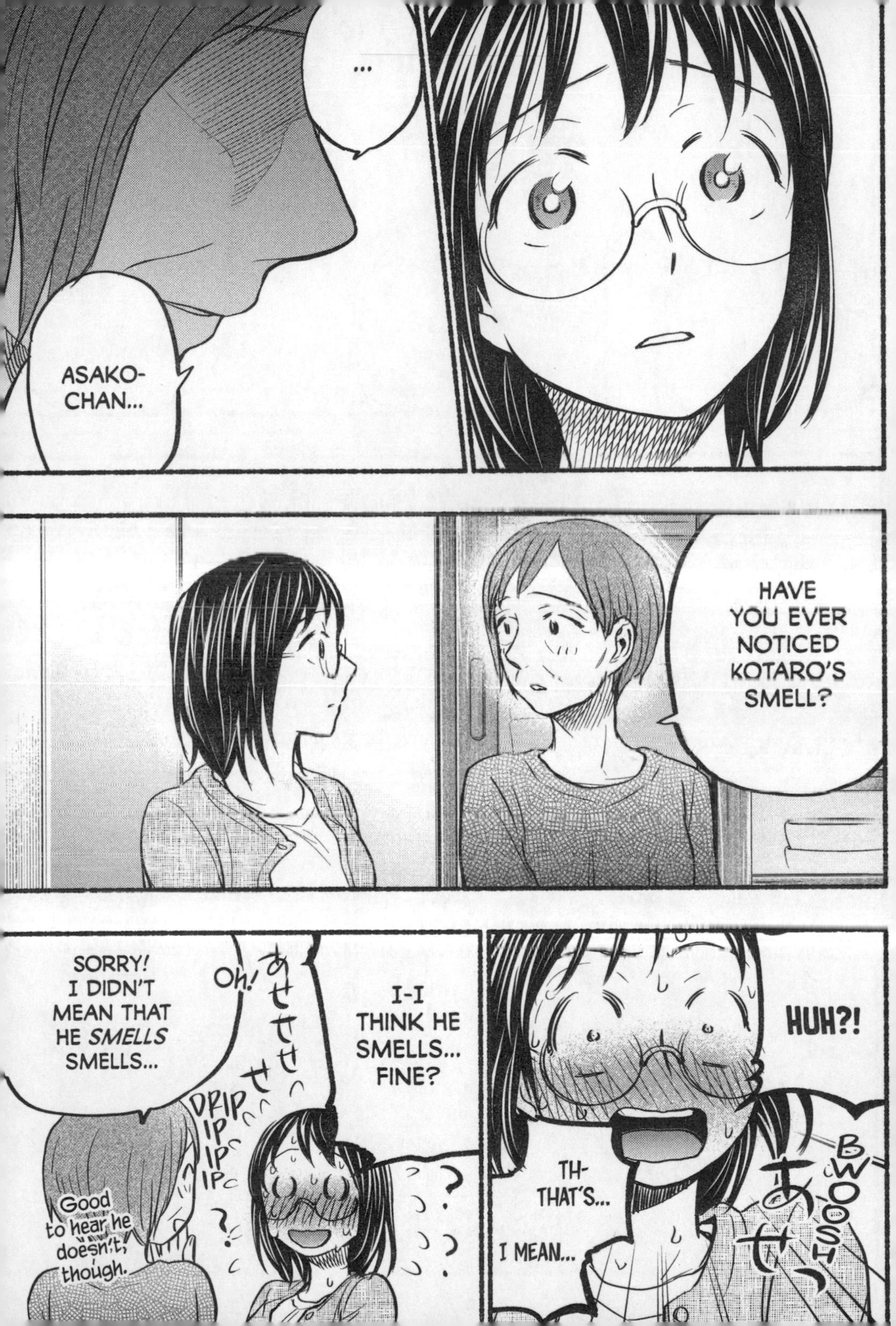
...
ASAKO-CHAN...
HAVE YOU EVER NOTICED KOTARO'S SMELL?
HUH?!
BWOOSH
あせっ
TH- THAT'S...
I MEAN...
I-I THINK HE SMELLS... FINE?
あせせせせ
Oh!
SORRY! I DIDN'T MEAN THAT HE *SMELLS* SMELLS...
DRIP IP IP IP
Good to hear he doesn't, though.

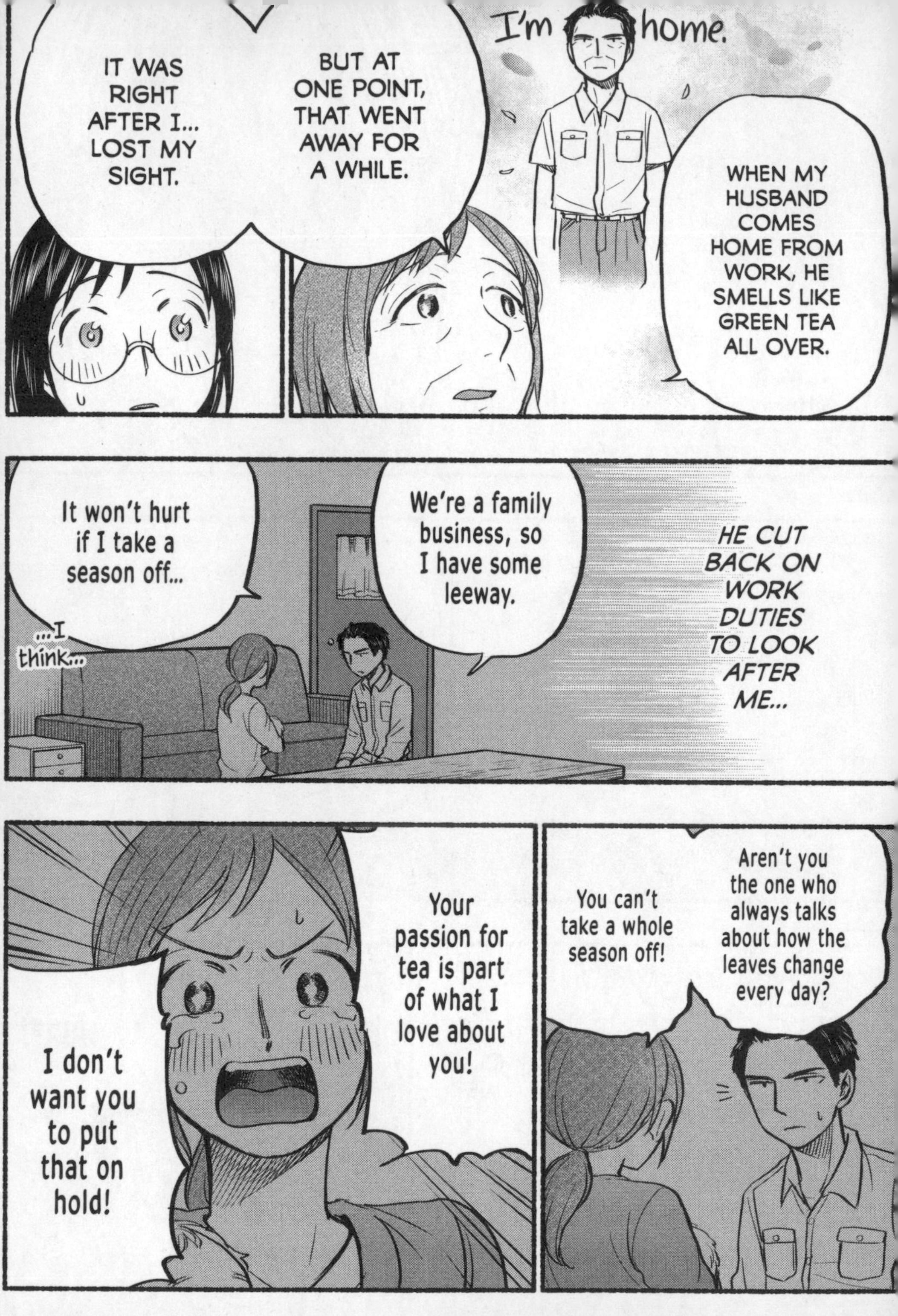
I'm home.
WHEN MY HUSBAND COMES HOME FROM WORK, HE SMELLS LIKE GREEN TEA ALL OVER.
BUT AT ONE POINT, THAT WENT AWAY FOR A WHILE.
IT WAS RIGHT AFTER I... LOST MY SIGHT.
HE CUT BACK ON WORK DUTIES TO LOOK AFTER ME...
We're a family business, so I have some leeway.
It won't hurt if I take a season off...
...I think...
Aren't you the one who always talks about how the leaves change every day?
You can't take a whole season off!
Your passion for tea is part of what I love about you!
I don't want you to put that on hold!

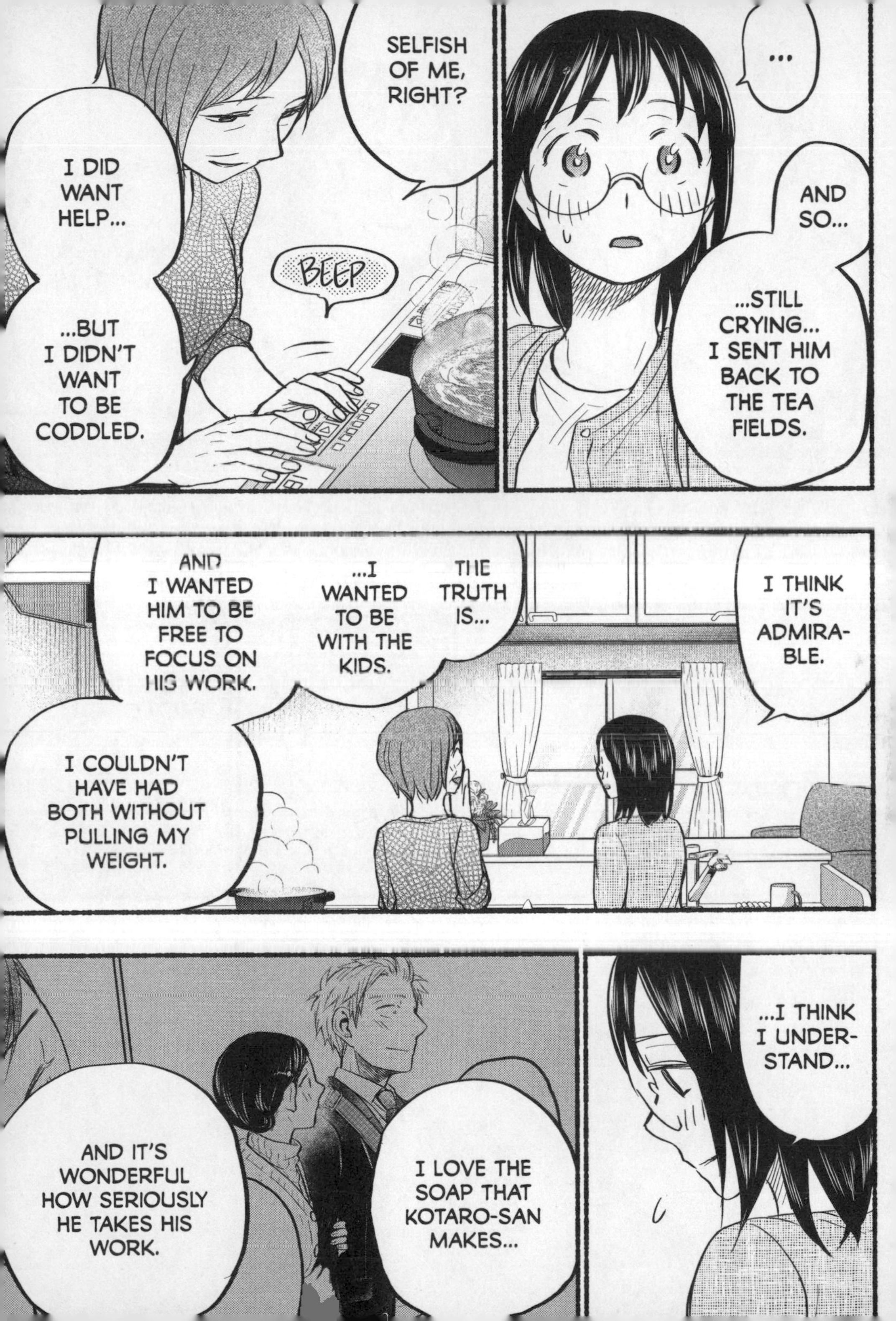
...
AND SO...
...STILL CRYING... I SENT HIM BACK TO THE TEA FIELDS.
SELFISH OF ME, RIGHT?
I DID WANT HELP...
BEEP
...BUT I DIDN'T WANT TO BE CODDLED.
I THINK IT'S ADMIRA-BLE.
THE TRUTH IS...
...I WANTED TO BE WITH THE KIDS.
AND I WANTED HIM TO BE FREE TO FOCUS ON HIS WORK.
I COULDN'T HAVE HAD BOTH WITHOUT PULLING MY WEIGHT.
...I THINK I UNDER-STAND...
I LOVE THE SOAP THAT KOTARO-SAN MAKES...
AND IT'S WONDERFUL HOW SERIOUSLY HE TAKES HIS WORK.

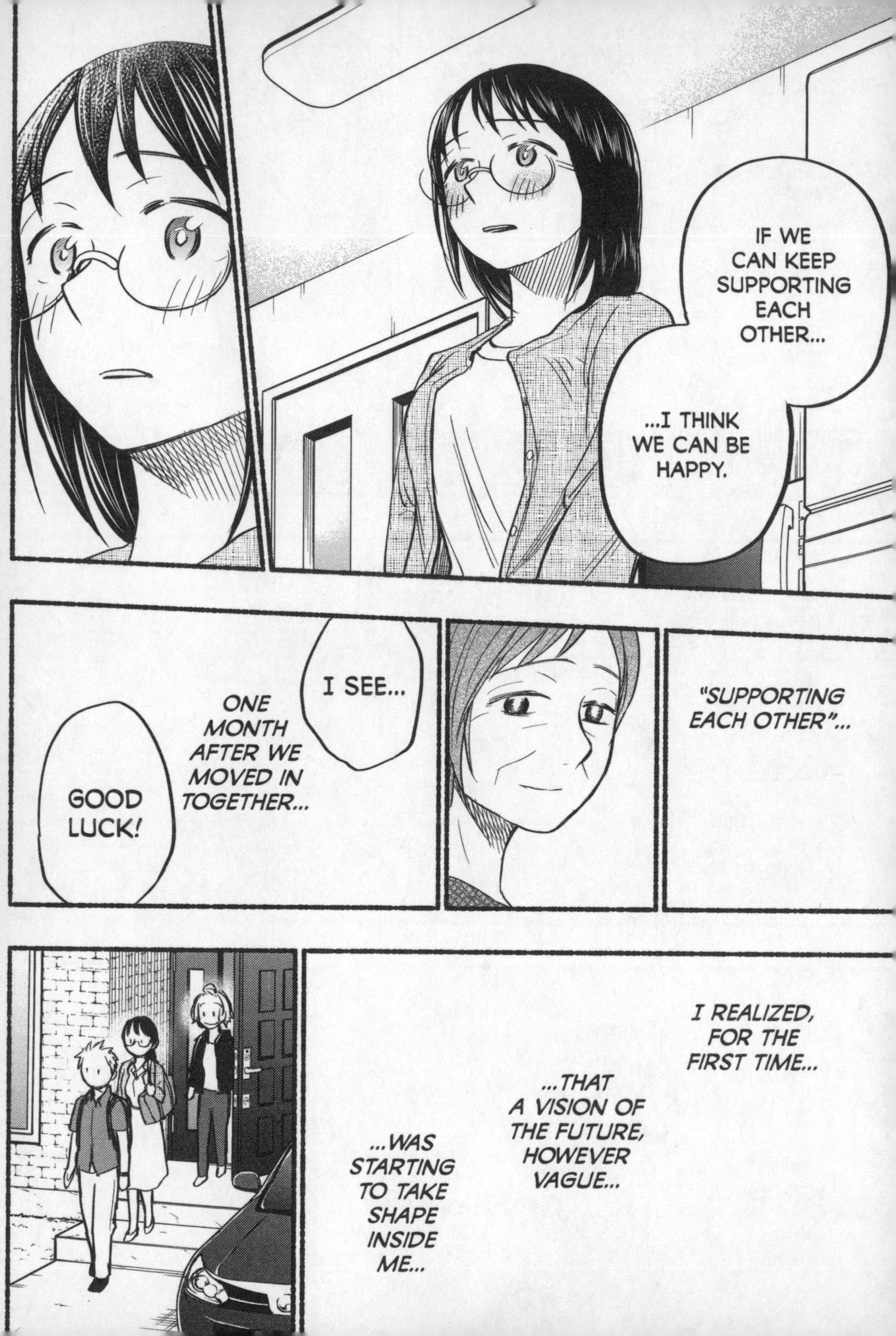
IF WE CAN KEEP SUPPORTING EACH OTHER...
...I THINK WE CAN BE HAPPY.
"SUPPORTING EACH OTHER"...
I SEE...
ONE MONTH AFTER WE MOVED IN TOGETHER...
GOOD LUCK!
I REALIZED, FOR THE FIRST TIME...
...THAT A VISION OF THE FUTURE, HOWEVER VAGUE...
...WAS STARTING TO TAKE SHAPE INSIDE ME...

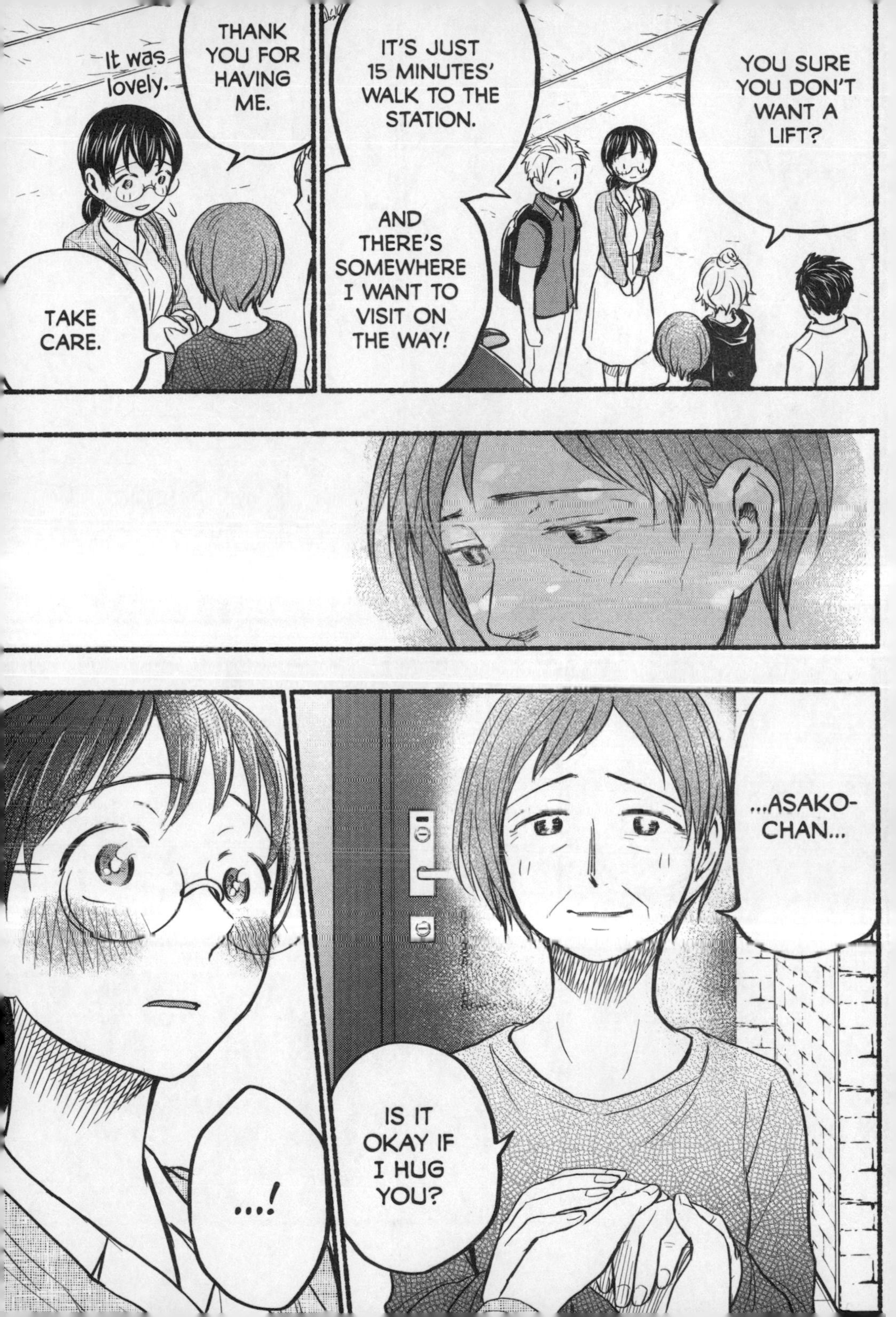
YOU SURE YOU DON'T WANT A LIFT?
IT'S JUST 15 MINUTES' WALK TO THE STATION.
AND THERE'S SOMEWHERE I WANT TO VISIT ON THE WAY!
THANK YOU FOR HAVING ME.
It was lovely.
TAKE CARE.
...ASAKO-CHAN...
IS IT OKAY IF I HUG YOU?
...!

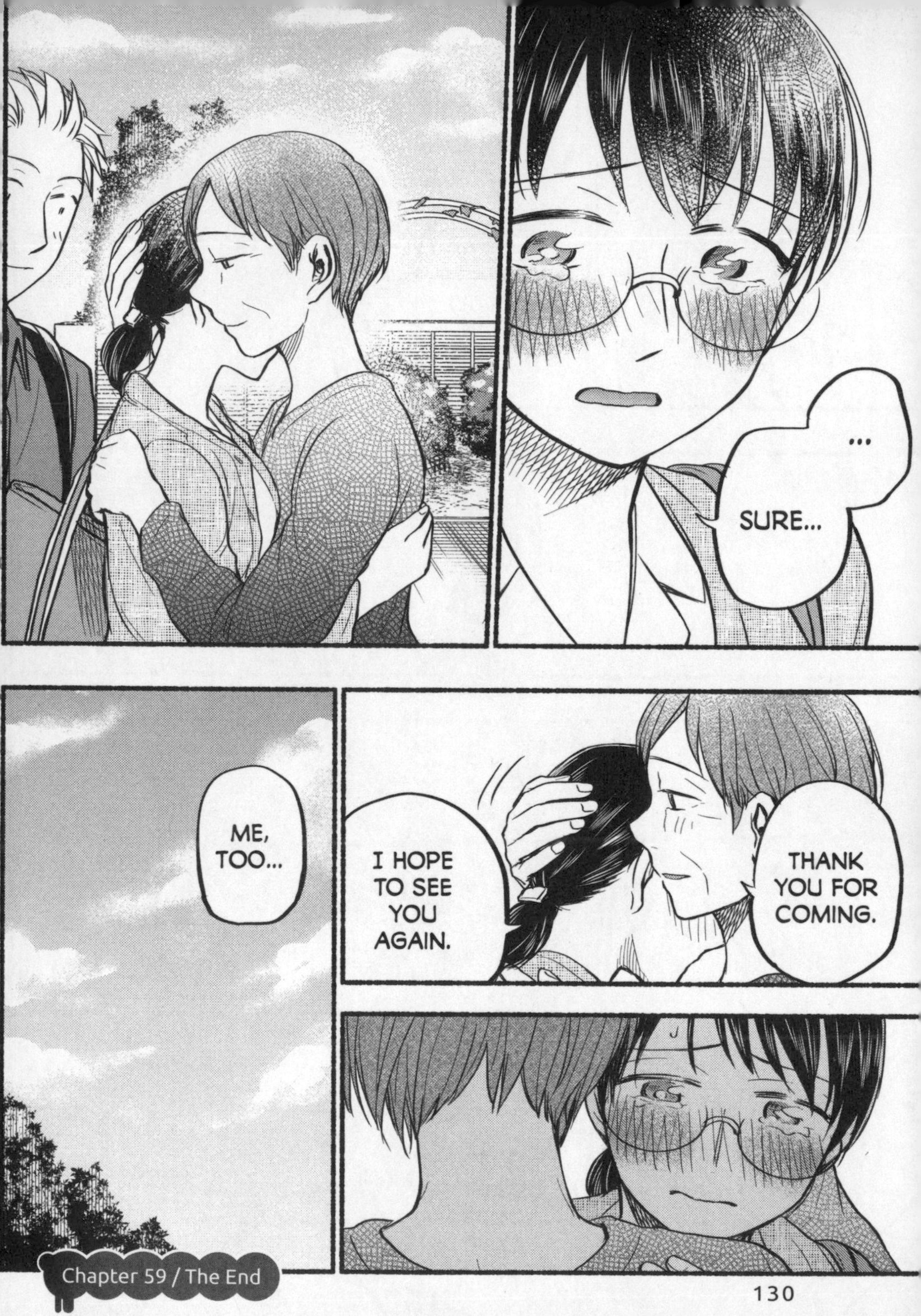
...
SURE...
THANK YOU FOR COMING.
I HOPE TO SEE YOU AGAIN.
ME, TOO...
Chapter 59 / The End

chapter 60
The Road Home

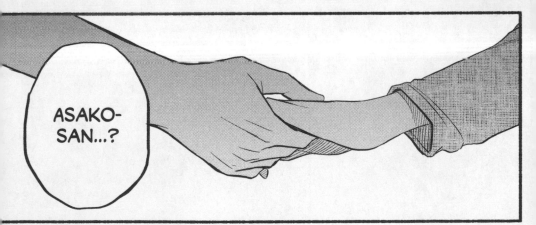

ASAKO-SAN...?

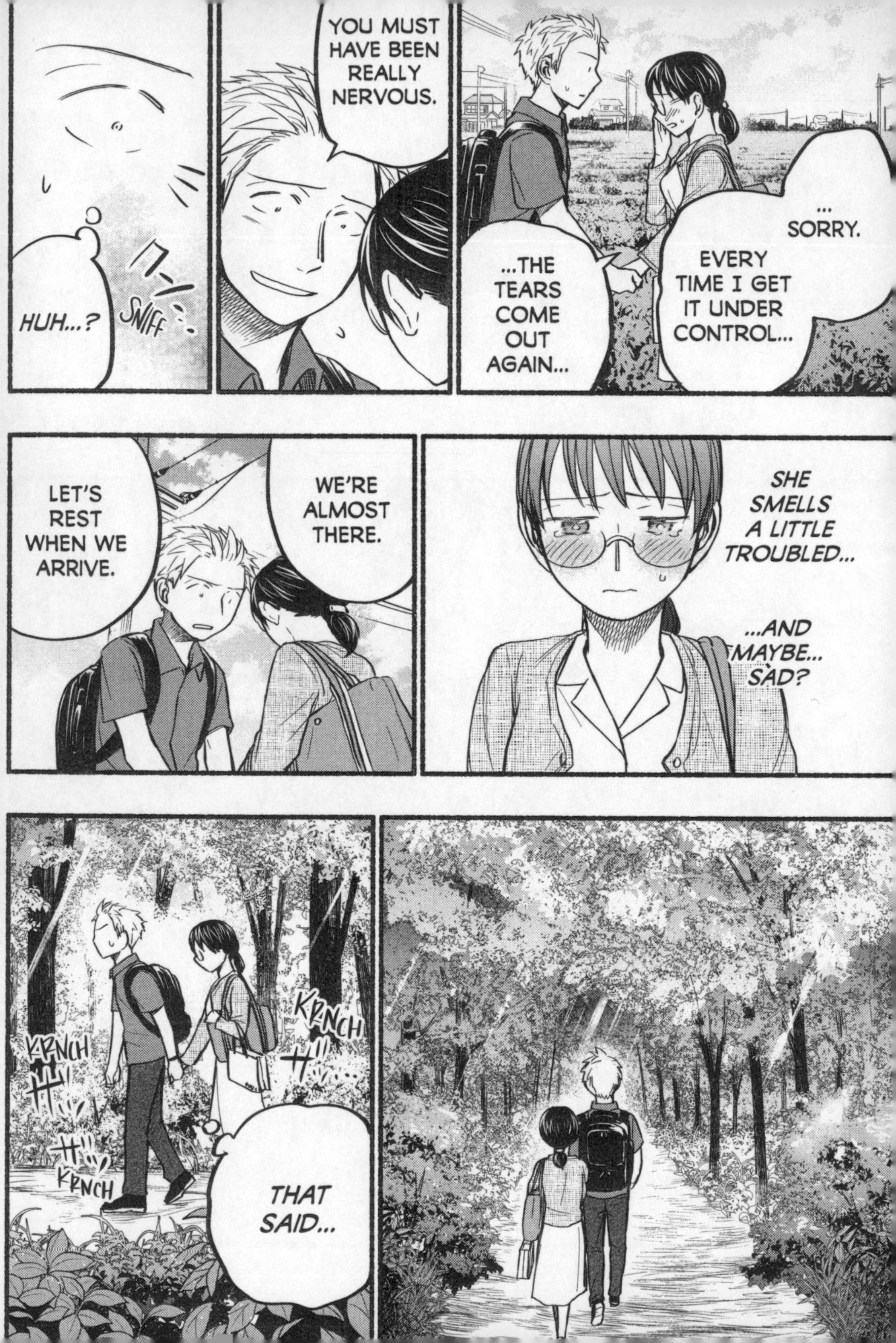
... SORRY.
EVERY TIME I GET IT UNDER CONTROL...
...THE TEARS COME OUT AGAIN...
YOU MUST HAVE BEEN REALLY NERVOUS.
SNIFF
HUH...?
SHE SMELLS A LITTLE TROUBLED...
...AND MAYBE... SAD?
WE'RE ALMOST THERE.
LET'S REST WHEN WE ARRIVE.
KRNCH
KRNCH
KRNCH
THAT SAID...

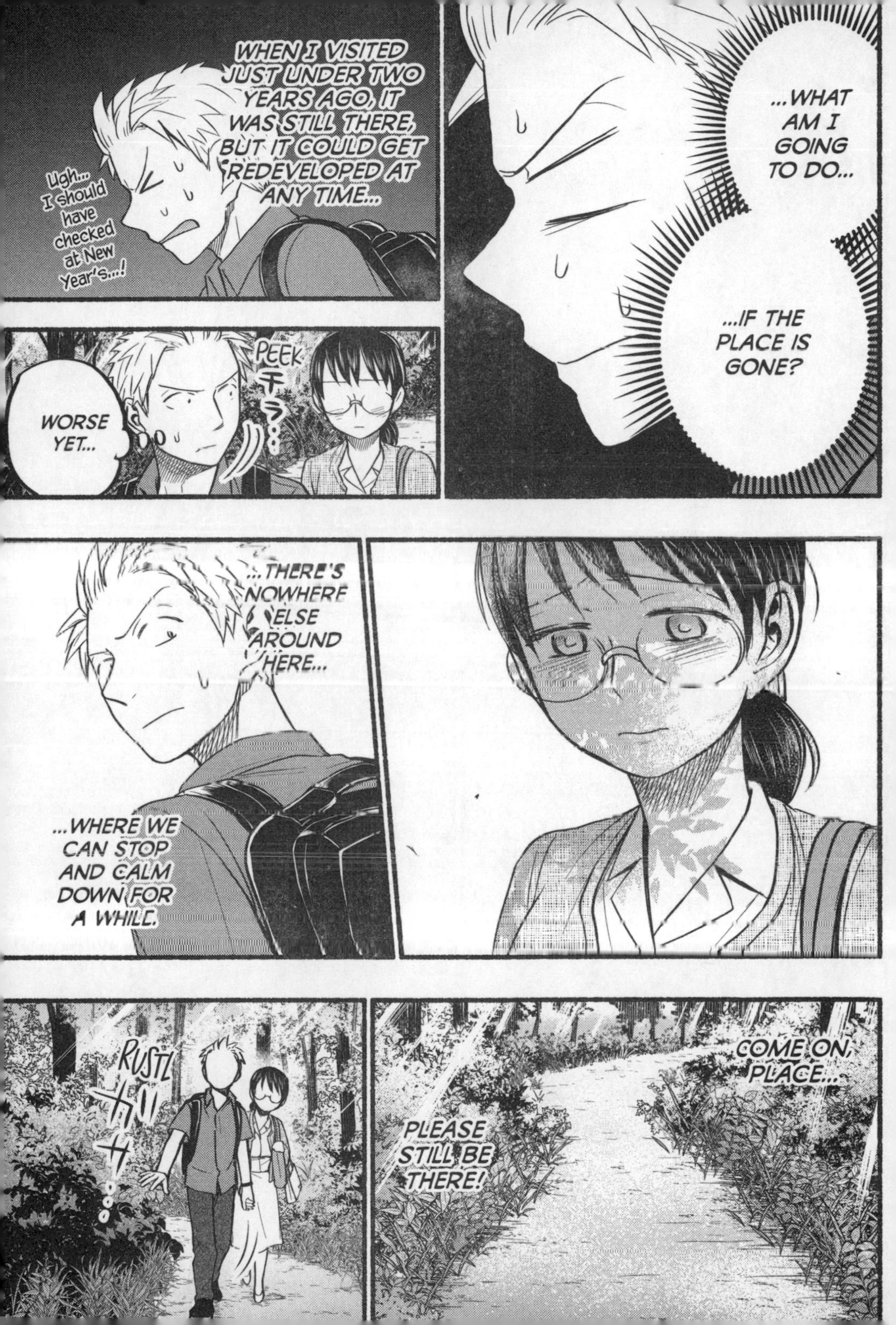
...WHAT AM I GOING TO DO...
...IF THE PLACE IS GONE?
WHEN I VISITED JUST UNDER TWO YEARS AGO, IT WAS STILL THERE, BUT IT COULD GET REDEVELOPED AT ANY TIME...
Ugh... I should have checked at New Year's...!
PEEK
チラ...
WORSE YET...
...THERE'S NOWHERE ELSE AROUND HERE...
...WHERE WE CAN STOP AND CALM DOWN FOR A WHILE.
COME ON, PLACE...
PLEASE STILL BE THERE!
RUSTL

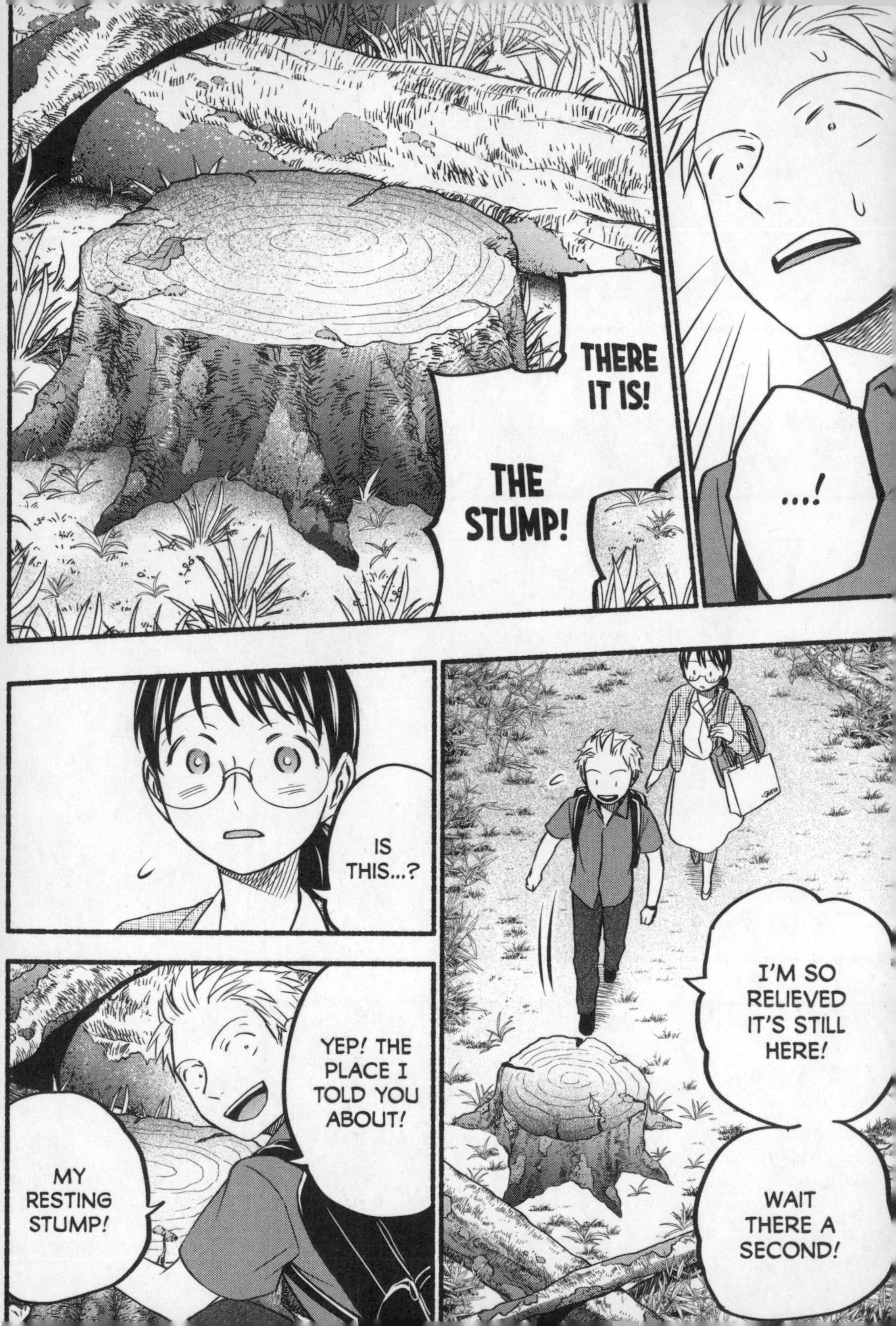
...!
THERE IT IS!
THE STUMP!
I'M SO RELIEVED IT'S STILL HERE!
WAIT THERE A SECOND!
IS THIS...?
YEP! THE PLACE I TOLD YOU ABOUT!
MY RESTING STUMP!

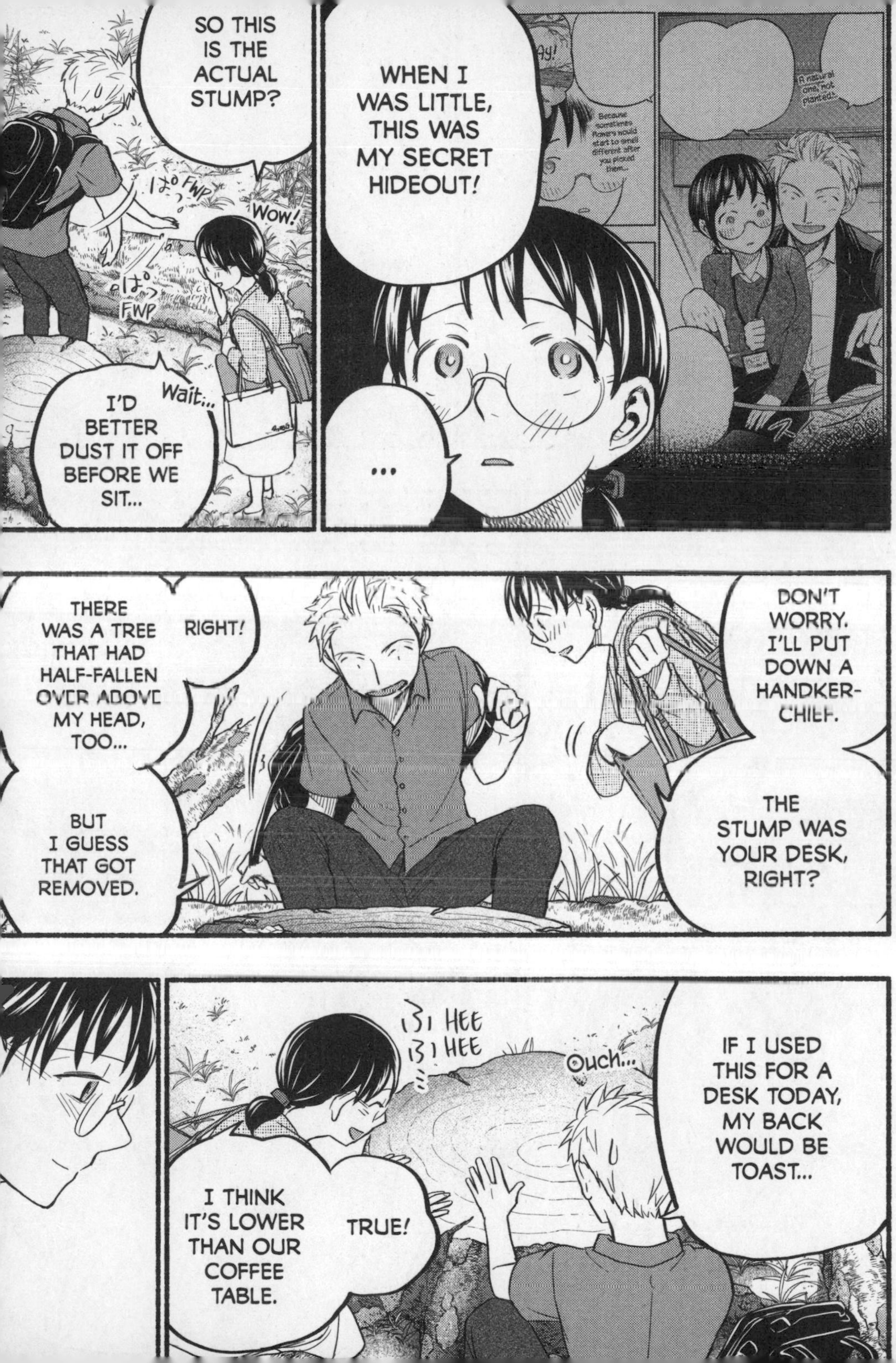
A natural one, not planted!...
Ay!
Because sometimes flowers would start to smell different after you picked them...
WHEN I WAS LITTLE, THIS WAS MY SECRET HIDEOUT!
...
SO THIS IS THE ACTUAL STUMP?
ぱっ FWP
Wow!
ぱっ FWP
Wait...
I'D BETTER DUST IT OFF BEFORE WE SIT...
DON'T WORRY. I'LL PUT DOWN A HANDKER-CHIEF.
THE STUMP WAS YOUR DESK, RIGHT?
RIGHT!
THERE WAS A TREE THAT HAD HALF-FALLEN OVER ABOVE MY HEAD, TOO...
BUT I GUESS THAT GOT REMOVED.
IF I USED THIS FOR A DESK TODAY, MY BACK WOULD BE TOAST...
Ouch...
ふ HEE ふ HEE
TRUE!
I THINK IT'S LOWER THAN OUR COFFEE TABLE.

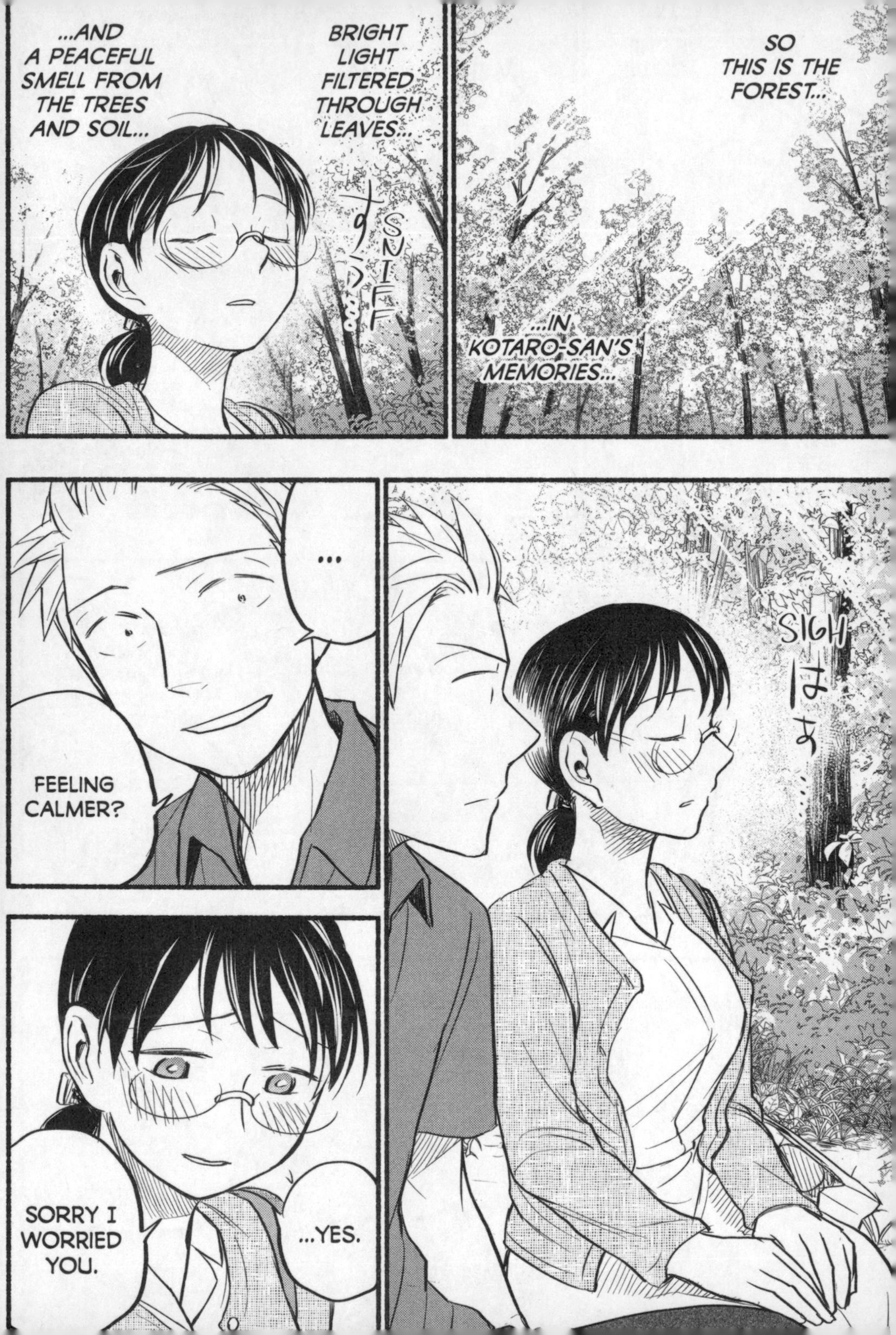
SO THIS IS THE FOREST...
...IN KOTARO-SAN'S MEMORIES...
BRIGHT LIGHT FILTERED THROUGH LEAVES...
...AND A PEACEFUL SMELL FROM THE TREES AND SOIL...
SNIFF
SIGH
...
FEELING CALMER?
...YES.
SORRY I WORRIED YOU.

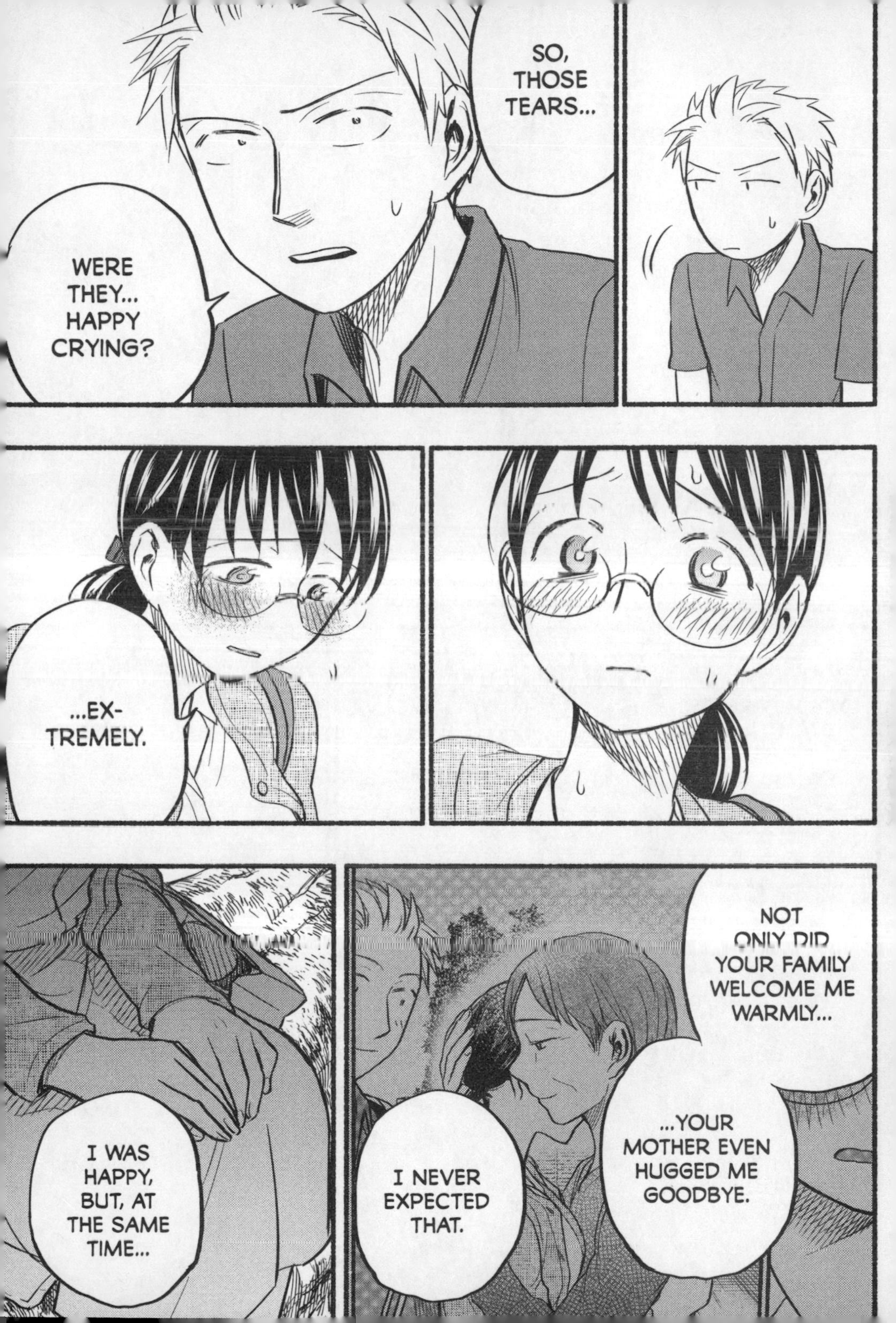
SO, THOSE TEARS...
WERE THEY... HAPPY CRYING?
...EX-TREMELY.
NOT ONLY DID YOUR FAMILY WELCOME ME WARMLY...
...YOUR MOTHER EVEN HUGGED ME GOODBYE.
I NEVER EXPECTED THAT.
I WAS HAPPY, BUT, AT THE SAME TIME...

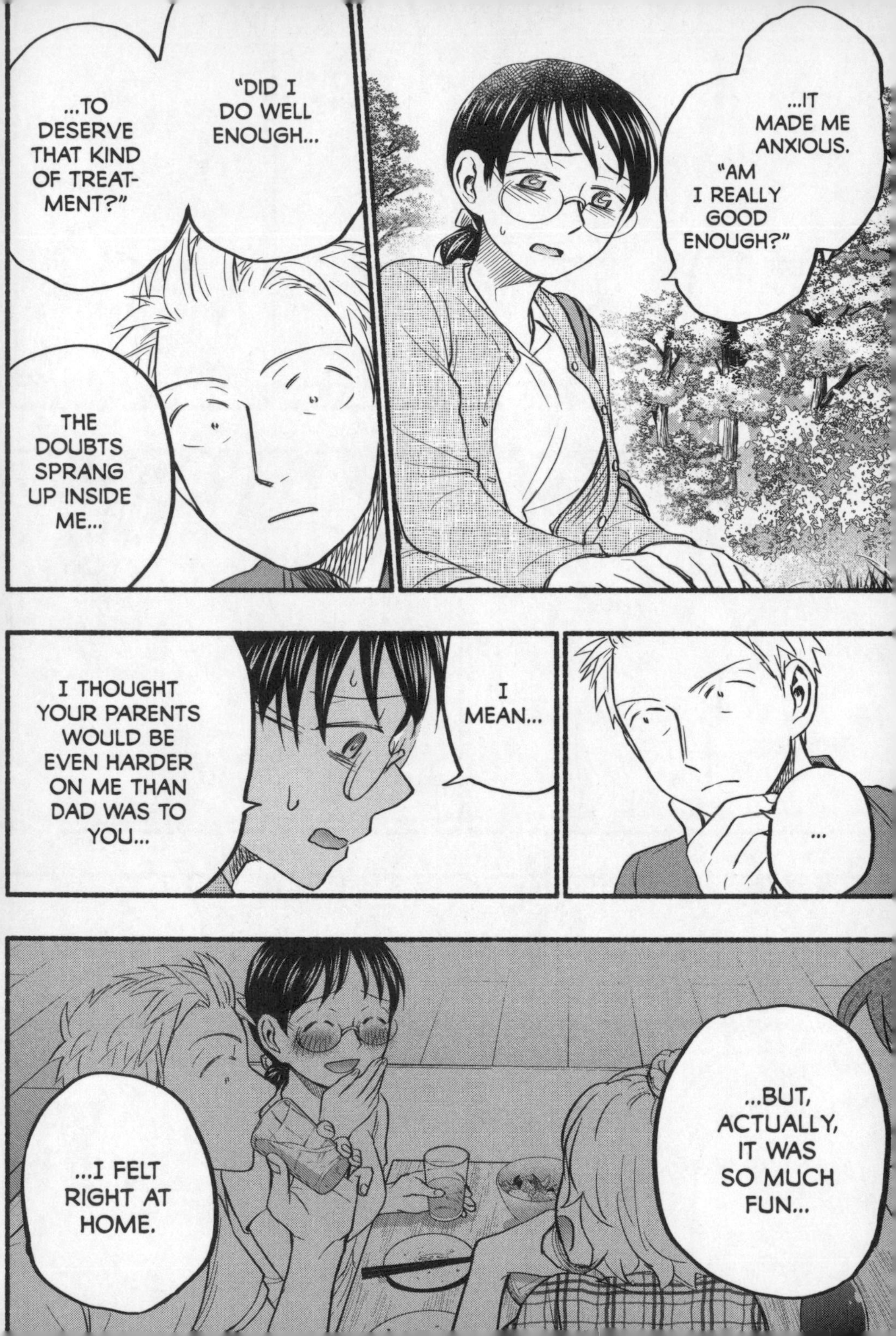
...IT MADE ME ANXIOUS. "AM I REALLY GOOD ENOUGH?"
"DID I DO WELL ENOUGH...
...TO DESERVE THAT KIND OF TREAT-MENT?"
THE DOUBTS SPRANG UP INSIDE ME...
...
I MEAN...
I THOUGHT YOUR PARENTS WOULD BE EVEN HARDER ON ME THAN DAD WAS TO YOU...
...BUT, ACTUALLY, IT WAS SO MUCH FUN...
...I FELT RIGHT AT HOME.

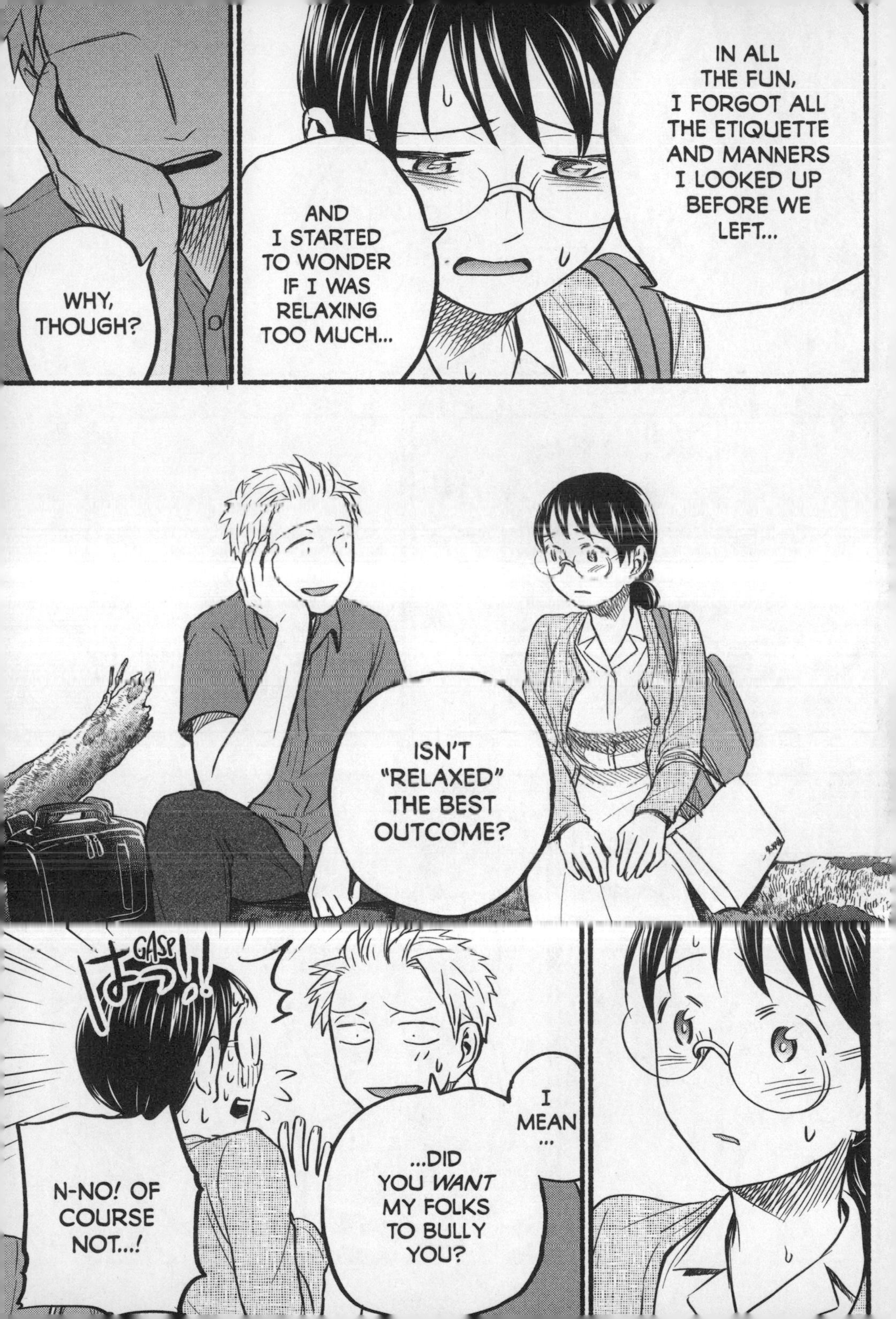
IN ALL THE FUN, I FORGOT ALL THE ETIQUETTE AND MANNERS I LOOKED UP BEFORE WE LEFT...
AND I STARTED TO WONDER IF I WAS RELAXING TOO MUCH...
WHY, THOUGH?
ISN'T "RELAXED" THE BEST OUTCOME?
I MEAN...
...DID YOU *WANT* MY FOLKS TO BULLY YOU?
GASP!
N-NO! OF COURSE NOT...!

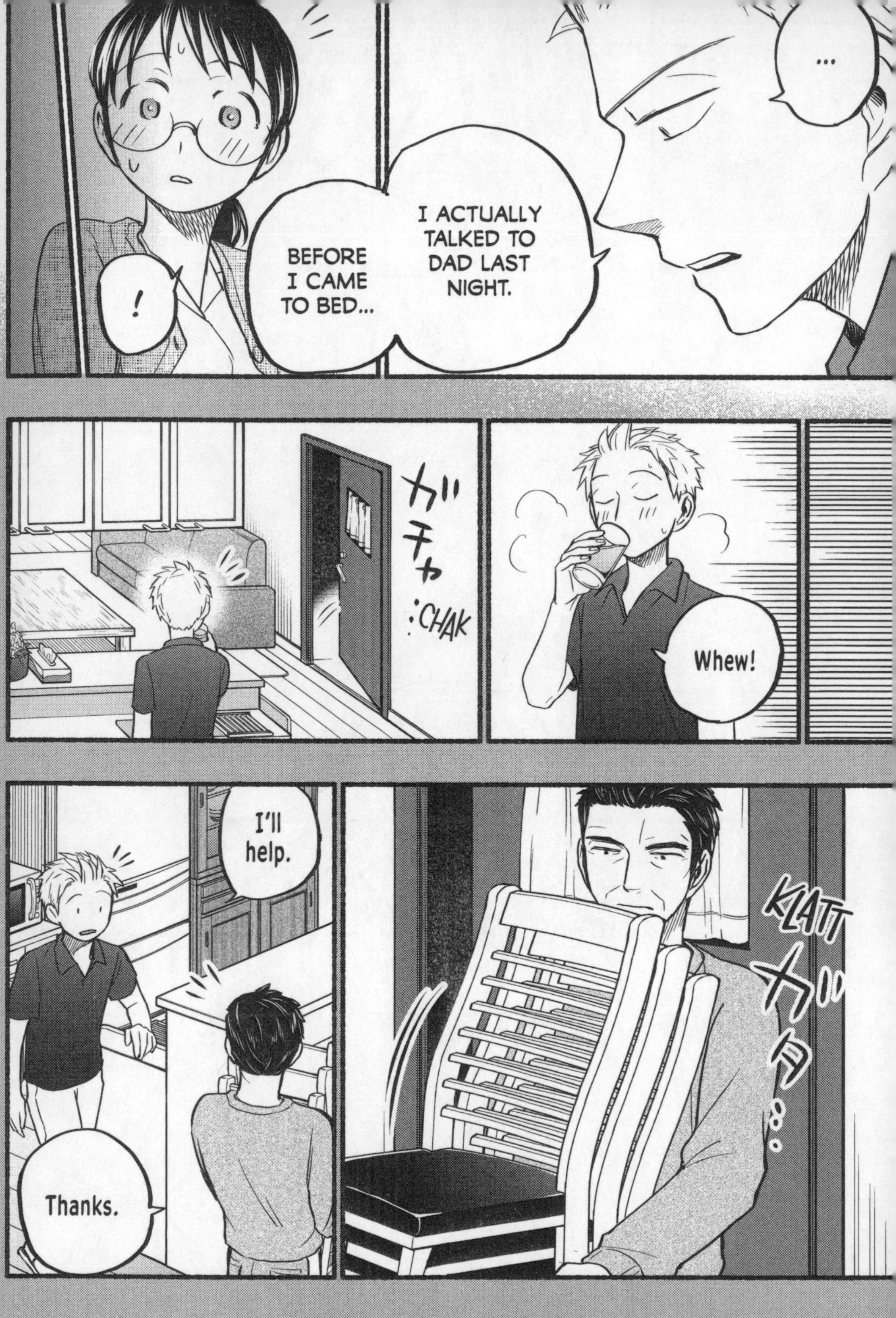
...
I ACTUALLY TALKED TO DAD LAST NIGHT.
BEFORE I CAME TO BED...
!
Whew!
ガチャ
CHAK
KLATT
ガタ...
I'll help.
Thanks.

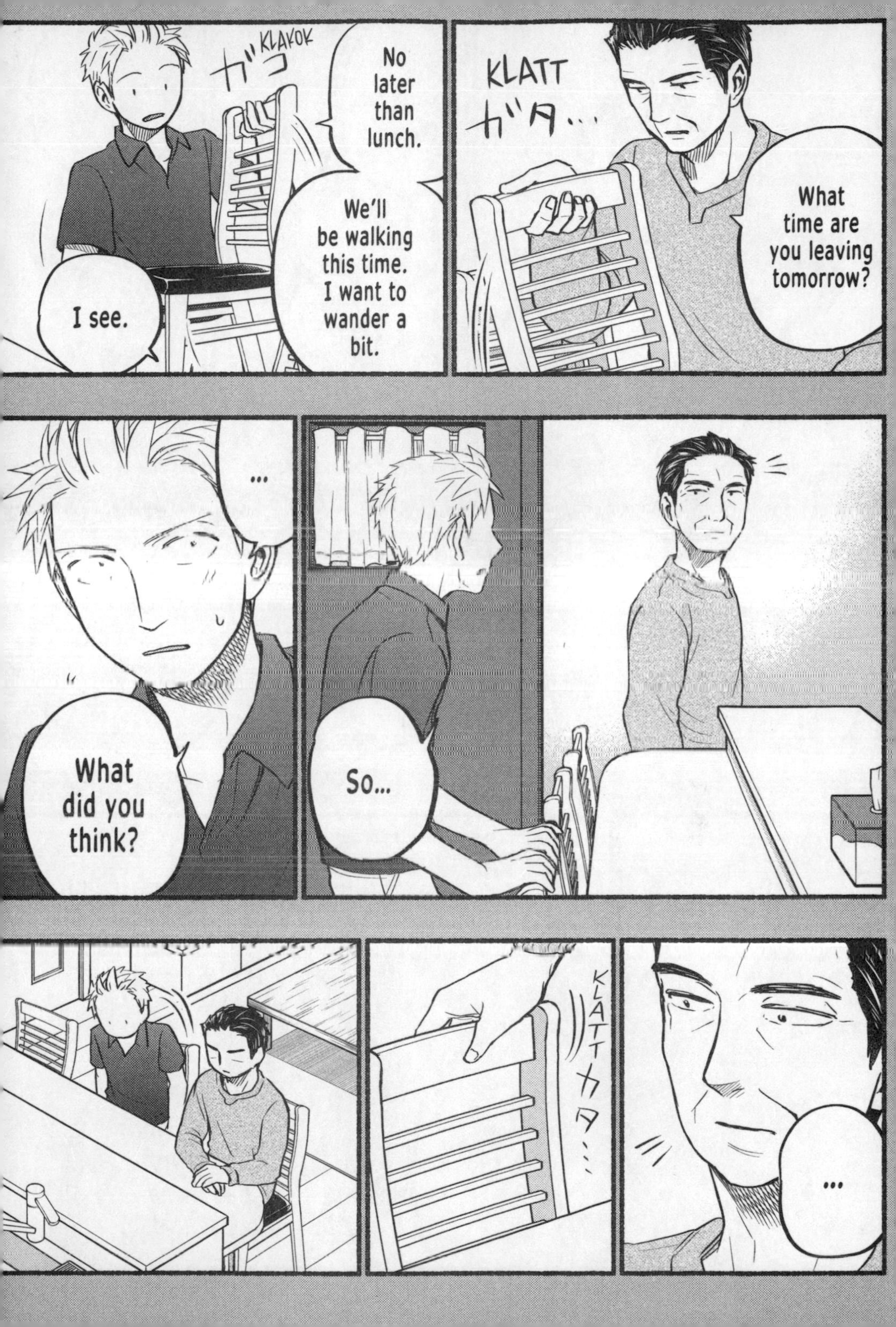
KLATT
ガタ…
What time are you leaving tomorrow?
ガコ
KLAKOK
No later than lunch.
We'll be walking this time. I want to wander a bit.
I see.
So...
...
What did you think?
...
KLATT
カタ…

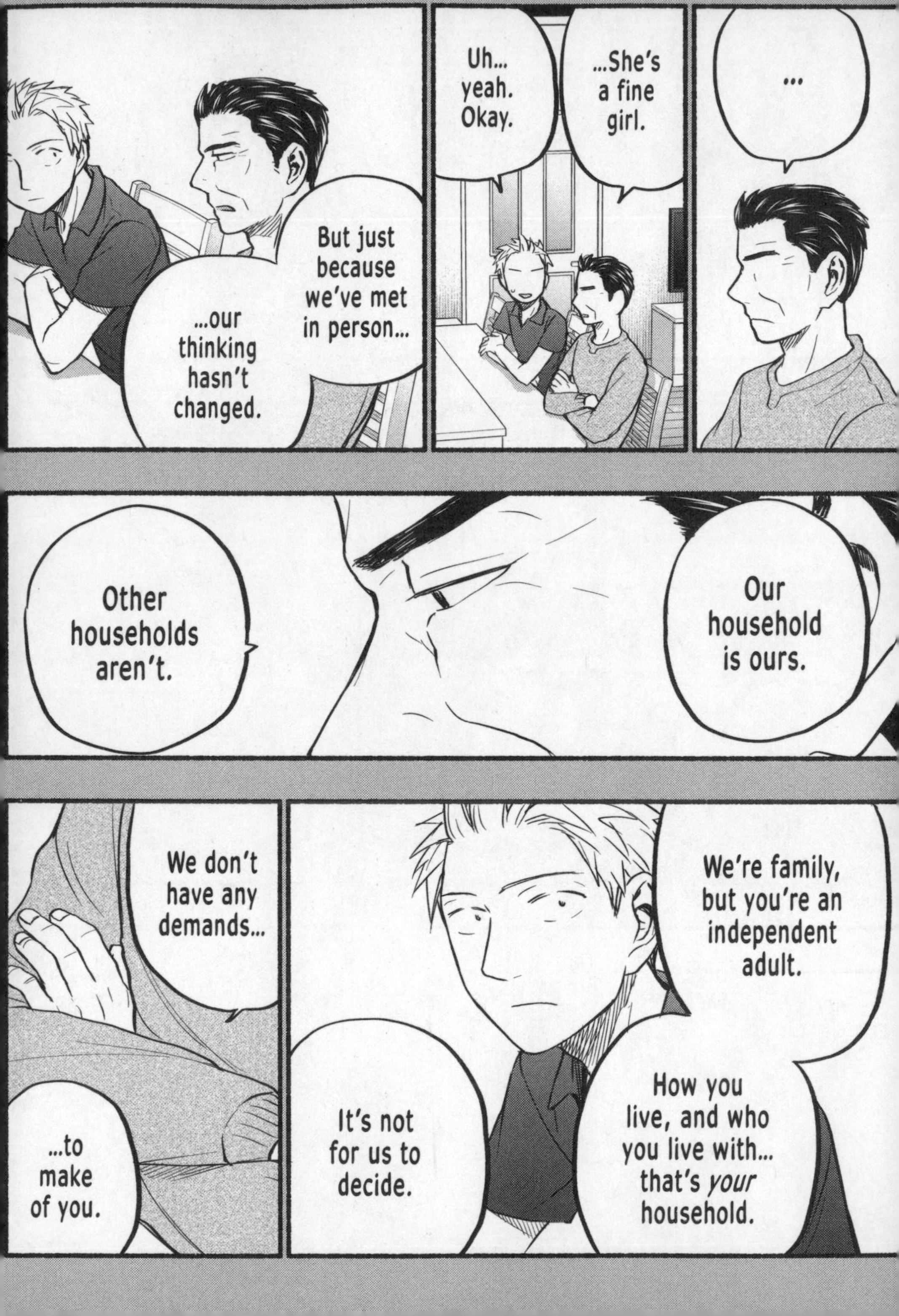
...
...She's a fine girl.
Uh... yeah. Okay.
But just because we've met in person...
...our thinking hasn't changed.
Our household is ours.
Other households aren't.
We're family, but you're an independent adult.
How you live, and who you live with... that's *your* household.
It's not for us to decide.
We don't have any demands...
...to make of you.

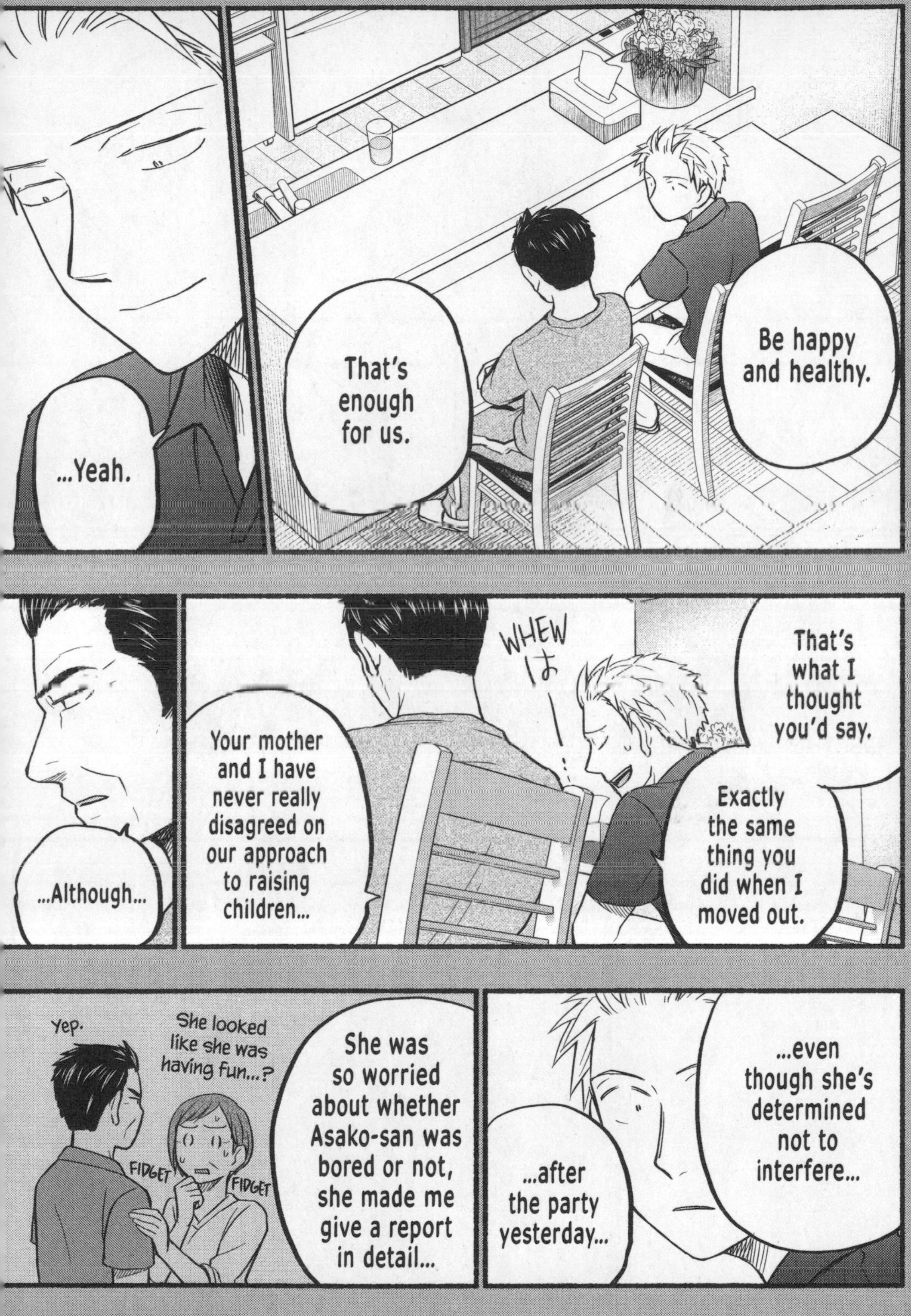

Be happy and healthy.
That's enough for us.
...Yeah.
That's what I thought you'd say.
Exactly the same thing you did when I moved out.
WHEW
は
Your mother and I have never really disagreed on our approach to raising children...
...Although...
...even though she's determined not to interfere...
...after the party yesterday...
She was so worried about whether Asako-san was bored or not, she made me give a report in detail...
She looked like she was having fun...?
Yep.
FIDGET
FIDGET

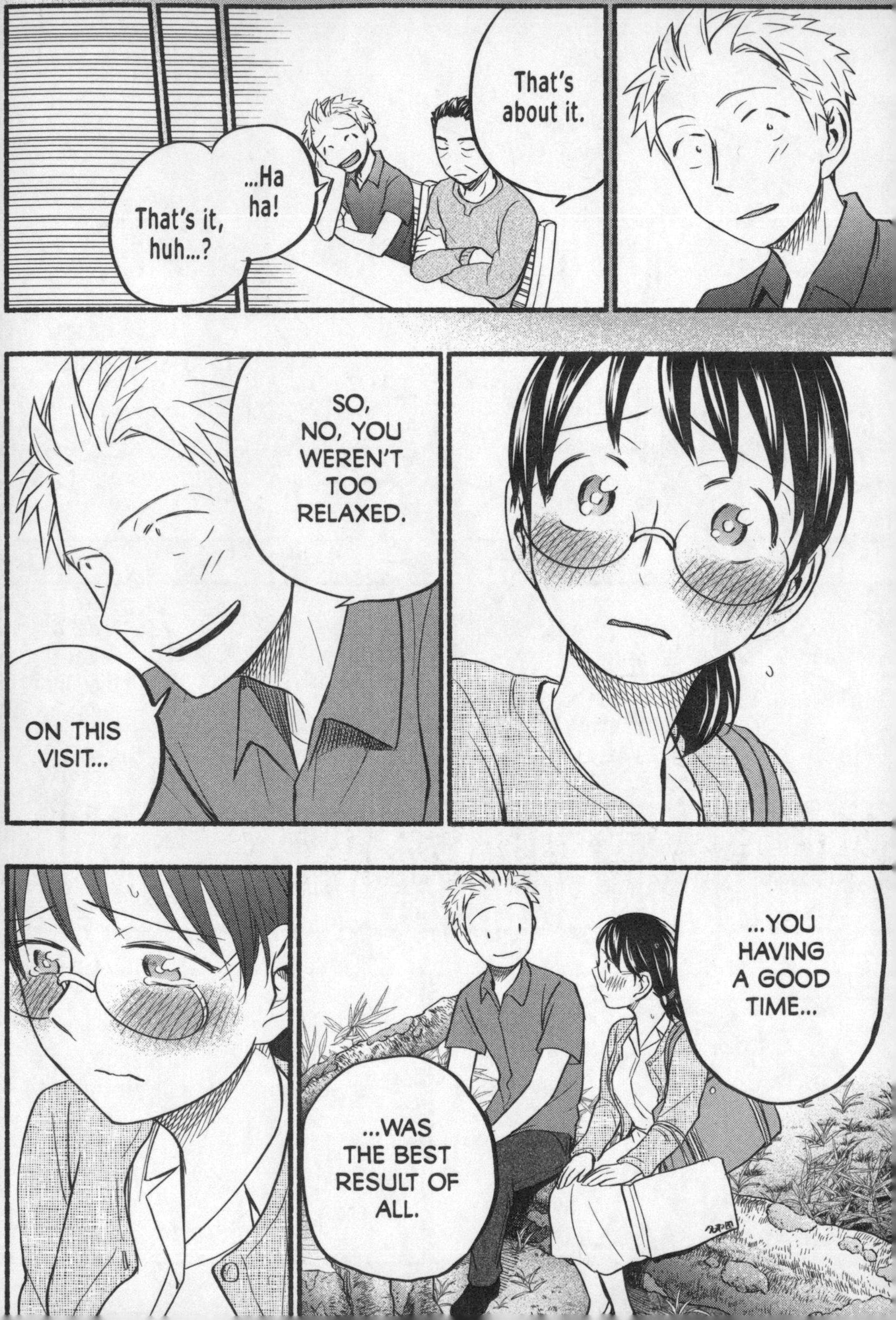
That's about it.
...Ha ha!
That's it, huh...?
SO, NO, YOU WEREN'T TOO RELAXED.
ON THIS VISIT...
...YOU HAVING A GOOD TIME...
...WAS THE BEST RESULT OF ALL.

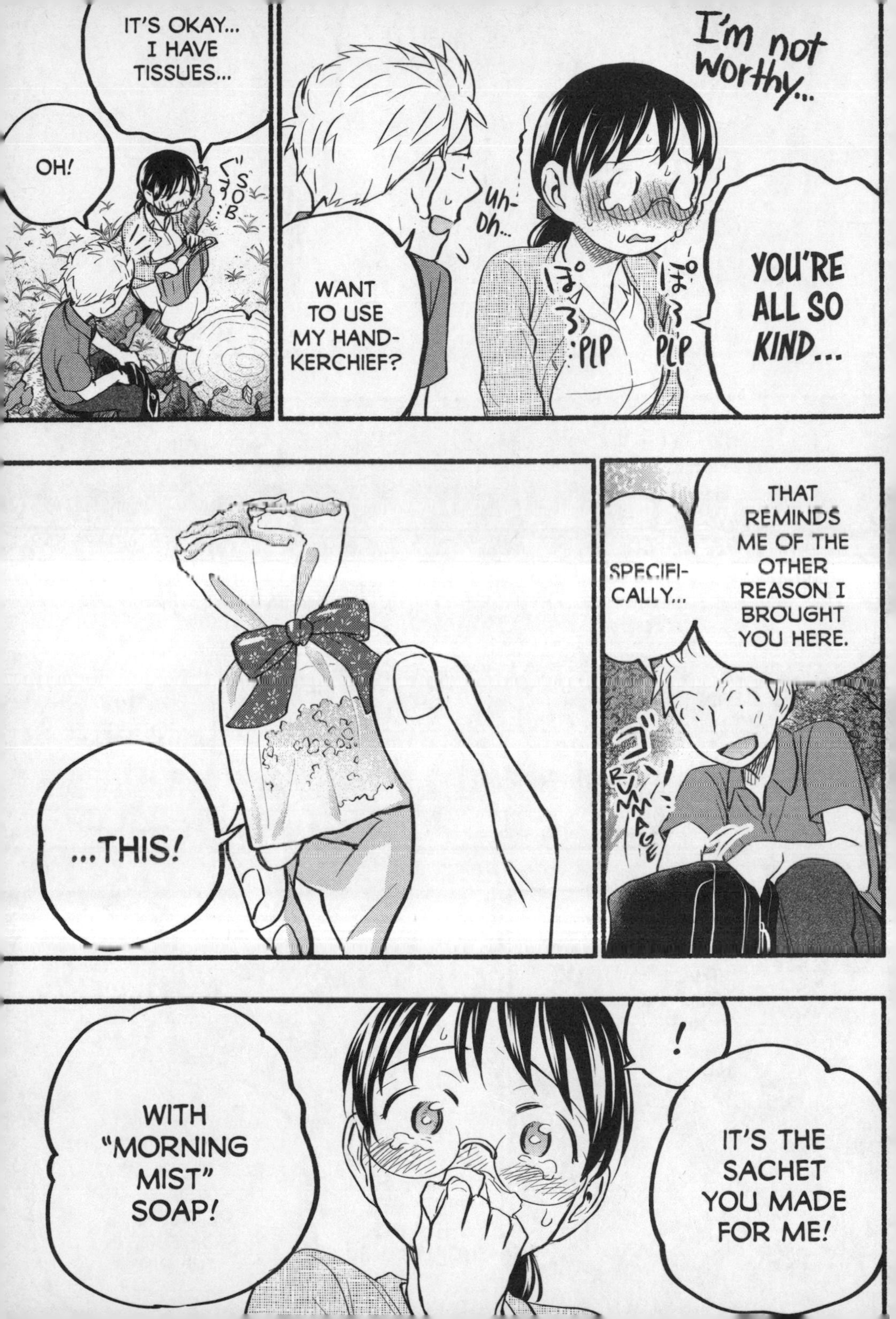
I'm not worthy...
YOU'RE ALL SO KIND...
ぽろ PLP
ぽろ PLP
Uh-Oh...
WANT TO USE MY HAND-KERCHIEF?
IT'S OKAY... I HAVE TISSUES...
SOB
OH!
THAT REMINDS ME OF THE OTHER REASON I BROUGHT YOU HERE.
SPECIFI-CALLY...
RUMMAGE
...THIS!
!
IT'S THE SACHET YOU MADE FOR ME!
WITH "MORNING MIST" SOAP!

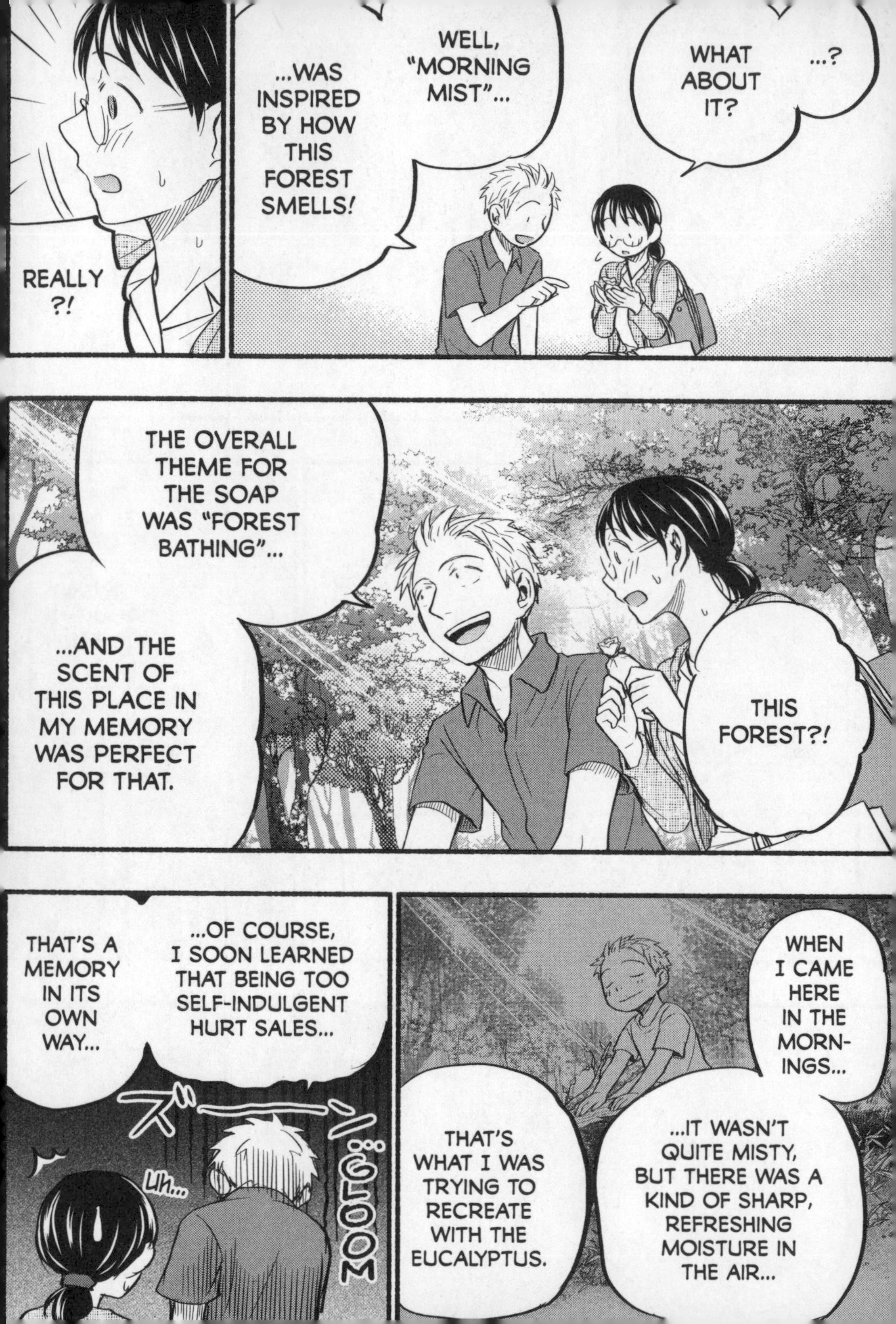
WHAT ABOUT IT?
...?
WELL, "MORNING MIST"...
...WAS INSPIRED BY HOW THIS FOREST SMELLS!
REALLY?!
THIS FOREST?!
THE OVERALL THEME FOR THE SOAP WAS "FOREST BATHING"...
...AND THE SCENT OF THIS PLACE IN MY MEMORY WAS PERFECT FOR THAT.
WHEN I CAME HERE IN THE MORN-INGS...
...IT WASN'T QUITE MISTY, BUT THERE WAS A KIND OF SHARP, REFRESHING MOISTURE IN THE AIR...
THAT'S WHAT I WAS TRYING TO RECREATE WITH THE EUCALYPTUS.
...OF COURSE, I SOON LEARNED THAT BEING TOO SELF-INDULGENT HURT SALES...
THAT'S A MEMORY IN ITS OWN WAY...
ズーーーン
GLOOM...
Uh...

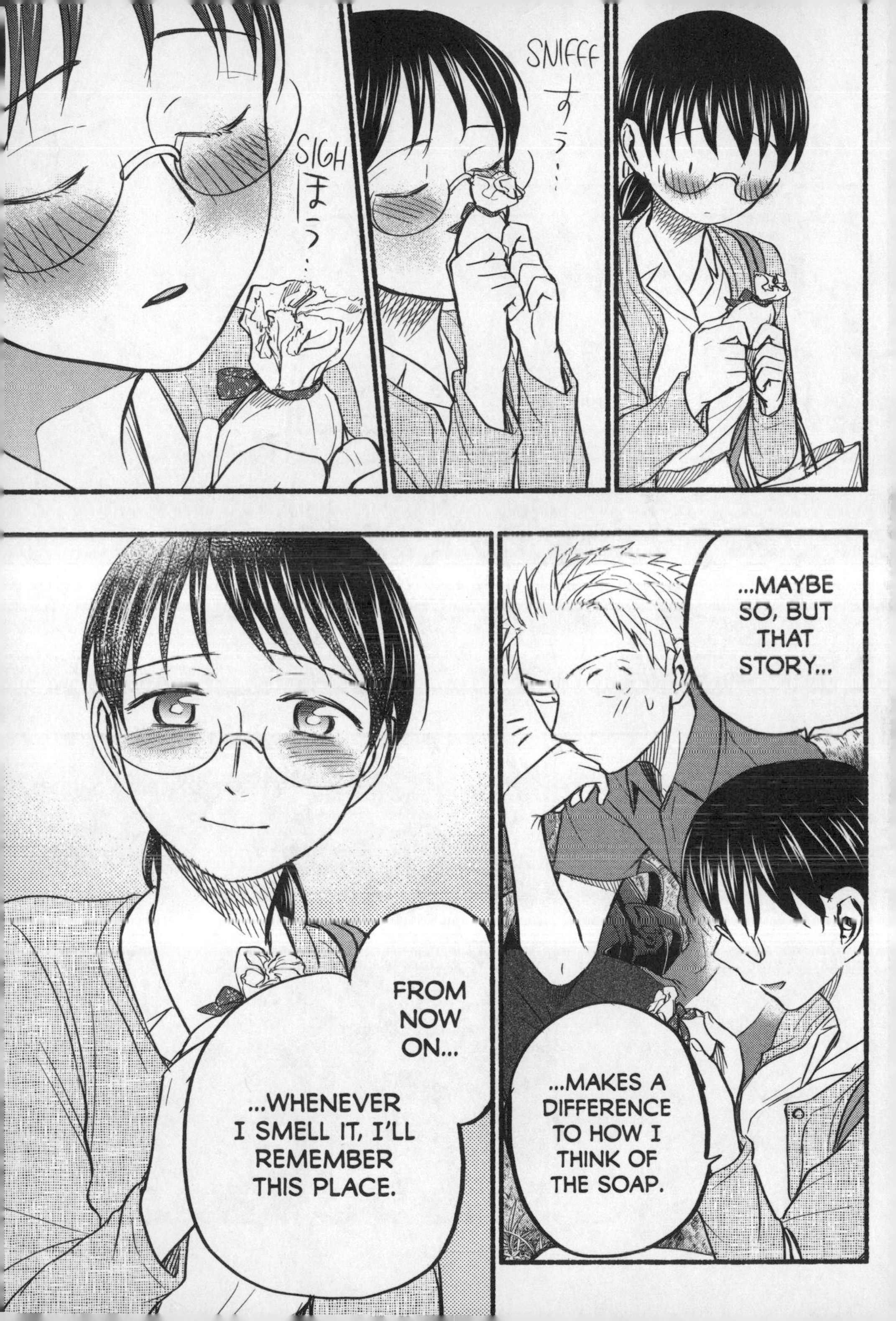
SNIFFF
すう…
SIGH
ほう…
...MAYBE SO, BUT THAT STORY...
...MAKES A DIFFERENCE TO HOW I THINK OF THE SOAP.
FROM NOW ON...
...WHENEVER I SMELL IT, I'LL REMEMBER THIS PLACE.

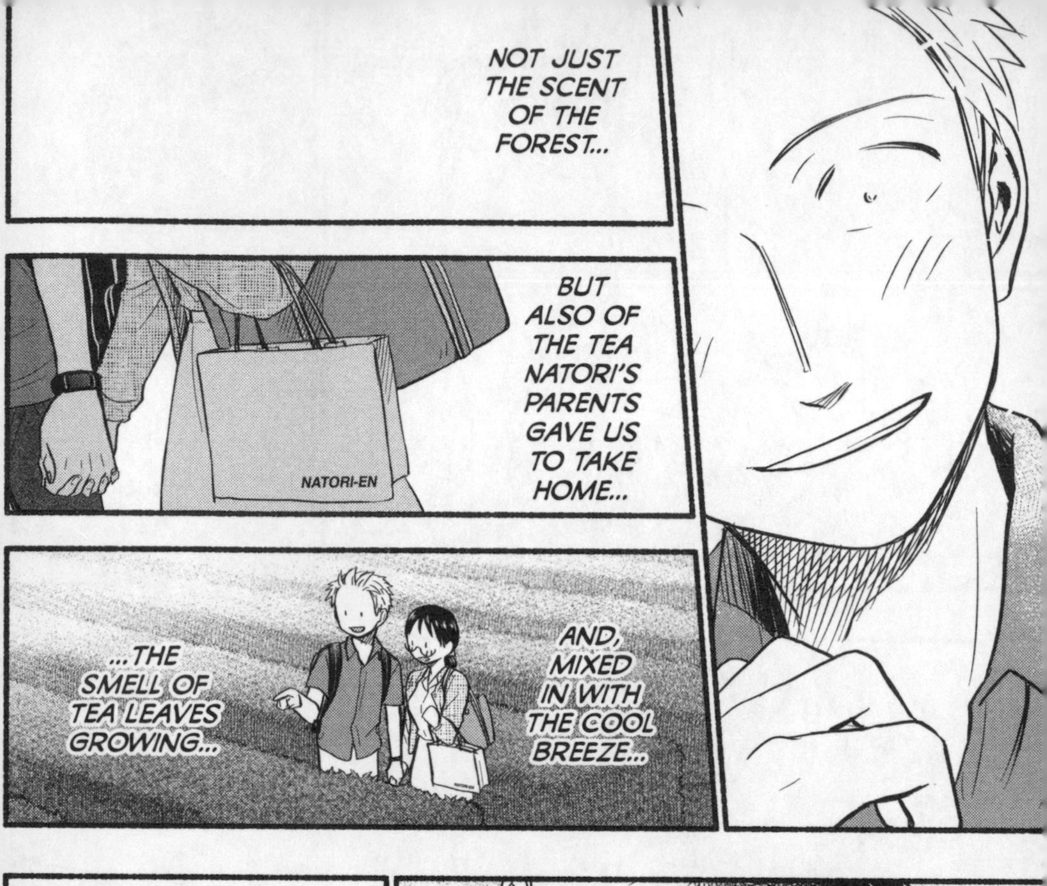
NOT JUST THE SCENT OF THE FOREST...
BUT ALSO OF THE TEA NATORI'S PARENTS GAVE US TO TAKE HOME...
NATORI-EN
AND, MIXED IN WITH THE COOL BREEZE...
...THE SMELL OF TEA LEAVES GROWING...
MY NOSE...
...MAY NOT BE AS GOOD AS KOTARO-SAN'S...
...BUT THE FRAGRANCE OF THE PLACE WHERE HE WAS BORN AND RAISED...
...IS NOW ENGRAVED IN MY MEMORY.

Chapter 60 / The End

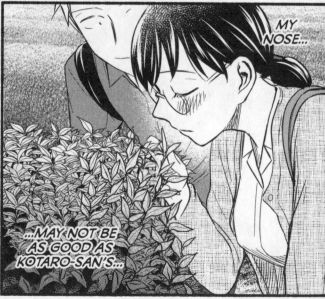

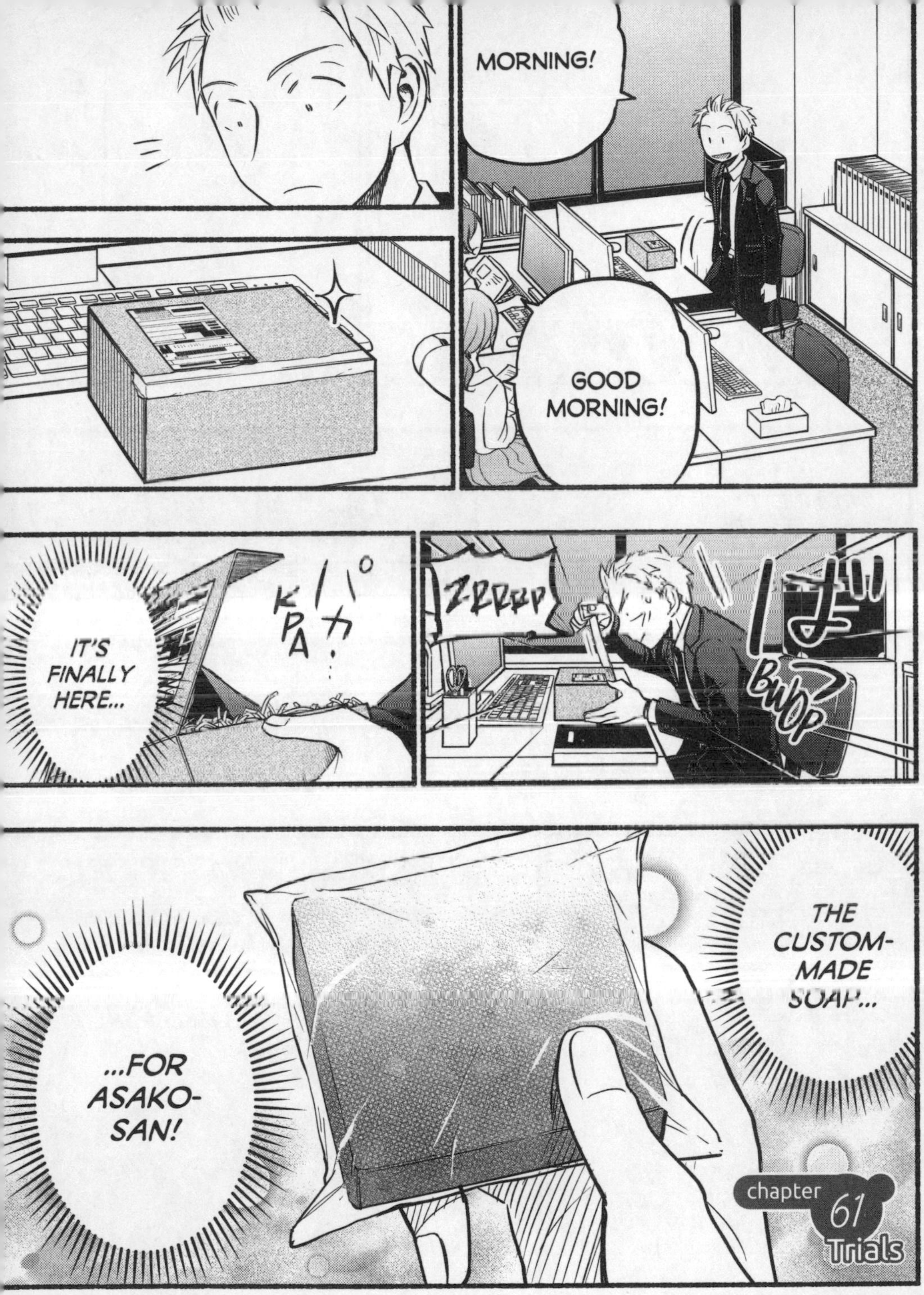
MORNING!
GOOD MORNING!
ZRRRP
BUDOP
IT'S FINALLY HERE...
KPA
THE CUSTOM-MADE SOAP...
...FOR ASAKO-SAN!
chapter 61 Trials

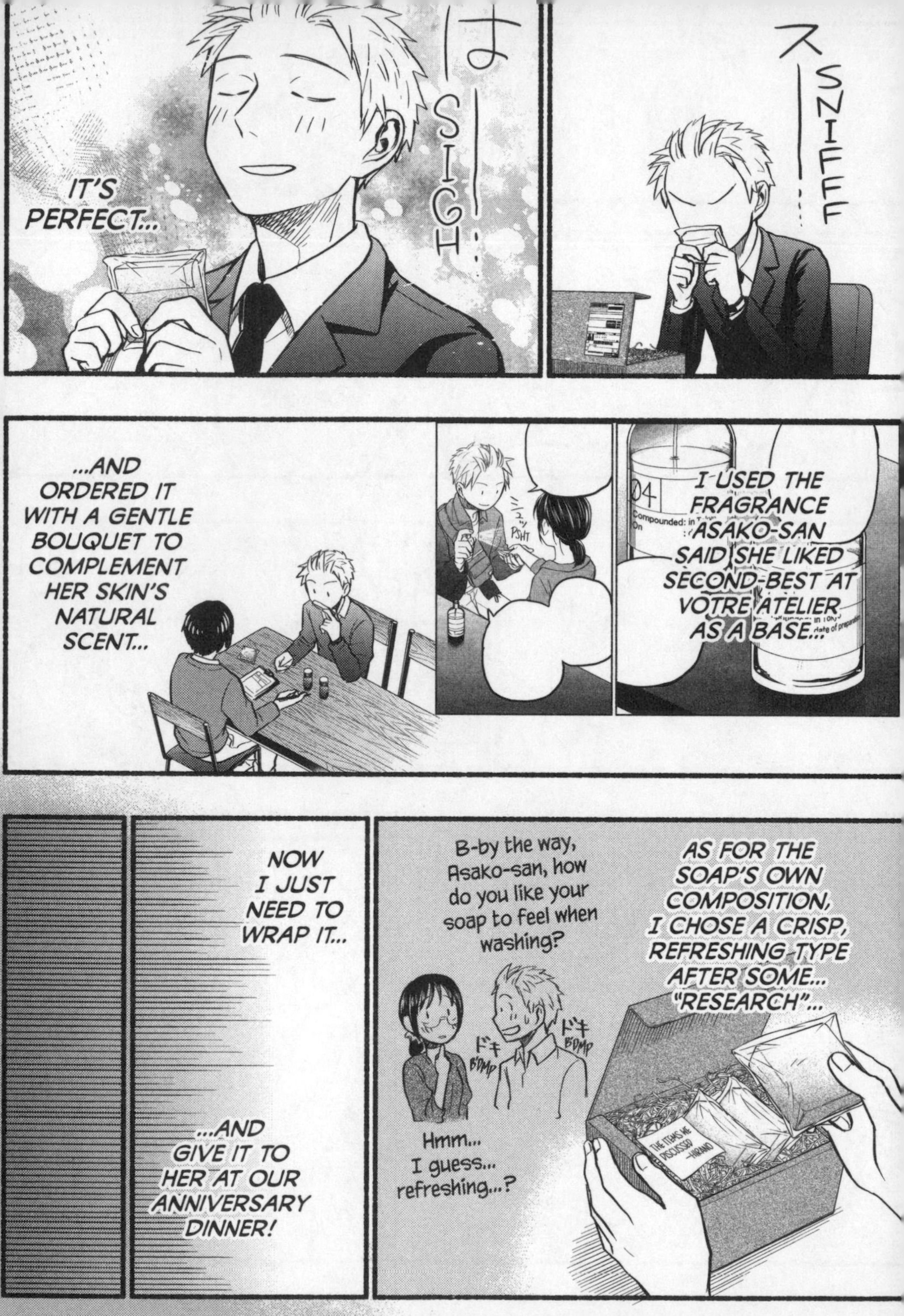
スーー
SNIFFF
はーー
SIGH
IT'S PERFECT...
I USED THE FRAGRANCE ASAKO-SAN SAID SHE LIKED SECOND-BEST AT VOTRE ATELIER AS A BASE...
シュッ
PSHT
...AND ORDERED IT WITH A GENTLE BOUQUET TO COMPLEMENT HER SKIN'S NATURAL SCENT...
AS FOR THE SOAP'S OWN COMPOSITION, I CHOSE A CRISP, REFRESHING TYPE AFTER SOME... "RESEARCH"...
B-by the way, Asako-san, how do you like your soap to feel when washing?
ドキ
BDMP
ドキ
BDMP
Hmm... I guess... refreshing...?
THE ITEMS WE DISCUSSED -HIRANO
NOW I JUST NEED TO WRAP IT...
...AND GIVE IT TO HER AT OUR ANNIVERSARY DINNER!

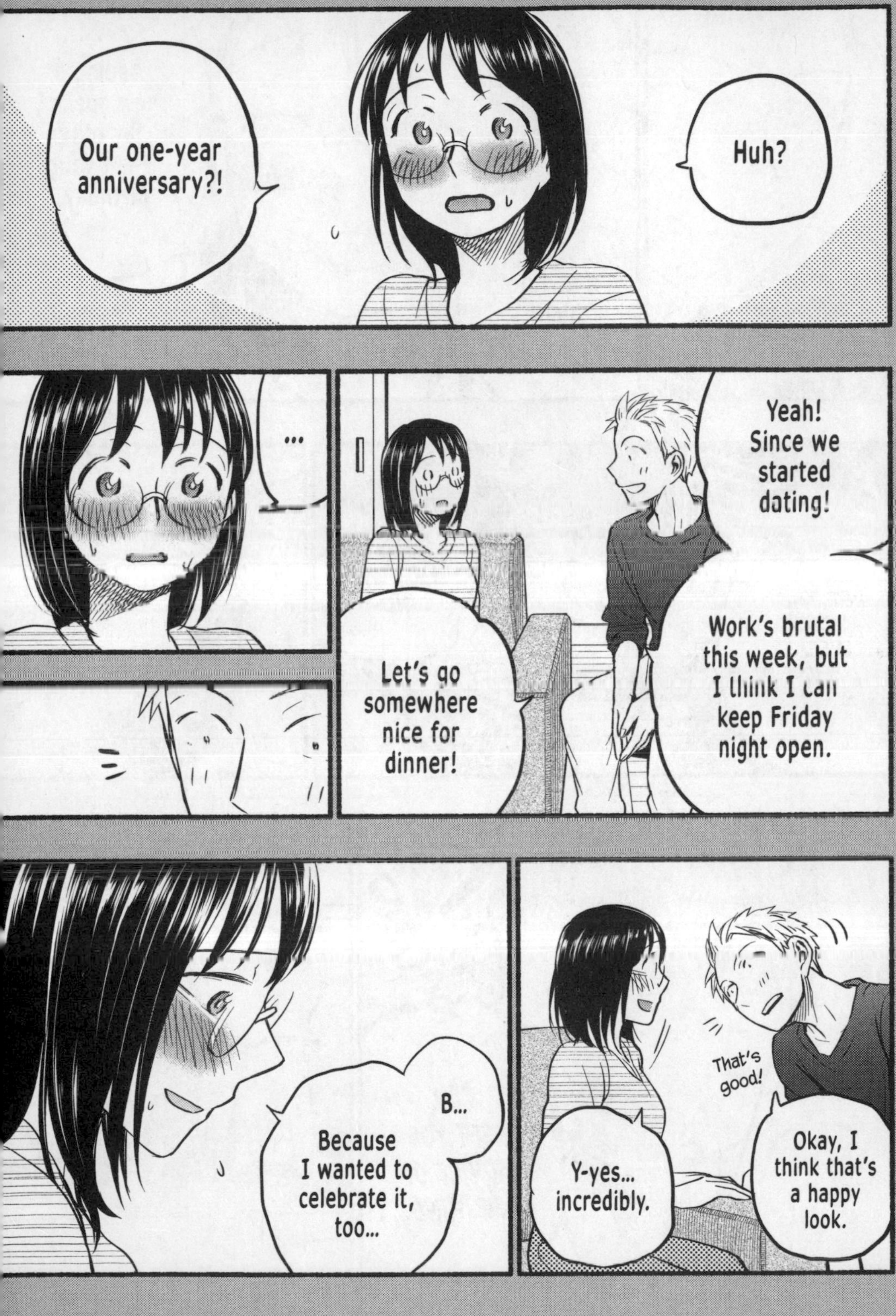
Huh?
Our one-year anniversary?!
Yeah! Since we started dating!
Work's brutal this week, but I think I can keep Friday night open.
Let's go somewhere nice for dinner!
...
That's good!
Okay, I think that's a happy look.
Y-yes... incredibly.
B...
Because I wanted to celebrate it, too...

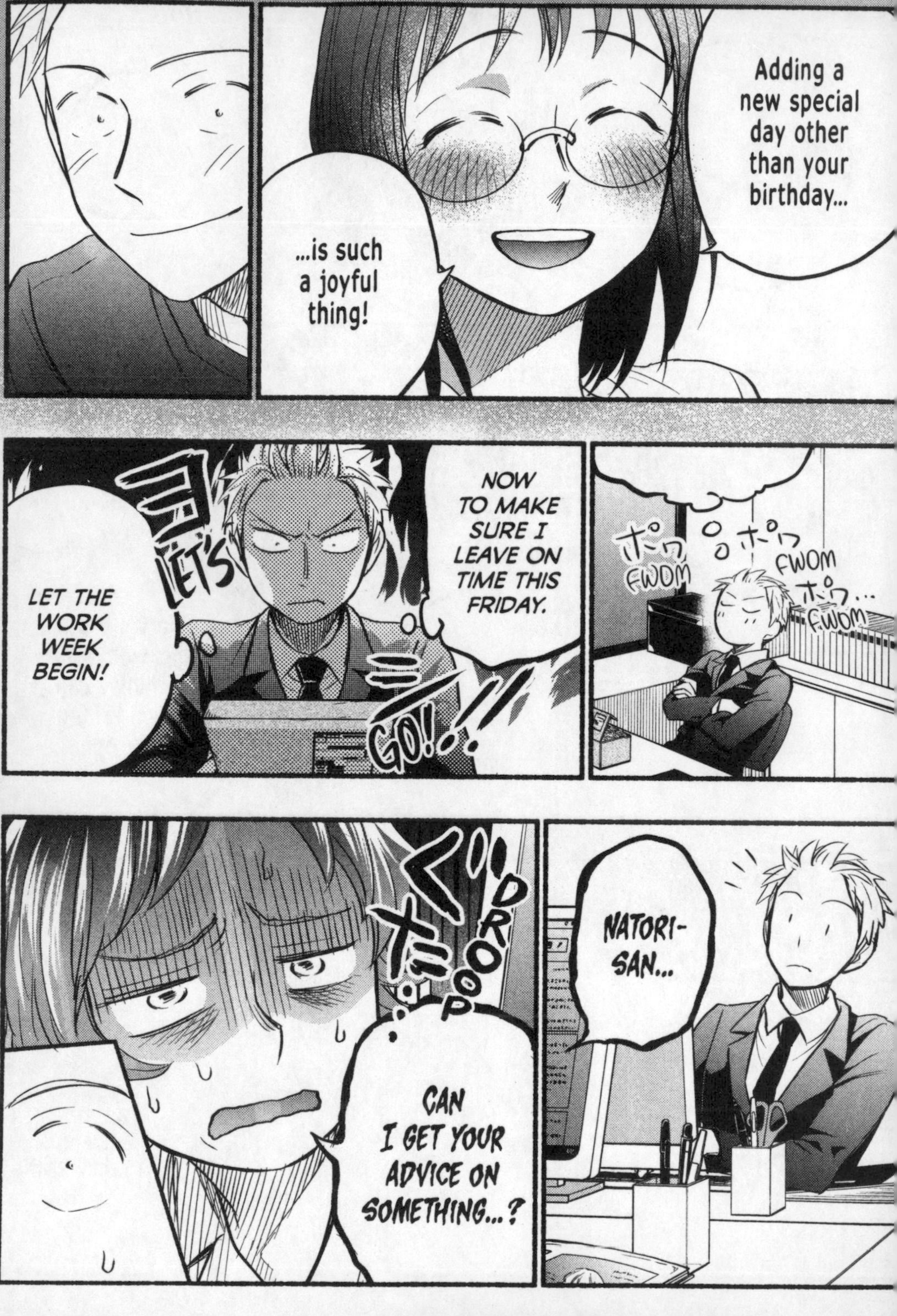
Adding a new special day other than your birthday...
...is such a joyful thing!
FWOM
FWOM
FWOM
NOW TO MAKE SURE I LEAVE ON TIME THIS FRIDAY.
LET THE WORK WEEK BEGIN!
LET'S
GO!!
NATORI-SAN...
CAN I GET YOUR ADVICE ON SOMETHING...?
DROOP

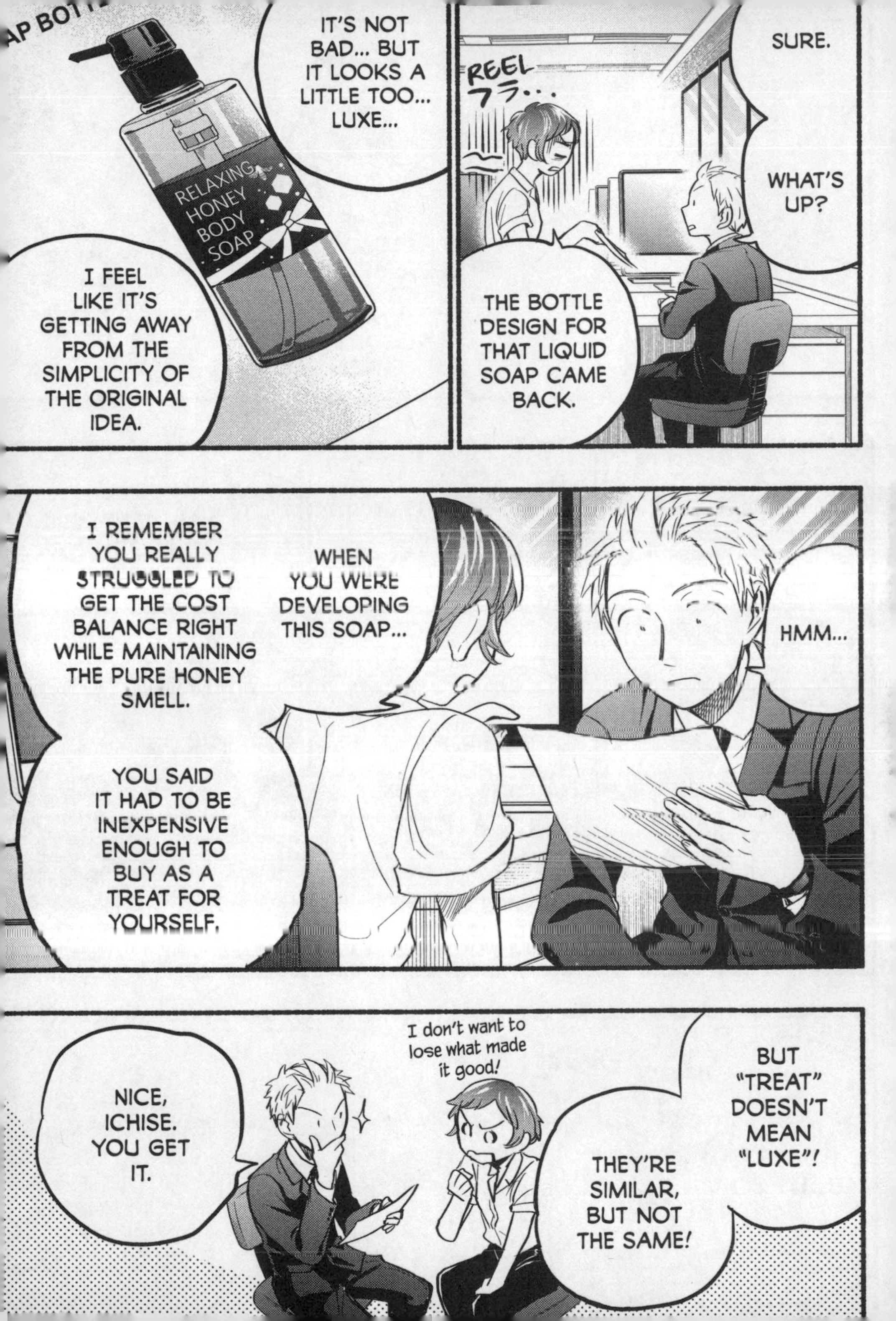
SURE.
WHAT'S UP?
REEL
THE BOTTLE DESIGN FOR THAT LIQUID SOAP CAME BACK.
AP BOTT
IT'S NOT BAD... BUT IT LOOKS A LITTLE TOO... LUXE...
RELAXING HONEY BODY SOAP
I FEEL LIKE IT'S GETTING AWAY FROM THE SIMPLICITY OF THE ORIGINAL IDEA.
HMM...
WHEN YOU WERE DEVELOPING THIS SOAP...
I REMEMBER YOU REALLY STRUGGLED TO GET THE COST BALANCE RIGHT WHILE MAINTAINING THE PURE HONEY SMELL.
YOU SAID IT HAD TO BE INEXPENSIVE ENOUGH TO BUY AS A TREAT FOR YOURSELF.
BUT "TREAT" DOESN'T MEAN "LUXE"!
THEY'RE SIMILAR, BUT NOT THE SAME!
I don't want to lose what made it good!
NICE, ICHISE. YOU GET IT.

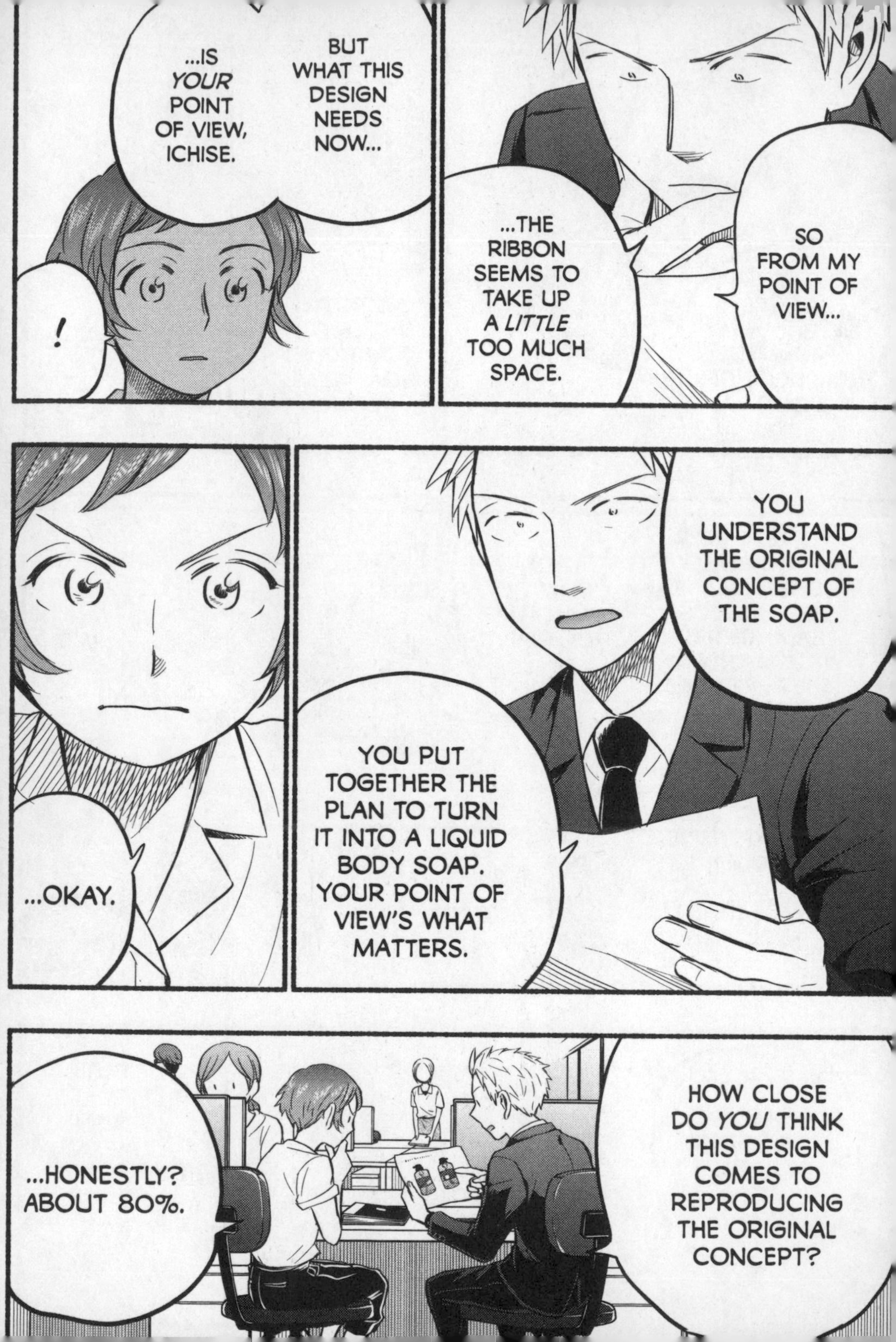
SO FROM MY POINT OF VIEW...
...THE RIBBON SEEMS TO TAKE UP A *LITTLE* TOO MUCH SPACE.
BUT WHAT THIS DESIGN NEEDS NOW...
...IS *YOUR* POINT OF VIEW, ICHISE.
!
YOU UNDERSTAND THE ORIGINAL CONCEPT OF THE SOAP.
YOU PUT TOGETHER THE PLAN TO TURN IT INTO A LIQUID BODY SOAP. YOUR POINT OF VIEW'S WHAT MATTERS.
...OKAY.
HOW CLOSE DO *YOU* THINK THIS DESIGN COMES TO REPRODUCING THE ORIGINAL CONCEPT?
...HONESTLY? ABOUT 80%.

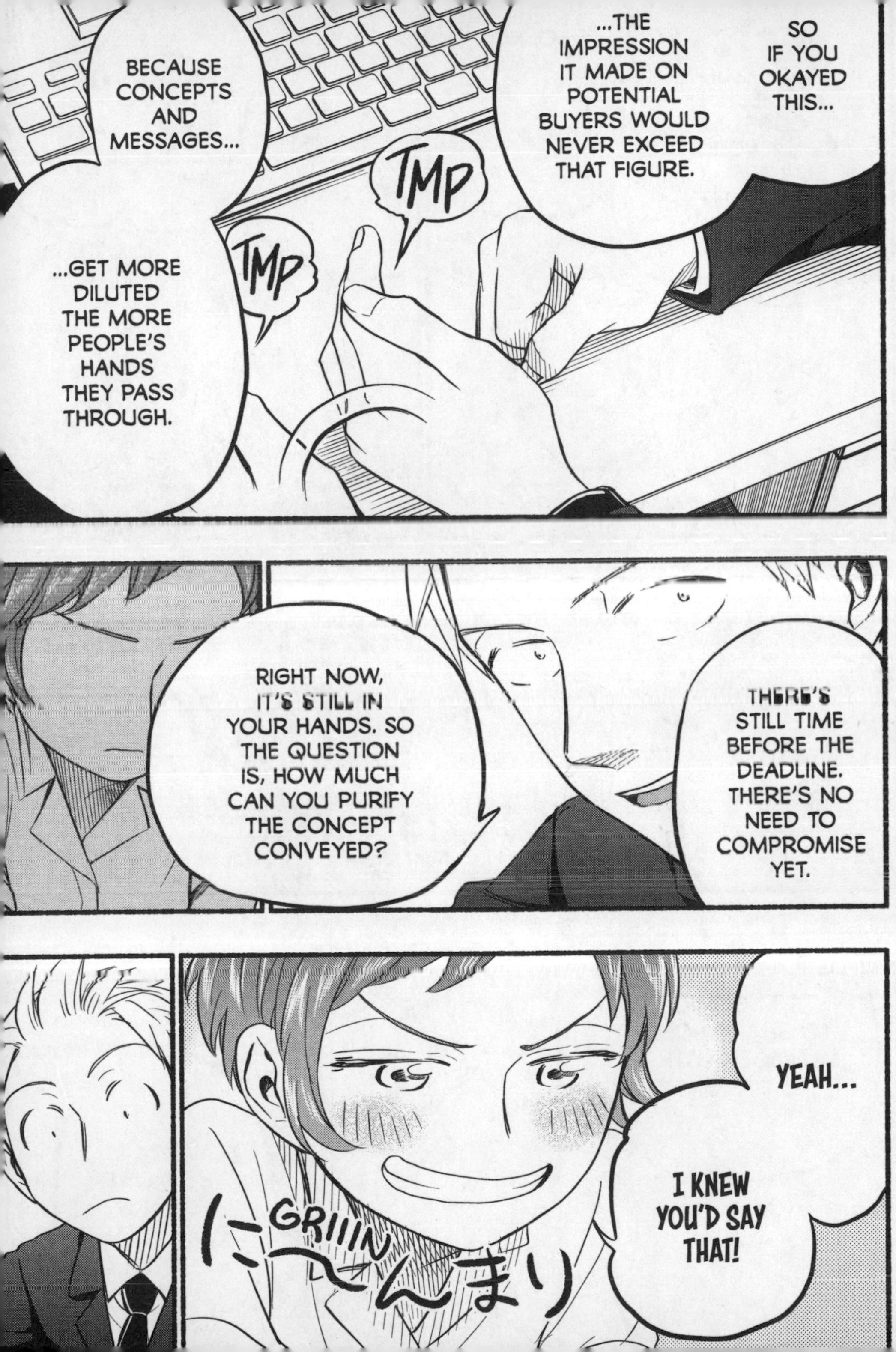
SO IF YOU OKAYED THIS...
...THE IMPRESSION IT MADE ON POTENTIAL BUYERS WOULD NEVER EXCEED THAT FIGURE.
TMP
TMP
BECAUSE CONCEPTS AND MESSAGES...
...GET MORE DILUTED THE MORE PEOPLE'S HANDS THEY PASS THROUGH.
THERE'S STILL TIME BEFORE THE DEADLINE. THERE'S NO NEED TO COMPROMISE YET.
RIGHT NOW, IT'S STILL IN YOUR HANDS. SO THE QUESTION IS, HOW MUCH CAN YOU PURIFY THE CONCEPT CONVEYED?
YEAH...
I KNEW YOU'D SAY THAT!
GRIIIN

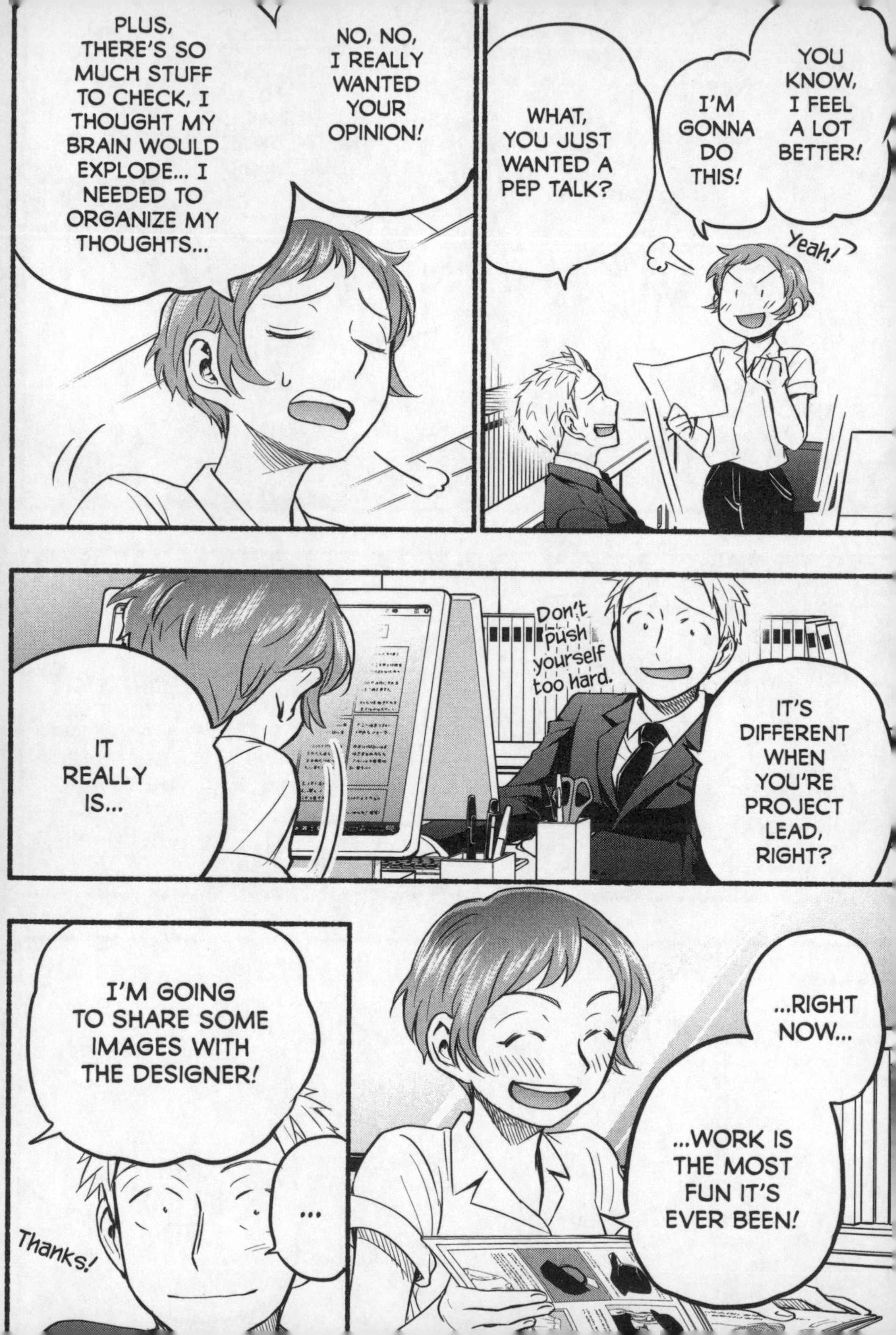
YOU KNOW, I FEEL A LOT BETTER!
I'M GONNA DO THIS!
WHAT, YOU JUST WANTED A PEP TALK?
Yeah!
NO, NO, I REALLY WANTED YOUR OPINION!
PLUS, THERE'S SO MUCH STUFF TO CHECK, I THOUGHT MY BRAIN WOULD EXPLODE... I NEEDED TO ORGANIZE MY THOUGHTS...
IT'S DIFFERENT WHEN YOU'RE PROJECT LEAD, RIGHT?
Don't push yourself too hard.
IT REALLY IS...
...RIGHT NOW...
...WORK IS THE MOST FUN IT'S EVER BEEN!
I'M GOING TO SHARE SOME IMAGES WITH THE DESIGNER!
...
Thanks!

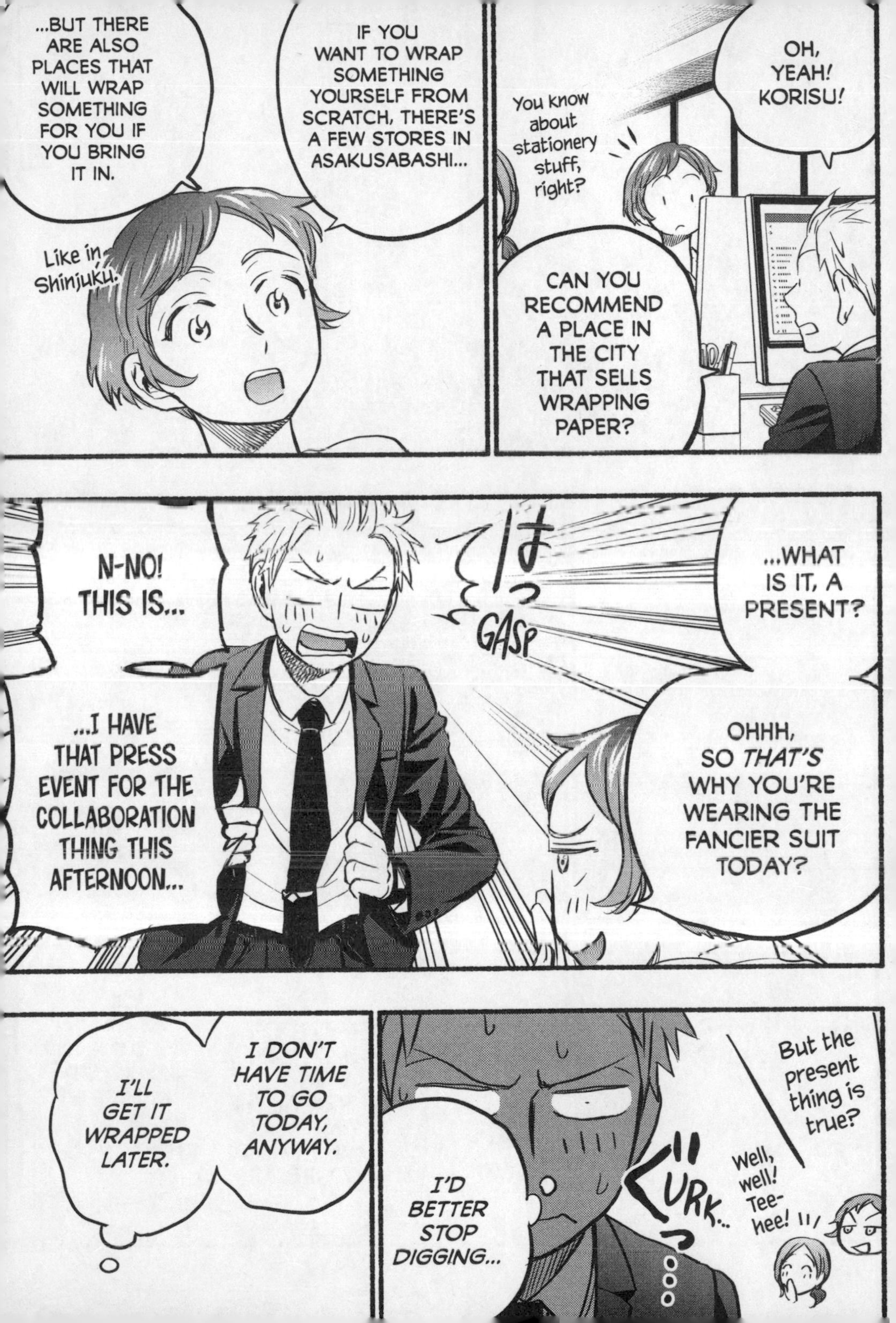
OH, YEAH! KORISU!
You know about stationery stuff, right?
CAN YOU RECOMMEND A PLACE IN THE CITY THAT SELLS WRAPPING PAPER?
IF YOU WANT TO WRAP SOMETHING YOURSELF FROM SCRATCH, THERE'S A FEW STORES IN ASAKUSABASHI...
...BUT THERE ARE ALSO PLACES THAT WILL WRAP SOMETHING FOR YOU IF YOU BRING IT IN.
Like in Shinjuku.
...WHAT IS IT, A PRESENT?
OHHH, SO *THAT'S* WHY YOU'RE WEARING THE FANCIER SUIT TODAY?
はっ
GASP
N-NO! THIS IS...
...I HAVE THAT PRESS EVENT FOR THE COLLABORATION THING THIS AFTERNOON...
But the present thing is true?
Well, well! Tee-hee!
URK...
I'D BETTER STOP DIGGING...
I DON'T HAVE TIME TO GO TODAY, ANYWAY.
I'LL GET IT WRAPPED LATER.

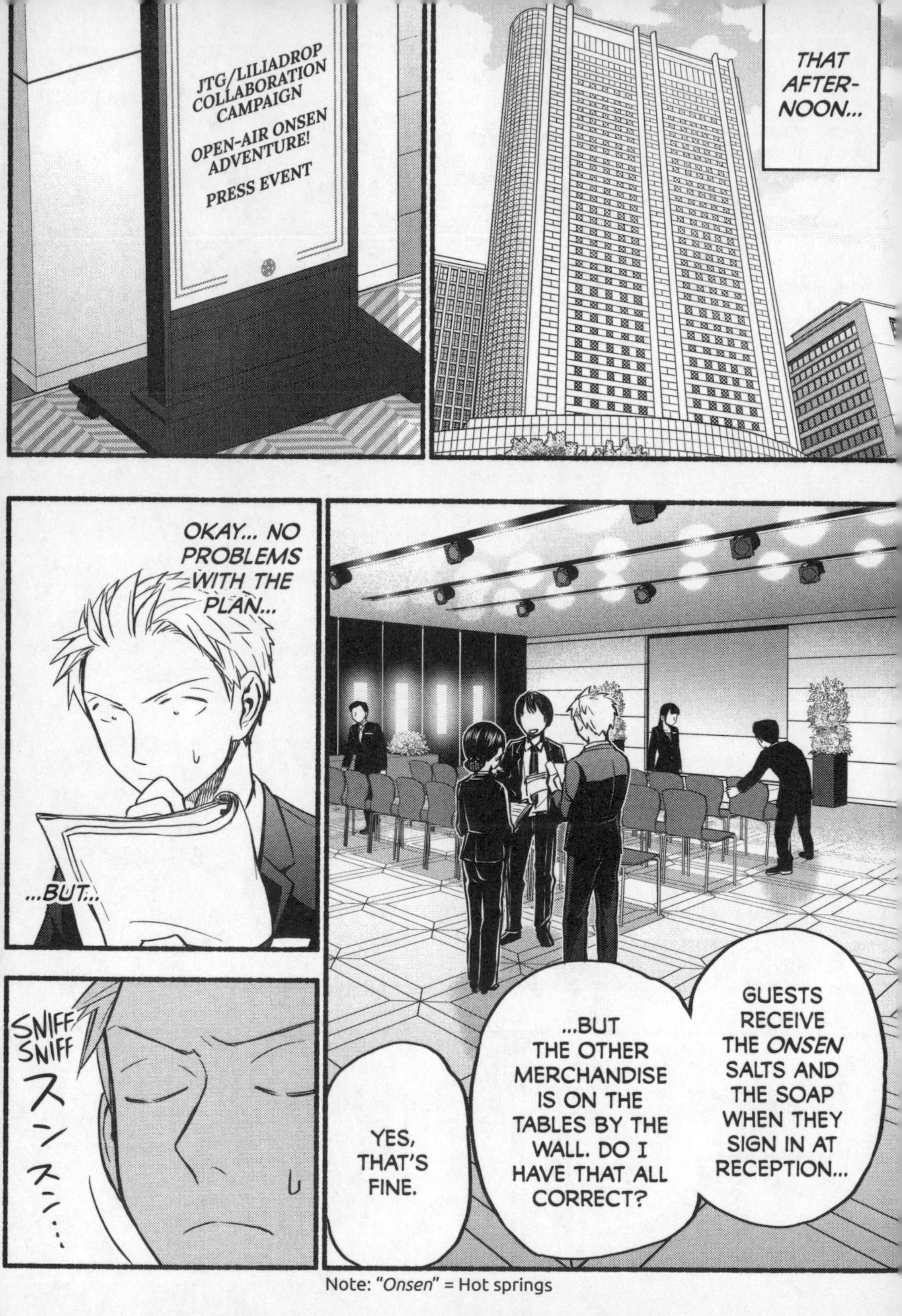
THAT AFTERNOON...
JTG/LILIADROP COLLABORATION CAMPAIGN
OPEN-AIR ONSEN ADVENTURE!
PRESS EVENT
GUESTS RECEIVE THE *ONSEN* SALTS AND THE SOAP WHEN THEY SIGN IN AT RECEPTION...
...BUT THE OTHER MERCHANDISE IS ON THE TABLES BY THE WALL. DO I HAVE THAT ALL CORRECT?
YES, THAT'S FINE.
OKAY... NO PROBLEMS WITH THE PLAN...
...BUT...
SNIFF SNIFF
スン スン...

Note: "*Onsen*" = Hot springs

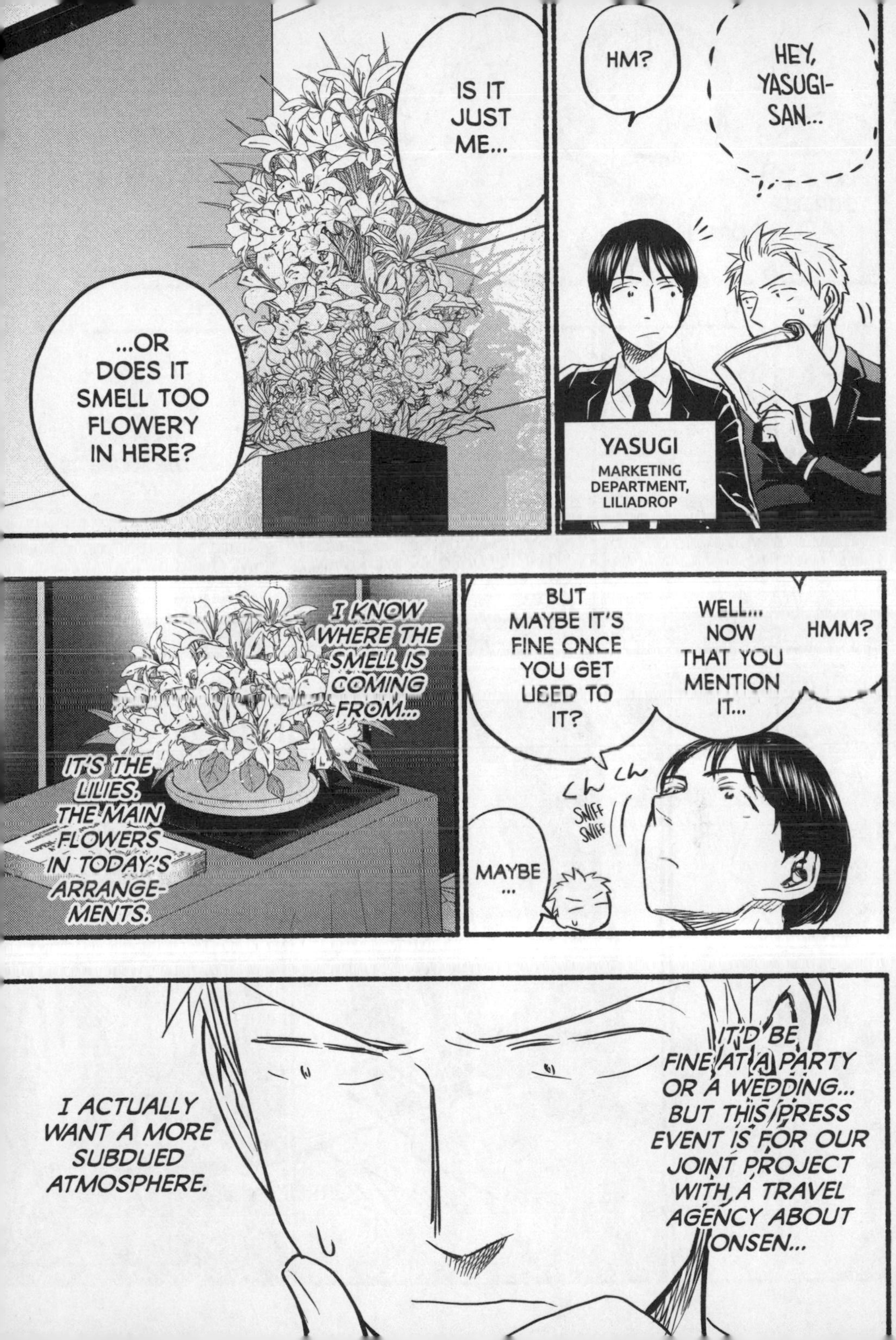
HEY, YASUGI-SAN...
HM?
YASUGI
MARKETING DEPARTMENT, LILIADROP
IS IT JUST ME...
...OR DOES IT SMELL TOO FLOWERY IN HERE?
HMM?
WELL... NOW THAT YOU MENTION IT...
BUT MAYBE IT'S FINE ONCE YOU GET USED TO IT?
SNIFF SNIFF
MAYBE ...
I KNOW WHERE THE SMELL IS COMING FROM...
IT'S THE LILIES. THE MAIN FLOWERS IN TODAY'S ARRANGEMENTS.
IT'D BE FINE AT A PARTY OR A WEDDING... BUT THIS PRESS EVENT IS FOR OUR JOINT PROJECT WITH A TRAVEL AGENCY ABOUT ONSEN...
I ACTUALLY WANT A MORE SUBDUED ATMOSPHERE.

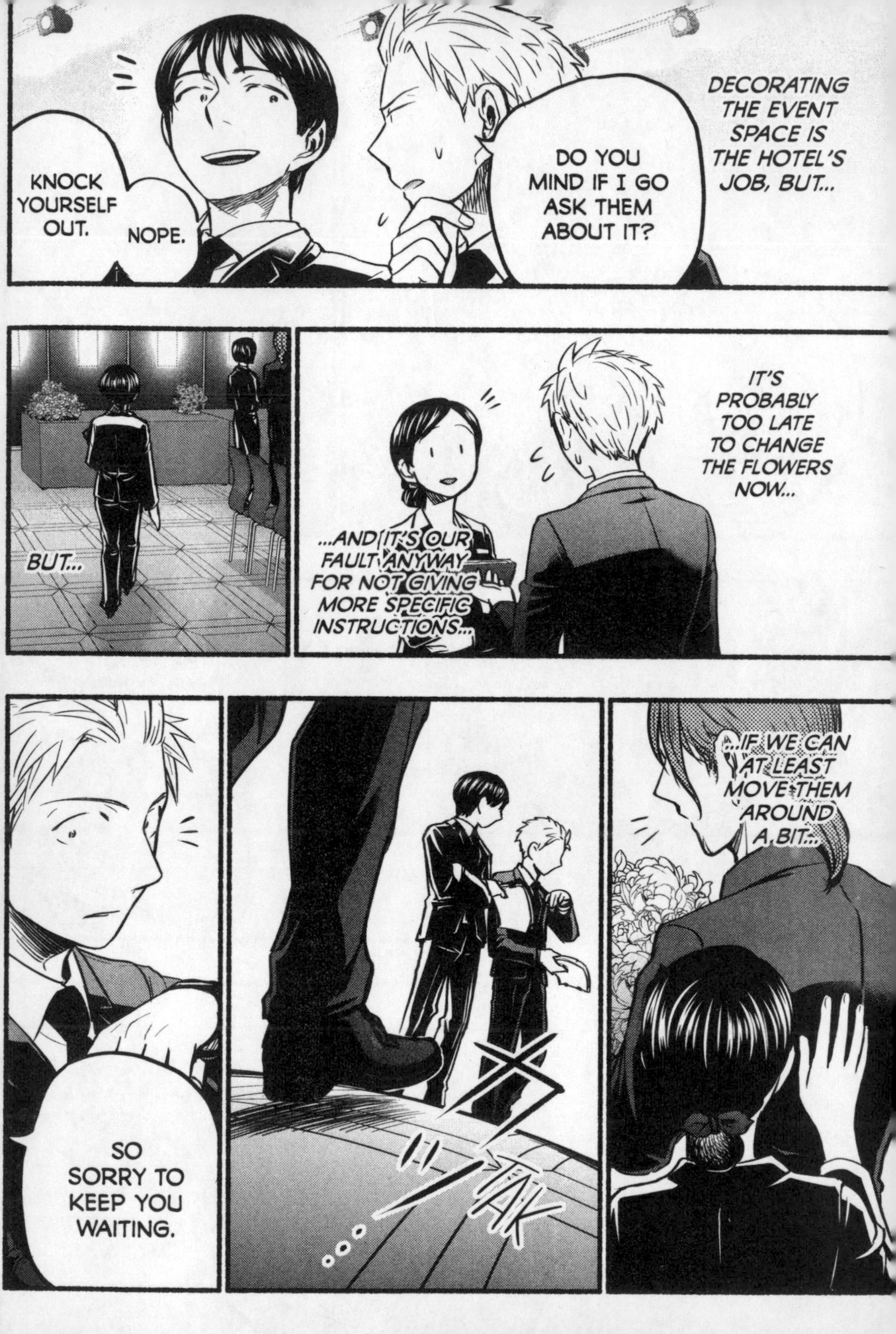
DECORATING THE EVENT SPACE IS THE HOTEL'S JOB, BUT...
DO YOU MIND IF I GO ASK THEM ABOUT IT?
NOPE.
KNOCK YOURSELF OUT.
IT'S PROBABLY TOO LATE TO CHANGE THE FLOWERS NOW...
...AND IT'S OUR FAULT ANYWAY FOR NOT GIVING MORE SPECIFIC INSTRUCTIONS...
BUT...
...IF WE CAN AT LEAST MOVE THEM AROUND A BIT...
SO SORRY TO KEEP YOU WAITING.

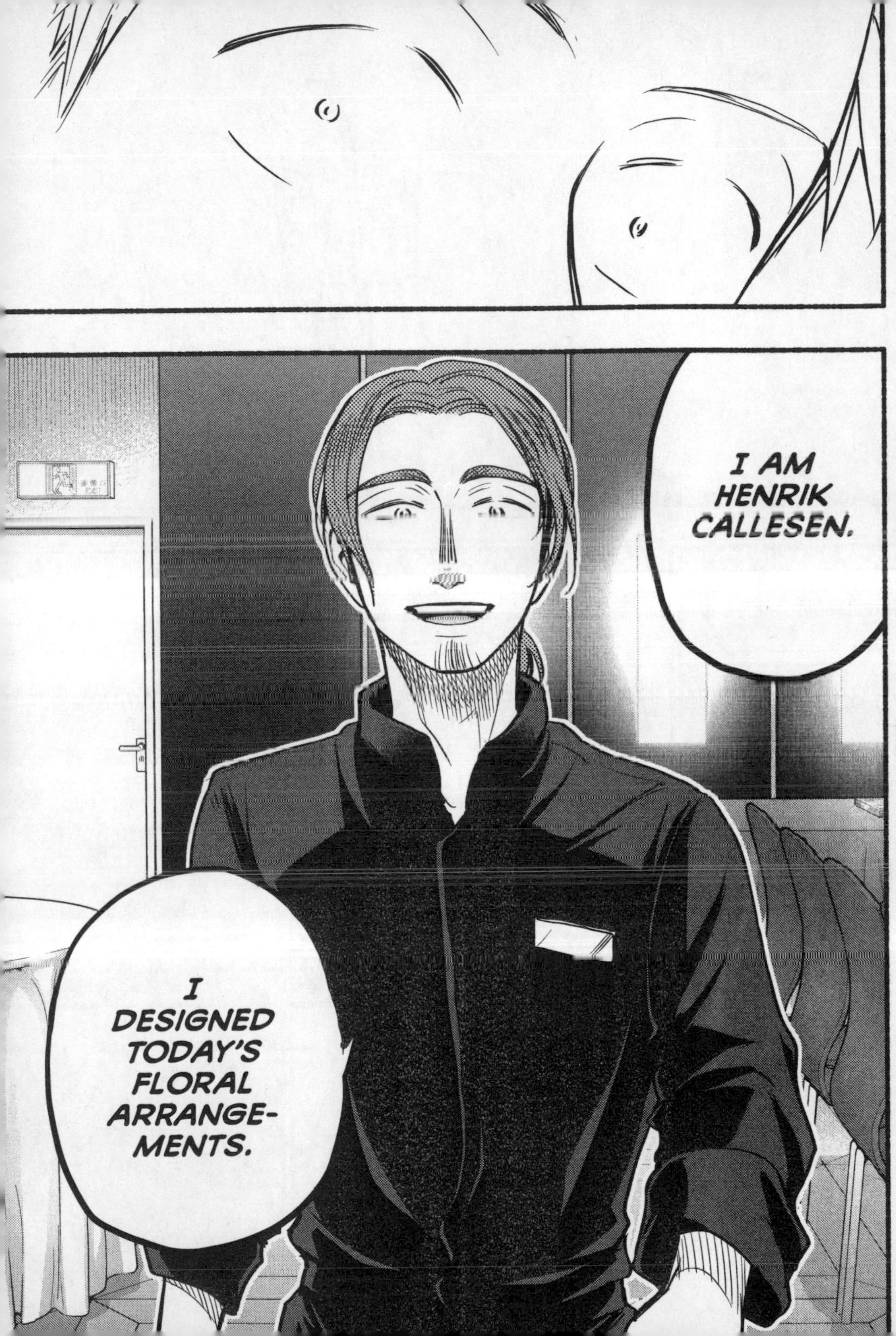
I AM HENRIK CALLESEN.
I DESIGNED TODAY'S FLORAL ARRANGE-MENTS.

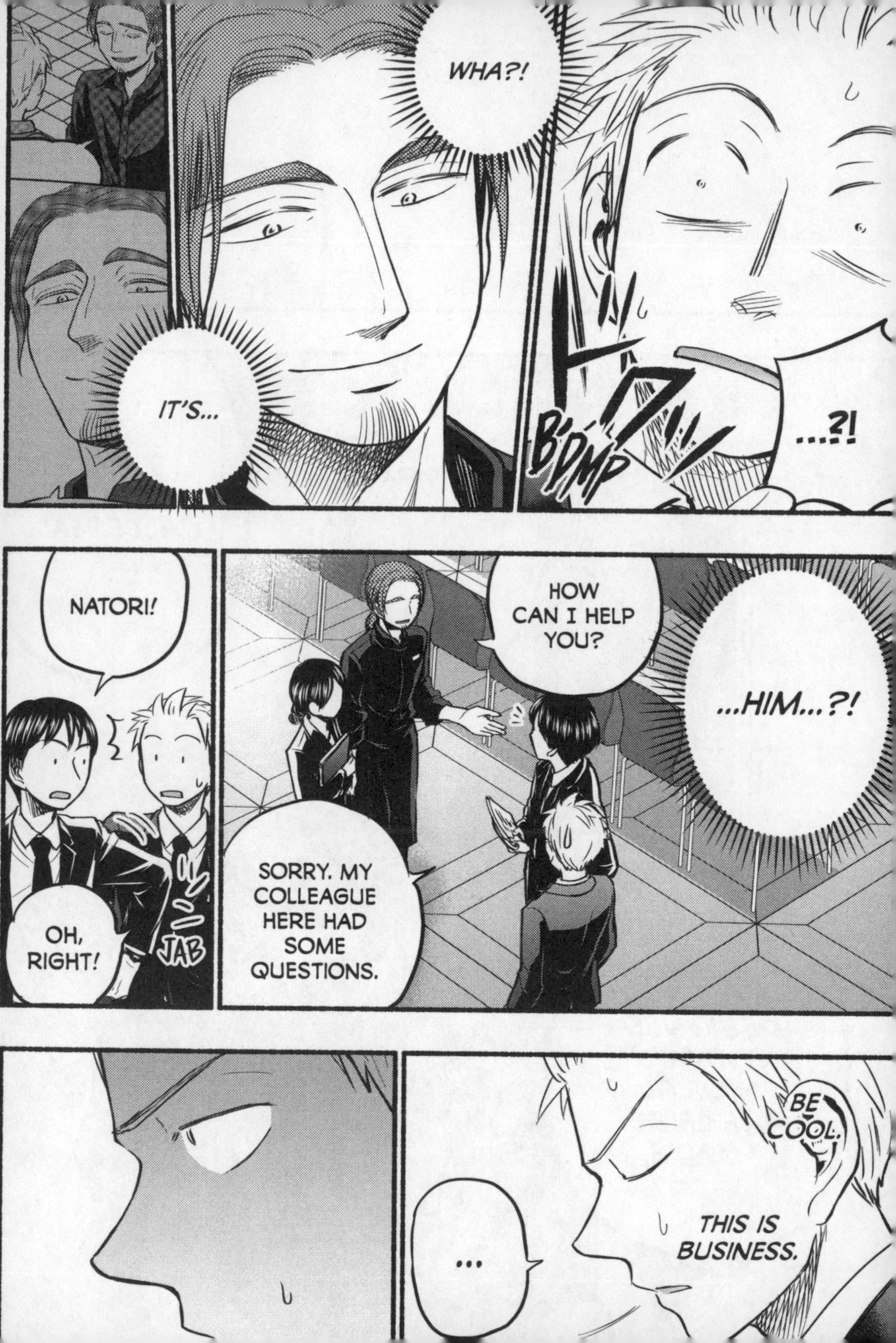
...?!
B'DMP
WHA?!
IT'S...
...HIM...?!
HOW CAN I HELP YOU?
SORRY. MY COLLEAGUE HERE HAD SOME QUESTIONS.
NATORI!
JAB
OH, RIGHT!
BE COOL.
THIS IS BUSINESS.
...

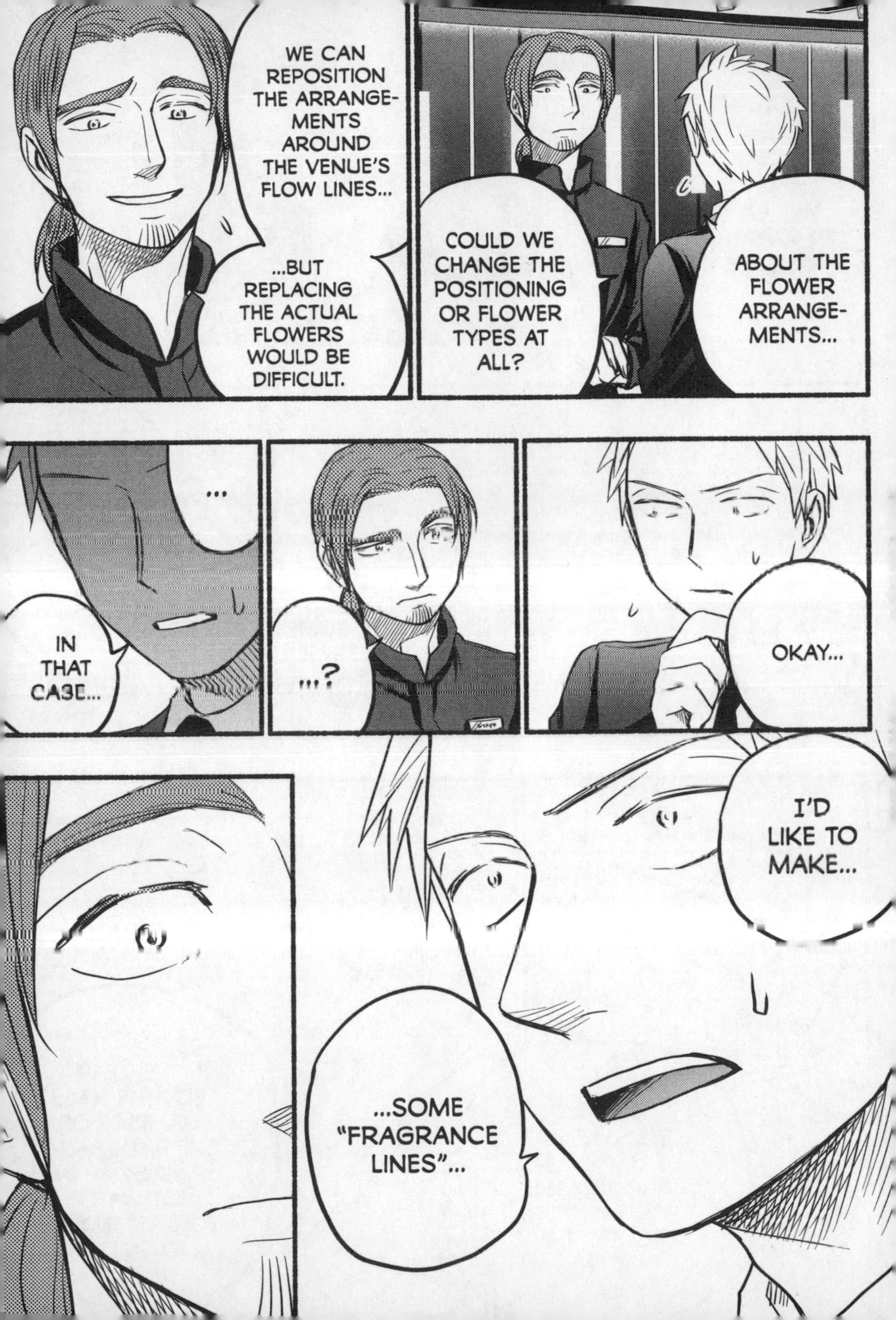
ABOUT THE FLOWER ARRANGE-MENTS...
COULD WE CHANGE THE POSITIONING OR FLOWER TYPES AT ALL?
WE CAN REPOSITION THE ARRANGE-MENTS AROUND THE VENUE'S FLOW LINES...
...BUT REPLACING THE ACTUAL FLOWERS WOULD BE DIFFICULT.
OKAY...
...?
...
IN THAT CASE...
I'D LIKE TO MAKE...
...SOME "FRAGRANCE LINES"...

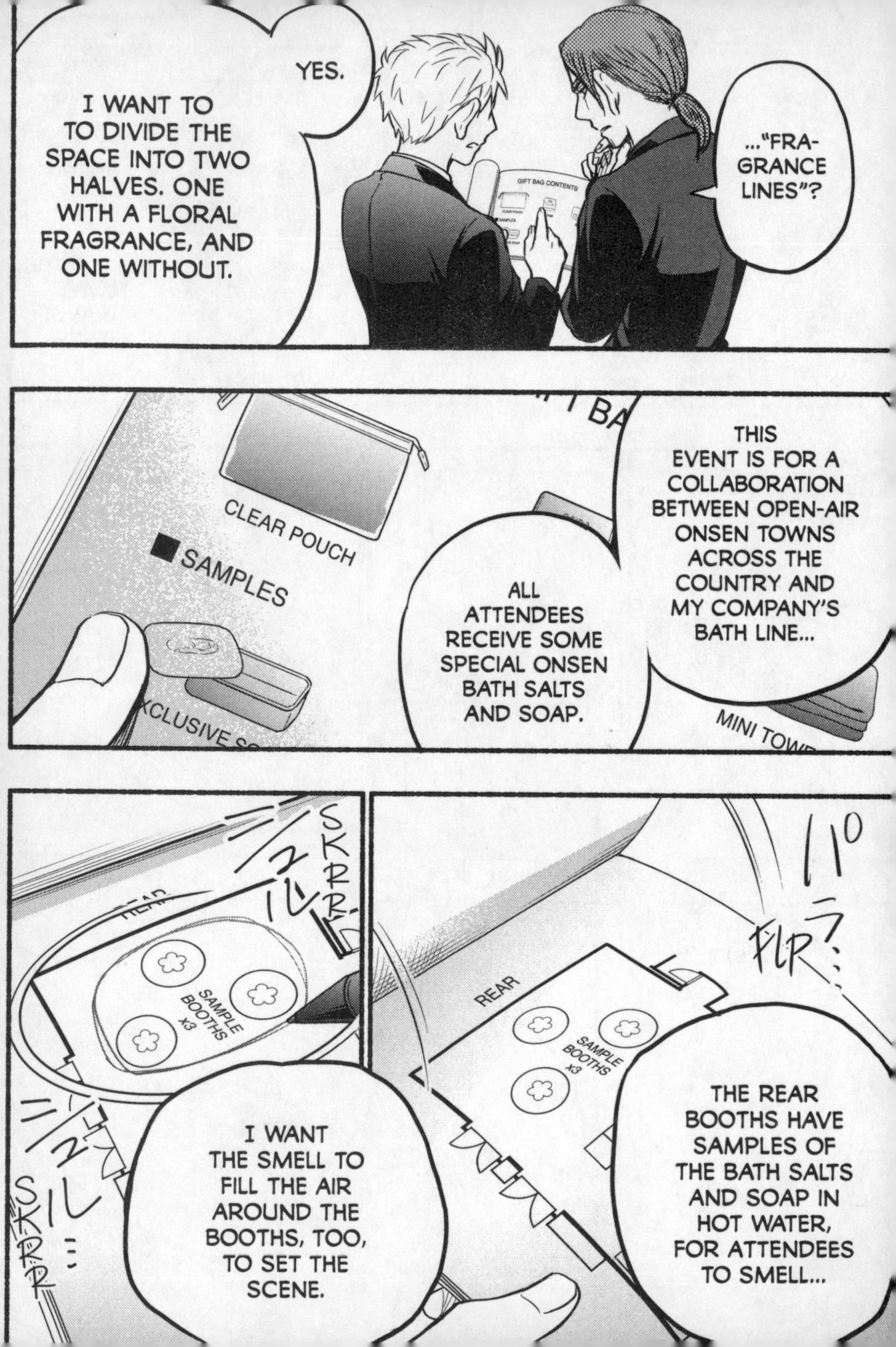
..."FRA-GRANCE LINES"?
YES.
I WANT TO TO DIVIDE THE SPACE INTO TWO HALVES. ONE WITH A FLORAL FRAGRANCE, AND ONE WITHOUT.
GIFT BAG CONTENTS
THIS EVENT IS FOR A COLLABORATION BETWEEN OPEN-AIR ONSEN TOWNS ACROSS THE COUNTRY AND MY COMPANY'S BATH LINE...
ALL ATTENDEES RECEIVE SOME SPECIAL ONSEN BATH SALTS AND SOAP.
CLEAR POUCH
■ SAMPLES
FLR
REAR
SAMPLE BOOTHS x3
THE REAR BOOTHS HAVE SAMPLES OF THE BATH SALTS AND SOAP IN HOT WATER, FOR ATTENDEES TO SMELL...
SKRR
SAMPLE BOOTHS x3
I WANT THE SMELL TO FILL THE AIR AROUND THE BOOTHS, TOO, TO SET THE SCENE.
SKRR

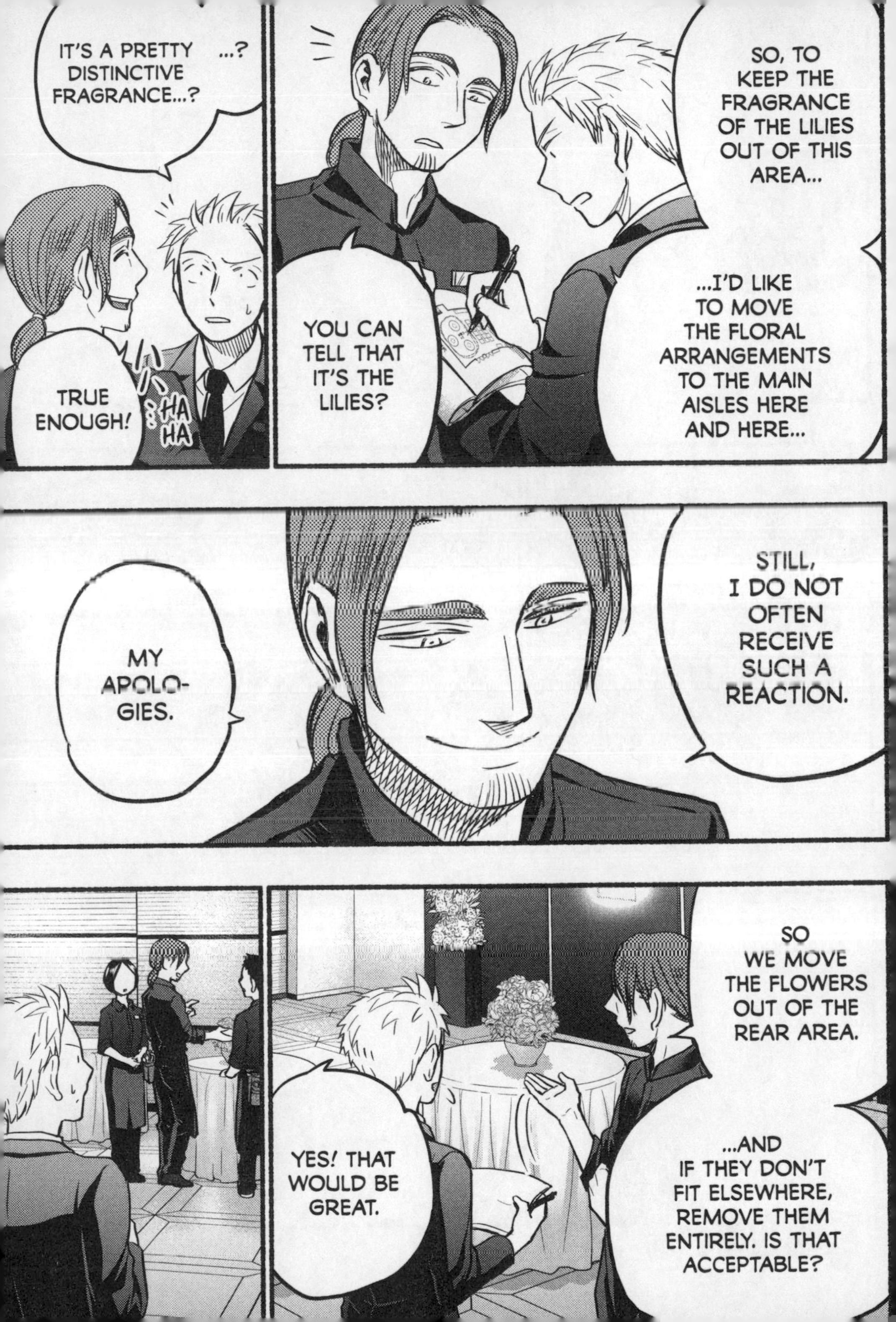
SO, TO KEEP THE FRAGRANCE OF THE LILIES OUT OF THIS AREA...
...I'D LIKE TO MOVE THE FLORAL ARRANGEMENTS TO THE MAIN AISLES HERE AND HERE...
YOU CAN TELL THAT IT'S THE LILIES?
IT'S A PRETTY DISTINCTIVE FRAGRANCE...?
...?
TRUE ENOUGH!
HA HA
STILL, I DO NOT OFTEN RECEIVE SUCH A REACTION.
MY APOLOGIES.
SO WE MOVE THE FLOWERS OUT OF THE REAR AREA.
...AND IF THEY DON'T FIT ELSEWHERE, REMOVE THEM ENTIRELY. IS THAT ACCEPTABLE?
YES! THAT WOULD BE GREAT.

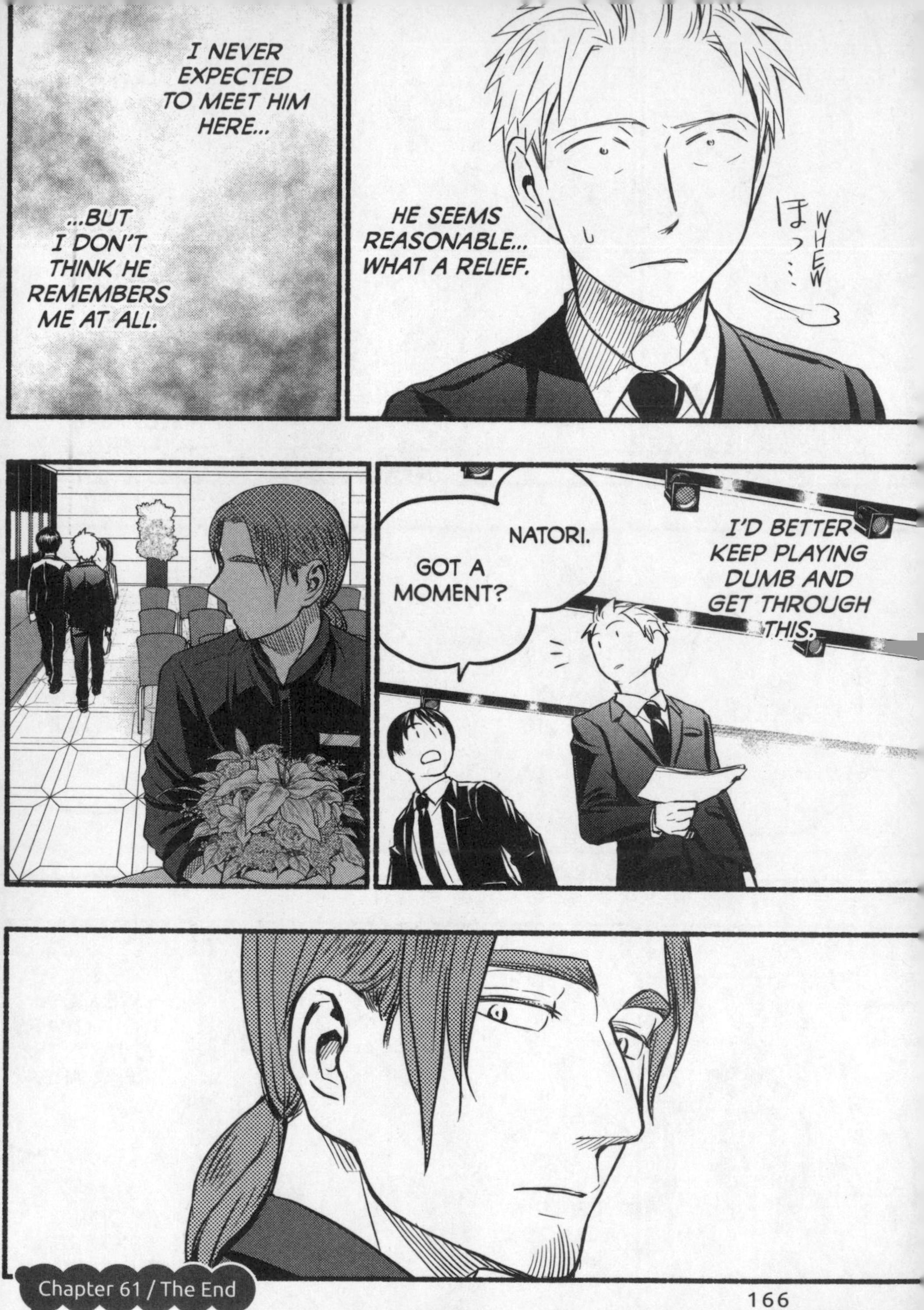
HE SEEMS REASONABLE... WHAT A RELIEF.
ほっ…
WHEW
I NEVER EXPECTED TO MEET HIM HERE...
...BUT I DON'T THINK HE REMEMBERS ME AT ALL.
I'D BETTER KEEP PLAYING DUMB AND GET THROUGH THIS.
NATORI.
GOT A MOMENT?

Chapter 61 / The End

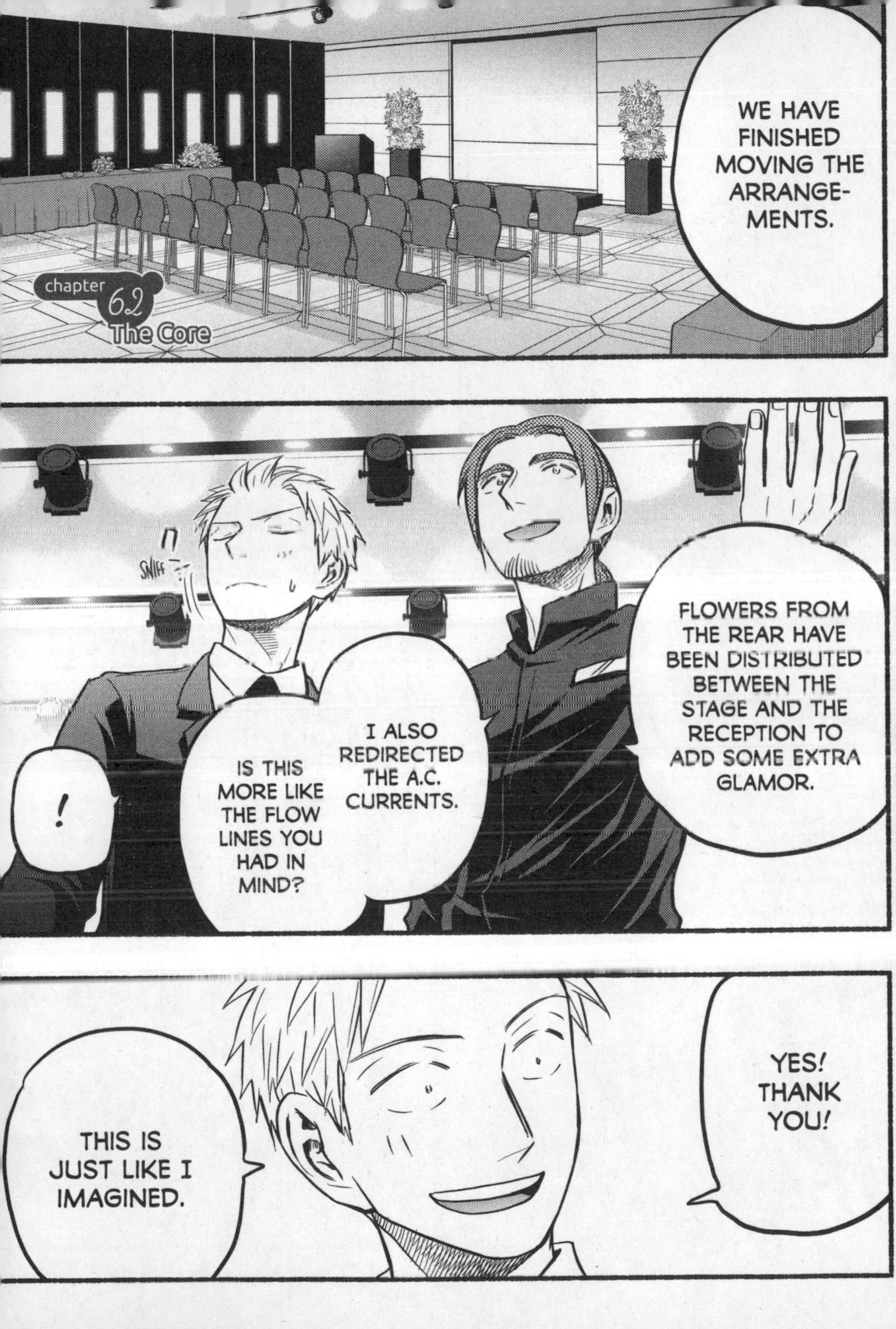
chapter 62
The Core
WE HAVE FINISHED MOVING THE ARRANGE-MENTS.
FLOWERS FROM THE REAR HAVE BEEN DISTRIBUTED BETWEEN THE STAGE AND THE RECEPTION TO ADD SOME EXTRA GLAMOR.
I ALSO REDIRECTED THE A.C. CURRENTS.
IS THIS MORE LIKE THE FLOW LINES YOU HAD IN MIND?
SNIFF
!
YES! THANK YOU!
THIS IS JUST LIKE I IMAGINED.

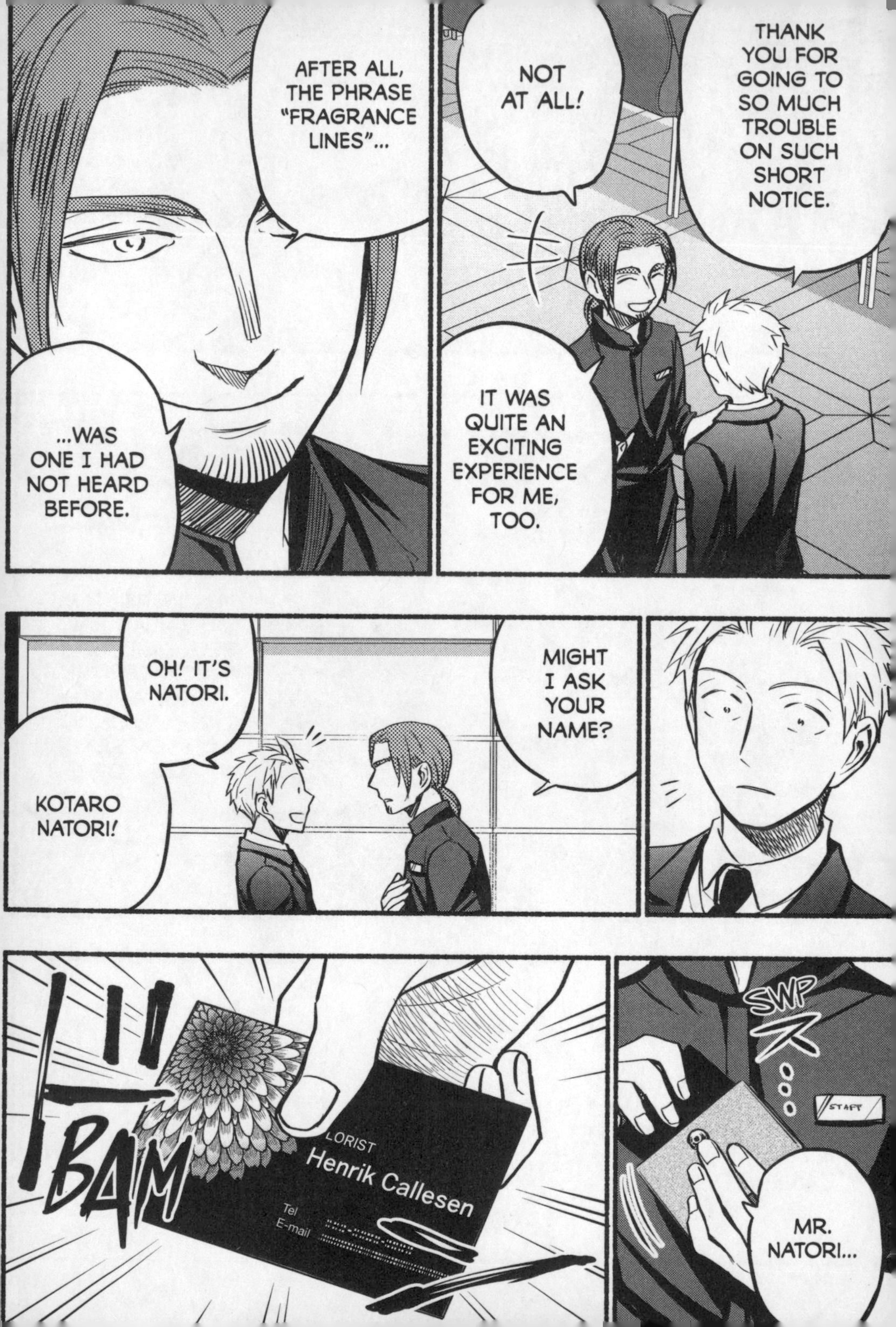
THANK YOU FOR GOING TO SO MUCH TROUBLE ON SUCH SHORT NOTICE.
NOT AT ALL!
IT WAS QUITE AN EXCITING EXPERIENCE FOR ME, TOO.
AFTER ALL, THE PHRASE "FRAGRANCE LINES"...
...WAS ONE I HAD NOT HEARD BEFORE.
MIGHT I ASK YOUR NAME?
OH! IT'S NATORI.
KOTARO NATORI!
SWP
STAFF
MR. NATORI...
BAM
LORIST
Henrik Callesen
Tel
E-mail

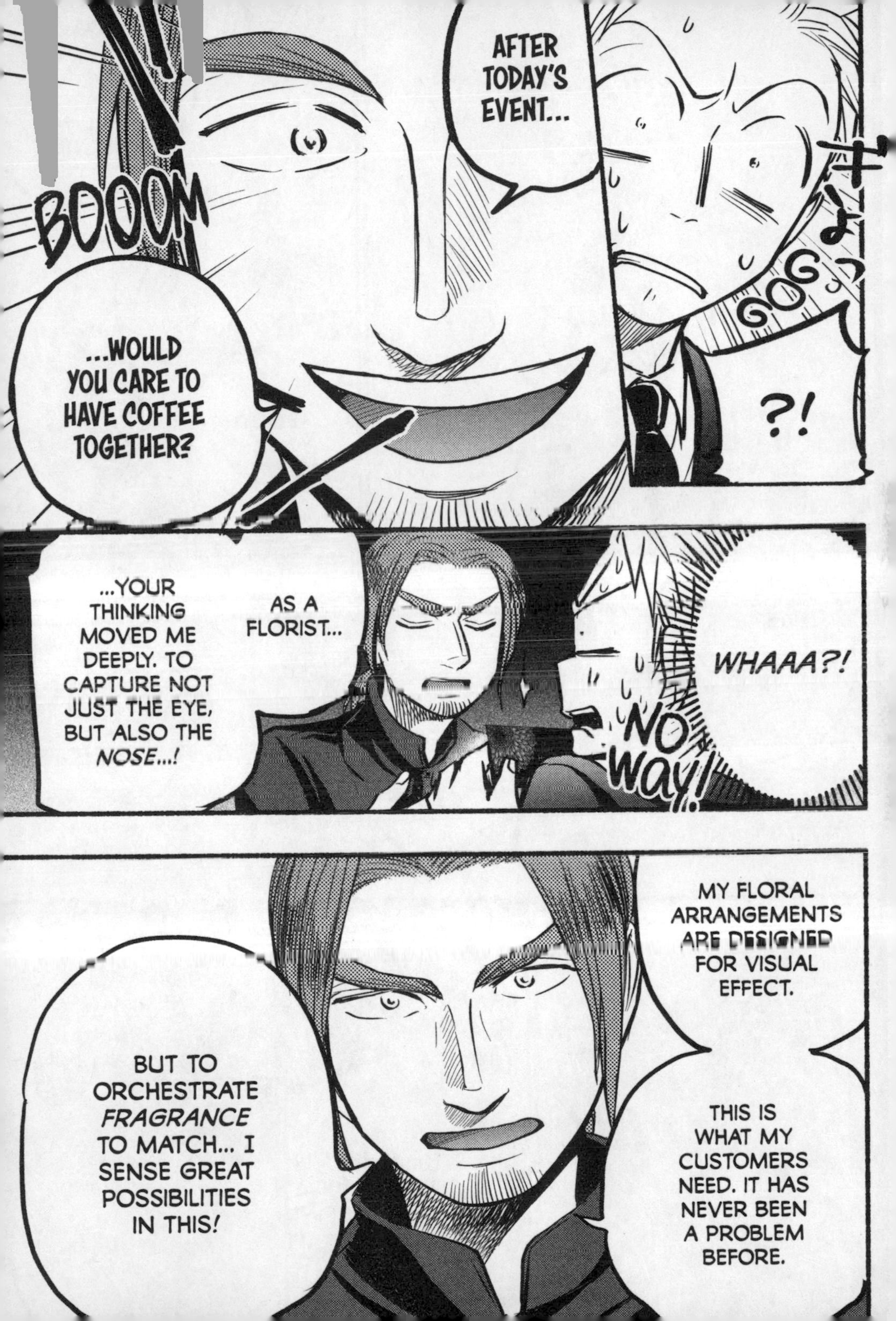
AFTER TODAY'S EVENT...
BOOOM
...WOULD YOU CARE TO HAVE COFFEE TOGETHER?
ギョ
GOGO
?!
WHAAA?!
NO WAY!
AS A FLORIST...
...YOUR THINKING MOVED ME DEEPLY. TO CAPTURE NOT JUST THE EYE, BUT ALSO THE *NOSE*...!
MY FLORAL ARRANGEMENTS ARE DESIGNED FOR VISUAL EFFECT.
THIS IS WHAT MY CUSTOMERS NEED. IT HAS NEVER BEEN A PROBLEM BEFORE.
BUT TO ORCHESTRATE *FRAGRANCE* TO MATCH... I SENSE GREAT POSSIBILITIES IN THIS!

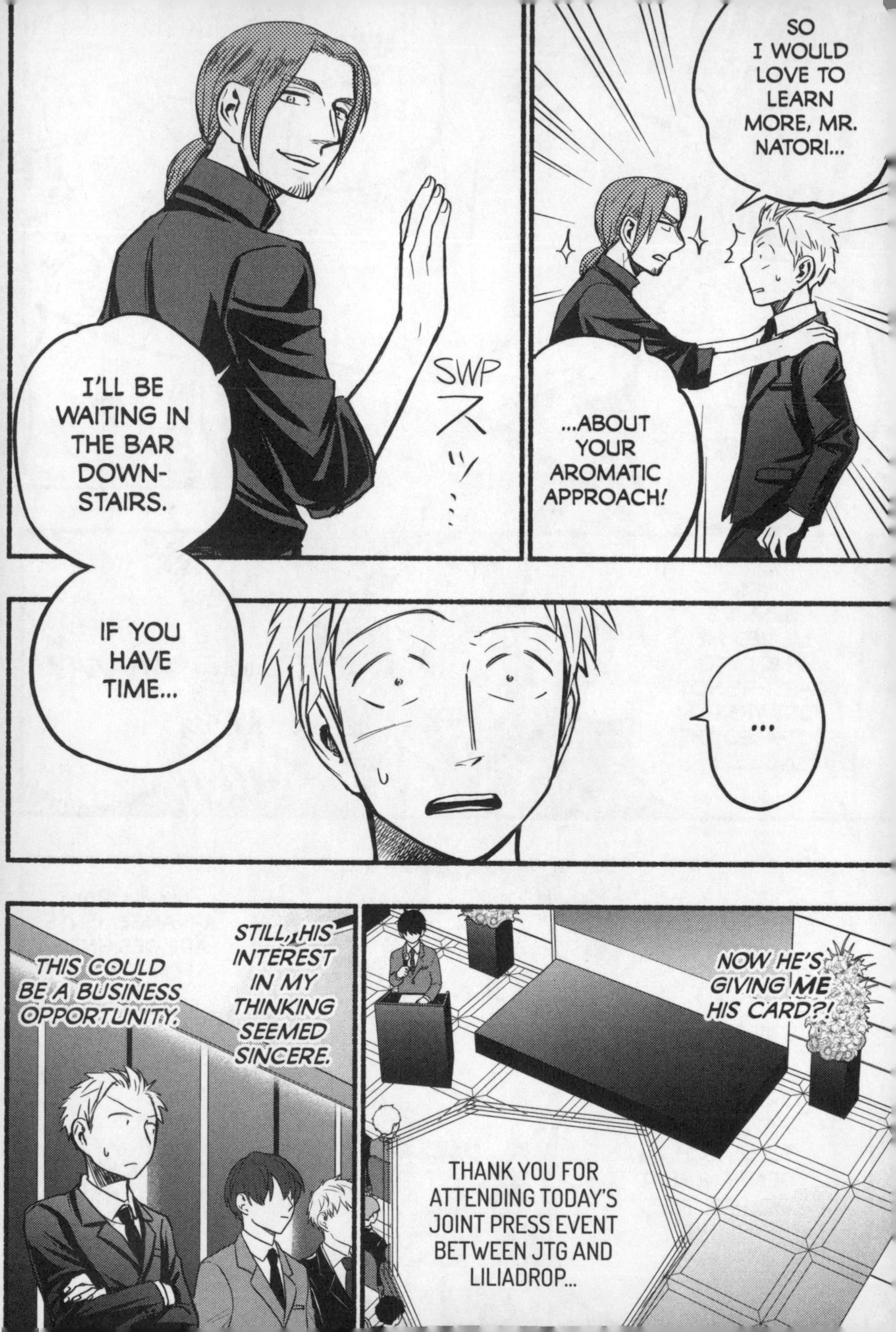
SO I WOULD LOVE TO LEARN MORE, MR. NATORI...
...ABOUT YOUR AROMATIC APPROACH!
I'LL BE WAITING IN THE BAR DOWN-STAIRS.
SWP
スッ
IF YOU HAVE TIME...
...
NOW HE'S GIVING ME HIS CARD?!
THANK YOU FOR ATTENDING TODAY'S JOINT PRESS EVENT BETWEEN JTG AND LILIADROP...
STILL, HIS INTEREST IN MY THINKING SEEMED SINCERE.
THIS COULD BE A BUSINESS OPPORTUNITY.

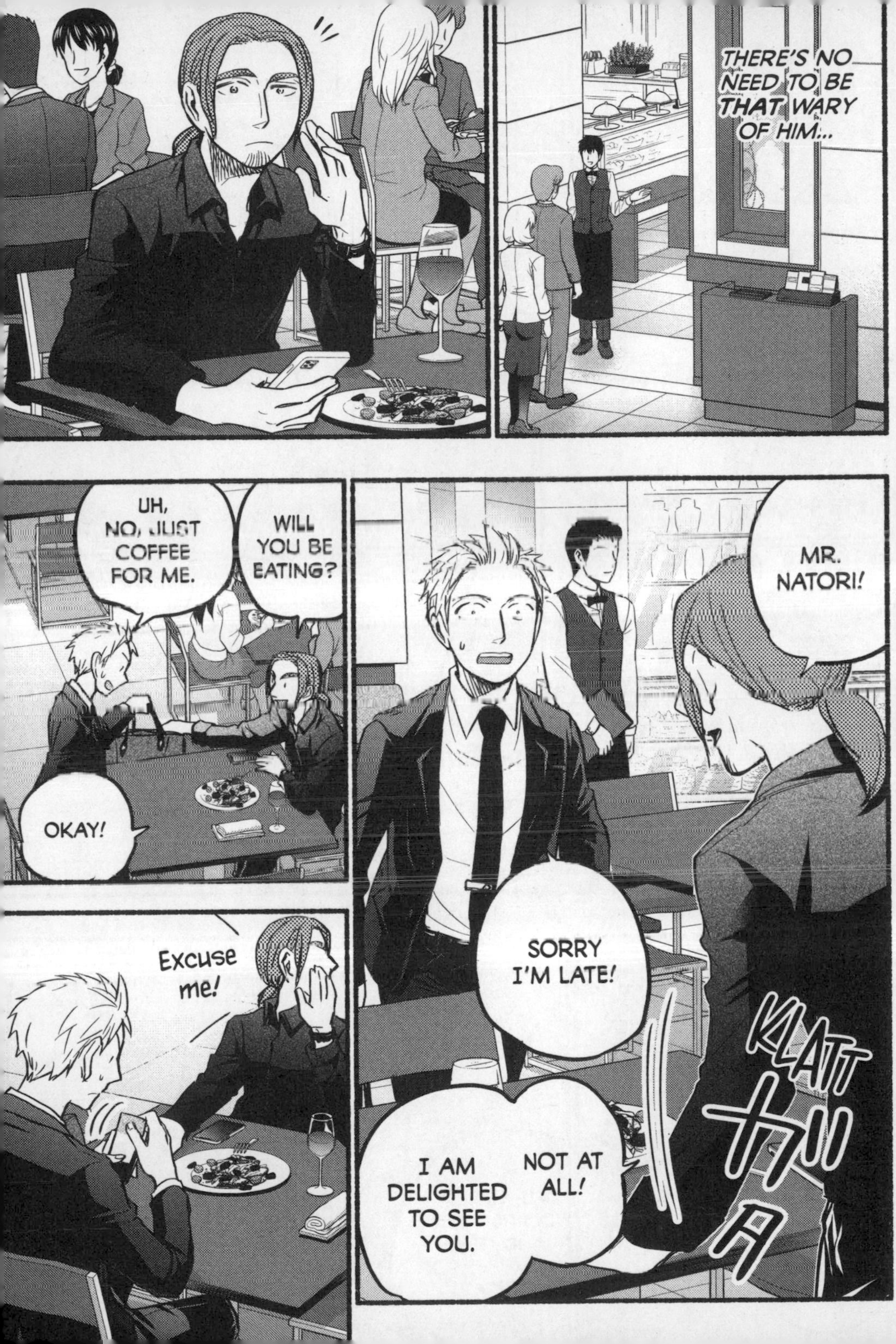
THERE'S NO NEED TO BE THAT WARY OF HIM...
MR. NATORI!
SORRY I'M LATE!
KLATT
NOT AT ALL!
I AM DELIGHTED TO SEE YOU.
WILL YOU BE EATING?
UH, NO, JUST COFFEE FOR ME.
OKAY!
Excuse me!

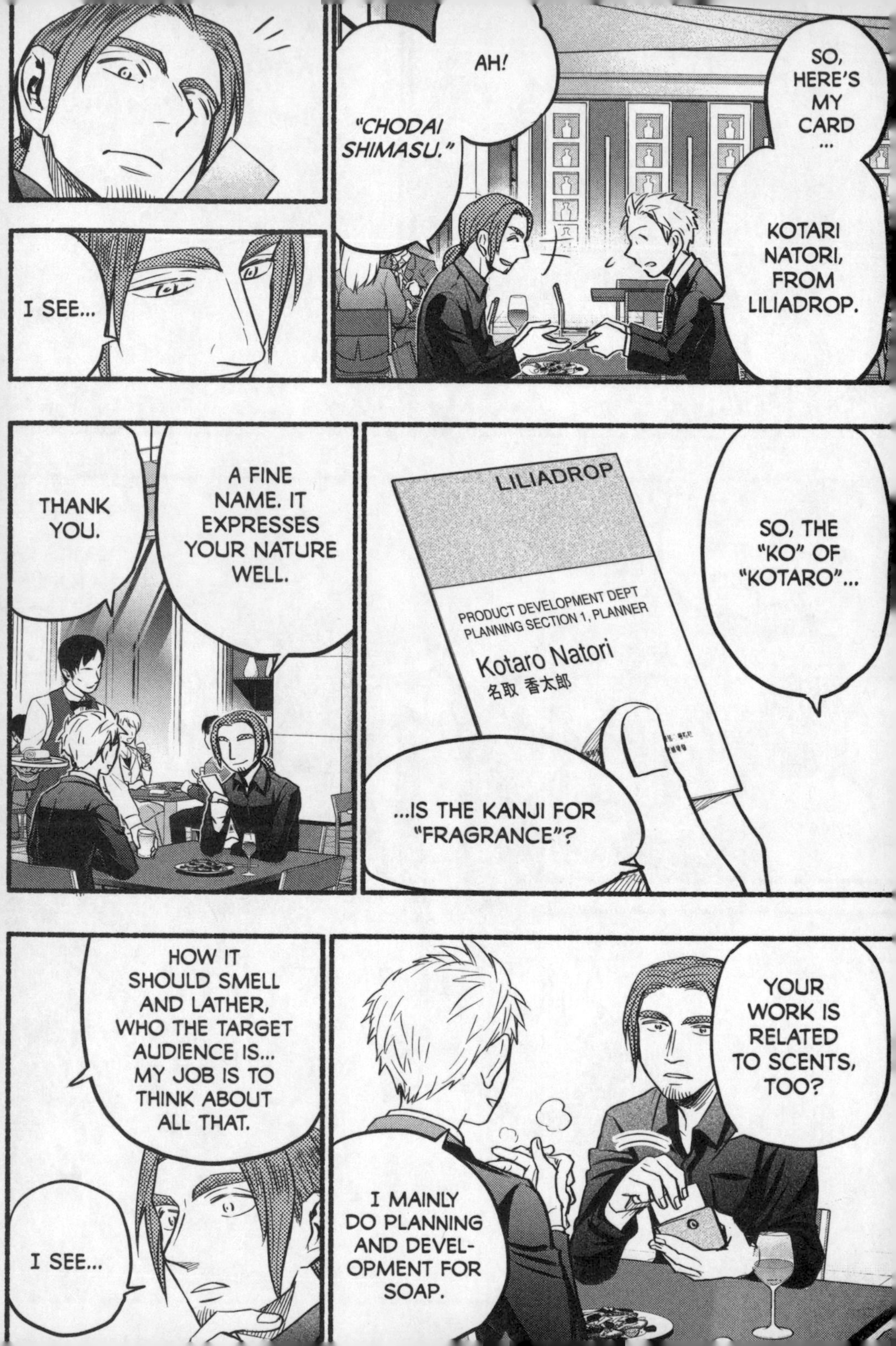
SO, HERE'S MY CARD ...
KOTARI NATORI, FROM LILIADROP.
AH!
"CHODAI SHIMASU."
I SEE...
LILIADROP
PRODUCT DEVELOPMENT DEPT
PLANNING SECTION 1, PLANNER
Kotaro Natori
名取 香太郎
SO, THE "KO" OF "KOTARO"...
...IS THE KANJI FOR "FRAGRANCE"?
A FINE NAME. IT EXPRESSES YOUR NATURE WELL.
THANK YOU.
YOUR WORK IS RELATED TO SCENTS, TOO?
I MAINLY DO PLANNING AND DEVEL-OPMENT FOR SOAP.
HOW IT SHOULD SMELL AND LATHER, WHO THE TARGET AUDIENCE IS... MY JOB IS TO THINK ABOUT ALL THAT.
I SEE...

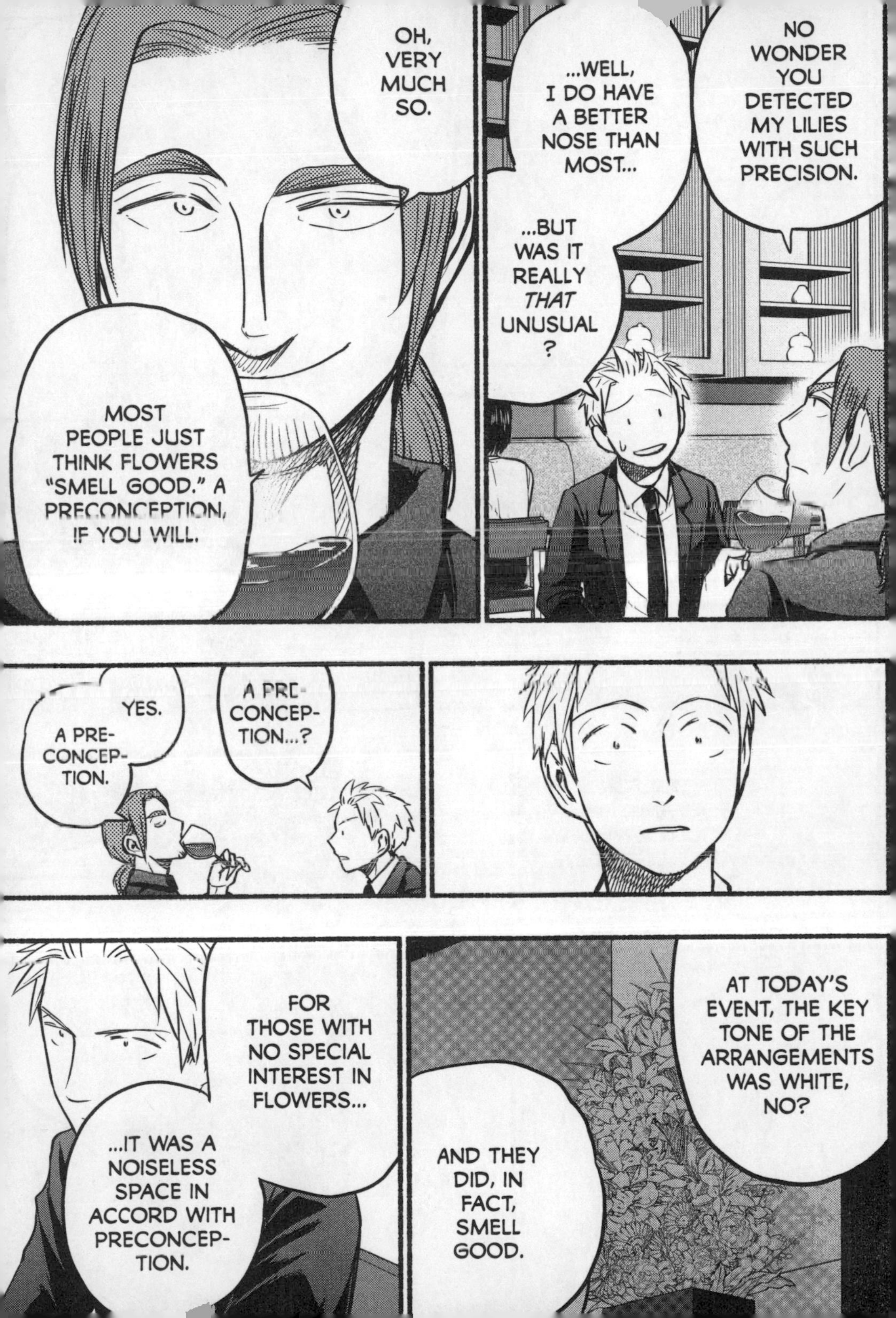
NO WONDER YOU DETECTED MY LILIES WITH SUCH PRECISION.
...WELL, I DO HAVE A BETTER NOSE THAN MOST...
...BUT WAS IT REALLY *THAT* UNUSUAL?
OH, VERY MUCH SO.
MOST PEOPLE JUST THINK FLOWERS "SMELL GOOD." A PRECONCEPTION, IF YOU WILL.
A PRE-CONCEPTION...?
YES. A PRE-CONCEPTION.
AT TODAY'S EVENT, THE KEY TONE OF THE ARRANGEMENTS WAS WHITE, NO?
AND THEY DID, IN FACT, SMELL GOOD.
FOR THOSE WITH NO SPECIAL INTEREST IN FLOWERS...
...IT WAS A NOISELESS SPACE IN ACCORD WITH PRECONCEPTION.

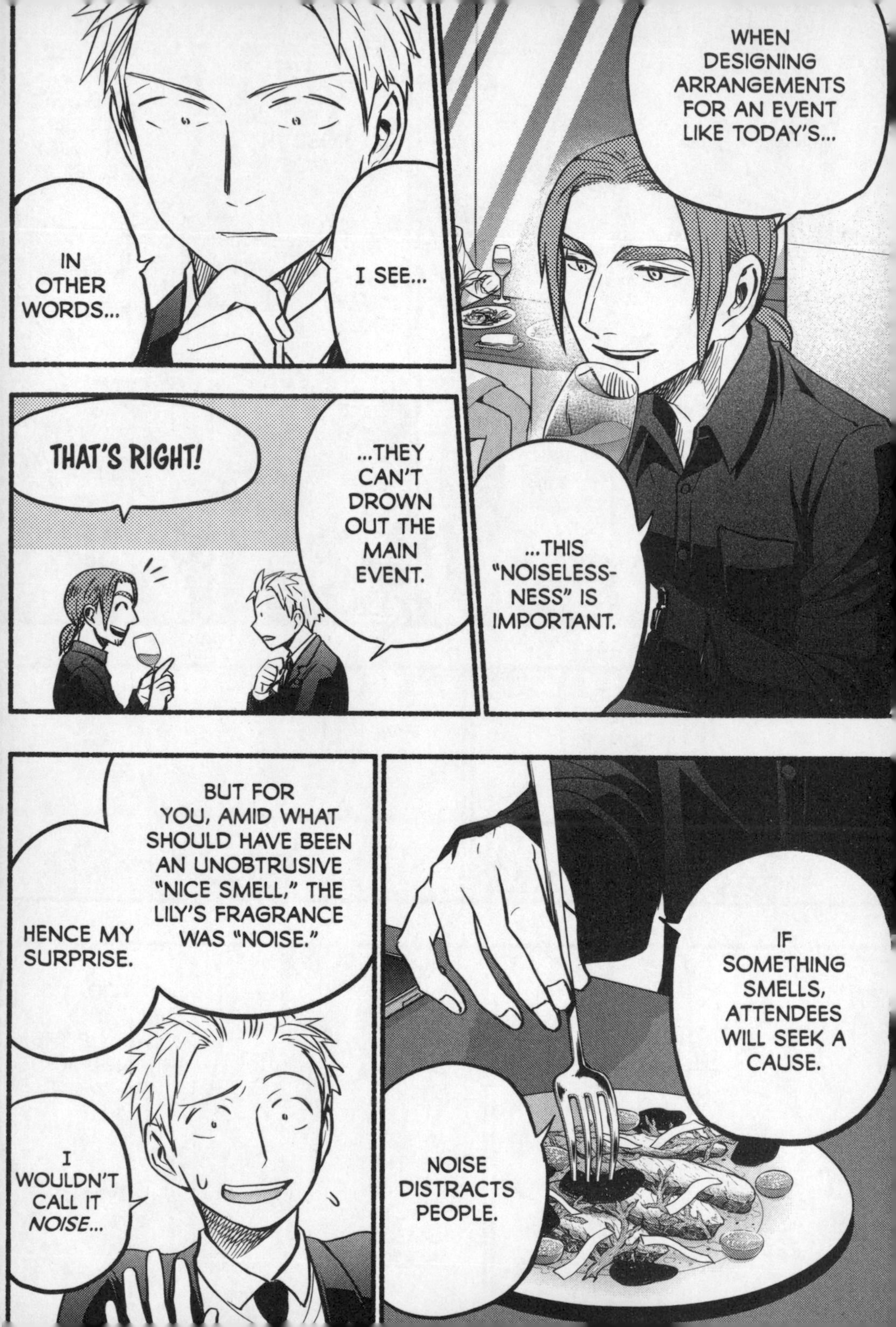
WHEN DESIGNING ARRANGEMENTS FOR AN EVENT LIKE TODAY'S...
...THIS "NOISELESS-NESS" IS IMPORTANT.
I SEE...
IN OTHER WORDS...
...THEY CAN'T DROWN OUT THE MAIN EVENT.
THAT'S RIGHT!
IF SOMETHING SMELLS, ATTENDEES WILL SEEK A CAUSE.
NOISE DISTRACTS PEOPLE.
BUT FOR YOU, AMID WHAT SHOULD HAVE BEEN AN UNOBTRUSIVE "NICE SMELL," THE LILY'S FRAGRANCE WAS "NOISE."
HENCE MY SURPRISE.
I WOULDN'T CALL IT *NOISE*...

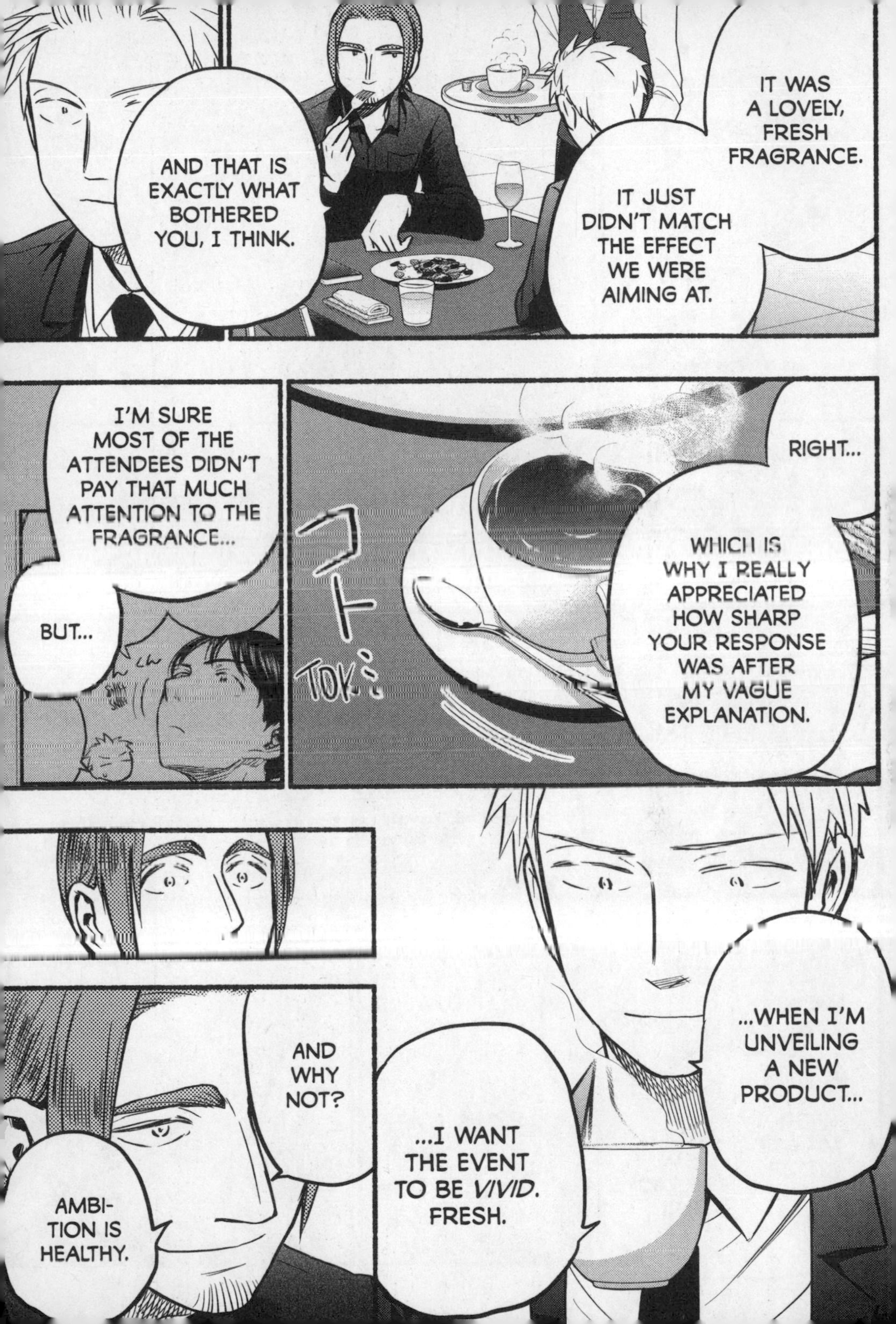
IT WAS A LOVELY, FRESH FRAGRANCE.
IT JUST DIDN'T MATCH THE EFFECT WE WERE AIMING AT.
AND THAT IS EXACTLY WHAT BOTHERED YOU, I THINK.
RIGHT...
WHICH IS WHY I REALLY APPRECIATED HOW SHARP YOUR RESPONSE WAS AFTER MY VAGUE EXPLANATION.
コト
TOK
I'M SURE MOST OF THE ATTENDEES DIDN'T PAY THAT MUCH ATTENTION TO THE FRAGRANCE...
BUT...
...WHEN I'M UNVEILING A NEW PRODUCT...
...I WANT THE EVENT TO BE *VIVID*. FRESH.
AND WHY NOT?
AMBI-TION IS HEALTHY.

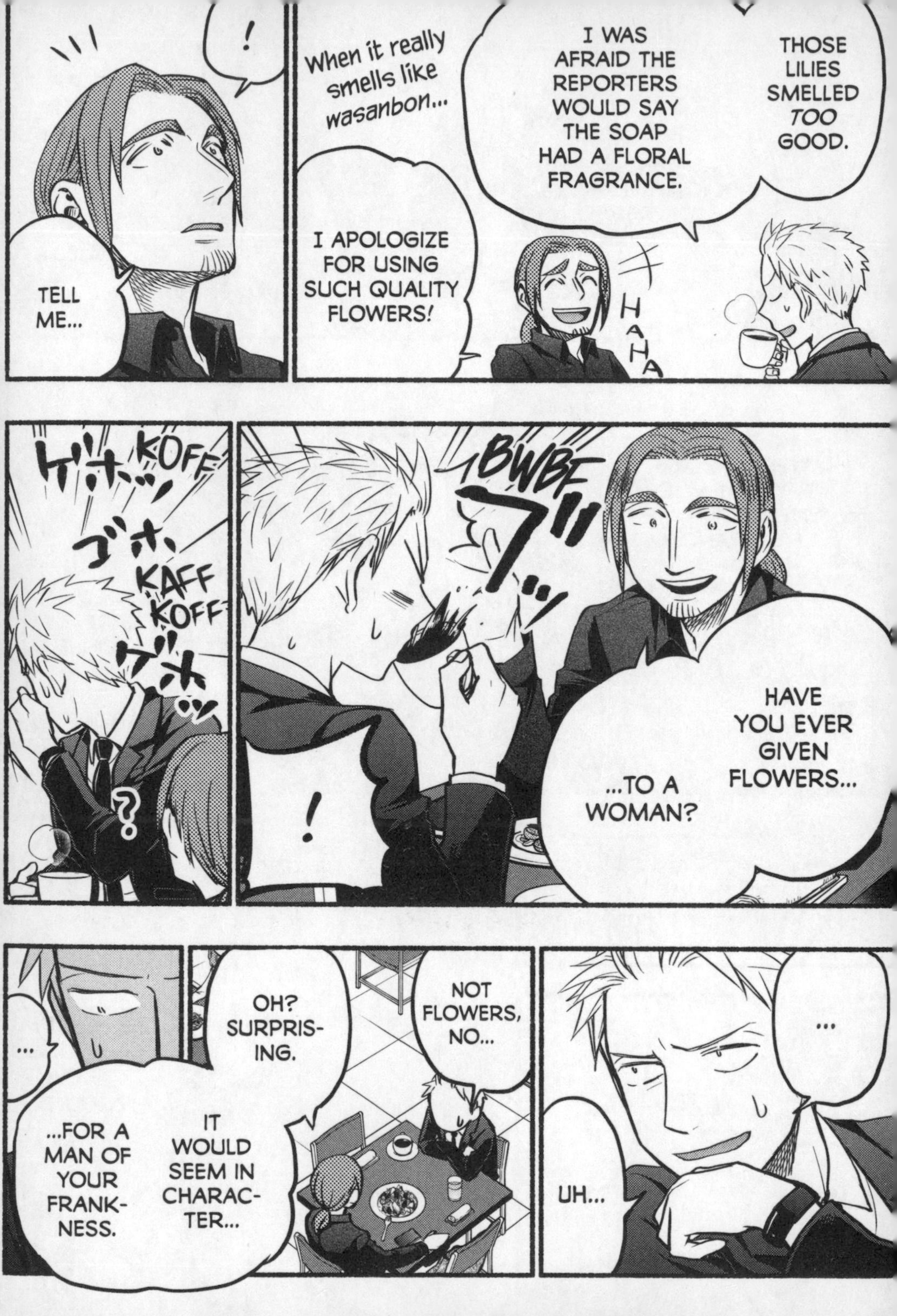
THOSE LILIES SMELLED TOO GOOD.
I WAS AFRAID THE REPORTERS WOULD SAY THE SOAP HAD A FLORAL FRAGRANCE.
When it really smells like wasanbon...
I APOLOGIZE FOR USING SUCH QUALITY FLOWERS!
HAHAHA
!
TELL ME...
BWBF
HAVE YOU EVER GIVEN FLOWERS...
...TO A WOMAN?
!
KOFF
KAFF
KOFF
?
...
UH...
NOT FLOWERS, NO...
OH? SURPRISING.
IT WOULD SEEM IN CHARACTER...
...
...FOR A MAN OF YOUR FRANKNESS.

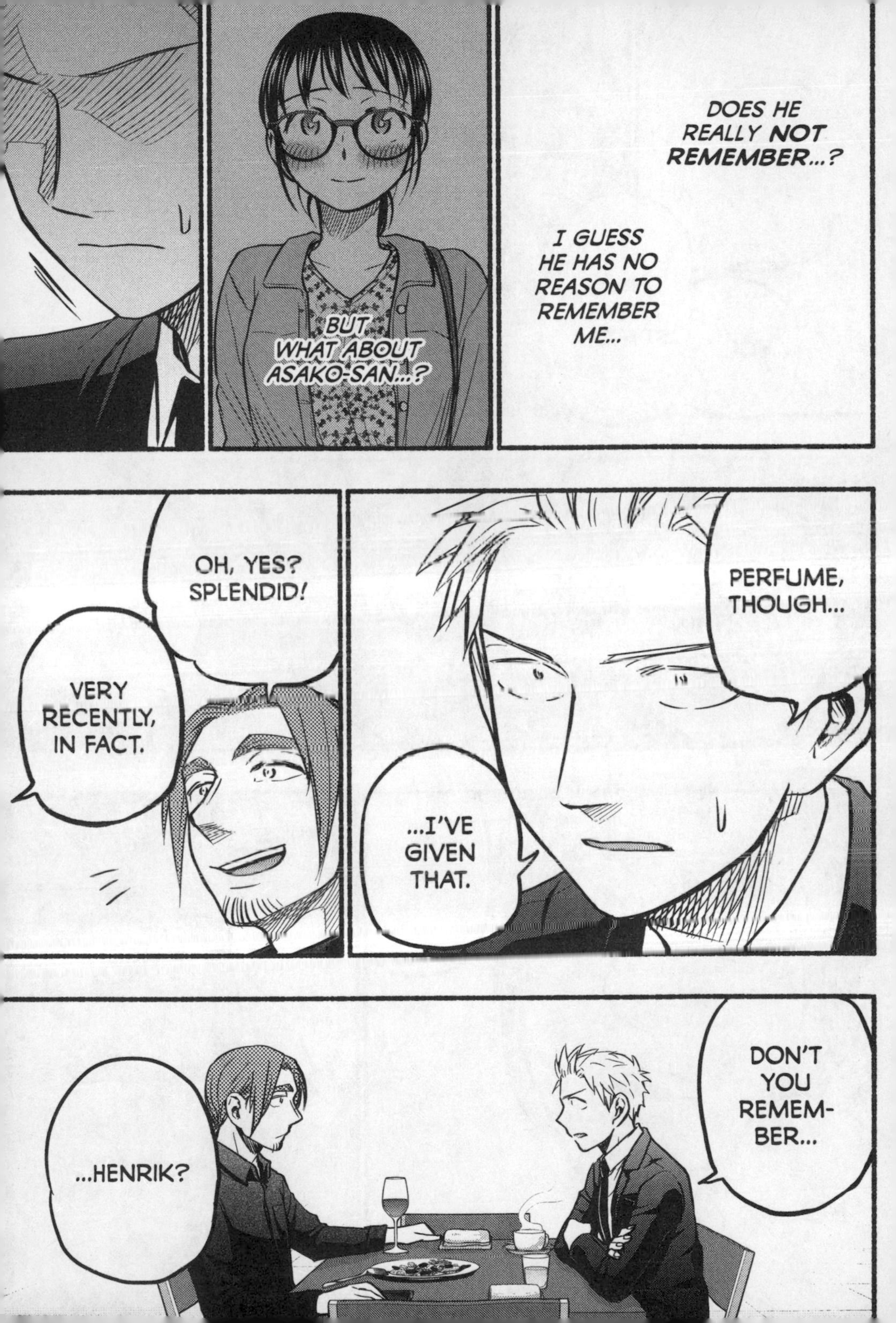
DOES HE REALLY NOT REMEMBER...?
I GUESS HE HAS NO REASON TO REMEMBER ME...
BUT WHAT ABOUT ASAKO-SAN...?
PERFUME, THOUGH...
...I'VE GIVEN THAT.
OH, YES? SPLENDID!
VERY RECENTLY, IN FACT.
DON'T YOU REMEM-BER...
...HENRIK?

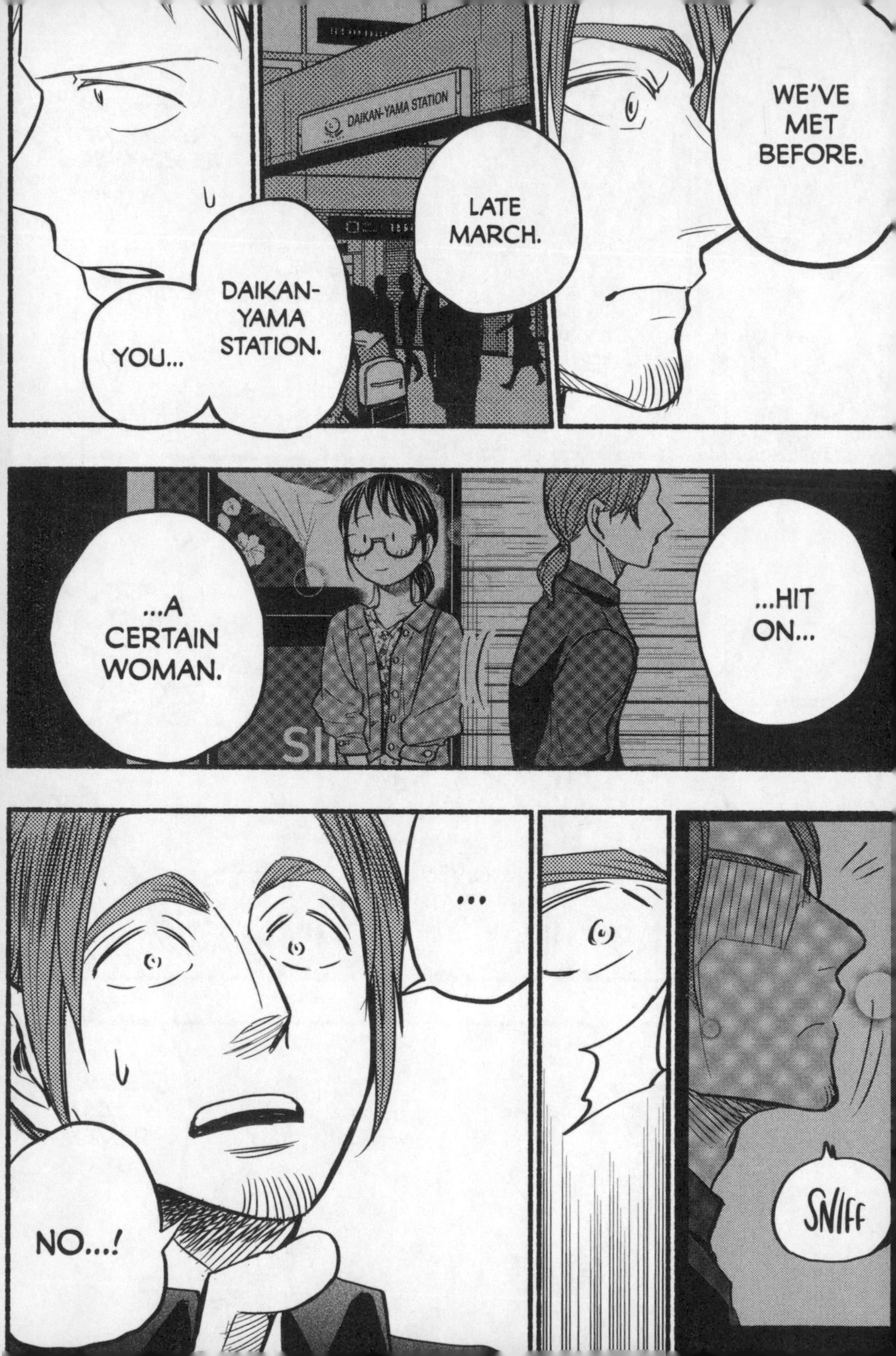
WE'VE MET BEFORE.
DAIKAN-YAMA STATION
LATE MARCH.
DAIKAN-YAMA STATION.
YOU...
...HIT ON...
...A CERTAIN WOMAN.
SNIFF
...
NO...!

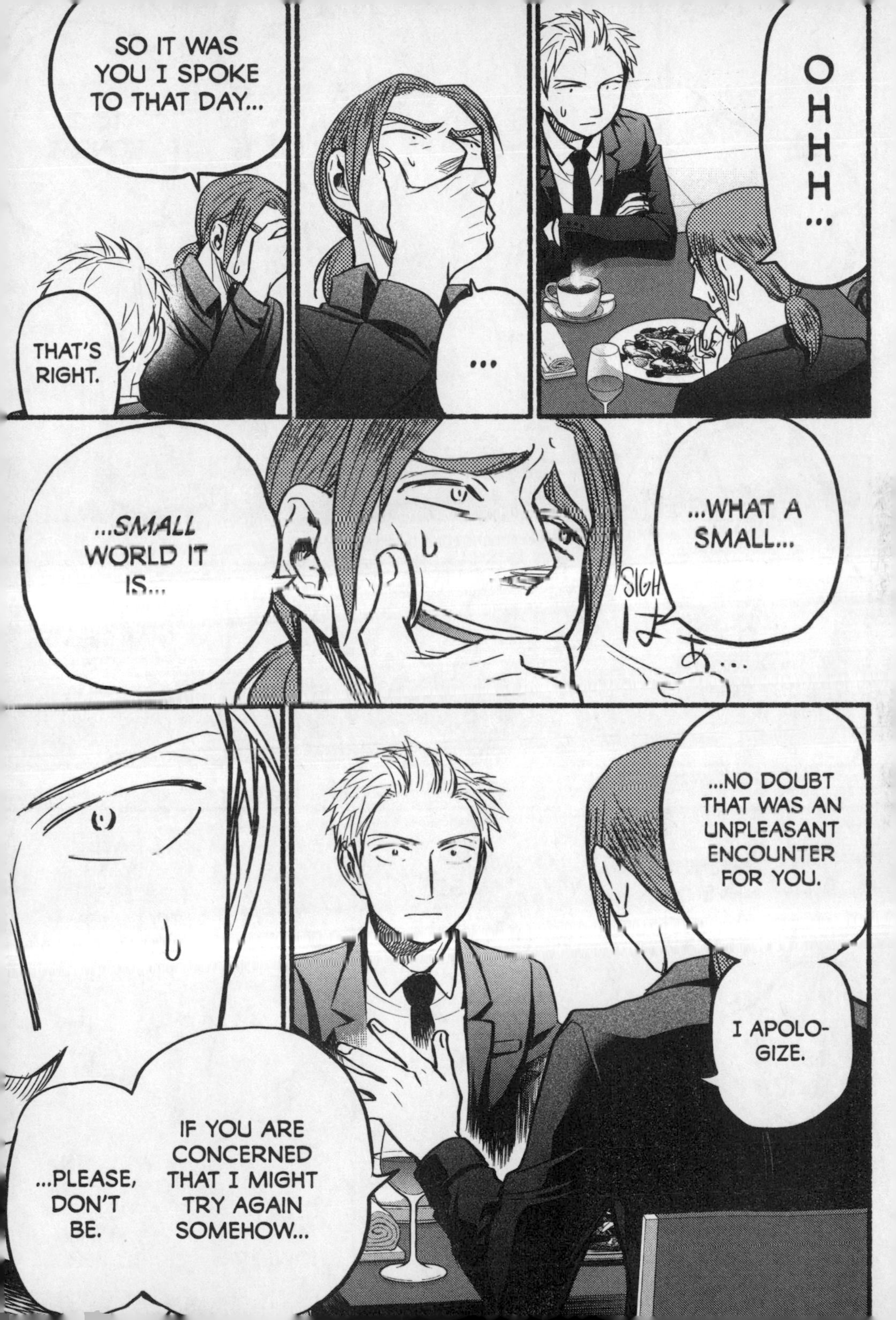
OHHH...
...
SO IT WAS YOU I SPOKE TO THAT DAY...
THAT'S RIGHT.
...WHAT A SMALL...
SIGH
はぁ...
...*SMALL* WORLD IT IS...
...NO DOUBT THAT WAS AN UNPLEASANT ENCOUNTER FOR YOU.
I APOLO-GIZE.
IF YOU ARE CONCERNED THAT I MIGHT TRY AGAIN SOMEHOW...
...PLEASE, DON'T BE.

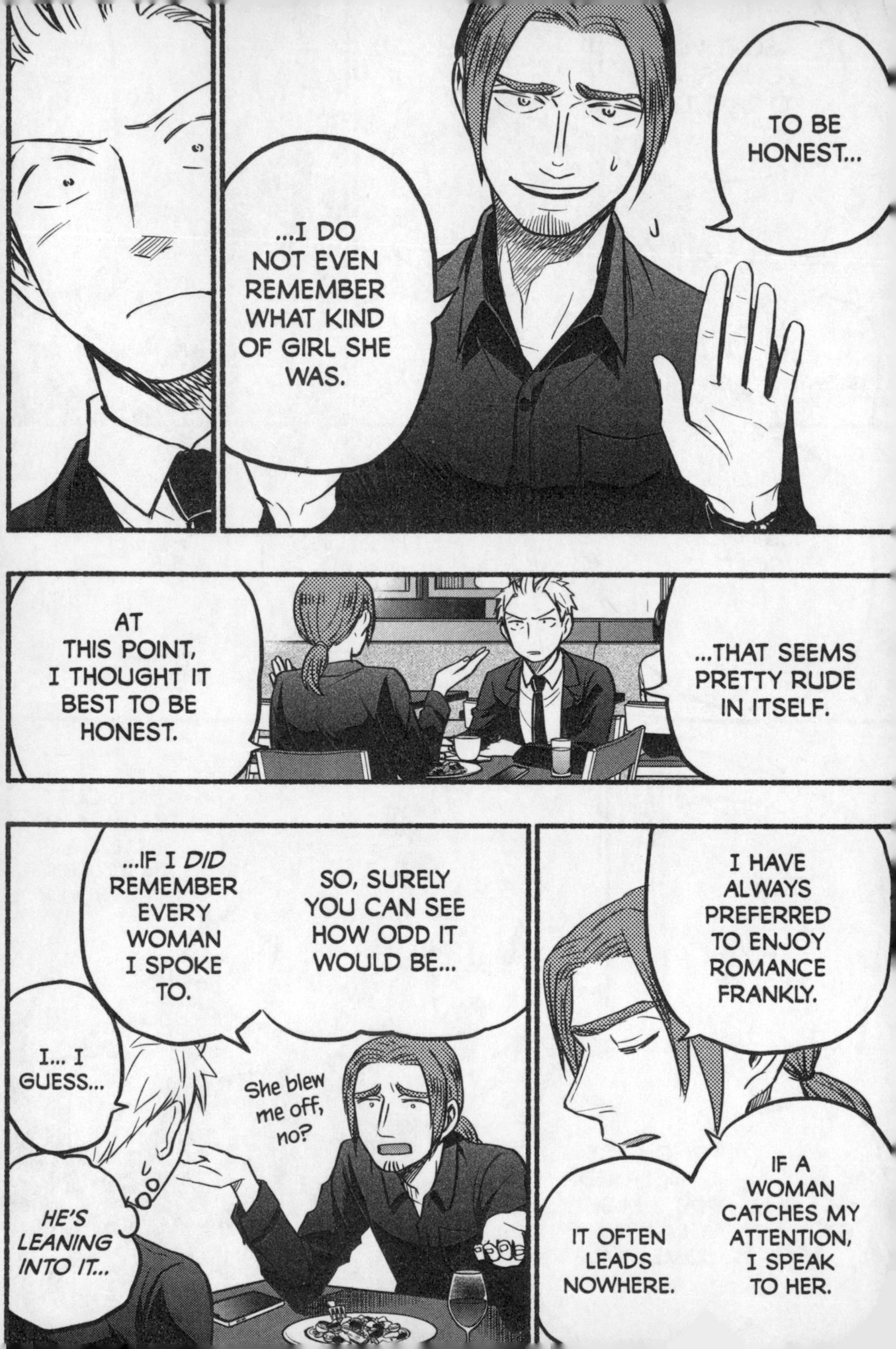
TO BE HONEST...
...I DO NOT EVEN REMEMBER WHAT KIND OF GIRL SHE WAS.
...THAT SEEMS PRETTY RUDE IN ITSELF.
AT THIS POINT, I THOUGHT IT BEST TO BE HONEST.
I HAVE ALWAYS PREFERRED TO ENJOY ROMANCE FRANKLY.
IF A WOMAN CATCHES MY ATTENTION, I SPEAK TO HER.
IT OFTEN LEADS NOWHERE.
SO, SURELY YOU CAN SEE HOW ODD IT WOULD BE...
...IF I *DID* REMEMBER EVERY WOMAN I SPOKE TO.
She blew me off, no?
I... I GUESS...
HE'S LEANING INTO IT...

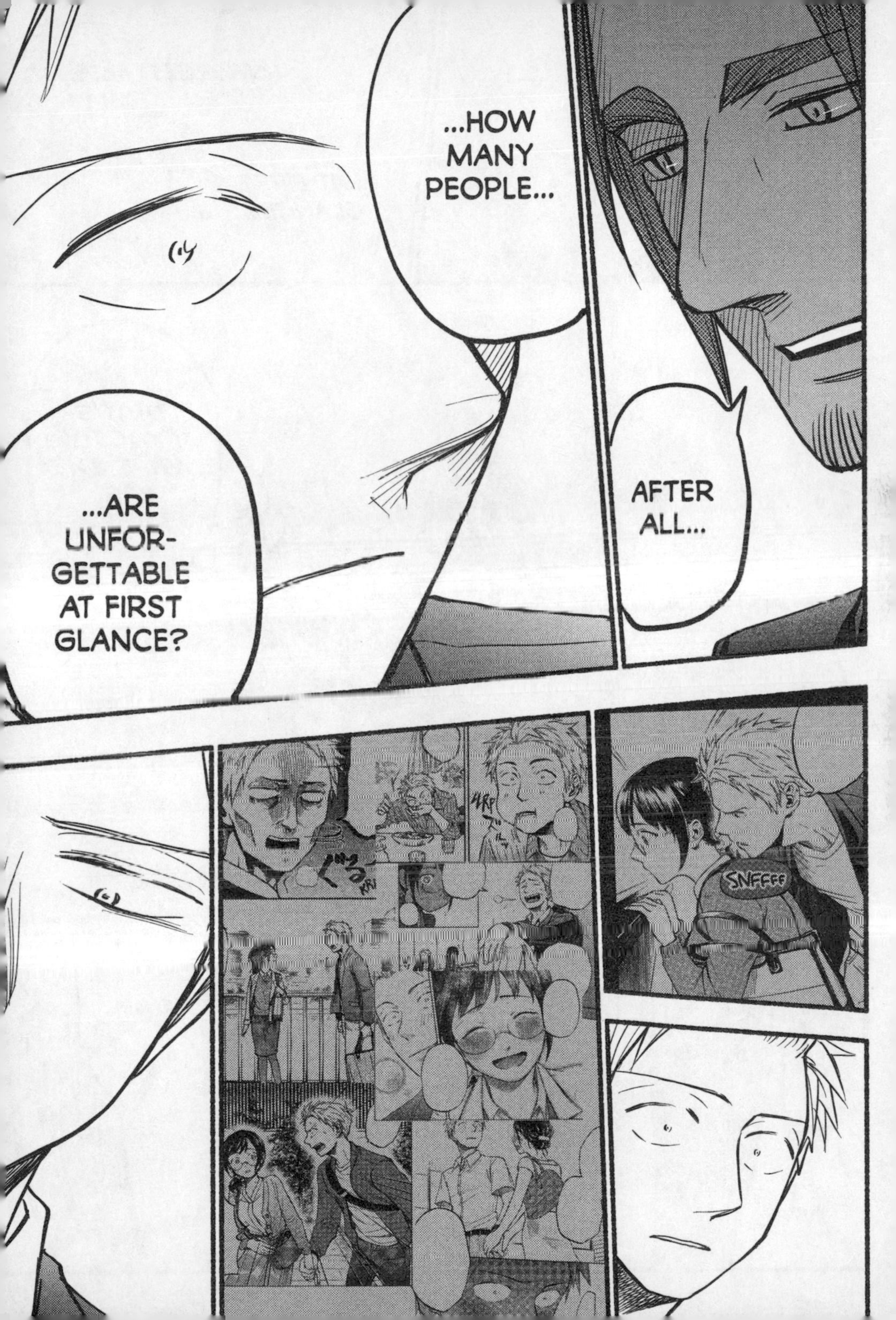
AFTER ALL...
...HOW MANY PEOPLE...
...ARE UNFOR-GETTABLE AT FIRST GLANCE?
SNFFFF

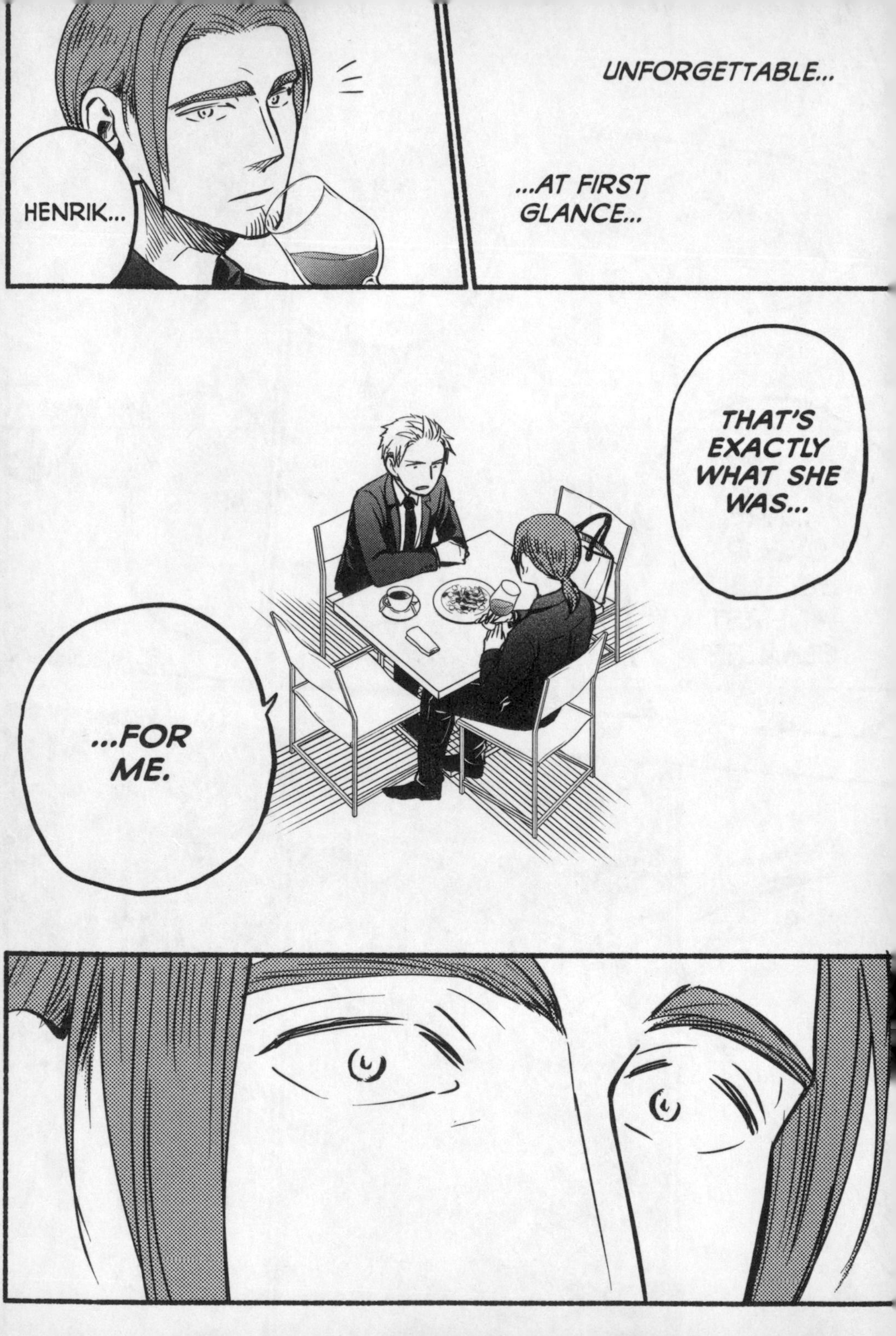
UNFORGETTABLE...
...AT FIRST GLANCE...
HENRIK...
THAT'S EXACTLY WHAT SHE WAS...
...FOR ME.

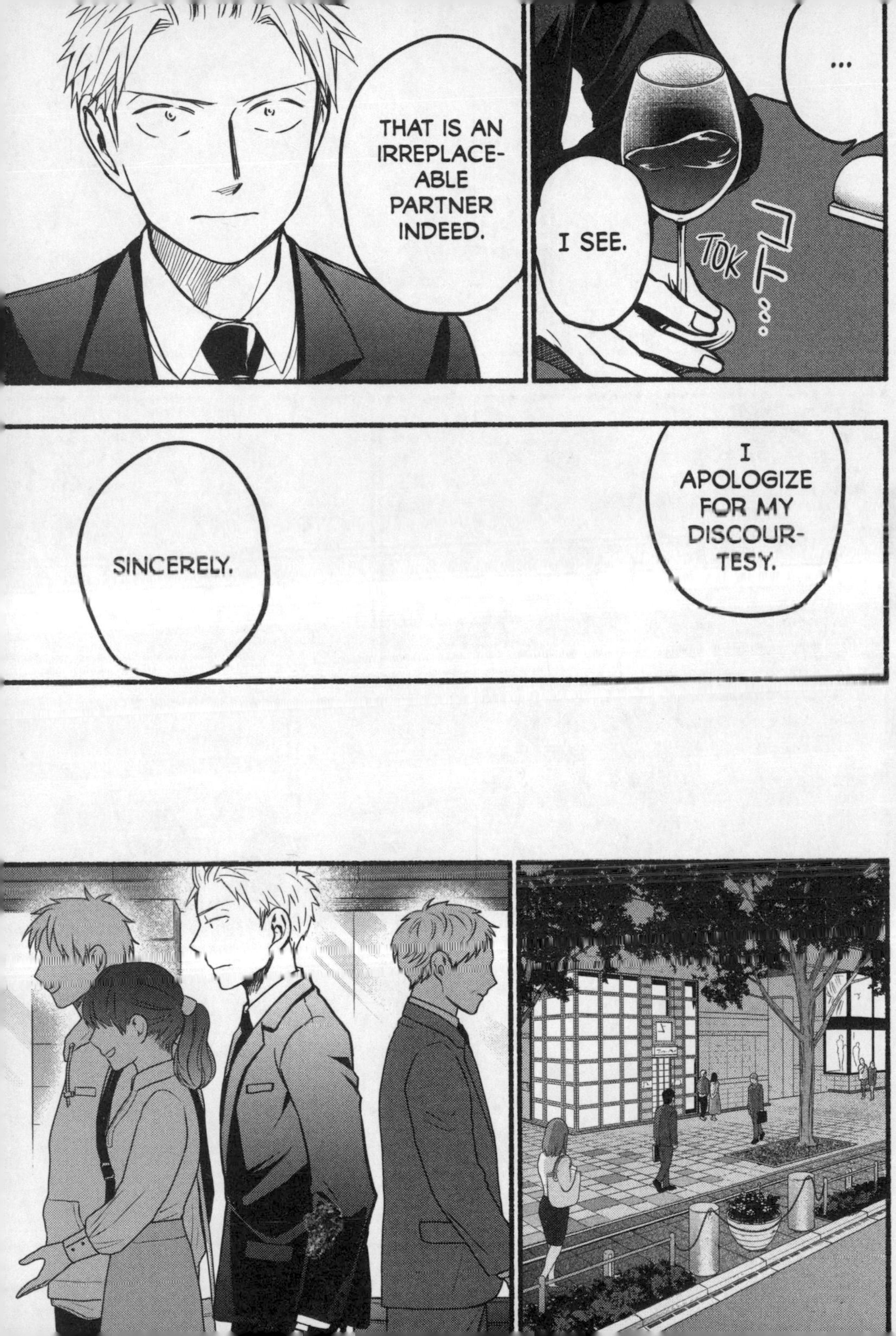
...
I SEE.
TOK
コト…
THAT IS AN IRREPLACEABLE PARTNER INDEED.
I APOLOGIZE FOR MY DISCOURTESY.
SINCERELY.

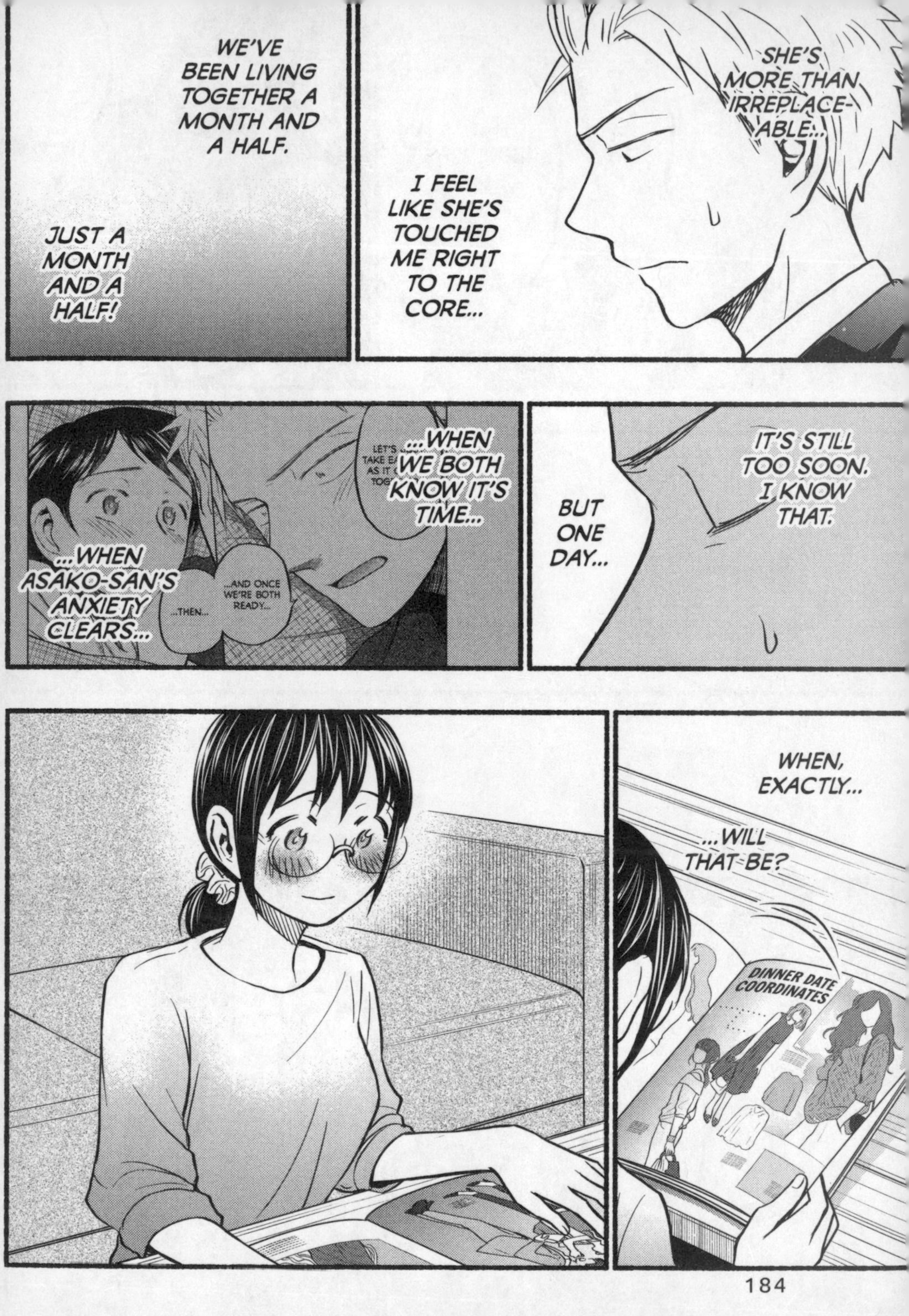
SHE'S MORE THAN IRREPLACE-ABLE...
I FEEL LIKE SHE'S TOUCHED ME RIGHT TO THE CORE...
WE'VE BEEN LIVING TOGETHER A MONTH AND A HALF.
JUST A MONTH AND A HALF!
IT'S STILL TOO SOON. I KNOW THAT.
BUT ONE DAY...
...WHEN WE BOTH KNOW IT'S TIME...
...AND ONCE WE'RE BOTH READY...
...THEN...
...WHEN ASAKO-SAN'S ANXIETY CLEARS...
WHEN, EXACTLY...
...WILL THAT BE?
DINNER DATE COORDINATES

Sweat and Soap, Volume 7 / The End

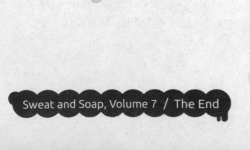

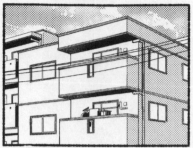

↑ THIS IS WHAT THE APARTMENT BUILDING LOOKS LIKE FROM OUTSIDE. THEY LIVE ON THE TOP (3RD) FLOOR.

NATORI AND ASAKO'S LOVE NEST...

THE FLOOR PLAN!

NOW THAT OUR TWO LEADS HAVE SETTLED INTO LIVING TOGETHER, THEIR NEW PLACE IS STARTING TO APPEAR MORE OFTEN. SO, ALLOW ME TO INTRODUCE THE FLOOR PLAN OF THEIR APARTMENT!

LIVING ROOM + BATHROOM

SHELVES
SOAP RACK
DESK
WINDOW
WHITE BUREAU
KITCHEN SHELVES
WASHING MACHINE
SINK
PC
TV
MAT
LAUNDRY BASKET
TOILET
COFFEE TABLE
CHAIR
SO FA
VERANDA
BATH AREA
RUG
MAT
TO LIVING ROOM
SHOE BOX
FRIDGE
KITCHEN
ENTRY-WAY
TO BEDROOM

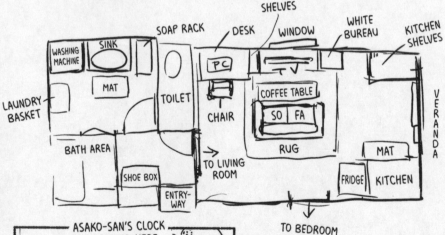

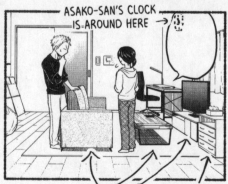

ASAKO-SAN'S CLOCK IS AROUND HERE
NATORI-SAN'S STUFF
ASAKO-SAN'S STUFF

↑ THIS IS THE FLOOR PLAN I USE WHEN EXPLAINING THINGS TO MY STAFF. THE BASIC LAYOUT DOESN'T CHANGE, BUT THINGS LIKE NEW FURNITURE GRADUALLY APPEAR EACH CHAPTER. THE AREA AROUND THE TV HAS A LOT OF NATORI-SAN'S STUFF, BUT SOME OF ASAKO-SAN'S IS THERE, TOO.

● BEDROOM

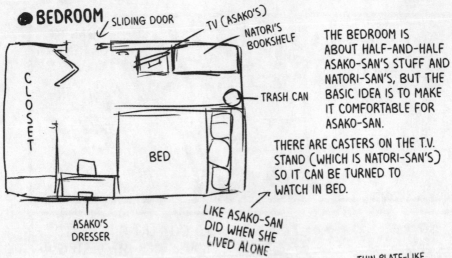

SLIDING DOOR

TV (ASAKO'S)

NATORI'S BOOKSHELF

CLOSET

TRASH CAN

BED

ASAKO'S DRESSER

LIKE ASAKO-SAN DID WHEN SHE LIVED ALONE

THE BEDROOM IS ABOUT HALF-AND-HALF ASAKO-SAN'S STUFF AND NATORI-SAN'S, BUT THE BASIC IDEA IS TO MAKE IT COMFORTABLE FOR ASAKO-SAN.

THERE ARE CASTERS ON THE T.V. STAND (WHICH IS NATORI-SAN'S) SO IT CAN BE TURNED TO WATCH IN BED.

● SINK AND SOAP DISH

THIN PLATE-LIKE BLACK SHEET COPPER

WET SOAP SITS HERE TO DRAIN AND DRY

ROUND CORNERS

SOAP DISH

MADE OF DIATOMITE— GOOD DRAINAGE

THE CLOTH HANGING FROM THE STAND IS USED TO WIPE THE SOAP DRY AFTER USING IT. IT'S LIKE A CLOTH FOR THE KITCHEN: YOU CAN WASH IT IN WATER AND REUSE IT (IT DRIES QUICKLY) AND VERY ABSORBENT. THE TOP DRAWER HOLDS ASAKO-SAN'S SOAP COLLECTION!

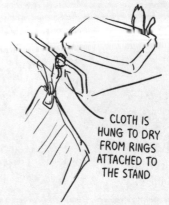

CLOTH IS HUNG TO DRY FROM RINGS ATTACHED TO THE STAND

OUT OF PAGES

AFTERWORD

KINTETSU YAMADA

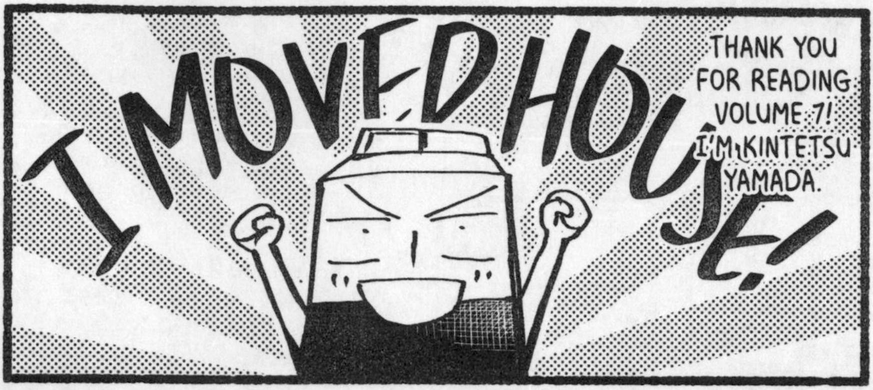
THANK YOU FOR READING VOLUME 7! I'M KINTETSU YAMADA.
I MOVED HOUSE!

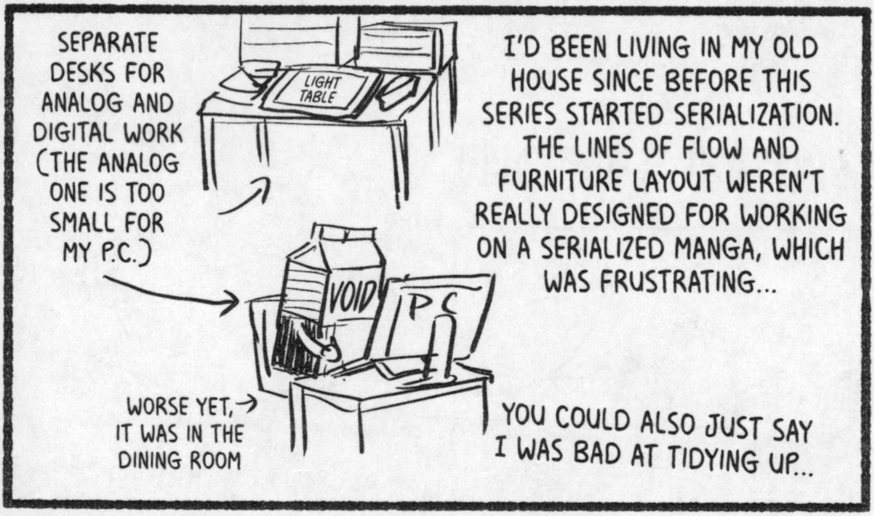
I'D BEEN LIVING IN MY OLD HOUSE SINCE BEFORE THIS SERIES STARTED SERIALIZATION. THE LINES OF FLOW AND FURNITURE LAYOUT WEREN'T REALLY DESIGNED FOR WORKING ON A SERIALIZED MANGA, WHICH WAS FRUSTRATING...
LIGHT TABLE
SEPARATE DESKS FOR ANALOG AND DIGITAL WORK (THE ANALOG ONE IS TOO SMALL FOR MY P.C.)
VOID
PC
YOU COULD ALSO JUST SAY I WAS BAD AT TIDYING UP...
WORSE YET, IT WAS IN THE DINING ROOM

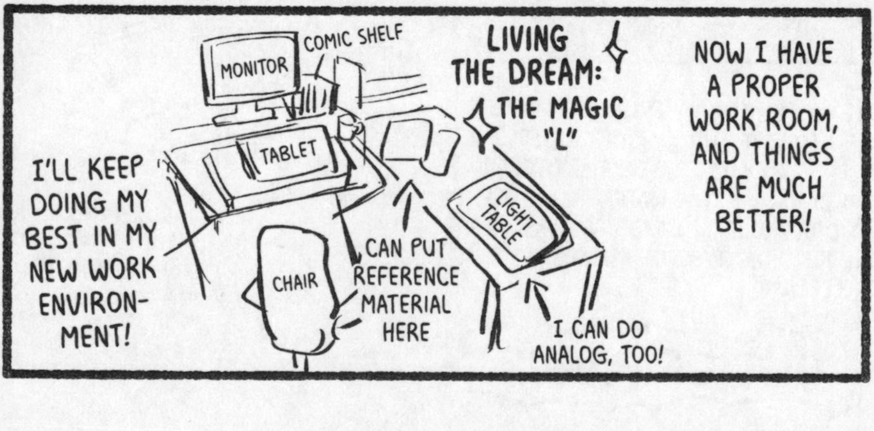
NOW I HAVE A PROPER WORK ROOM, AND THINGS ARE MUCH BETTER!
LIVING THE DREAM: THE MAGIC "L"
COMIC SHELF
MONITOR
TABLET
LIGHT TABLE
I CAN DO ANALOG, TOO!
CAN PUT REFERENCE MATERIAL HERE
CHAIR
I'LL KEEP DOING MY BEST IN MY NEW WORK ENVIRONMENT!

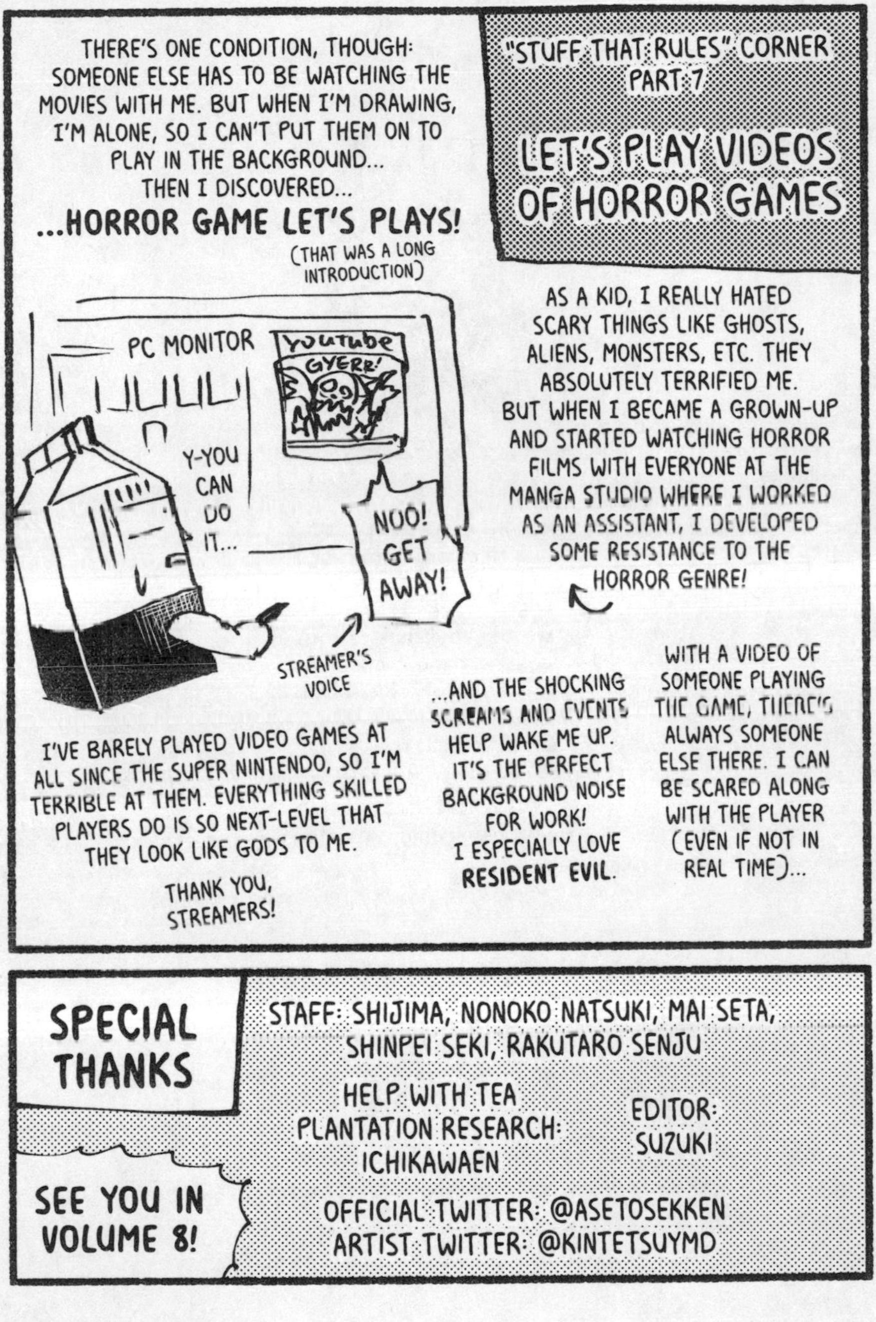
"STUFF THAT RULES" CORNER PART 7
LET'S PLAY VIDEOS OF HORROR GAMES
AS A KID, I REALLY HATED SCARY THINGS LIKE GHOSTS, ALIENS, MONSTERS, ETC. THEY ABSOLUTELY TERRIFIED ME. BUT WHEN I BECAME A GROWN-UP AND STARTED WATCHING HORROR FILMS WITH EVERYONE AT THE MANGA STUDIO WHERE I WORKED AS AN ASSISTANT, I DEVELOPED SOME RESISTANCE TO THE HORROR GENRE!
THERE'S ONE CONDITION, THOUGH: SOMEONE ELSE HAS TO BE WATCHING THE MOVIES WITH ME. BUT WHEN I'M DRAWING, I'M ALONE, SO I CAN'T PUT THEM ON TO PLAY IN THE BACKGROUND... THEN I DISCOVERED...
...HORROR GAME LET'S PLAYS!
(THAT WAS A LONG INTRODUCTION)
PC MONITOR
YouTube
GYERR!
NOO! GET AWAY!
Y-YOU CAN DO IT...
STREAMER'S VOICE
WITH A VIDEO OF SOMEONE PLAYING THE GAME, THERE'S ALWAYS SOMEONE ELSE THERE. I CAN BE SCARED ALONG WITH THE PLAYER (EVEN IF NOT IN REAL TIME)...
...AND THE SHOCKING SCREAMS AND EVENTS HELP WAKE ME UP. IT'S THE PERFECT BACKGROUND NOISE FOR WORK! I ESPECIALLY LOVE RESIDENT EVIL.
I'VE BARELY PLAYED VIDEO GAMES AT ALL SINCE THE SUPER NINTENDO, SO I'M TERRIBLE AT THEM. EVERYTHING SKILLED PLAYERS DO IS SO NEXT-LEVEL THAT THEY LOOK LIKE GODS TO ME.
THANK YOU, STREAMERS!
SPECIAL THANKS
STAFF: SHIJIMA, NONOKO NATSUKI, MAI SETA, SHINPEI SEKI, RAKUTARO SENJU
HELP WITH TEA PLANTATION RESEARCH: ICHIKAWAEN
EDITOR: SUZUKI
OFFICIAL TWITTER: @ASETOSEKKEN
ARTIST TWITTER: @KINTETSUYMD
SEE YOU IN VOLUME 8!

kintetsu yamada

When I drew this picture ↑
I was thinking, "This time I'm
gonna write about milk," but
when I checked I found that
I wrote about milk cartons in
volume 1 and 2, *and* about
how thick Hokkaido milk is in
volume 3, and it was, like...we
get it, you like milk already.
So that was a shock.
MILK IS DELICIOUS.
I hope you enjoy volume 7!

THIS TIME, I WAS DETERMINED TO GIVE A RECIPE FOR ASAKO-SAN'S HANDMADE GYOZA IN CHAPTER 54, BUT WHEN IT COMES TO GYOZA YOUR AUTHOR HAS, OF LATE, BEEN HUMBLY ACCEPTING ONLY THE BLESSINGS OF THE FROZEN VARIETY, AND I DIDN'T HAVE A RECIPE...
SO INSTEAD OF THAT, I'D LIKE TO OFFER YOU...

"THIS IS HOW I EAT 'EM!"
TOP 3 RECOMMENDED GYOZA DIPPING SAUCES

1. PONZU AND GARLIC RAYU (CHILI OIL)

START OUT WITH JUST THE PONZU FOR A FEW LIGHT JABS. THEN, WHEN YOU'RE READY TO GO TO TOWN (STOMACH-WISE), ADD THE GARLIC RAYU. A GOOD BALANCE OF "LIGHT AND REFRESHING" AND "GOING TO TOWN."

2. VINEGAR AND PEPPER

AN EVEN LIGHTER OPTION WITH THE FRAGRANCE OF PEPPER FOR EXTRA PUNCH. NORMAL PEPPER OR BLACK PEPPER ARE BOTH FINE, BUT THE MORE FRAGRANT STUFF FEELS MORE LUXURIOUS SOMEHOW.

3. MELTED BUTTER AND BLACK PEPPER

UNAPOLOGETICALLY FATTENING. I ONLY EAT THIS ONCE OR TWICE A YEAR, WHEN I WANT SOMETHING THAT'LL MAKE ME REALLY FEEL GUILTY. TASTES OF SIN.

COVER CONVERSATION

PLEASE READ THIS AFTER READING CHAPTER 55.
-KINTETSU YAMADA

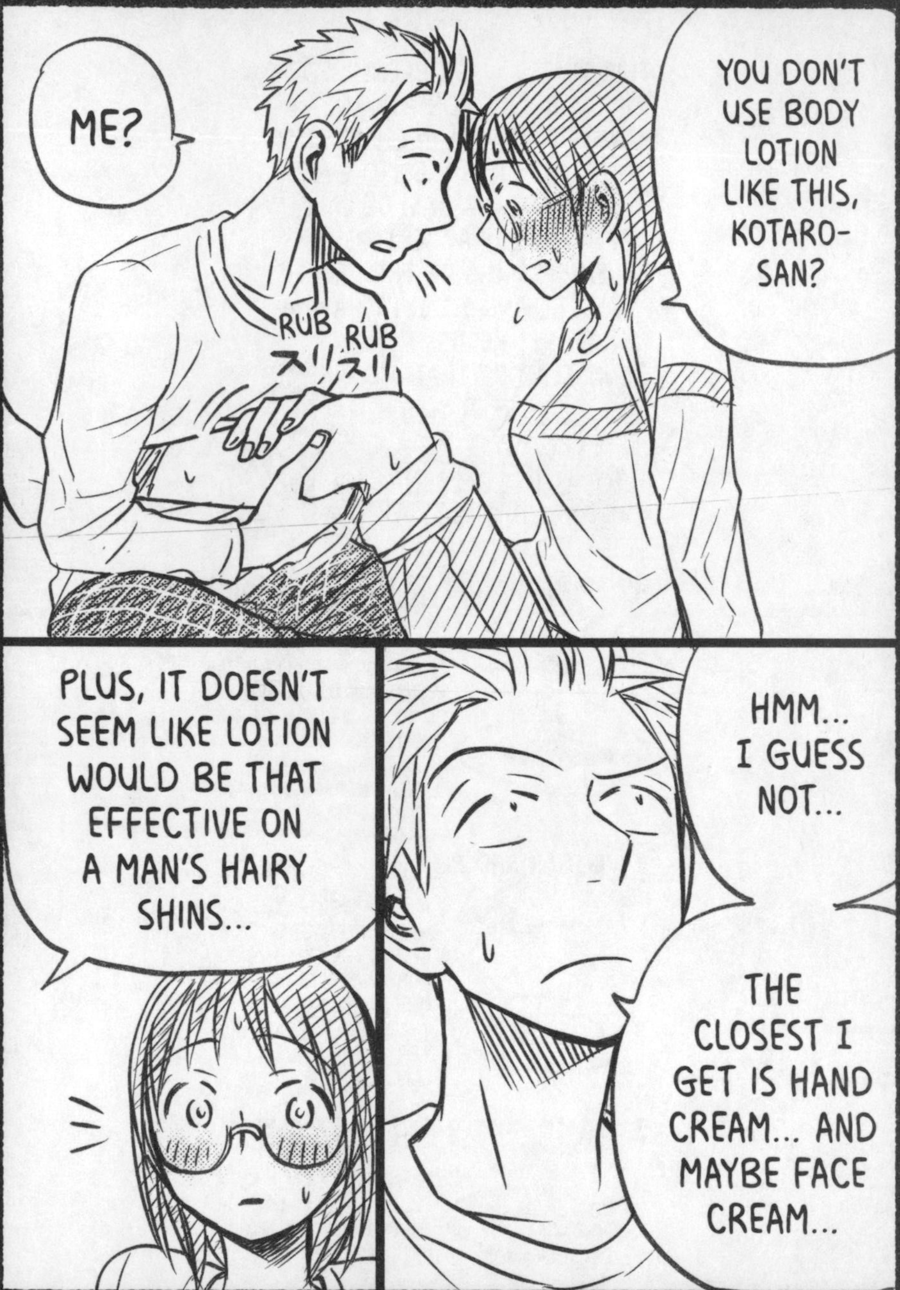

YOU DON'T USE BODY LOTION LIKE THIS, KOTARO-SAN?
ME?
RUB RUB
スリスリ
HMM... I GUESS NOT...
THE CLOSEST I GET IS HAND CREAM... AND MAYBE FACE CREAM...
PLUS, IT DOESN'T SEEM LIKE LOTION WOULD BE THAT EFFECTIVE ON A MAN'S HAIRY SHINS...

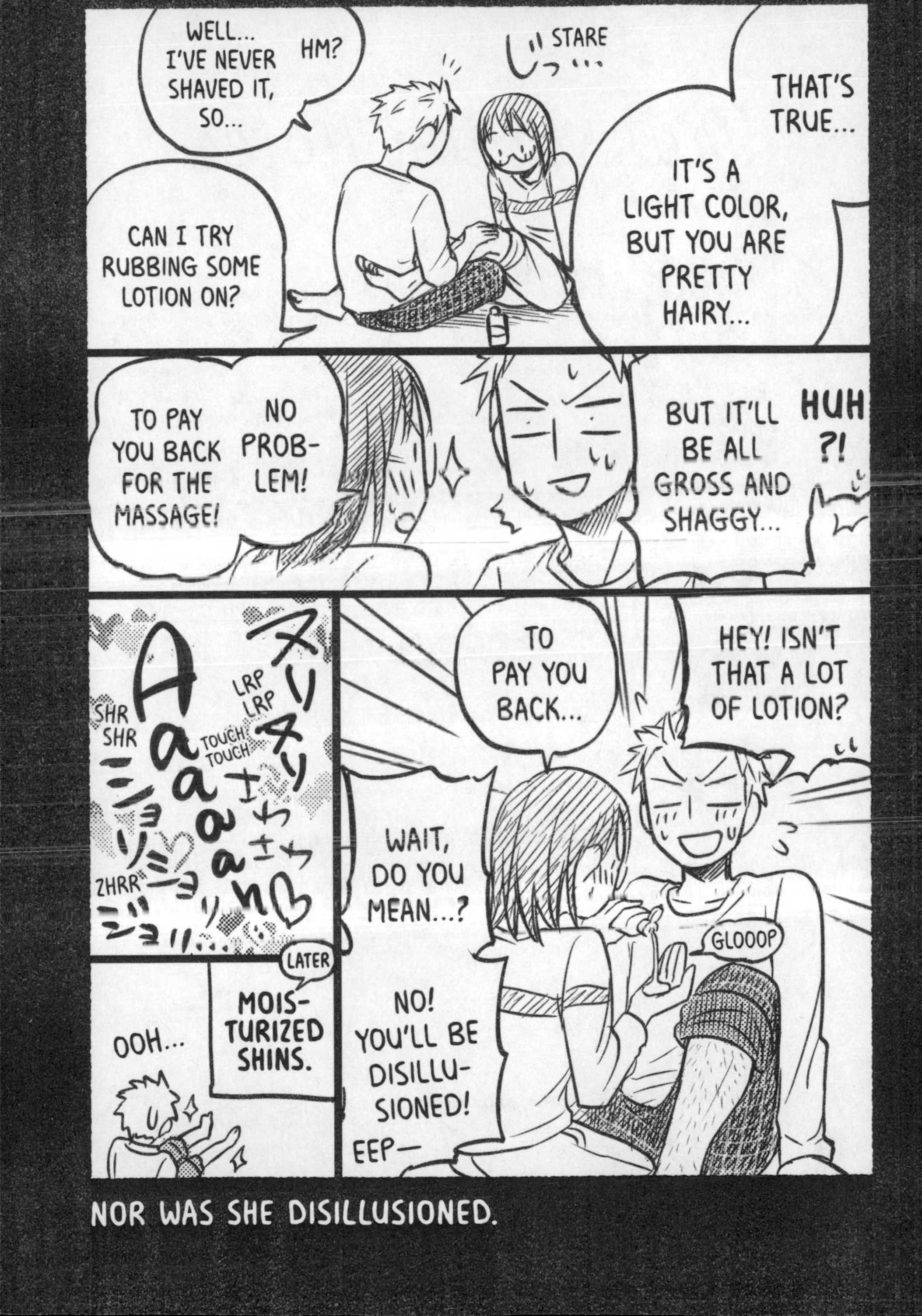
THAT'S TRUE...
IT'S A LIGHT COLOR, BUT YOU ARE PRETTY HAIRY...
STARE
HM?
WELL... I'VE NEVER SHAVED IT, SO...
CAN I TRY RUBBING SOME LOTION ON?
HUH ?!
BUT IT'LL BE ALL GROSS AND SHAGGY...
NO PROB-LEM!
TO PAY YOU BACK FOR THE MASSAGE!
HEY! ISN'T THAT A LOT OF LOTION?
TO PAY YOU BACK...
WAIT, DO YOU MEAN...?
GLOOOP
NO! YOU'LL BE DISILLU-SIONED!
EEP—
Aaaaaaah
LRP LRP
SHR SHR
TOUCH TOUCH
ZHRR
LATER
MOIS-TURIZED SHINS.
OOH...

NOR WAS SHE DISILLUSIONED.

Translation Notes

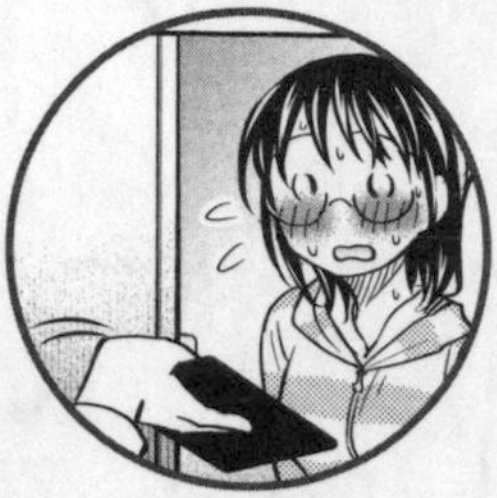

Seal or signature, page 16
Traditionally Japan has used personal seals (*hanko*) instead of signatures. Even today, people usually "sign" for deliveries with a seal. Actual signatures are also accepted, though, and since they are replacements for seals, it's acceptable—even expected—to sign the actual recipient's name rather than your own.

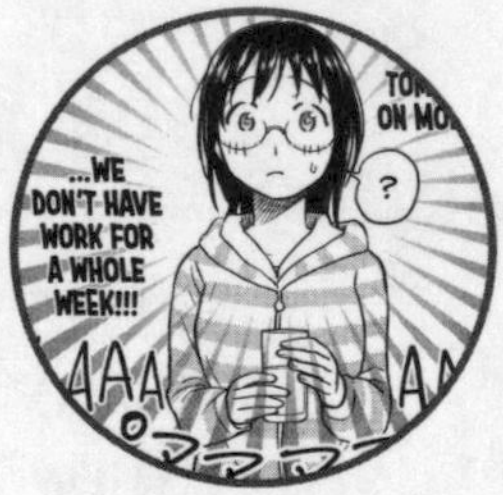
...WE DON'T HAVE WORK FOR A WHOLE WEEK!!!
?

Golden Week, page 19
A week from late April to early May that contains a string of public holidays. Most office workers get at least a full week off, although the exact combination of holidays and weekends changes every year.

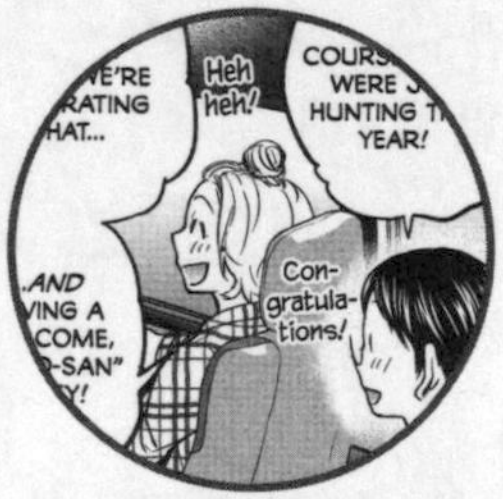
Heh heh!
Con-gratula-tions!

You were job hunting this year, page 71
In Japan, college students try to find a job before they graduate. For most students, fourth year is the year of serious job hunting.

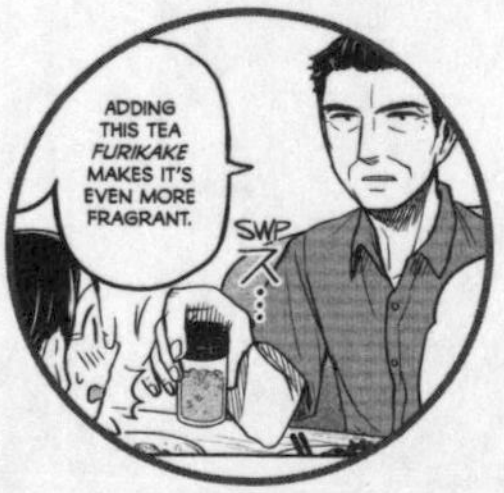
ADDING THIS TEA FURIKAKE MAKES IT'S EVEN MORE FRAGRANT.
SWP

***Furikake*, page 82**
Dry seasoning made of anything from fish flakes to tea leaves (as in this case), to be sprinkled over rice and other foods.

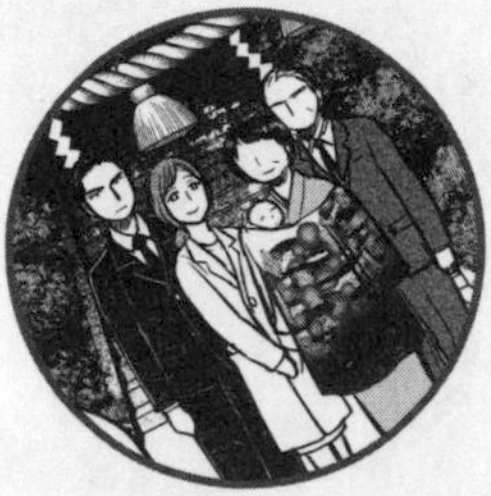

First shrine visit, page 87
When Japanese babies are about one month old, their parents traditionally take them to a local shrine to receive its blessings.

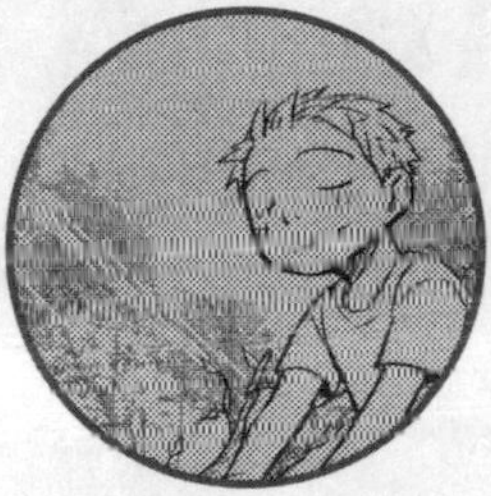

Forest bathing, page 146
Also known by its Japanese name of *shinrin-yoku*, "forest bathing" is a form of nature therapy: spending time in a forest as a therapeutic practice.

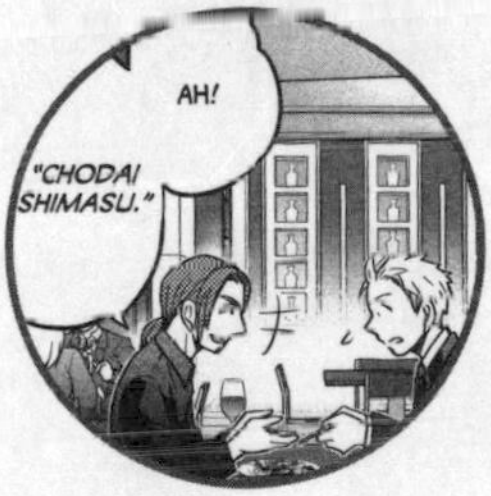
AH!
"CHODAI SHIMASU."

"*Chodai shimasu*," page 172
The standard formula recited when accepting a business card, literally meaning, "I humbly receive it." Henrik makes an ironically exaggerated show of using the correct phrase to show respect for Natori and acknowledge the "business" side of their conversation without making things too formal.

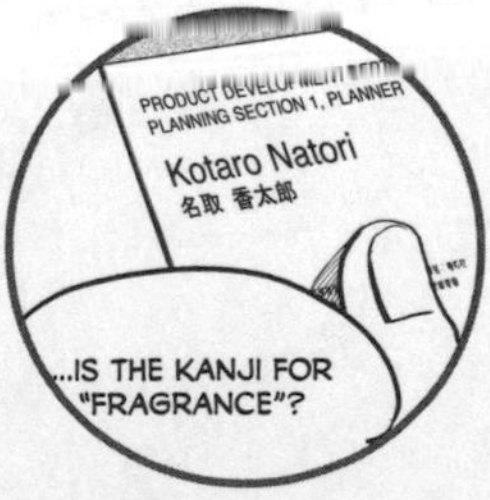
PLANNING SECTION 1, PLANNER
Kotaro Natori
名取 香太郎
...IS THE KANJI FOR "FRAGRANCE"?

The kanji that means "fragrance," page 172
Although not all Japanese names have a transparent meaning, in this story Kotaro's name is written with kanji (Chinese characters) that literally mean "fragrance boy."

Knight of the ICE

Knight of the Ice ©Yayoi Ogawa/Kodansha Ltd.

Yayoi Ogawa

PERFECT WORLD

Rie Aruga

A TOUCHING NEW SERIES ABOUT LOVE AND COPING WITH DISABILITY

An office party reunites Tsugumi with her high school crush Itsuki. He's realized his dream of becoming an architect, but along the way, he experienced a spinal injury that put him in a wheelchair. Now Tsugumi's rekindled feelings will butt up against prejudices she never considered — and Itsuki will have to decide if he's ready to let someone into his heart...

"Depicts with great delicacy and courage the difficulties some with disabilities experience getting involved in romantic relationships... Rie Aruga refuses to romanticize, pushing her heroine to face the reality of disability. She invites her readers to the same tasks of empathy, knowledge and recognition."
—Slate.fr

"An important entry [in manga romance]... The emotional core of both plot and characters indicates thoughtfulness... [Aruga's] research is readily apparent in the text and artwork, making this feel like a real story."
—Anime News Network

THE WORLD OF CLAMP!

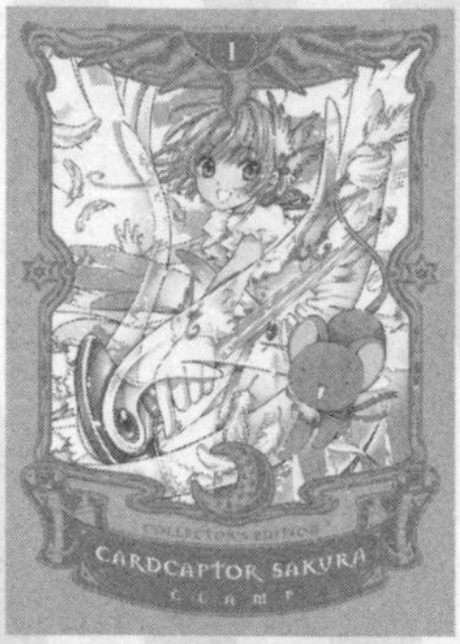
CARDCAPTOR SAKURA
CLAMP

Cardcaptor Sakura
Collector's Edition

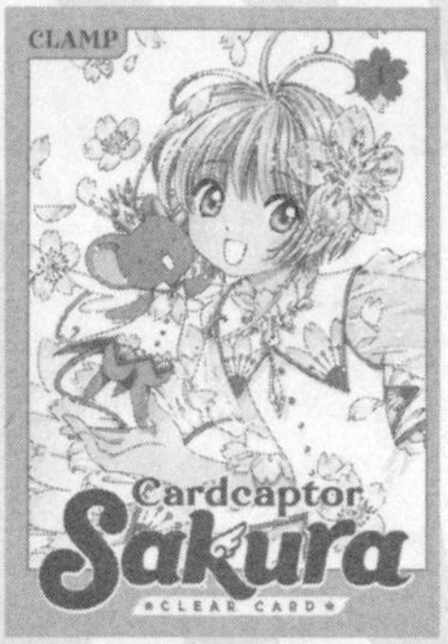
CLAMP
Cardcaptor
Sakura
CLEAR CARD

Cardcaptor Sakura:
Clear Card

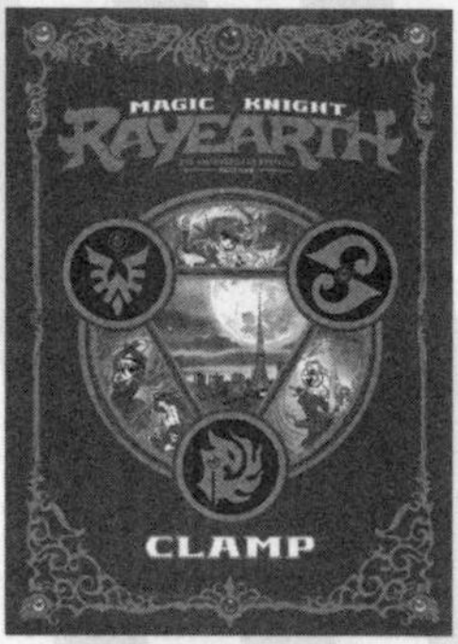
MAGIC KNIGHT
RAYEARTH
CLAMP

Magic Knight Rayearth
25th Anniversary Box Set

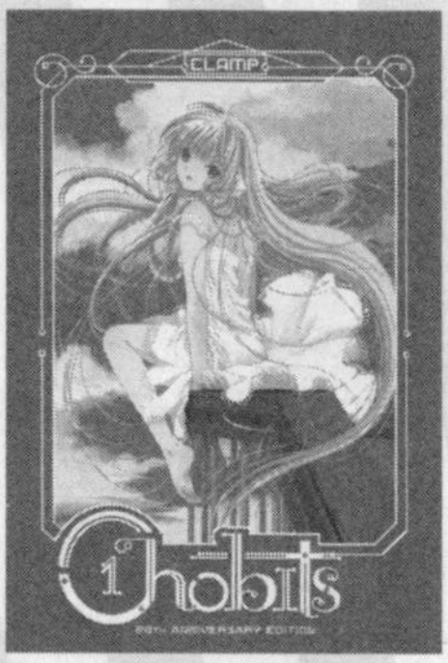
CLAMP
Chobits

Chobits

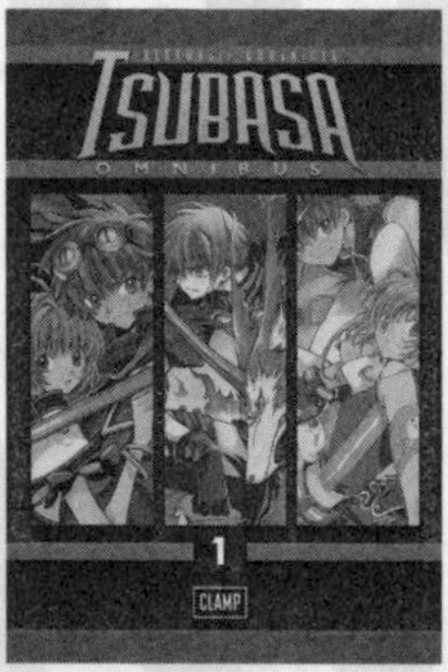
TSUBASA
OMNIBUS
1
CLAMP

TSUBASA Omnibus

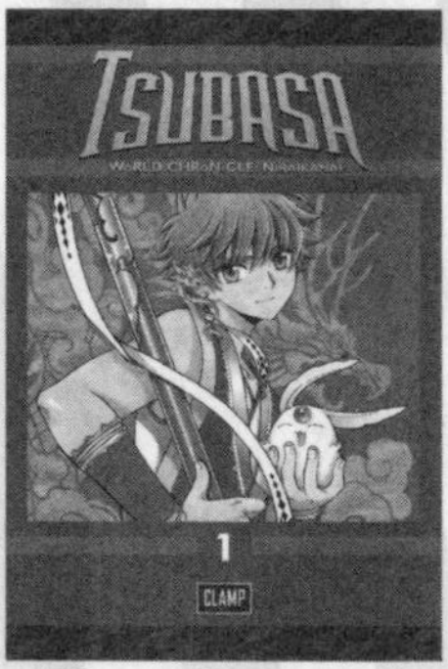
TSUBASA
1
CLAMP

TSUBASA WoRLD CHRoNiCLE

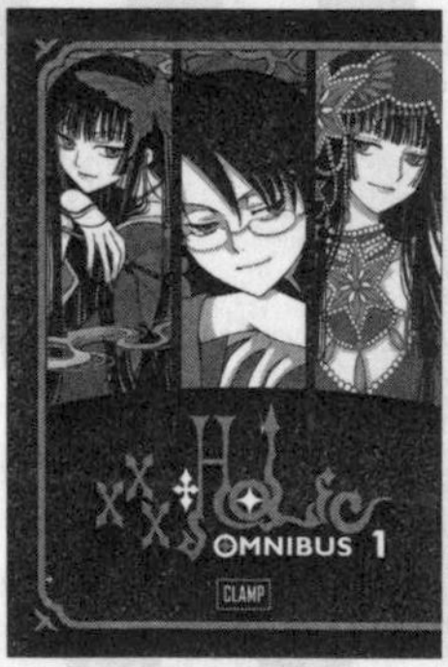
xxxHOLiC
OMNIBUS 1
CLAMP

xxxHOLiC Omnibus

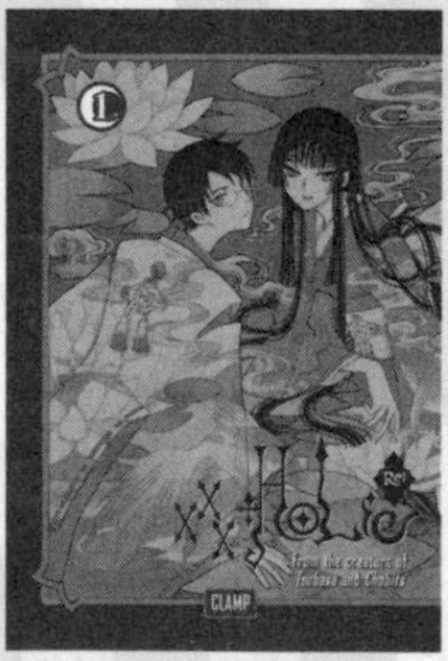
CLAMP

xxxHOLiC Rei

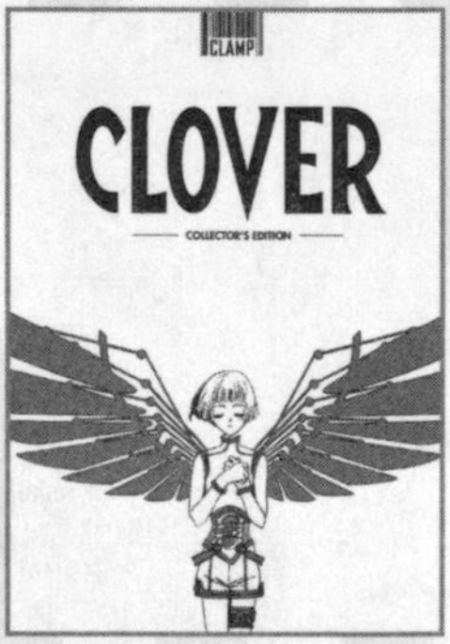
CLAMP
CLOVER
COLLECTOR'S EDITION

CLOVER Collector's Edition

KC KODANSHA COMICS

Kodansha Comics welcomes you to explore the expansive world of CLAMP, the all-female artist collective that has produced some of the most acclaimed manga of the century. Our growing catalog includes icons like *Cardcaptor Sakura* and *Magic Knight Rayearth*, each crafted with CLAMP's one-of-a-kind style and characters!

Poor college student Hideki is down on his luck. All he wants is a good job, a girlfriend, and his very own "persocom"—the latest and greatest in humanoid computer technology. Hideki's luck changes one night when he finds Chi—a persocom thrown out in a pile of trash. But Hideki soon discovers that there's much more to his cute new persocom than meets the eye.

The art-deco cyberpunk classic from the creators of *xxxHOLiC* and *Cardcaptor Sakura*!

CLOVER © CLAMP·ShigatsuTsuitachi CO.,LTD./Kodansha Ltd.

Su was born into a bleak future, where the government keeps
tight control over children with magical powers—codenamed
"Clovers." With Su being the only "four-leaf" Clover in the
world, she has been kept isolated nearly her whole life. Can
ex-military agent Kazuhiko deliver her to the happiness she
seeks? Experience the complete series in this hardcover
edition, which also includes over twenty pages of ravishing
color art!

KC
KODANSHA
COMICS

The beloved characters from *Cardcaptor Sakura* return in a brand new, reimagined fantasy adventure!

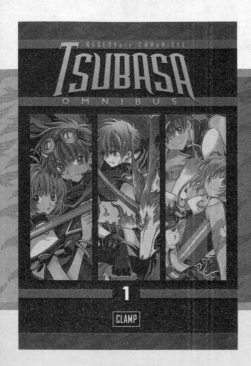

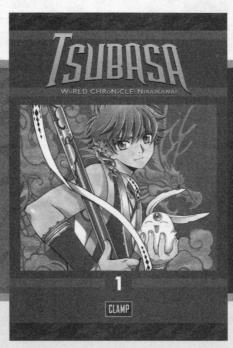

"[*Tsubasa*] takes readers on a fantastic ride that only gets more exhilarating with each successive chapter." —Anime News Network

In the Kingdom of Clow, an archaeological dig unleashes an incredible power, causing Princess Sakura to lose her memories. To save her, her childhood friend Syaoran must follow the orders of the Dimension Witch and travel alongside Kurogane, an unrivaled warrior; Fai, a powerful magician; and Mokona, a curiously strange creature, to retrieve Sakura's dispersed memories!

SAINT ☆ YOUNG MEN

A LONG AWAITED ARRIVAL IN PREMIUM 2-IN-1 HARDCOVER

After centuries of hard work, Jesus and Buddha take a break from their heavenly duties to relax among the people of Japan, and their adventures in this lighthearted buddy comedy are sure to bring mirth and merriment to all!

"Brilliant…the physical comedy and facial expressions will make you literally LOL."

—Sam Humphries
(host of *DC Daily*;
writer, *Green Lanterns*,
Legendary Star-Lord)

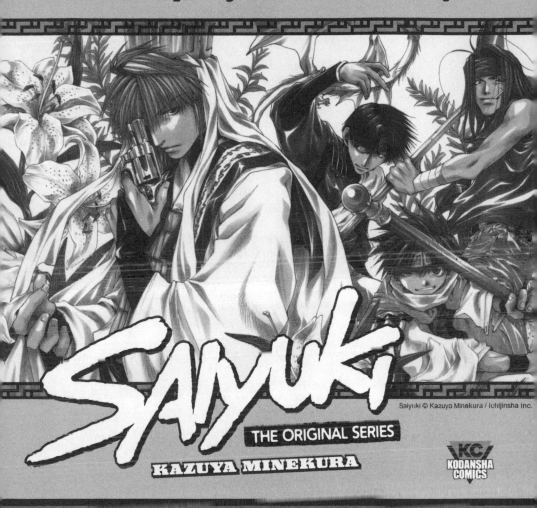

A Kodansha Comics Trade Paperback Original
Sweat and Soap 7 copyright © 2020 Kintetsu Yamada
English translation copyright © 2021 Kintetsu Yamada

Published in the United States by Kodansha Comics, an imprint of Kodansha USA Publishing, LLC, New York.

Publication rights for this English edition arranged through Kodansha Ltd., Tokyo.

First published in Japan in 2020 by Kodansha Ltd., Tokyo as Ase to Sekken volume 7.

ISBN 978-1-64651-166-2

Printed in the United States of America.

www.kodansha.us

2nd Printing
Translation: Matt Treyvaud
Lettering: Sara Linsley
Editing: Kristin Osani
Kodansha Comics edition cover design by Phil Balsman

Publisher: Kiichiro Sugawara

Director of publishing services: Ben Applegate
Associate director of operations: Stephen Pakula
Publishing services associate managing editor: Madison Salters
Production Managers: Emi Lotto, Angela Zurlo